SOUTHDOWN AT WAR

COLIN DRUCE

Capital Transport

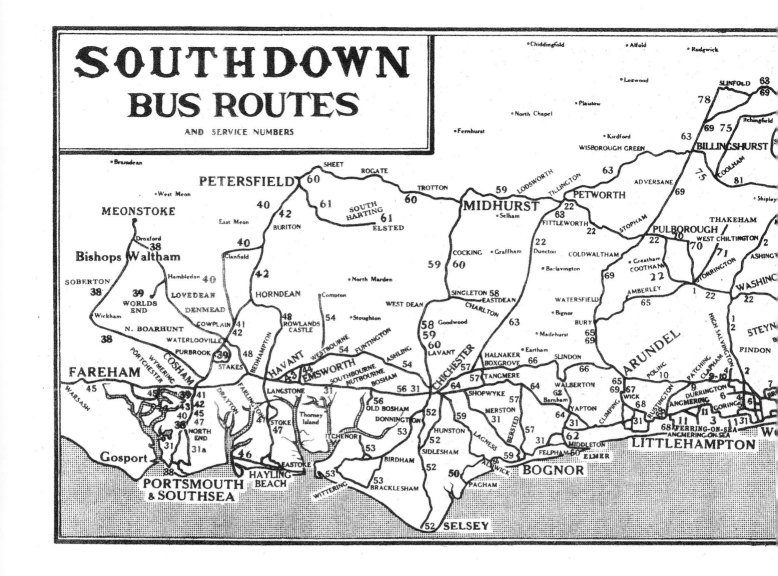

SOUTHDOWN BUS ROUTES
AND SERVICE NUMBERS

First published 2015

Published by
Capital Transport
Publishing Ltd
www.capitaltransport.com

Printed by 1010 Printing
International Ltd

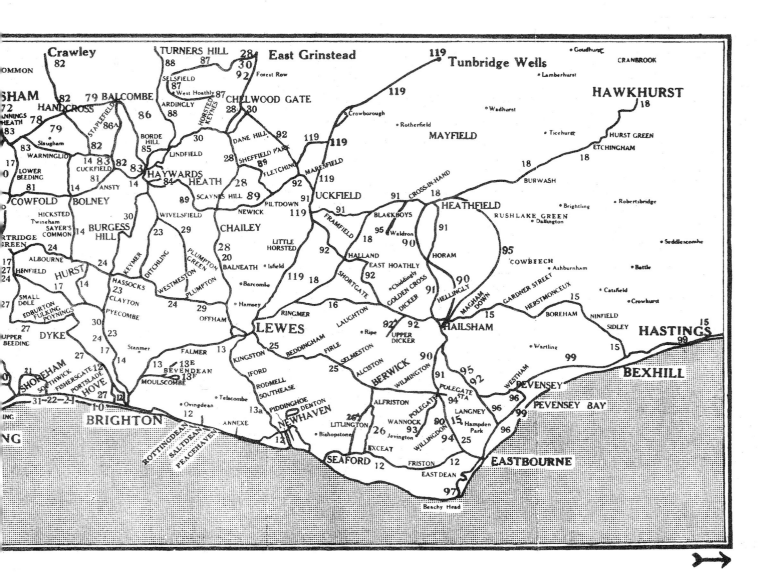

Front cover With France about to seek an Armistice, the South Coast of England is poised to become the front line against a ruthless enemy poised just across the English Channel – although, fortunately, no serious plans for an invasion had so far been prepared by Hitler! A Southdown Leyland Titan with lowbridge Park Royal body on service 119 bound for Tunbridge Wells has been stopped at a roadblock believed to be near Falmer on the A27 road between Brighton and Lewes. Along with most vehicles in the fleet it has already gained a dark green roof but otherwise retains fully lined prewar livery. This scene on 15 June 1940 will be repeated many times in the coming months as invasion fears grow across the Southdown area. *Brighton & Hove Museums*

Title page It is January 1943 and Southdown have decided to show off their first Leyland Titan TD2 adapted to run on producer gas. Car 952 (UF 8852) – Southdown referred to all its vehicles as cars – is about to cross the eastern end of North Street on its trial run in Brighton. Service 13B was at this time weekday short journeys on the 13 between Brighton Pool Valley and North Moulscombe, Coldean Lane but most routes in Brighton were far too hilly for gas buses and Southdown's small fleet were all operated on town services in Worthing. On the left is a Brighton, Hove & District Tilling bodied AEC Regent while ahead is a Brighton Corporation trolleybus with grey roof.

During its long existence Southdown Motor Services Ltd was generally held in great regard by its customers, transport professionals and enthusiasts alike. Perhaps it was the smart apple green and cream buses which could be seen in all the towns and resorts between Hastings in the east and Fareham in the west and inland for up to 20 miles. Their routes served busy coastal towns, rural communities, picture postcard villages and traversed rolling downland. Perhaps it was because their buses and coaches evoked fond memories of seaside trips or holidays on the south coast. In short, Southdown mostly seemed to serve 'nice' places that people liked to visit!

This book describes the everyday difficulties and dangers faced by Southdown and those living and working in its area during the Second World War. It is not just about the buses and coaches but includes details of the devastating air raids that affected the coastal towns. The imposition at various times of Defence Areas, Curfews and Visitor Bans all brought major changes to everyday life including the provision of bus services. With the outbreak of war expected at any time the summer visitors and holidaymakers returned home at the end of August 1939 only to be replaced by many thousands of young evacuees who travelled from London to safe billets across the Southdown area – except in Portsmouth where local schoolchildren were evacuated to the Isle of Wight or inland areas in Hampshire and Wiltshire. As the expected bombing raids failed to materialise most evacuees returned home and in spring 1940 many hoped for a near normal summer.

Suddenly, at the end of May 1940 Southdown found itself on the frontline against an apparently unstoppable enemy across the channel. The last of the London evacuees were moved to the north and west and thousands of local schoolchildren and others who could get away left for safer homes. After Dunkirk a German landing on the Kent and Sussex coast seemed almost inevitable. In the bombing raids that followed Portsmouth and Eastbourne were singled out for some of the worst attacks to affect the Southdown area. From summer 1941 'Hit & Run' attacks often by single aircraft which approached the coast at wave level and evaded detection by radar caused widespread damage and loss of life as people were often caught out in the streets in machine gun attacks. Sussex and Hampshire were involved with the preparations for D-Day and for months large parts of the area were used for training camps and Military stores. Then in June 1944 came the first of Hitler's new weapons as the V1 flying bombs fell mainly across the eastern half of the Southdown area.

Throughout all the destruction Southdown appeared to lead a charmed existence with only three vehicles seriously damaged of which one was rebodied. In many cases the company's garages, especially in Eastbourne and Portsmouth, were surrounded by bomb ravaged buildings but Southdown was fortunate not to sustain serious damage. When victory finally came in May 1945 the company quickly set about restoring its services and fleet. The story continues postwar until summer 1947 and illustrates how successfully Southdown was able to quickly restore and expand its services to meet the hugely increased post war demand for travel.

Acknowledgements

There are already excellent histories of the company and of Sussex and Portsmouth during the war but I wanted to tell the detailed story of Southdown in wartime along with how unfolding events affected its operating area. An early response from John Allpress, Chairman of the Southdown Enthusiasts Club to one of my first pleas for help in 2004 should have rung alarm bells as he warned me that, compared to many other bus companies, there remained little official detail from Southdown's wartime operations. What there was had largely been published already and there were few people still around to add much detail based on personal experiences. I soon discovered that this was true and have had to look far and wide for sources of information that might be relevant to the story. Perhaps that's why it has taken so long!

This book would not have been possible without the generous assistance of many people to whom I would like to offer my sincere thanks. Firstly, renowned Southdown expert Alan Lambert has most generously assisted me in resolving numerous queries which have arisen during the course of my research. After much searching I am pleased to say that, eventually, it has been possible to amend and add significantly to earlier information. John Allpress, long time Chairman of SEC, has kindly given encouragement, advice and allowed me access to his Route History records. Anyone interested in more detailed vehicle information is recommended to the excellent Fleet History series produced by the Southdown Enthusiasts Club which have proved invaluable in compiling this book. Many hours were spent in research at both the Omnibus Society library in Walsall and at the Kithead Archive in Droitwich Spa and I would like to thank Alan Mills and Peter Jacques respectively for their help in providing access to all the material requested. I was extremely fortunate to have access to the unique archive material held by the late Roger Funnell without whom the story of the London Express Services would have been impossible to compile. His willingness to assist me at a very difficult time in his life will always be remembered and greatly appreciated. The wartime schoolboy jottings of the late Norman Read and David Kaye have been invaluable in providing additional detailed information for the Worthing area. I was delighted to meet Norman Read in August 2011 and discuss his recollections. My long term friend John Card has bravely accompanied me on several marathon research missions and saved me many extra visits to distant archives for which I am very grateful. And, finally my wife has (mostly) cheerfully accepted several years of my leisure time spent in my 'office' researching and drafting this project since 2004!

Colin Druce
Torquay 2014

Photographs
Following the passing of the Emergency Powers Defence Act in August 1939, just prior to the declaration of war, the government published a list of some 104 emergency regulations for the defence of Great Britain and one of these dealt with carrying a camera in certain designated areas. Although this was primarily aimed at German agents or sympathisers taking images of sensitive Military or Defence works or personnel movements which could assist the enemy it meant that as from June 1940 when a large part of the Southdown operating territory was designated a Defence Area the taking of photographs without an appropriate pass was strictly forbidden. Fortunately a small number of official press photographers managed to include some buses in their street scenes whilst, due to the various alterations in restricted areas as the war progressed, the regulations were not as strictly applied in towns such as East Grinstead, Haywards Heath and Horsham as in the coastal towns.

Despite these difficulties I have been able to assemble what I believe to be a representative selection of illustrations covering Southdown's operations between 1939 and 1947. I have again been assisted greatly by Alan Lambert who kindly made available his extensive collection for my perusal and answered many requests for help in identifying locations. The photographic archives of the Omnibus Society and Southdown Enthusiasts Club have provided the great bulk of the photographs and I would like to thank Alan Oxley of OS for his patience in dealing with my many requests. The archive held by West Sussex County Council at Worthing Library proved very useful and fortunately the photographs of Walter Gardiner included many wartime scenes which included Southdown buses. I would especially thank Martin Hayes of WSCC for all his help. Despite extensive searches it has not been possible to identify all of the photographers from whom I have obtained images in the 50 or so years.

Use of Bold Type
In the text route numbers which were new or being revised are shown in bold as are the commencing dates of new timetable publications. Although the 24 hour clock has been used throughout to avoid confusion between a.m. and p.m. times, Southdown used the 12 hour clock in all its publications during the period covered by this book.

At the outbreak of war in September 1939 some 36 of the once large standard fleet of Tilling-Stevens Express B10A2s saloons dating from 1929/30 remained in service with Southdown together with 12 special lightweight versions used on Hayling Island services where the weight restricted Langstone Bridge precluded standard heavier buses. Car 660 (UF 4660) with Short Bros bodywork is seen outside the Southdown garage in Richmond Road in Bognor Regis on the Circular Town Service 51 which was one of the final haunts of these buses before withdrawal in 1939/40 although car 660 was sold in March 1939. *C F Klapper © Omnibus Society*

In the final months before the second major European war in twenty five years the company took delivery of a further 43 Leyland Titan TD5 double-deck buses. All were fitted with 8.6 litre diesel engines and composite six-bay 52 seat bodies similar to those purchased since 1936. As in the previous year there were three body types with cars 206, 207, 208, 210, 211, 218 to 227 and 240 to 249 having highbridge bodywork by Park Royal, while cars 228 to 239 had identical highbridge bodies by Beadle. Cars 212 to 217 had lowbridge bodies by Park Royal with the usual 4 seats to each row on the upper deck and offside gangway sunk into the lower saloon.

In July 1939 Southdown took delivery of two more vehicles for use on the Worthing Tramocars services. Cars 80 and 81 were based on a newly introduced Dennis Falcon chassis powered by the Dennis 3.77 litre petrol engine and fitted with Harrington porch style centre entrance bus bodywork seating 30. The chassis frame was raised over the axles to give a lowered floor level suitable for these routes. The outbreak of war meant their stay on the Tramocars routes was short as they were delicensed during 1942 and stored out of use until at least June 1945. On their postwar return to service in Worthing they were used mainly on the local service 31F to South Ferring but in June 1950 both were transferred to the Portsmouth area and joined the postwar Dennis Falcons at Hayling Island.

For the last summer season before the outbreak of war Southdown took delivery of 14 Tiger TS8 coaches, again with 8.6 litre diesel engines and Harrington bodywork developed from the stylish curved waist rail design introduced on car 1212 in the previous year. Cars 1213 to 1226 arrived during June and July and were for use on excursions being fitted with cove windows in place of a cream band incorporating the coach service roof board. Their life on front line duties was to be very short as within just a few weeks their intended duties were severely curtailed. They were to be the last new coaches delivered to Southdown until 1947. During the Second World War the diesel engines were exchanged with the petrol engines from cars 1400 to 1429. After the war these coaches were held in such esteem that during 1949 and 1950 nine of them – 1218 to 1226 – were reseated to C21R at Portslade Works to operate a new programme of European luxury tours and to augment the ageing Lionesses and Tigresses then used on luxury tours in the U.K. Another six lightweight vehicles for Hayling Island were purchased for the 1939 season. Cars 505 to 510 were Cheetah LZ4 coaches with the 4.7 litre petrol engines and fitted with Park Royal 24 seat centre entrance bodywork.

A further 14 Harrington bodied Leyland TS8 single deck buses were on order for 1939 but all arrived after the war had commenced.

Sixteen TD5s with Park Royal bodies remained on order for delivery after the outbreak of war. Six of the Park Royal bodied Titans delivered earlier in 1939 had lowbridge bodies as shown by car 215 (FCD 515) which is awaiting departure in North Street, Midhurst after the war on the hourly service 60 to Petersfield via Rogate. This service actually passed under a low railway bridge in Petersfield so in this case there was a genuine need for a lowbridge bus. Car 215 was rebodied with a new East Lancs highbridge body in January 1950 and lasted in service until sale in January 1962. *Southdown Enthusiasts Club – W J Haynes Collection*

Southdown acquired two Harrington bodied Dennis Falcons for the former Tramocars services in May 1939. Although painted in normal livery they carried Tramocars names at the front and also featured script fleetnames normally only found on coaches. Car 81 (FUF 181) is waiting at the terminus of services T1 and T2 at Splash Point in Worthing during the summer of 1939 in front of the more traditional Tramocars vehicles. As the war progressed the Falcons became surplus to requirements and the services subject to significant reduction and diversion away from the sea front roads. After postwar service on Hayling Island car 81 was finally sold in 1958 and eventually passed into preservation.
Omnibus Society

Car 1224 (FUF 324) is one of a batch of 14 Leyland Tiger TS8s with attractive Harrington bodies delivered in May 1939. They only had a few months normal service before the outbreak of war severely curtailed seaside Excursion duties until they were eventually suspended in 1941. All were delivered with diesel engines, which helped them avoid the attention of the Military Authorities when requisitioning began in 1940, but exchanged these for petrol engines to allow the conversion of buses to diesel power. This car was one that was converted to a 21 seat touring coach in 1949/50 and remained with Southdown until March 1957.
Southdown Enthusiasts Club – Clark/Surfleet Collection

Further Park Royal bodied Leyland Titan TD5 models joined the fleet during the summer of 1939 including car 226 (FUF 226) which arrived in June. It is seen after the war loading passengers at Shoreham High Street on the popular hourly service 10 between Brighton and Arundel. All of the Titans delivered in 1939 were included in the postwar rebodying programme with car 226 receiving a replacement Beadle body in December 1949.
Southdown Enthusiasts Club – Clark/Surfleet Collection

The last week of peace

On Monday 28 August the British Ambassador to Germany, Sir Neville Henderson, flew back to Berlin with the Government's latest message to Hitler, although Britain's policy remained the protection of Poland's independence and opposition to any form of aggression.

Following the passing of the Emergency Powers Defence Act the government published a list of 104 emergency regulations for the defence of Great Britain and allowing it the means of putting the country onto a war footing. These were split into several sections, the first dealing with the security of the state including spying or interfering with essential services. It also covered impersonating police officers, interfering with radio communications, carrying a camera in certain designated areas and stricter control of homing pigeons. The second section dealt with public safety by providing for the compulsory evacuation of people, animals and moveable property on the orders of the Secretary of State. It also included the precautions to be taken in the event of an air attack, such as the use of shelters, the co-ordination of fire brigades and police forces, and the control of lighting during the hours of darkness. The third section gave the Admiralty control over merchant shipping and provided for the control of aircraft. Finally the regulations contained some very wide reaching powers for the requisitioning of land and property, the control of industry as well as the control of rail and road traffic. Immediately the war started, the public would be faced with a string of prohibitions as to what they could not do and requirements as to what they had to do. Despite the grave situation the new laws attracted considerable criticism even within Parliament.

A full scale rehearsal of evacuation plans took place throughout the country as 900 schools in London and those from about 30 other vulnerable areas were involved. Many secondary school children, whose term did not begin for another two weeks, were away on holiday and so missed the rehearsal, since returning home especially was not thought necessary by the Board of Education. A statement after the rehearsal stated that it had involved a school population of over a million children throughout the country and had been a marked success.

In the House of Commons on Tuesday 29 August the Prime Minister confirmed that the British Government felt they must hold fast to the Pact they signed with Poland last week, which would involve Britain immediately, should Poland be attacked by another country. Under the Emergency Powers Defence Act the British Admiralty assumed control of all British registered merchant ships including the Southern Railway ferries that ran from ports along the south coast to the Isle of Wight, Channel Islands and France. In London on Wednesday 30 August there were still hopes of a peaceful settlement and during the day the official German News Agency announced that Germany was still hoping for a peaceful solution, but that the 'issue now depends on the decision in London which must be awaited'. There was some mystery about this statement as Britain had not been called upon to make any fresh decision.

Delivered in August 1939 just a few weeks before the outbreak of war were 12 Leyland Titan TD5s with Beadle highbridge bodies similar in appearance to the Park Royal examples. Car 234 (FUF 234) is seen in Bognor after the war on a westbound working on the busy cross town service 50 which, along with the 50A, provided a combined 15 minute frequency between Elmer and Pagham Beach. A new Northern Counties body was fitted in April 1950 and in this form car 234 survived in Southdown service until January 1962. *Southdown Enthusiasts Club – W J Haynes Collection*

For millions of people across Europe, Thursday 31 August 1939 would be the last 'normal' day of peace for many years to come. Much to the complete surprise of everyone involved in the international negotiations of the last few days, Germany announced a 16 point plan for a settlement between Germany and Poland although the Polish Government was completely unaware of the German proposals and continued its military preparations. In Britain the situation had become serious enough for the Government to decide on the evacuation of over three million children and other priority classes as from the following day although in a Ministerial broadcast earlier in the evening the Minster of Health, Walter Elliot, explained that the evacuation was only a precaution. He stated "The Prime Minister has asked me to make it quite clear that this does not mean that war is inevitable. The tension abroad has gone on for some time; it may go on for some time yet. This is an insurance, this is a thing which ought to be done now because it's a very big thing. It will mean, as you hear, moving nearly three million people. It will take nearly four days to carry through. It will make tremendous demands on the patience, skill, cheerfulness – yes especially the cheerfulness – of the whole nation. Of course, we can put this thing through and by Monday night, no later, we shall have given the world another example of what a free people can do that puts its back into the work and puts its heart into the job." Despite this mild optimism the British fleet was put on full alert and the remainder of the naval reservists called for duty. Air Raid Precautions were brought into

force at once by an order sent to the Local Authorities who would operate them. Later in the day Hitler received the Polish Ambassador to Berlin but the talks lasted only a few minutes as Hitler had already made up his mind that German Armed Forces would invade Poland at 0445 on 1 September 1939. Finally, the German radio station at Gliewitz on the German-Polish border was 'attacked' by Polish troops although in fact these soldiers were actually concentration camp inmates, dressed in Polish uniforms and organised by the German SS to give Hitler a pretext for invading Poland.

At dawn on Friday 1 September 1939 Germany began its invasion of Poland. The attack was launched without warning, and without a declaration of war. During the day, German troops crossed Poland's borders with the Reich, and Warsaw and other major cities were bombed. In Britain the evacuation of school children, pregnant women, hospital patients and others from the London area began as announced on the previous day and was to have a major effect on Southdown's bus and coach services as shown in chapters 2 to 7.

Evacuation

As early as May 1938 a committee was set up to consider evacuation from the cities in the event of war. With the expectation of heavy bombing raids immediately after any declaration of war the Government had, by August 1938, finalised extensive plans for the evacuation of Priority Classes from likely target areas. These were described as children of school age or below,

In 1936 Southdown turned to the coachbuilder H.V. Burlingham for a batch of nine coaches on Leyland Tiger TS7 chassis to be used on the company's Express Services. Unlike the current Harrington and Beadle bodies they carried a brighter livery with cream roof and deeper than usual waist band but were not fitted with the customary roof luggage racks. At the outbreak of war all acquired a dark green roof to help make them less conspicuous to enemy raiders. Car 1156 (CUF 156) is seen loading at Victoria Coach Station on the Gosport service and remained with Southdown until sale in May 1957. *Southdown Enthusiasts Club – W J Haynes Collection*

expectant mothers and blind or crippled people. Children under school age were to be evacuated with their mothers or some other responsible adult while children of school age were to be evacuated in school parties under the charge of their teachers. The country was divided into three categories:

Evacuation – people living in urban districts where heavy bombing raids could be expected

Neutral – areas that would neither send nor take evacuees

Reception – rural areas where evacuees would be sent

The Reception areas where the evacuees would be sent were to be the safer parts of the English shire counties mainly in the country and coastal areas away from major industrial towns or cities that were under the threat of bombing raids.

In Southern England the 'evacuable' areas under the government scheme were:

London *including West Ham, East Ham, Walthamstow, Leyton, Ilford and Barking in Essex and Tottenham, Hornsey, Willesden, Acton and Edmonton in Middlesex*

The Medway towns of Chatham, Gillingham and Rochester

Portsmouth, Gosport and Southampton

At that time it was anticipated that any bombing raids would operate from bases within Germany and therefore the Southdown area – apart from around the important Naval base at Portsmouth – was seen as a safe reception area. It was envisaged that the prime target of any German bombing would be the city of London and posters were to be seen all over the capital advising 'Mothers, send them out of London' with a picture of helpless and forlorn children looking up in bewilderment. Most of the evacuees who found their way to the Southdown area came from London and its suburbs.

With war now inevitable, the Government had issued the order to 'Evacuate forthwith' at 1107 on Thursday 31 August 1939. Prepared plans for evacuation would commence at dawn on 1 September 1939 but few realised that within a week, a quarter of the population of Britain would have a new address. The Government estimated that 3,500,000 people would be evacuated in this period alone although in the first four days of September 1939 only 1,500,000 people took up the offer to move to safer areas away from the major towns. The Government had always stressed that evacuation was purely voluntary and many preferred to stay at home and take their chances rather than saying goodbye to their loved ones. Many others who were in a position to do so, decided they would make their own arrangements for evacuation and soon country and seaside hotels in the south and west enjoyed a steady stream of evacuees seeking refuge from the expected bombing.

The official evacuation of schools from the London area usually involved the children marching from their school to a point where they boarded buses, trams or trolleybuses which conveyed them mostly to suburban railheads such as Richmond, Wimbledon, Clapham Junction and New Cross Gate. Revised Monday to Friday train services ran on the three main evacuation days – 1 to 3 September – to release rolling stock and line capacity for the evacuation specials. From London – the main evacuation area as far as Sussex was concerned – almost half the schoolchildren joined the exodus. The rate of take-up varied widely among the various places scheduled for evacuation although the serious shortfall was not admitted publicly at the time. In addition patients in London hospitals who could be moved were taken to establishments in the Home Counties – often by converted coach ambulances or specially adapted ambulance trains – freeing up space for the expected air raid casualties. Broadly speaking the four day official exodus worked surprisingly well although it was soon apparent that nothing like the expected number had turned up for evacuation. Whilst, in theory, this shortfall meant that the exercise should have been easier to achieve than had been anticipated, in fact it led to serious problems in reception areas. When it was clear that only half the number expected needed transport, train timetables and destinations were often hurriedly rescheduled to get the evacuees away as fast as possible, although this meant the evacuation parties that finally arrived at towns and villages in the reception areas were sometimes quite different from those that had been expected.

On arrival by train at one of the eleven railheads in Sussex the evacuees were then normally transported by buses and coaches to a reception centre where the billeting officer attempted the sometimes difficult job of matching evacuees to billets. Eastbourne's experience was probably typical. For three days the railway station saw the arrival of a seemingly unending succession of trains and the orderly movement of some 17,000 children and hospital patients to waiting buses, cars and ambulances for transport to billeting centres and on to private homes or hospitals. In Brighton, said to be the biggest reception area in the country with 30,000 evacuees, some 40 BH&D and Corporation buses were requisitioned for the three day task of transporting them from Brighton and Hove stations to distributing centres located in the suburbs. Parties arrived by train at all the main towns along the coast from Hastings to Bognor and inland from Crowborough and East Grinstead in the east to Horsham, Petersfield and Chichester in the west. Whilst life by the seaside might be appealing, some school parties from inner London areas found themselves evacuated to small towns and villages including Petworth, Hassocks, Burgess Hill, Pulborough, Chailey and Balcombe with very limited local school facilities. In prewar days most children walked to local schools and now transport would clearly be required for

Seen operating on the London Express Service in Angerstein Road, Portsmouth just days before the outbreak of war is car 1099 (BCD 899), a Harrington bodied Leyland Tiger TS7 fitted with folding sunroof and roof luggage rack. Delivered to Southdown in April 1935 it will very soon have white markings applied to the front wings and be fitted with headlamp masks. And, loading luggage onto the rear roof racks in the blackout will become a new challenge for Southdown crews! Portsmouth's first bombs of the war fell nearby at Kingston Cross in July 1940.
Omnibus Society

many to reach schools in the nearby towns each day. Some minor country services suddenly became important routes requiring larger buses, earlier journeys and even duplication at peak times.

Not all evacuees were heading ***into*** Southdown territory. In Portsmouth, the first of some 12,000 children along with their teachers were taken by special trains to reception centres in places such as Winchester, Salisbury and the New Forest or on boats to the Isle of Wight. The Southern Railway provided 16 special services from Clarence Pier and a total of 5,281 adults and children were carried to the Isle of Wight.

During the day the full machinery of Britain's civil defence was set in motion. Local authorities were instructed to put the air raid warning system into operation, and warned that the sounding of factory hooters and sirens was prohibited except in an air raid. The public was reminded that an 'air raid warning' was given by a series of short blasts on a siren, while the 'all clear' was a long steady blast lasting two minutes. There were three types of warning:

Yellow – issued by Fighter Command as a preliminary warning to all areas over which raiders might pass

Purple – issued at night to areas over which raiders might pass. On receipt of this warning all exposed lighting in factories, docks and railway sidings etc was to be extinguished

Red – a public warning on receipt of which the sirens were to be sounded

Later in the evening the Prime Minister, Neville Chamberlain, told a packed House of Commons that British and French Ambassadors in Berlin had given the German Foreign Minister an ultimatum stating that unless the Nazis withdraw from Poland, Britain and France would fulfil their promise of support to Poland. As dusk

fell a complete blackout came into effect over the whole country from sunset through to sunrise the following morning. Nobody could now doubt the situation was grave. It had an immediate and profound effect on the lives of everyone in Britain and caused a huge increase in road casualties. The effect on Southdown's operations is detailed in chapters 2 and 7.

As the country recovered from its first night of blackout, the evacuation from towns and cities continued by road and rail during Saturday 2 September. The blackout was considered only a partial success, according to the London Regional Transport Commissioner, who announced that not enough care had been taken to obscure house and vehicle lights. The National Service Act came into force meaning that all fit males aged 18 to 41 were liable for conscription into the army, navy or air force. Following the previous day's announcement that British forces had been mobilised there was plenty of military activity as soldiers and sailors from the reserves rejoined their ships or units. In the House of Commons there was an outcry when the Prime Minister was asked why Britain was not standing by Poland. Mr Chamberlain assured the House that the Government was bound to take action unless German forces were withdrawn from Polish territory although no reply had been received in response to the warning message sent the previous day. Arthur Greenwood, acting leader of the opposition, concluded by saying: "I hope, therefore, that tomorrow morning, however hard it may be to the Right Honourable Gentleman – and no one would care to be in his shoes tonight – we shall know the mind of the British Government".

Few could then have doubted that war would be declared on the following day.

'This country is at war with Germany'

In Britain, Sunday 3 September 1939 started bright and sunny with most of the population trying to go about their normal Sunday morning business. But, inevitably, the talk and gossip was about the possibility of war although the public was unaware of the British ultimatum "that German troops be withdrawn from Poland" had been handed to the German Government at 0900. It was due to expire at 1100 but no reply came. At 1000 the BBC advised its listeners to standby for an announcement of national importance and at 1115 the Prime Minister, Neville Chamberlain, spoke to the nation:

"I am speaking to you from the Cabinet Room at 10 Downing Street. This morning the British Ambassador in Berlin handed the German Government a final note stating that, unless we heard from them by eleven o'clock that they were prepared at once to withdraw their troops from Poland, a state of war would exist between us. I have to tell you now that no such undertaking has been received and consequently this country is at war with Germany".

Following Chamberlain's broadcast, a series of short official announcements instructed listeners that the blowing of whistles or sounding of horns was now forbidden since these could be mistaken for an air raid siren. They were told that all theatres, cinemas, music halls and other places of entertainment were to be closed forthwith, and football matches and other events that attracted large crowds were forbidden – measures intended to minimise the chances of a large number of people being killed by a single bomb. This concern was later proved by subsequent events in Brighton, Portsmouth and East Grinstead when cinemas received direct hits resulting in many casualties. Every citizen was warned of his or her wartime responsibilities: to observe the blackout from dusk to dawn, to listen regularly to the BBC news broadcasts, to carry a gas mask at all times and to make sure every member of the family was labelled with his or her name and address.

At 1130, only minutes after the Prime Minister had finished his broadcast to the nation, an unidentified aircraft passed over No 1 Observer Group at Maidstone at 5000 feet moving north easterly. This prompted the first air raid warnings being sounded across Southern England although subsequently it was confirmed that the plane was French and had failed to file a flight plan. The All Clear sounded at 1150. The public had already been warned that when air raids threatened, warning would be given in towns by sirens or hooters and in some cases by the police or air raid wardens blowing short blasts on whistles. They were advised to take cover immediately they heard the warning and stay under cover until the 'Raiders Passed' siren was sounded. In the previous few days 'Public Shelter' notices had been pasted on buildings such as town halls, railway stations, offices and shops and purpose built brick public shelters had started to appear in the streets. Work was resumed on the trenches in the parks and other open spaces, which had been abandoned after the Munich crisis the previous autumn.

The four Main Line Railway companies, London Passenger Transport Board and several minor railways were effectively taken over by the Government on 1 September 1939 under the Emergency Powers (Defence) Act, 1939 – Order No. 1197. They were placed under the control of the Minister of War Transport who appointed the Railway Executive Committee to be his agents for the purpose of giving orders. The railway companies' management and staffs carried on their duties subject to the direction and orders of the Government. Southdown did not come directly under State control but its operations and fleet would 'for the duration' be under the stern governance of various Government departments.

At the outbreak of war the Traffic Commissioners were renamed Regional Transport Commissioners (RTCs) with the South Eastern Area based at Tunbridge Wells. The Southern Area – including Portsmouth and Fareham – which had earlier been absorbed into the South Eastern Area was resurrected under wartime regulations at Reading and continued in existence until the end of the hostilities. Their duties were vastly expanded and included supervision of the evacuation of children and others if

The former Sargent's Limited Stop service between East Grinstead and Brighton was an early casualty of war and was never replaced. This is the timetable for the last summer of operation dated 16 July 1939. Note that unusually it started from the coach station in Steine Street and then ran via Pool Valley. Premium fares applied over some sections and Period Returns were available.

LIMITED STOP

28 BRIGHTON — LEWES — EAST GRINSTEAD 28

via CHAILEY and DANEHILL.

For additional buses between East Grinstead and Chelwood Gate see Services 30 and 92.

Brighton *Steine Street*	...	...	...	10 10	12 10	2 10	4 10	6 10	9 0	... ...
Brighton *Pool Valley*	...	...	...	10 12	12 12	2 12	4 12	6 12	9 2	... ...
Lewes *County Hall*	...	...	...	10 35	12 35	2 35	4 35	6 35	9 25	... ...
Chailey *King's Head*	...	...	...	11 0	1 0	3 0	5 0	7 0	9 53	... ...
Sheffield Park *Station S.R.*			...	11 5	1 5	3 5	5 5	7 5	9 57	... ...
Sheffield Arms	...		...	11 9	1 9	3 9	5 9	7 9	10 1	... ...
Danehill *Post Office*			...	11 14	1 14	3 14	5 14	7 14	10 5	... ...
Chelwood Gate *Red Lion*	...		...	11 20	1 20	3 20	5 20	7 20	10 10	... ...
Wych Cross			...	11 22	1 22	3 22	5 22	7 22	10 12	... ...
Forest Row *The Swan*	...		...	11 30	1 30	3 30	5 30	7 30	10 20	... ...
Ashurst Wood *Three Crowns*			...	11 34	1 34	3 34	5 34	7 34	10 24	... ...
East Grinstead *The Crown*			...	11 40	1 40	3 40	5 40	7 40	10 30	... ...
East Grinstead *The Crown*			...	9 0	11 45	2 0	3 45	5 45	7 45	... ...
Ashurst Wood *Three Crowns*			...	9 6	11 51	2 6	3 51	5 51	7 51	... ...
Forest Row *The Swan*	...		...	9 10	11 55	2 10	3 55	5 55	7 55	... ...
Wych Cross	...		...	9 18	12 3	2 18	4 3	6 3	8 3	... ...
Chelwood Gate *Red Lion*	...		...	9 20	12 5	2 20	4 5	6 5	8 5	... ...
Danehill *Post Office*			...	9 26	12 11	2 26	4 11	6 11	8 11	... ...
Sheffield Arms	...		...	9 31	12 16	2 31	4 16	6 16	8 16	... ...
Sheffield Park *Station S.R.*			...	9 35	12 20	2 35	4 20	6 20	8 20	... ...
Chailey *King's Head*			...	9 40	12 25	2 40	4 25	6 25	8 25	... ...
Lewes *County Hall*			...	10 5	12 50	3 5	4 50	6 50	8 50	... ...
Brighton *Steine Street*			...	10 30	1 15	3 30	5 15	7 15	9 15	... ...

and when necessary. The RTCs had the power to curtail services that were mostly intended for pleasure and to allow new services to be started under a wartime permit without reference to a traffic court as the normal licensing regulations were suspended. They also allocated the much sought after petrol and diesel fuel coupons to operators initially using a basic allowance linked to the route miles that an operator covered in 1938 plus a discretionary amount for new essential routes to strategic locations and could issue a permit to any person to act as a driver or conductor of a public service vehicle for a period of one year from the date of the permit. Defence Permits costing £2 per vehicle and £1 per service per annum replaced the PSV licensing system but modifications to existing road service licences were free.

Most Southdown stage carriage licences expired on 28 February 1940 and those that remained in operation were replaced by Defence Permits starting next day (29 February 1940) in the South Eastern area and from 1 March 1940 in the Southern area which gained reference numbers prefixed by the letter 'J'. The permit for service 31 was issued only in the South Eastern area but permits for all other services in Portsmouth, Havant, Emsworth and Hayling Island were issued in the Southern area. Defence Permits were issued for some 'temporarily suspended' services such as the 28, 62 and 65 although never in practice reintroduced. Annual one year permits were again issued in 1941 and

1942 but under the Emergency Powers (Defence) Road Vehicles and Drivers Order 1942, which came into force on 31 July 1942 all valid licences and permits for buses, drivers and conductors at that time were automatically renewed for 12 months from their expiry dates. In practice they remained in force until normal road service licensing was reintroduced starting during 1946. Many detailed changes do not appear to have been added to the licence files and often the authorisation dates were several weeks after changes had been implemented. The fortnightly publication of 'Notices and Proceedings' ceased at the outbreak of war and the Traffic Courts procedure established since 1930 was suspended for the duration. In the Southdown area this led to some dissatisfaction on the part of smaller operators who felt they had been cheated under the new system.

At the outbreak of war Southdown's full summer timetable had just three weeks operation remaining. The inevitable drift towards war over several months had given the company some time to prepare its plans for bus services in the hostile conditions that were expected. The first major impact on Southdown was the arrival of thousands of evacuees in Sussex starting on Friday 1 September as parties of school children, mainly from the London area, were taken by train to all the main towns along the coast from Hastings to Bognor Regis and inland from Crowborough and East Grinstead in the east to Horsham, Petersfield and Chichester in the west.

Brighton Railway Station was used to welcoming thousands of summer visitors but these young arrivals on Friday 1 September 1939 have been hastily transported by train from the London area as war seemed inevitable and, with it, the threat of heavy German bombing. Brighton was the biggest reception area in the country with 30,000 evacuees arriving over three days. Not all the children seem as enthusiastic as the young man who cheerfully waves to the camera as they wait to board almost new Brighton Corporation AEC Regents in Queens Road.
The Argus

Many were then taken by bus to billets in small towns and villages including Petworth, Hassocks, Burgess Hill, Pulborough, Chailey and Balcombe with very limited local school facilities.

As dusk fell on Friday 1 September 1939 Britain was plunged into complete darkness as all street lighting was turned off. The total darkness meant that for most people, trying to get around after dark was confusing, frightening and often dangerous. Going out in the blackout was very soon restricted to journeys of necessity and bus patronage in the evenings reduced dramatically especially as places of entertainment were all temporarily closed down at the outbreak of war. Road accidents were quickly on the increase and in September 1939, despite much reduced traffic on the roads, the total number of people killed increased by nearly one hundred per cent.

During the wartime period many changes to services were introduced at short notice to meet new situations. Timetables warned that Defence Area restrictions (from 1940), the regulation of fuel supplies and other circumstances made inevitable constant adjustment of the services to meet the changing conditions. These alterations were usually publicised by means of locally distributed leaflets in the areas affected and many of these have not survived. Therefore the dates of changes quoted are often the dates when the next timetable book was produced although the revisions may have been introduced at some earlier date. Given the loss of traffic as holiday visitors returned home and with normal places of entertainment closed it appears that reductions to Southdown bus services began in early September particularly affecting evening frequencies and times of last buses which were generally brought forward by around an hour. The alterations listed for the first weeks of war have mainly been confirmed by leaflets but as few of these appear to have been saved from wartime salvage it must therefore be assumed that many other detailed changes took place.

The evacuation from the cities was completed on the first working day of war, Monday 4 September, and hailed a great success although the numbers of school age children choosing to remain in the danger areas such as Portsmouth was soon to cause problems for the authorities. Starting on Tuesday 5 September 1939 winter timetables were introduced on some services including (at least) 11, 12, 27, 31G, 38, 47, 50, 50A, 52, 53, 55, 98 and 99 while services 62 between Bognor

Regis and Arundel and 65 between Littlehampton and Storrington were temporarily suspended. In addition all Southdown and Portsmouth Corporation services departing from Southsea after 2030 were withdrawn due, according to the local press, to Police complaints about interior lights. It would appear that these problems were promptly resolved and some limited evening services restored. The withdrawal of service 65 left the village of Amberley dependent on the Southern Railway and made travel from Storrington to Arundel a lengthy affair.

A National Registration Bill was given Royal assent on Thursday 7 September, providing for government control over the use of labour and the introduction of identity cards for all UK citizens – both of which would affect Southdown operations in the future. One week after the start of hostilities there were still no devastating bombing raids although the nightly blackout was causing many casualties on the roads. Evening journeys on service 31 were altered from Saturday 9 September with the last through bus from Brighton to Portsmouth departing at 1745 instead of 1915. The last bus from Brighton to Bognor became 2045 instead of 2145 and the final bus as far as Littlehampton was half hour earlier at 2145. From Southsea the last bus to Brighton ran 30 minutes earlier at 1922 while the final service as far as Littlehampton was advanced by an hour to 1952. Running times were unchanged at this time. The extra seasonal journeys on Beachy Head service 97 were withdrawn from Tuesday 12 September and services 28 (Brighton to East Grinstead) and 32 (Brighton Station to Devils Dyke) temporarily suspended from Thursday 14 September. Neither of these was reinstated and the service numbers quickly re-used at the end of the war.

Starting on Saturday 16 September Hayling Island service 47 was curtailed to operate a circular route between HAVANT STATION and HAYLING with an hourly frequency each way around the loop including a two hourly service via Northney. Previously it had run through to Southsea South Parade Pier although otherwise a similar service was provided on Hayling Island as in winter 1938. The timetable for service 12 was altered from Sunday 17 September with the through frequency between Brighton and Eastbourne reduced from half hourly to hourly. Last buses were brought forward with the final departure from Brighton Station to Seaford advanced from 0004 to 2249 and the last 12B to Saltdean Mount leaving Brighton Station at 2141 instead of 2309. The last through bus from Eastbourne was advanced from 2200 to 2045. Running times were unchanged at this time. Commencing Thursday 21 September service 38 was withdrawn between Droxford, Meonstoke and Hambledon and also between Southsea Clarence Pier and Theatre Royal. Four through journeys ran daily plus two journeys as far as Wickham.

In the early weeks of war many services had minor reductions especially in the evenings but service 65 was withdrawn completely leaving the adjacent railway as the only alternative for travellers to Amberley. Note the first bus of the day left Storrington at 1103 and arrived in Littlehampton at 1201! After the war it would be reintroduced as part of a long north to south link from Horsham to Littlehampton.

Bus Service 65 LITTLEHAMPTON, AMBERLEY, and STORRINGTON

Connecting at Storrington with buses for Worthing.

WEEK DAYS AND SUNDAYS. †Change buses at Washington

Littlehampton ...	9 48	12 48	2 48	4 48	6 48	8 48	...	...	...
Forester's Arms ...	9 50	12 50	2 50	4 50	6 50	8 50	...		
Cemetery ...	9 52	12 52	2 52	4 52	6 52	8 52	...		
Wick "Globe" ...	9 54	12 54	2 54	4 54	6 54	8 54	...		
Lyminster Church	9 58	12 58	2 58	4 58	6 58	8 58	...		
Crossbush...	10 1	1 1	3 1	5 1	7 1	9 1	...		
Arundel ...	10 5	1 5	3 5	5 5	7 5	9 5	...		
Whiteways Lodge	1017	1 17	3 17	5 17	7 17	9 17	...		
Houghton...	1021	1 21	3 21	5 21	7 21	9 21	...		
Amberley ...	1027	1 27	3 27	5 27	7 27	9 27	...		
Rackham Lane ...	1032	1 32	3 32	5 32	7 32	9 32	...		
Cootham Lane ...	1037	1 37	3 37	5 37	7 37	9 37	...		
Storrington arr	1044	1 44	3 44	5 44	7 44	9 44	...		
Storrington dep	1110	2 10	4 10	6 10	8 10	1010	. .	...	
Worthing arr	1151	2 51	4 51	6 51	8 51	1051	...		
Worthing dep	1016	12†46	2†46	4†46	6†46	9 16	...		
Storrington arr	11 0	1 30	3 30	5 30	7 30	10 0	...		
Storrington dep	11 3	1 48	3 48	5 48	7 48	10 3	...		
Cootham Lane ...	1110	1 55	3 55	5 55	7 55	10 9	...		
Rackham Lane ...	1115	2 0	4 0	6 0	8 0	1013	...		
Amberley ...	1120	2 5	4 5	6 5	8 5	1018	...		
Houghton...	1125	2 10	4 10	6 10	8 10	1023	...		
Whiteways Lodge	1134	2 19	4 19	6 19	8 19	1031	...		
Arundel ...	1144	2 29	4 29	6 29	8 29	1040	...		
Crossbush...	1147	2 32	4 32	6 32	8 32	1043	...		
Lyminster Church	1150	2 35	4 35	6 35	8 35	1046	...		
Wick "Globe" ...	1154	2 39	4 39	6 39	8 39	1050	...		
Cemetery ...	1156	2 41	4 41	6 41	8 41	1052	...		
Forester's Arms ...	1158	2 43	4 43	6 43	8 43	1054	...		
Littlehampton	12 1	2 46	4 46	6 46	8 46	1057	...		

SOUTHDOWN MOTOR SERVICES, LTD.

SERVICE 47.   HAVANT—HAYLING ISLAND—HAVANT

(with Connections from and to Portsmouth)

Starting on Saturday, September 16th, the following Time Table will be operated until further notice :—

47	HAVANT—HAYLING ISLAND HAVANT (With Connections from and to Portsmouth)														47
		NS	NS	NS											
Southsea *S. Parade Pier*..	..											9 12	9 42	10 12	
Portsmouth *Theatre Royal*	6 12	6 a 55	7 32		8 2	8 *22	8 †52		9 12	9 22	9 52	10 22			
North End *Junction*	6 21	7	7 41		8 11	8 *31	9 †1		9 31	10 1	10 31				
Cosham *Station S.R.*	6 28	7 15	7 48		8 18	8 *38	9 †8		9 38	10 8	10 38				
Havant *Church* ... arr.	6 46	7 34	8 7		8 37	8 *57	9 †27		9 57	10 27	10 57				
Havant *Station S.R.*	6 56	7 33	8 3	8 33	9 3	9 33	10 3	10 33	11 3						
Havant *Church* ... dep.	6 57	7 34	8 † 4	8† 4	9 4	9 34	10 4	10 34	11 4						
Langstone *Ship*	7 2	7 39	8 9	8 39	9 9	9 39	10 9	10 39	11 *9						
Northney *Camp*				8 13				10 13							
Stoke *Yew Tree*	7 9	7 46	8 19	8 46	9 16	9 46	10 19	10 46	11 16						
Manor *Corner*	7 12	7 49	8 22	8 49	9 19	9 49	10 22	10 49	11 19						
Hayling *Bus Station*	7 18		8 27		9 24		10 27		11 24						
Eastoke *Post Office*	7 23		8 31		9 28		10 31		11 28						
Gable *Head*	7 28	7 51	8 36	8 51	9 33	9 51	10 36	10 51	11 33						
Eastoke *Post Office* ·				8 56				10 56							
Hayling *Bus Station*		8 1		9 1		10 1		11 1							
Manor *Corner*	7 30	8 7	8 38	8 *7	9 35	10 7	10 38	11 7	11 35						
Stoke *Yew Tree*	7 33	8 10	8 41	9 10	9 38	10 10	10 41	11 10	11 38						
Northney *Camp*			8 47		9 44				11 44						
Langstone *Ship*	7 40	8 17	8 51	9 17	9 48	10 17	10 48	11 17	11 48						
Havant *Church* ... arr.	7 45	8 22	8 57	9 22	9 52	10 22	10 52	11 22	11 52						
Havant *Station S.R.*	7 47	8 24	8 57	9 24	9 54	10 24	10 54	11 24	11 54						
Havant *Church* ... dep.	7 55	8 22	8 59	9 29	9 59	10 29	10 59	11 29	11 59						
Cosham *Bridge*	8 12	8 40	9 17	9 47	10 17	10 47	11 17	11 47	12 17						
North End *Junction*	8 19	8 47	9 24	9 54	10 24	10 54	11 24	11 54	12 24						
Portsmouth *Theatre Royal*	8 28		9 33	10 3	10 33	11 3	11 33	12 3	12 33						
Southsea *S. Parade Pier*	...	9 4	9 43	10 13	10 43	11 13	11 43	12 13	12 43						

SOUTHDOWN MOTOR SERVICES, LTD.

SERVICE 22 : REVISION OF TIMES & CONNECTIONS

STARTING ON THURSDAY, SEPTEMBER 28th, 1939

Attention is particularly directed to the altered Service between Petworth and Duncton, the connections at Petworth to and from both Midhurst and Haslemere, and the timing of the first morning bus from Pulborough to Petworth.

22	BRIGHTON—Steyning—Pulborough—PETWORTH Also showing Service 22 and 63 buses between Petworth and Duncton.	22

(timetable grid)

*—Not Sundays.   †—by Service 63 bus.   §—by Service 59 bus.   ‡—by Aldershot & District bus.

22	PETWORTH—Pulborough—Steyning—BRIGHTON Also showing Service 22 and 63 buses between Duncton and Petworth.	22

(timetable grid)

*—Not Sundays.   †—by Service 63 bus.   §—by Service 59 bus.   ‡—by Aldershot & District bus.

The Southern Publishing Co., Ltd., 130, North Street, Brighton—B8192

SOUTHDOWN MOTOR SERVICES, LTD.

SERVICE 38 : REVISION OF TIMES & CURTAILMENT OF ROUTE.

STARTING ON THURSDAY, SEPTEMBER 21st, 1939.

It is regretted that circumstances make it necessary for this Service to be considerably curtailed. A reduced Time Table, as shown below, will be operated between Portsmouth (Theatre Royal) and Droxford only. Between Hambledon and Droxford, Droxford and Meonstoke, and Portsmouth (Theatre Royal) and Clarence Pier, the Service will, for the present, be entirely suspended.

38	PORTSMOUTH—Southwick—Wickham—DROXFORD							38
		NS						
Portsmouth *Theatre Royal*	...	10 35	1 35	2 35	4 35	5 35	7 35	...
North End *Bus Office*	...	10 44	1 44	2 44	4 44	5 44	7 44	...
Cosham *Station S.R.*	...	10 51	1 51	2 51	4 51	5 51	7 51	...
Portsdown *The George*	...	10 55	1 55	2 55	4 55	5 55	7 55	...
Southwick *Church*	...	11 2	2 2	3 2	5 2	6 2	8 2	...
Boarhunt *Garage*	...	11 11	2 11	3 11	5 11	6 11	8 11	...
Wickham *The Square*	8 10	11 16	2 16	3 16	5 16	6 16	8 16	...
Roebuck *Inn*	8 15	11 30	2 30	...	5 30	6 30	...	...
The Bold *Forester*	8 20	11 35	2 35	...	5 35	6 35	...	...
Soberton *The Falcon*	8 25	11 40	2 40	...	5 40	6 40	...	...
Soberton *White Lion*	8 31	11 46	2 46	...	5 46	6 46	...	...
Droxford *The Square*	8 40	11 55	2 55	...	5 55	6 55	...	...

		NS	SO	NS	SO								
Droxford *The Square*	...	10 0	10 0	1 0	...	4 0	6 0	8 0					
Soberton *White Lion*	...	10 5	10 9	1 9	...	4 9	6 9	8 9					
Soberton *The Falcon*	...	10 15	...	1 15	...	4 15	6 15	8 15					
The Bold *Forester*	...	10 20	...	1 20	...	4 20	6 20	8 20					
Roebuck *Inn*	...	10 25	...	1 25	...	4 25	6 25	8 25					
Wickham *The Square*	8 5	9 30	10 30	11 30	1 30	3 30	4 30	6 30	8 30				
Boarhunt *Garage*	8 14	9 39	10 39	11 39	1 39	3 39	4 39	6 39	...				
Southwick *Church*	8 23	9 48	10 48	11 48	1 48	3 48	4 48	6 48	...				
Portsdown *The George*	8 35	10 0	11 0	12 0	2 0	4 0	5 0	7 0	...				
Cosham *Railway Bridge*	8 39	10 4	11 4	12 4	2 4	4 4	5 4	7 4	...				
North End *Bus Office*	8 46	10 11	11 11	12 11	2 11	4 11	5 11	7 11	...				
Portsmouth *Theatre Royal*	8 55	10 20	11 20	12 20	2 20	4 20	5 20	7 20	...				

SO—Sundays only.   NS—Not Sundays.

Most service changes were notified by the issue of leaflets distributed locally and unfortunately not many have survived. There is little detail or explanation included but companies were under enormous pressure in the early days of the war with drastic fuel rationing expected at any moment.

Service 38 was one of the first to be significantly curtailed, losing the sections of route beyond Droxford to Meonstoke and Hambledon and also between Clarence Pier and Theatre Royal. Previously the last bus from Clarence Pier far as Wickham had been at 2305. At this time no adjustments had been made for blackout running.

SOUTHDOWN MOTOR SERVICES, LTD.

SERVICE 81.   REVISION OF TIMES AND CURTAILMENT OF ROUTE

STARTING ON THURSDAY, SEPTEMBER 28th, 1939

It is regretted that circumstances make it necessary for this Service to be considerably curtailed. A reduced Time Table, as shown below, will be operated between Haywards Heath and Cowfold only. Between Cowfold and Billingshurst, this Service will, for the present, be entirely suspended. Buses to and from Coolham, Coneyhurst and Billinghurst, will continue to be available, via Horsham.

81	HAYWARD SHEATH—COWFOLD With connections at Cowfold to and from Horsham and Henfield.	81

(timetable grid)

NS—Not Sundays.   ‡ Henfield bus leaves Cowfold at 8.50 a.m.

§ Bus from Henfield arr. Cowfold 8.26 a.m.

FARES

Haywards Heath *Station S.R.* 24.

1	Tylor's Green. **22.**										
2	1	Wheatsheaf. **21.**									
3	2	1	Cuckfield *Clock*. **20.**								
5	4	3	2	Ansty. **19.**							
6	5	4	3	1	Pickwell Cross Roads. **18.**						
8	7	6	5	3	2	Bolney Cross Roads. **17.**					
9	8	7	6	4	3	1	Crosspost. **16.**				
10	9	8	7	5	4	2	1	Homewood Hbuse. **15.**			
11	10	9	8	6	5	3	2	1	Lyeland Cross Roads. **14.**		
1/-	11	10	9	7	6	4	3	2	1	Oakdean Letter Box. **13.**	
1/1	1/-	11	10	8	7	5	4	3	2	1	Cowfold. **12.**

RETURN FARES.

Haywards Heath *Station S.R.* and Cowfold	... 1/8
„ „ „ „ „ „ Horsham *Carfax* (via Cowfold)	2/6
Cuckfield *Clock* and Horsham *Carfax* (via Cowfold)	... 2/2

Whilst food rationing would not commence for over three months, the rationing of petrol and diesel fuel began on Saturday 23 September 1939 (after being delayed from 17 September) and the large bus companies were obliged to reduce operations by at least 25% with immediate effect. In the normal course of events some bus services would have been withdrawn or reduced in frequency from Monday 25 September 1939 when the winter timetable was due to commence. Although many changes occurred before this date, summer only services **26A** and **46** along with any remaining seasonal journeys were withdrawn no later than Sunday 24 September 1939.

Starting on Thursday 28 September evening journeys were reduced on service **22** with the last bus from Brighton advanced from 2220 (2300 on Saturdays) to 2120. Although a basic hourly daytime service continued to run between Brighton and Petworth the number of buses to Duncton was cut to four. Service **59** gained a lengthy extension over former service 63 from PETWORTH to HORSHAM STATION via Wisborough Green, Billingshurst, Slinfold and Broadbridge Heath. With a journey time of 2 hours 53 minutes it became one of the longest Southdown routes. An hourly service ran between Bognor and Midhurst – partly replacing Aldershot & District's 19 which was curtailed from the north at Midhurst – with alternate journeys continuing to and from Horsham. On the alternate hour buses changed to service 60 at Midhurst and ran to Petersfield. As a consequence service **63** was reduced to run only between Petworth and Chichester. The frequency of service **60** running between Midhurst (Grammar School) and Petersfield Station was halved from hourly to two hourly daily. Two additional afternoon journeys (not shown on the surviving leaflet) ran on Saturdays only between Petersfield and Rogate 'if traffic required and circumstances permit' but these appeared on a new leaflet dated Saturday 7 October. In addition service **61** was curtailed to operate only between PETERSFIELD STATION and EAST HARTING (TURKEY ISLAND) being withdrawn from Elsted Church. The company stated that the service between East Harting and Elsted was for the present entirely suspended. It is likely that many others followed.

Although service **81** between Haywards Heath and Billingshurst may have appeared as a strategic cross county link on the route map, the western section traversed some very unpromising bus territory which struggled to support a regular daily service even in the post war boom years. Accordingly, from Thursday 28 September the Cowfold to Billingshurst section was suspended without replacement and the frequency of the Haywards Heath to Cowfold section halved to two hourly. Again, the company apologised for the 'considerable curtailment' of the service.

The National Registration system under which all civilians were centrally registered was set up on Friday 29 September using the machinery devised for the Census of 1941 which was cancelled due to the war. This was followed in October by the issue of the identity card, a small document containing one's name, address and a six or seven digit National Registration number. On 22 May 1940, as the war in Europe took a serious turn for the worse, the Ministry of Home Security instructed every civilian to carry their card at all times as proof of identity and address. They had to be produced on demand to the police, members of the Armed Forces on duty and national registration officers. Identity cards remained in use in the UK until 22 February 1952.

The 'Phoney War' September 1939 – April 1940

The term 'Phoney War' is usually applied to the period from late September 1939 to April 1940 when, after the successful German attack on Poland at the start of September, little seemed to happen. Many experts in the UK had predicted major German air attacks on towns and cities leading to massive casualties and destruction from the outset of war. The feared bombing did not occur and by October many of the London evacuees had already returned home to their families.

The next known revision to services occurred on Thursday 19 October affecting service **45** which was withdrawn between Southsea South Parade Pier and Theatre Royal or Bradford Road junction (Fratton journeys). Journey times were revised and blackout journey times introduced after 1800. The main daytime westbound service consisted of:

1 journey per hour Theatre Royal – direct – Fareham – Warsash

2 journeys per hour Bradford Road – Fratton – direct – Cornaway Lane, Portchester

2 journeys per hour Theatre Royal – Castle Street – Fareham

2 journeys per hour Theatre Royal – Castle Street – Cornaway Lane, Portchester

3 journeys per hour Theatre Royal – direct – Fareham

There were still ten journeys per hour overall but two extra journeys were extended beyond Cornaway Lane to Fareham while the westbound Fratton journeys no longer served Castle Street. A slightly different pattern of service applied for eastbound journeys. The terminus at Bradford Road was better known locally as Bradford Junction but at this time Southdown did not have a destination screen for this point and buses showed instead:

NORTH END
FRATTON BRIDGE

It is notable that Southdown made no attempt to distinguish the route variations by means of suffix letters as it did on the Havant and A3 route corridors in the Portsmouth area.

24	**BRIGHTON, HURSTPIERPOINT, PLUMPTON, LEWES, BRIGHTON** CIRCULAR SERVICE.	24

Brighton *Pool Valley* ...	8 48	1024	1224	2 24	4 24	6 27	8 40	...
N. Moulscombe ...	9 4	1040	1240	2 40	4 40	6 44	8 57	...
Falmer	9 8	1044	1244	2 44	4 44	6 49	9 2	...
Kingstonridge ...	9 16	1052	1252	2 52	4 52	6 58	9 12	...
Lewes *County Hall*	9 23	1059	1259	2 59	4 59	7 5	9 19	...
Offham	9 30	11 7	1 7	3 7	5 7	7 14	9 28	...
Plumpton *Half Moon* ...		1117	1 17	3 17	5 17	7 25	9 40	...
Westmeston ...		1122	1 22	3 22	5 22	7 31	9 46	
Ditchling *Church* ...		1127	1 27	3 27	5 27	7 36	9 51	
Hassocks *Cinema* ...		1132	1 32	3 32	5 32	7 42	9 57	
Hassocks *Stone Pound* ...		1134	1 34	3 34	5 34	7 44	9 59	
Hurstpierpoint ...		1140	1 40	3 40	5 40	7 50	10 5	
Albourne		...	...	...	...	...	10 9	
Henfield		...	...	...	...	...	1027	
Muddleswood Cross Roads		1144	1 44	3 44	5 44	7 55		
Pyecombe *Plough* ...		1152	1 52	3 52	5 52	8 4		
Patcham *Fountain* ...		12 0	2 0	4 0	6 0	8 12		
Brighton *Pool Valley* ...		1215	2 15	4 15	6 17	8 29		

Brighton *Pool Valley* ...	...	...	1124	1 24	3 24	5 24	7 33	...
Patcham *Fountain* ...	...	...	1139	1 39	3 39	5 39	7 49	...
Pyecombe *Plough* ...	...	...	1147	1 47	3 47	5 47	7 58	...
Muddleswood Cross Roads ...	...	...	1155	1 55	3 55	5 55	8 7	...
Henfield		9 15	...					...
Albourne		9 36	...					...
Hurstpierpoint ...		9 39	1159	1 59	3 59	5 59	8 11	...
Hassocks *Stone Pound* ...		9 44	12 4	2 4	4 4	4 6	5 8	8 17
Hassocks *Cinema* ...		9 46	12 6	2 6	4 6	6 7	8 19	
Ditchling *Church* ...		9 53	1212	2 12	4 12	4 12	6 14	8 26
Westmeston ...		10 0	1218	2 18	4 18	6 20	8 32	
Plumpton, *Half Moon* ...		10 6	1223	2 23	4 23	6 23	8 38	
Offham	9 34	1018	1234	2 34	4 34	6 38	8 50	
Lewes *County Hall*	9 43	1031	1243	2 43	4 43	6 48	9 0	
Kingstonridge ...	9 50	1038	1250	2 50	4 50	6 55	9 7	
Falmer	9 57	1045	1257	2 57	4 57	7 3	9 15	
N. Moulscombe ...	10 0	1048	1 0	3 0	5 0	7 6	9 18	
Brighton *Pool Valley* ...	1016	11 4	1 16	3 16	5 16	7 24	9 36	

For other buses between Hassocks, Hurstpierpoint and Brighton, see Services 14, 23, 30, 34 and 36.

From 3 November 1939 the official period of the blackout was reduced by one hour to begin half an hour after sunset and end half an hour before sunrise. British Summer Time continued until Sunday 19 November 1939 and was brought forward to commence from Sunday 25 February 1940. Clocks were not put back as usual in the autumn of 1940 and BST continued throughout the rest of the war. In addition Double Summer Time was introduced as from 4 May 1941 with clocks brought forward a further hour – two hours ahead of GMT – and continuing until 10 August 1941. In summer, Southern England became the land of the midnight sun with buses making the last journeys of the day in daylight.

Blackout regulations were making all travel after dark difficult and often hazardous. Southdown had long been renowned for its system of connecting services and in an effort to maintain this facility and cope with the blackout conditions, the company introduced new schedules from 16 November 1939. From this date all timings after 1800 were extended by 10%. Thus a journey of 1 hour would be given 1 hour 6 minutes and one of 90 minutes was rescheduled to take 1 hour 39 minutes. Services departing every 30 minutes would change to every 33 minutes after 1800 and hourly departures would, for example, become 1700, 1806, 1912, 2018, 2124 etc. The timetable for Service 31 was complicated as late afternoon journeys would start with the normal running time but from 1800 the time was gradually extended. The so called blackout running times continued until 12 May 1945 and

did not just operate during the hours of darkness, as might have been expected. The extension of BST throughout the year coupled with the withdrawal of late evening services by January 1943 meant that for several months of the year the last Southdown buses ran into their garages in daylight. Conversely in mid winter the morning rush hour could be completed in total darkness.

A complete system timetable book was issued dated **Thursday 16 November 1939** incorporating the new blackout timetables. It was described as *Emergency Timetable No 1* and was the first of the wartime series which would eventually reach No 9 in October 1942 before even greater demands for economy lead to the issue of three separate booklets for East Sussex, West Sussex and Hampshire/Portsmouth starting from 3 January 1943 and continuing until 13 May 1945. The new books were smaller than prewar, measuring 127mm by 87mm but still cost 2d – increased to 3d from Issue No 5 – and, in most cases, no longer included faretables or express coach timetables. The cover was a thin cream card with green print and the first edition ran to 196 pages as compared to 368 pages for the July 1939 publication. In addition to the blackout amendments a number of other changes were introduced throughout the Southdown area although it must be stressed that it most probably started earlier.

In Worthing the short journeys on service **1** between Worthing and Findon were reduced to operate during weekday peak periods only and cross town service **3** curtailed to terminate at GEORGE V AVENUE (GORING ROAD) although certain early morning weekday journeys continued to and from Goring Church and the frequency remained at 10 minutes daily. The frequency of service **4** was reduced to 20 minutes throughout daily – the winter service was normally every 10 minutes as far as Durrington. Not surprisingly the former Tramocars routes were also both reduced in frequency with both **T1** and **T2** dropping from a 10 minute service in

This timetable commenced on 16 November 1939 and shows the extra running time allowed after 1800 to cope with operation in the blackout although the same times applied throughout the year. A basic two hourly frequency was provided although no early morning journeys for workers or scholars were operated and the same timetable applied seven days a week. One of the buses operating on service 24 was provided from Henfield garage and ran to and from Albourne along roads otherwise unserved by any buses.

By the time car 257 (GCD 357) entered service in November 1939 the country had been at war for almost 3 months. It is a Park Royal bodied Leyland Titan TD5 and seen here after the war in Pool Valley, Brighton on service 14 to Haywards Heath via Bolney which ran every 2 hours. After being rebodied by Northern Counties in February 1950 it survived in service until sale in October 1962.
Southdown Enthusiasts Club – Clark/Surfleet Collection

About to leave Petersfield for its southward journey to Southsea is car 224 (FUF 224), a Leyland Titan TD5 with Park Royal 52 seat highbridge body new in May 1939. As was normal practice at this time there is no indication on the destination screen whether the bus is on service 40 via Clanfield or 42 via Horndean. During the early months of the war buses generally operated with only the nearside headlamp masked and the bulb removed from the offside lamp. Car 224 retains prewar lined livery but has already gained a dark green roof and white markings on the front wings. It was rebodied by Park Royal in 1949 and finally withdrawn in January 1962.
Alan Lambert collection

winter 1938 to a 15 minute service. The short **11A** between NORTH FERRING CORNER and FERRING (SOUTH DRIVE) was withdrawn and service **31** was once more diverted between Goring Station and Roundstone Gates to operate via Goring Street, Littlehampton Road, Ferring Lane, Langbury Lane, Littlehampton Road and Worthing Road thus reversing the change introduced on 25 May 1939.

The daytime frequency of service **12** was revised to provide:

1 journey per hour Tongdean to Eastbourne

3 journeys per hour Tongdean to Seaford

1 journey per hour Tongdean to Peacehaven, Rosemary

1 journey per hour Brighton Station to Peacehaven Annexe (12A)

1 journey per hour Brighton Station to Saltdean Mount (12B)

This represented a reduction of one Eastbourne to Seaford journey per hour compared to winter 1938 whilst the frequency of **12B** was reduced from two buses per hour in the previous winter to an hourly service daily. Service **12A** was again curtailed to operate only between BRIGHTON STATION and PEACEHAVEN ANNEXE. As work on Newhaven Bridge was completed, double deckers began to appear on other journeys and by 1 December 1939 the entire 12 group had been converted except service 12B which retained its 1400 class Tiger saloons. It was noted at the company Board Meeting on Thursday 14 March 1940 that Southdown had paid £4,000 to the Southern Railway as an agreed portion of the cost of renewal of moving parts of Newhaven Bridge. Among many frequency reductions service **13F** between BRIGHTON (POOL VALLEY) and LOWER BEVENDEAN (HAPPY VALLEY) had its frequency reduced from 20 minutes daily to 30 minutes on Weekdays and hourly on Sundays although at this stage other buses along the Lewes Road remained virtually unchanged.

As part of a reduction in frequency to Southsea, services **31B**, **31C** and **43** were withdrawn between South Parade Pier and Theatre Royal. Also in the Portsmouth area service **39** was withdrawn between HAMBLEDON and WORLD'S END. New service **42A** was introduced between PORTSMOUTH (THEATRE ROYAL) and HORNDEAN (SHIP & BELL) operating only late evenings as a renumbering of short journeys on service 42 as far as Horndean. Last buses from Portsmouth were generally at least 30 minutes earlier departing Theatre Royal at around 2230. In the Chichester area the frequency of service **52** was slightly reduced as compared to winter 1938 with an hourly service via Hunston but only four Selsey bound and five Chichester bound journeys operating via Donnington. The Witterings loop service **53** was reduced to a two hourly service each way daily similar to winter 1938. Service **69** was suspended between Littlehampton and Arundel but the frequency was increased from two hourly to 90 minutes.

In the north of the area service **86A** was curtailed to operate between HAYWARDS HEATH STATION and BROOK STREET being suspended between Brook Street and Balcombe although other services in the Haywards Heath remained unscathed at this time. At East Grinstead, service **87** was curtailed at TYES CROSS being suspended from its usual terminus in the midst of Ashdown Forest, an area which the Military were soon to use extensively for training purposes.

87	EAST GRINSTEAD—TYES CROSS via KINGSCOTE and WEST HOATHLY								87
		NS	NS	NS	SO	Sats			
East Grinstead *Crown*	...	8 0	10 5	1 5	2 5	2 35	4 35	6 6	9 5
Sainthill Green	...	8 7	10 12	1 12	2 12	2 42	4 42	6 14	9 13
Hazeldene Cross Roads	...	8 11	10 16	1 16	2 16	2 46	4 46	6 18	9 17
Kingscote *Station S.R.*		8 16	10 21	1 21	2 21	2 51	4 51	6 24	9 23
Selsfield	...	8 22	10 27	1 27	2 27	2 57	4 57	6 30	9 29
West Hoathly *The Cat*		8 27	10 32	1 32	2 32	3 2	5 2	6 36	9 35
Sharpthorne *Post Office*		8 30	10 35	1 35	2 35	3 5	5 5	6 39	9 38
Tyes Cross	...	8 33	10 38	1 38	2 38	3 8	5 8	6 42	...
		NS	NS	NS	SO	Sats			
Tyes Cross	...	8 35	10 50	1 50	2 50	3 20	5 20	6 55	...
Sharpthorne *Post Office*		8 38	10 53	1 53	2 53	3 23	5 23	6 59	9 40
West Hoathly *The Cat*		8 41	10 56	1 56	2 56	3 26	5 26	7 2	9 43
Selsfield	...	8 46	11 1	2 1	3 1	3 31	5 31	7 8	9 49
Kingscote *Station S.R.*		8 52	11 7	2 7	3 7	3 37	5 37	7 14	9 55
Hazeldene Cross Roads	...	8 57	11 12	2 12	3 12	3 42	5 42	7 20	10 1
Sainthill Green	...	9 1	11 16	2 16	3 16	3 46	5 46	7 24	10 5
East Grinstead *Crown*	...	9 8	11 23	2 23	3 23	3 53	5 53	7 32	10 13

NS—Not Sundays.   SO—Sundays only.   Sats.—Saturdays only.

88	HAYWARDS HEATH, TURNERS HILL EAST GRINSTEAD								88
		NS							
Haywards Heath Stn.	7 45	9 30	11 30	1 30	2 30	4 30	6 33	8 45	...
Lindfield P.O.	...	7 49	9 34	11 34	1 34	2 34	4 34	6 39	8 51	...
Ardingly P.O.	7 59	9 44	11 44	1 44	2 44	4 44	6 50	9 2	...
Stonehurst	...	...	9 48	11 48	1 48	2 48	4 48	6 54	9 6	...
Selsfield	...	...	9 53	11 53	1 53	2 53	4 53	7 0	9 13	...
Turners Hill	...	...	9 56	11 56	1 56	2 56	4 56	7 3	9 15	...
Turners Hill East Grinstead	For connections to East Grinstead see announcements by London Passenger Transport Board.								
East Grinstead Turners Hill	For connections from East Grinstead see announcements from East Grinstead see announcements by London Passenger Transport Board.								
		NS							
Turners Hill	...	...	10 4	12 4	2 4	3 4	4 5	4 7	10 9 22	...
Selsfield	...	...	10 7	12 7	2 7	3 7	5 7	7 13 9 25	...
Stonehurst	...	...	...	10 12	12 12	2 12	3 12	5 12	7 19 9 31	...
Ardingly P.O.	8 5	10 16	12 16	2 16	3 16	5 16	7 23 9 35	...
Lindfield P.O.	...	8 13	10 24	12 24	2 24	3 24	5 24	7 32 9 44	...
Haywards Heath Stn.	8 18	10 29	12 29	2 29	3 29	5 29	7 38 9 50	...

Further east, the timetable page for the Beachy Head service **97** stated "This service will be continued as long as circumstances permit, at times announced locally in Eastbourne. It is hoped in any event to maintain a service at fine weekends". For winter 1938 a two hourly basic service was increased to 30 minutes in fine weather but circumstances were now very different. The frequency of service **99** was reduced from two hourly daily in winter 1938 to 4 journeys daily with buses departing Eastbourne at 1030, 1230, 1430 and 1830 and Hastings at 1006, 1206, 1406 and 1806. A second edition of *Emergency Timetable No.1* was issued with some minor alterations from **Saturday 25 November 1939**.

Whilst on land in Western Europe very little of military importance was apparently taking place, the war at sea continued to affect supplies of valuable food and materials as magnetic mines laid by German U-boats sank 60,000 tons of shipping on the east coast of Britain in one week in mid November. The expected air attacks on Britain had not materialised allowing some degree of normality from mid September with the reopening of many cinemas and theatres. Most places of entertainment were allowed to reopen by 17 December 1939 in time for Christmas but this often caused problems for bus operators as most evening services had already been reduced in line with lower demand during the blackout. By late September children who had been evacuated earlier in the month from Portsmouth began to drift back to their homes in ever increasing numbers even though most schools in the city remained closed. With many families separated by military service and

evacuation, Christmas 1939 was very different to recent years. The blackout regulations meant the end of traditionally decorated Christmas trees in front windows and bright shop displays with lots of goods to tempt the shopper. But, with food rationing coming in January, everyone seemed determined to enjoy the festive season with restaurants and hotels fully booked. Anyone planning to get home for the festive season would have found their journeys difficult, as fuel rationing and travel restrictions began to affect road and rail services.

1940

In the first four months of the war a total of 4,133 people were killed on Britain's roads, and 2,657 of these were pedestrians. Road fatalities increased by 100% compared to the corresponding months in 1938. For some months German U-boats had been causing serious losses to Merchant shipping and, after much deliberation, the government introduced food rationing in Britain on Monday 8 January 1940. It came as a further blow to housewives and families and, although everyone had been warned about the rations, most found the amounts very small. One of the surprising effects of food rationing was that it generally improved the nation's health by encouraging a more balanced diet than most enjoyed in prewar days. The winter weather of 1939/40 proved to be some of the worst on record with many weeks of snow accompanied by very low temperatures and strong winds leading to major disruption of road and rail services. Snow began to fall on 12 December and continued to affect the Southdown area at intervals through until the middle of March adding to the misery caused by the blackout and rationing. Services were often seriously disrupted and a report in the Portsmouth Evening News on Wednesday 31 January told of a bus on the 54 from Chichester to Compton which left the depot around 1500 on Monday and had not been heard of since. It finally returned to Chichester at midday on Thursday!!

Southdown took over the old established services of Bannister and Evans on Thursday 1

Car 187 (EUF 187) is a Leyland Titan TD5 with Beadle lowbridge body new in May 1938 and seen working an eastbound service 89 somewhere between Haywards Heath and Uckfield. It still retains full lined out livery but has gained the standard headlamp masks introduced in early 1940. A new Beadle highbridge body was fitted in 1949 and the bus remained in the fleet until sale in May 1959.
Alan Lambert collection

Southdown acquired the businesses of Bannister of Burgess Hill and Evans of Ditchling in February 1940 along with their stage carriage services between Hassocks and Ditchling. One of the two vehicles used on the service was UR 9874 a Commer Invader with Strachan 20 seat body new in 1931 and latterly owned by Evans t/a Red Bus of Ditchling. Both were acquired by Southdown but not operated and sold in March 1940 before serious restrictions on the sale of Motor Vehicles had been enforced.
A Norris © Omnibus Society

Southdown provided a one man operated Leyland Cub to operate its new service 33 between Hassocks Station and Ditchling. Car 17 (CUF 517) with Park Royal 20 seat body new in July 1936 is seen here with an early type of nearside headlamp mask and white blackout markings but still retaining a cream roof. At this early stage of the war and before any air raids had occurred this may not have been seen by the company as a top priority on country routes!
J F Parke © Omnibus Society

An interesting early wartime view at Storrington of a 1400 class Leyland Tiger which still retains its Southdown fleetname above the front destination screen. The vehicle has been fitted with (at least) a nearside headlamp mask and had white paint added to the front wings but still retains a cream roof and rear glass corner windows. The offside destination displays have, however, already been painted over in cream suggesting that the adoption of dark green roofs was not an immediate priority in the early days of war when no enemy attacks had materialised. At this time one Storrington based bus provided an irregular service on both the 70 to Pulborough and 71 to Thakeham Cross Roads although these local routes would be absorbed or extended in the early postwar years.
Frank Willis

February 1940 running between HASSOCKS STATION and DITCHLING (BULL INN) via Station Approach, B2116, Keymer Church and B2116 OR Station Approach, B2116, Grand Avenue, Burgess Hill Road, Keymer Church and B2116. Numbered **33** by Southdown, the journey time was 7 minutes direct or 10 minutes via Grand Avenue and a 1 or 2 hourly service ran daily via each route.

Emergency timetable No. 2 was issued to include all amendments up to and including **Thursday 15 February 1940**. Although many of the evacuees had already returned home, Southdown still found it necessary to transport hundreds of children billeted in small rural villages where the school was just large enough for the local children. Many of the village schools were in any case unsuitable for those London children who had previously been studying for various technical jobs. Where schools were forced to share buildings Southdown had to provide special school journeys around midday as well as morning and afternoon and, if only small buses could be used, some scholars were transported in shifts and school hours had to be staggered to suit. In addition there were large numbers of troops billeted in the area, often in isolated camps, requiring transport into such towns as

Brighton, Worthing and Haywards Heath in the evenings. More and more households were also obliged to lay up their cars for the duration and travel by bus to the shops or railway station. While faced with these increased demands for travel the company was obliged to reduce its overall mileage.

Some of the November cutbacks had proved too severe and a few were gradually reinstated. For instance, the short workings between Worthing and Findon on service **1**, which had been reduced to operate only in peak periods, were increased to operate hourly on weekdays only from 1256 with the last journey at 1829. The Findon area was soon to become a major training area for Canadian troops. Some minor revisions also took place in the Newhaven and Eastbourne areas.

Although many of those evacuated in September 1939 had already returned to their homes, further evacuations from British towns and cities started on Saturday 17 February 1940. Some degree of normality began to return to operations as the severe winter gave way to spring and the hours of blackout became shorter and more tolerable. To most people in Britain things were still uneventfully quiet and for many it was – almost – business as usual. People went to work in the same way as they had done for years, they caught the same bus or train, shopped at the same shops, and still went to local football matches. The Minister of War Transport accepted the need for some seasonal increase in bus operations, and therefore allowed the fuel ration to be augmented in line with prewar seasonal consumption, providing total consumption did not go above 75% of that level. Bus operators in the South of England enjoyed record breaking passenger numbers over the Easter weekend from 22 to 25 March 1940. Crowds travelled to the south coast towns to enjoy the attractions of the seaside unaware of the problems that lay just ahead. Within a few weeks

Britain really would be at war and this was the last 'normal' Bank Holiday to be celebrated until Whitsun 1945.

On Friday 5 April the Prime Minister, Neville Chamberlain, told the British people that Hitler has "missed the bus", meaning that a German invasion of the west was now unlikely to succeed. Unfortunately this ill informed prophecy proved short lived as just three days later on Monday 8 April Germany invaded Norway and Denmark. The so called 'Phoney War' was coming to an end. Tuesday 23 April was Budget Day and taxes were raised on beer by 1d, whisky by 1/9d and postage by 1d. The estimates of the 1940 war expenditure were given as £2,000 million but criticised by many MPs for being too low. A new evacuation scheme was launched on Thursday 25 April as a Ministry of Health survey showed that only 8% of eligible children had been registered although by the time the scheme was implemented Sussex would no longer be considered a safe reception area.

A second edition of *Emergency timetable No. 2* included some minor changes to services which were introduced as from **Thursday 2 May 1940**, a little over a week before the Germans invaded the Low Countries and any prospects of an early end to hostilities finally faded. In Eastbourne services **93** and **94** were sensibly curtailed to terminate at Pevensey Road having continued to Langley Road since being taken over from Twines Services in 1929. Service **97** to Beachy Head gained an hourly service – increased to 30 minutes in fine weather – but by August all journeys would be suspended for the duration.

Frontline County
May – July 1940

Momentous events which would change the south coast of England from a reception area to the front line of war now began to unfold across Europe. On Friday 10 May German forces invaded Holland, Belgium and Luxembourg by air and land while in Britain there was political drama as Prime Minister Neville Chamberlain announced his resignation. He was replaced by the First Lord of the Admiralty, Winston Churchill, who formed a coalition government including all the three main parties. On Saturday 11 May King George V1 signed a proclamation cancelling the Whitsun bank holiday throughout the UK although this did not stop many from visiting the south coast. Southdown announced that during the holiday buses will run to 'ordinary schedules' but will be duplicated where the fuel supplies permit. Later an official of the company said that they were a little busier than at a normal weekend and buses had to be duplicated on certain country routes to popular destinations such as Arundel. France was invaded on Whit Monday 13 May and Holland surrendered two days later. The serious situation unfolding across the English Channel led the British Secretary of State for War, Anthony Eden

to call for volunteers to form a Local Defence Volunteers force (LDV), later to be known as the Home Guard. Southdown's significant involvement is described in chapter 11.

As May progressed the military situation became even more serious as the Germans attacked further into North Eastern France while Luftwaffe attacks brought havoc across Northern France and Belgium as refugees began to stream west, clogging the roads and delaying the movement of allied forces. By Monday 20 May the Germans had completed their advance to the Channel coast thus separating the British Expeditionary Force, French 1st Army and the Belgian Army from the rest of the French forces to the south of the river Somme. German aircraft now started bombing the Channel ports. The Emergency Powers (Defence) Act was passed on Wednesday 22 May allowing the government to make new defence rules without the consent of Parliament. It was also announced that the previously issued identity cards 'must now be carried at all times'. In Britain all coastal towns from Great Yarmouth to Folkestone were declared evacuation areas – many of them still providing 'safe' homes for evacuees from the cities. On Saturday 25 May there was a tense atmosphere on Worthing sea front as fishing boats were removed from the beach and the pier was closed to the public and placed under military guard. Strollers along the promenade were kept moving by the police and all seats within 100 yards of the pier were turned upside down to prevent their use.

With over 300,000 British and French soldiers trapped in north east France needing evacuation from Dunkirk and the surrounding beaches, Operation 'Dynamo' began on Sunday 26 May. At first Royal Naval ships attempted to take on survivors from the port but after serious losses a call went out for assistance from smaller craft. The result was a flotilla of more than 800 small rescue vessels, partly crewed by civilians, which assembled at the Kent ports to make the perilous voyage across the Channel to Dunkirk and nearby beaches. The British public were still unaware of the desperate situation across the Channel until a news broadcast on Friday 31 May when they were told that "All night and all day men of the undefeated British Expeditionary Force have been coming home". From the many reports of their arrival and of interviews with the men, it was clear that they were not returning in triumph. Despite heavy losses the evacuation continued until German troops finally entered Dunkirk on Tuesday 4 June. Prime Minister, Winston Churchill, described the "miracle of deliverance" from Dunkirk and ended with a defiant message to Hitler's armies. "We shall defend our island whatever the cost may be. We shall fight on the beaches, we shall fight on the landing grounds, we shall fight in the fields and in the streets, we shall fight in the hills. We shall never surrender."

Sussex was now in the frontline with a powerful, and apparently unstoppable, enemy poised just across the English Channel. A German invasion of Southern England seemed a distinct possibility and those remaining London evacuees still on the South Coast were quickly moved to other safe havens further north and west. The Army, often assisted by thousands of willing volunteers, set to work on improving defences by constructing hundreds of pill boxes, tank traps and all kinds of barriers and barbed wire which sprung up along the roads of Sussex. It is believed that the first High Explosive (HE) bomb in the Southdown area fell on the village of Cowfold at 0300 on Wednesday 29 May. In Worthing the pier was closed and guarded by sentries with fixed bayonets and on the same day barricades, consisting of bathing machines partially filled with shingle, were erected across Montague Place and South Street and other streets leading to the sea front.

On Saturday 1 June a letter was sent to all RTCs warning of new Defence Regulation 16A which may require them to take action in the near future. Although not to be implemented immediately this would give powers to prohibit visits for the purpose of Holidays, Recreation or Pleasure to designated Defence (also known as Restricted) Areas. It would allow the public to be excluded from beaches and the neighbourhood of fortifications and other military works and to impose a curfew in any place where the Military authorities could show cause for such action. On Tuesday 4 June, Holiday Camps were banned in an area within 10 miles of the east and south east coasts of England presumably meaning the closure of the remaining sites in the Southdown area such as those around Selsey and Bracklesham Bay.

It was announced on Wednesday 5 June that small groups of highly mobile, armed men called 'Ironsides' had been created for defence against parachutists which were then seen as the main invasion threat. On the same day the Germans began 'Operation Red', the Battle of France with an offensive just 100 miles from Paris. Next day, the government announced that production of hundreds of household goods would be banned in Britain and air raids were reported along many parts of the East Coast of England. In Worthing a concrete strong point for guns was erected at Splash Point – and later painted to resemble a chalet – while the decorative glass lamps were removed from the promenade for safe storage. At 0140 on Friday 7 June the first air raid warning of the war was sounded in Worthing.

The third edition of *Emergency timetable No. 2* was issued including all changes up to **Thursday 6 June 1940** and, although recent events could not have been foreseen, there were none of the customary seasonal enhancements of previous years. Any optimism there may have been at Easter 1940 about the prospects of a near normal summer season on the South Coast had completely disappeared by now. As a result only one small service improvement took effect from this date and this was an increase on service **27** with the Devil's Dyke short workings rising to six each way daily. In summer 1939 a maximum of 23 journeys ran to Devils Dyke but within a few months much of this area would be out of bounds to the public for many years to come. It is also believed that the former Tramocars routes in Worthing were renumbered from this time with T1 becoming **3A** and T2 becoming **5A** although they had little in common with the existing Southdown routes 3 and 5. They were certainly altered by Saturday 13 July when

Brush bodied Leyland Titan TD1 car 820 (UF 4820) is in full wartime trim at Devils Dyke on service 27 in the summer of 1940 judging by the standard nearside headlamp mask introduced earlier in 1940. Although these buses were unlikely to see much use after blackout the bulb will have been removed from the offside lamp. Normal summer augmentation of service 27 did not occur for 1940 but six additional short journeys between Brighton and Devils Dyke were provided between June and late August by which time the grave situation facing the south coast towns brought such operations to an end for the duration.
Southdown Enthusiasts Club – Clark/Surfleet Collection

reduced late evening services were introduced as a result of the curfew. New destination screens including services 3A and 5A were produced in May 1940 and it therefore appears likely that the remaining SD Freighters were replaced by new 1400 class Leyland Tigers 1480/4/5 first licensed from 1 June 1940. The Dennis Falcons remained licensed into 1942 and probably continued in use on these services which, combined with the new Tigers, must have provided an awesome improvement in comfort over the old SD Freighters. Whilst contemporary reports suggest a gun emplacement had been built on the sea front turning circle by early June, buses somehow continued to terminate at Splash Point and ran every 15 minutes on each route during the day.

On Thursday 13 June the ringing of church bells was banned, in future they would only be rung by the military or the police to warn that an invasion – generally meaning by parachutists – was in progress. The French government moved from Tours for Bordeaux on Friday 14 June as German forces entered Paris and all remaining British troops in France were ordered to return to England. After further heavy losses the French government resigned and was replaced by one led by Marshal Petain who on Monday 17 June ordered the French to stop fighting and sue for 'honourable' peace terms. The following day Winston Churchill spoke to the House of Commons, declaring "let us so bear ourselves that . . . men will still say, this was their finest hour". The French Army was now in general retreat and on Wednesday 19 June the Germans invited the French to send a representative to discuss armistice terms. On the same day more than 100 German bombers made raids over Britain. Finally, an armistice between France and Germany was signed on Saturday 22 June – it was less than seven weeks since the start of the German invasion of the Low Countries and Britain now faced a very uncertain future.

As the new defences were constructed it sometimes became necessary to divert bus services where roads were obstructed or closed to non military traffic. In Brighton gun sites erected on Marine Parade, near the Aquarium, the junction with Lower Rock Gardens and another further east at the bottom of Paston Place forced the closure of the eastern end of Marine Parade with services **12, 12A, 12B** diverted as from Monday 17 June via Portland Place, St George's Road, Chesham Street, Rock Street and Eastern Road to Arundel Road.

As far as Southdown territory was concerned the first Defence Area was imposed by the Ministry of Home Security on Wednesday 19 June covering parts of East Kent along with the County Borough of Hastings and Borough of Bexhill although visitors were not banned immediately. The first restrictions on entry to the Southdown area were imposed from Friday 21 June as journeys for the purposes of Holidays,

5A	WORTHING FRONT—WEST STATION via Rowlands Road and Grand Avenue										5A
	NS	NS	NS	NS	NS	NS	NS	NS	NS	NS	NS
Splash Point	...	...	8 23	8 36	8 50	9 7	9 22	9 37	9 52	10 7	10 22
Worthing *Pier*	7 59	8 12	8 25	8 38	8 52	9 9	9 24	9 39	9 54	10 9	10 24
Plaza Cinema	8 3	8 16	8 29	8 42	8 56	9 13	9 28	9 43	9 58	10 13	10 28
Heene Road	8 4	8 17	8 30	8 43	8 57	9 14	9 29	9 44	9 59	10 14	10 29
Grand Avenue *Rowlands Road*...	8 6	8 19	8 32	8 45	8 59	9 16	9 31	9 46	10 1	10 16	10 31
West Worthing *Station S.R.* ...	8 10	8 23	8 36	8 49	9 3	9 20	9 35	9 50	10 5	10 20	10 35
	NS	NS	NS	NS	NS	NS	NS	NS	NS	NS	NS
Splash Point	10 37	10 52	11 7	11 22	11 37	11 52	12 7	12 22	12 37	12 52	1 7
Worthing *Pier*	10 39	10 54	11 9	11 24	11 39	11 54	12 9	12 24	12 39	12 54	1 9
Plaza Cinema	10 43	10 58	11 13	11 28	11 43	11 58	12 13	12 28	12 43	12 58	1 13
Heene Road	10 44	10 59	11 14	11 29	11 44	11 59	12 14	12 29	12 44	12 59	1 14
Grand Avenue *Rowlands Road*...	10 46	11 1	11 16	11 31	11 46	12 1	12 16	12 31	12 46	1 1	1 16
West Worthing *Station S.R.* ...	10 50	11 5	11 20	11 35	11 50	12 5	12 20	12 35	12 50	1 5	1 20
	NS										
Splash Point	1 22	1 37	1 52	and daily at	7	22	37	52	until	6 7	6 22
Worthing *Pier*	1 24	1 39	1 54	the following	9	24	39	54		6 9	6 24
Plaza Cinema	1 28	1 43	1 58	minutes past	13	28	43	58		6 13	6 28
Heene Road	1 29	1 44	1 59	each hour	14	29	44	59		6 14	6 29
Grand Avenue *Rowlands Road*...	1 31	1 46	2 1		16	31	46	1		6 16	6 31
West Worthing *Station S.R.* ...	1 35	1 50	2 5		20	35	50	5		6 21	6 36
Splash Point	6 37	6 58	7 38	8 18	8 58	9 38					
Worthing *Pier*	6 39	7 0	7 40	8 20	9 0	9 40			NS—Not Sundays.		
Plaza Cinema	6 43	7 5	7 45	8 25	9 5	9 45					
Heene Road	6 44	7 6	7 46	8 26	9 6	9 46					
Grand Avenue *Rowlands Road*...	6 46	7 8	7 48	8 28	9 8	9 48					
West Worthing *Station S.R.* ...	6 51	7 13	7 53	8 33	9 13	9 53					

Recreation and Pleasure were no longer permitted into parts of East Anglia, Kent and East Sussex as far west as Bexhill. Access to and from these areas, which stretched inland for up to 20 miles, was strictly controlled by police and military road blocks although the movement of existing residents was not affected. At first there was a reluctance to impose such restrictions at the height of the normal holiday season and it was still possible to buy bus and rail tickets for such journeys although warning notices were exhibited at stations and on some buses but it is not known if Southdown carried these. Police regularly boarded buses to carry out inspections and there was a police presence by the ticket barrier at all railway stations. Any person who was a non-resident or did not have official business in the restricted area was liable to be turned

This photograph was apparently taken on 15 June 1940, just a few days after Paris had fallen to German troops and fears of an invasion on the South Coast were growing. A Tunbridge Wells bound Leyland Titan with lowbridge Park Royal body has been stopped at a roadblock believed to be near Falmer on the A27 between Brighton and Lewes. It has already gained a dark green roof. Such delays were to become very common as further restrictions on entry to the coastal towns came in starting in July 1940.
Brighton & Hove Museums

back and notices warned that no refund of fares would be available to any passenger whose journey was terminated by the police or military authorities. The remainder of the Southdown area was not actually a 'prohibited area' at this time as there were no restrictions on travel, but the new regulations meant the end for many small businesses especially in the coastal towns. The familiar amusements, deck chairs and ice cream vendors closed for the duration. In anticipation of imminent invasion, a start was made on evacuating school children and non-essential local people from the Sussex coastal areas. Some 4000 people were evacuated from Portsmouth on 27-28 June to rural areas of Hampshire, Wiltshire and Surrey.

Although the sirens had sounded along the south coast on several occasions during the month, the first raid by enemy aircraft on Brighton or Hove occurred in the early hours of Sunday 30 June. Just after midnight enemy aircraft were heard followed by the sound of exploding bombs and machine gun fire. A single aircraft had dropped two small HE bombs which fell some distance from the clubhouse at West Hove golf course damaging windows on a nearby housing estate and shattering a number of chicken sheds. Another bomb fell at Sharpthorne Crescent in Portslade causing some damage but no deaths although three people were treated at the scene for cuts caused by flying glass. During the following day local people flocked to the golf course hoping to see something of this first air raid.

Events now began to move very quickly. Starting on Tuesday 2 July the beaches along the south coast were closed to the public and mines laid while barbed wire stretched the length of the seafronts as armed troops patrolled the promenades. Southsea sea front was among those placed under military control and the public banned from using the promenade or Common. Corporation trolleybuses were unable to serve Clarence Pier or South Parade Pier although Southdown buses continued to the latter point for several months probably using stops on the north side of South Parade. In Brighton the public was banned from the beaches and the southern side of the promenade between Black Rock and the West Sussex boundary although the northern sides were not affected at this time. In Worthing visitors were not even allowed to sit on the seats along the promenade near the pier causing the bus stops to be moved to the north side of the road. A neat row of 6 feet high concrete blocks was erected along the length of the promenade to delay enemy tanks coming ashore from invasion barges. All kinds of anti-invasion defences were built and gun emplacements constructed and manned at sites overlooking the English Channel. Many of the large seaside hotels were forced to close down or were requisitioned for military occupation and the popular piers had sections blown out of their centres to stop their use as enemy landing stages. The August Bank Holiday due to be on Monday 5 August was cancelled and Hitler now ordered the preparation of 'Operation Sea Lion', the plan for the invasion of Britain.

The first recorded attack on Newhaven was at 0920 on Wednesday 3 July when a single aircraft began machine gunning the town causing some minor damage but no casualties. At 1630 the first bombs dropped within the Eastbourne county borough boundary although no damage or injuries were caused. A far more sinister attack occurred a little later that day. At 1737 a steam hauled passenger train left Seaford bound for Lewes and Haywards Heath. After passing Bishopstone Beach Halt a single German aircraft opened fire and dropped six bombs. Although the train was not directly hit it took the force of the bombs and suffered blast damage. A splinter struck the driver, from which he died a short time later and the guard also suffered a serious

Starting on Tuesday 2 July 1940 the beaches along the south coast were closed to the public and became no go areas until later in 1944. Police or armed troops patrolled the promenades in case of a German invasion and two policemen can be seen here guarding the entrance to the beach at Bognor Regis. Although the usual seaside attractions were soon forced to close, the town was not actually closed to leisure visitors in 1940 leading many to complain of rather disappointing experiences! *West Sussex County Council Library Service*

back injury. The few passengers suffered only minor injuries, mainly as a result of flying glass but train services were suspended and passengers transferred to Southdown bus services.

By Thursday 4 July the restrictions on visitors were extended to include as far west as Newhaven thus closing the resorts of Eastbourne and Seaford to holiday visitors. Southern parts of Hampshire including Portsmouth followed on Saturday 6 July although it is clear from surviving records that dates of full implementation varied from place to place presumably depending on the military significance. Anyone wishing to travel from, say, Chichester to Portsmouth or Brighton to Eastbourne on non essential business would no longer be allowed access to the restricted areas. Leisure travel on many Southdown services in the coastal areas was now allowed only for those residents in the restricted areas who were permitted to go outside their zones. On Sunday 7 July a German aircraft dropped ten high explosive (HE) bombs in the Whitley Road area of Eastbourne. One man was killed outright and another man died in hospital three days later. A further 22 people were injured, nine houses were destroyed and sixty damaged. No warning had been sounded because of an edict made at national level that 'the air raid sirens are not to sound a general alert for the intrusion of single aircraft'. This ruling led to further loss of life as such raids became more common, leading eventually, to a separate local warning system. On the same day the Defence Area was extended to cover all of East and West Sussex and southern districts of Hampshire including Portsmouth. There were reports that people from just outside the zone were banned from visiting their normal shops in Portsmouth although, following protests to the Military authorities, essential shopping was not classified as a leisure activity. The ban on visitors was not extended, however, at this time to the towns between Brighton and Bognor causing much confusion and agitation from affected hoteliers in resorts such as Bournemouth who had lost their summer trade.

On Monday 8 July 1940 the South Eastern RTC imposed a curfew under which no person was allowed between half an hour after sunset and half an hour before sunset to be out of doors seaward of a given line, usually roughly 300 yards north of designated seafront areas, without a written permit. All Public houses and places of amusement and entertainment in these areas were required to close their doors before the start of the curfew. Within the Southdown area this initially extended from Hastings to the western boundary of Bognor UDC mainly following the line of the A259 road except where military installations dictated. Most other areas imposed specific times for their restrictions and eventually the South Eastern area came into line. No civilians or civilian vehicles were permitted to move about in the coastal areas

covered by the Order although all A and B classified roads had to remain open to essential freight traffic even where they were included in restricted areas. Anyone disobeying the curfew could be handed over by the police to the military. The Southern RTC introduced similar curfews in coastal areas which included Portsmouth and Southsea from around the same time. Details were not generally published in the press as it was felt that this would give the enemy information about where defences were being reinforced. During August the RTC for the Eastern area confirmed that buses and coaches operating on regular scheduled services could continue even where their route entered a dusk to dawn curfew area. This was to allow those engaged on essential war work to get to and from home although it is not clear from surviving records whether this arrangement applied in the South Eastern and Southern areas. Although Southdown buses continued to serve sea front terminals such as Pool Valley in Brighton, The Dome in Worthing and South Parade at Southsea after the curfew time, reductions to evening services were soon implemented. Not surprisingly the former Tramocars services from Splash Point which ran along Worthing sea front – now under complete curfew from half an hour after sunset – were among the first to be cut from Saturday 13 July. The last 3A now departed at 2128 from Splash Point with the last 5A at 2138. Other Worthing town services were affected from Monday 22 July when last buses departing after 2200 were cancelled on routes 3, 4, 5, 6 and 8. From Saturday 31 August the South Eastern curfew zone was extended to the West Sussex boundary bringing the whole of the Southdown coastal area within the restrictions.

One of the two Dennis Falcons for the former Tramocars services is seen near the Splash Point terminus in Worthing soon after delivery in summer 1939. Both were delicensed during 1942 and replaced by spare 1400 class Tigers. After the war car 80 (FUF 180) spent some time working on service 31F to Ferring, where the residents objected to larger, heavier buses on the estate roads, before transferring to Hayling Island to join the remainder of Southdown's lightweight buses. Note the ornate street lighting that was removed for safe keeping soon after the outbreak of war.
C F Klapper © Omnibus Society

By late May it was clear that Britain faced the real possibility of an invasion as the German forces maintained their rapid advance across France. The main threat was thought to be from airborne forces which would target and capture airfields in the east and south east of the country to allow further rapid reinforcements of troops and equipment. An attempted crossing of the English Channel or North Sea had to be accepted as a further possible threat although it would require the attackers to build up a suitable fleet of landing craft for the assault on the beaches. At the time this seemed a less likely threat mainly because of the disproportionate effect that the parachute landings in Belgium and Holland had on public morale. Many of the airborne troops were reputedly disguised as Nuns or wearing Dutch military uniforms leading to growing concerns that there may already be enemy agents ready to assist in any landings on British soil. In fact a small number of agents were landed on the south coast of Kent and East Sussex but all were soon rounded up after quickly arousing local suspicions.

On Monday 27 May, as the evacuation from Dunkirk got under way, Churchill appointed General Sir Edmund Ironside, Commander-in-Chief Home Forces, to organise Britain's defence. Although he had a significant force of men at his disposal consisting of fifteen infantry divisions and an incomplete Armoured division, they were mostly at half strength with inadequate arms and equipment, little transport and generally poorly trained. Ironside therefore chose to set up a static system of defence which, he hoped, could delay German invasion forces after landing and allow Britain time to bring its small mobile reserves into position. If the Germans could be delayed on the beaches and again as they attempted to move inland the British army might be able to mount an effective counter attack even though they would be principally relying on civilian buses and coaches to move them. A key objective in the plan was to assemble enough force against the Germans to stop them reaching London or the industrial heartlands of the Midlands and the North. Ironside identified the so called GHQ line, a fortified line running from The Wash through Cambridge and around London to Maidstone and then west to Basingstoke, Reading and Bristol to which forces would fall back if the initial lines of defence failed. In front of this, three advance stop lines ran through Surrey, Sussex and Kent, while others covered the approaches from East Anglia. There was to be a coastal 'crust' consisting of a thin screen of infantry deployed along the beaches which were intended to disrupt enemy landings long enough to allow the arrival of local reinforcements. The static defence lines formed by concrete pillboxes, gun emplacements, anti-tank obstacles, trench systems, minefields and barbed wire entanglements mostly used natural obstacles such as watercourses, railway embankments and steep hills to increase their delaying effect. At best they were designed to confine and delay the invaders until better equipped troops could be moved forward.

As the invasion fears grew across Southern England, orders were given on Friday 31 May for all signs which might be helpful to enemy parachutists landing in Britain to be removed throughout the UK. All milestones were to be uprooted and names of streets, towns and villages, railway stations, vehicles and hoardings obliterated in the hope of confusing the enemy. Bus companies were ordered by the Ministry of Transport that destination indicators must not show a terminus at which a Government establishment, camp or aerodrome was situated. For Portsmouth Corporation this meant that buses and trolleybuses could no longer show 'Dockyard' as their destination. Meanwhile across Britain anti-invasion defences were being planned and built with incredible speed. Areas of the countryside on which an invading plane could land were covered with obstacles, such as old cars, buses, carts and even iron bedsteads. Bridges were prepared for demolition. Pill boxes – small concrete huts for housing machine guns – and tank traps began to be erected along the main roads of Kent and Sussex. Giant concrete blocks were placed in vast numbers along the seaside promenades to try and disrupt any seaborne

This view looking west along the main A259 coast road near Lancing illustrates the anti-invasion defences which were erected in summer 1940. Concrete blocks are visible along the top of the beach to the left while on the opposite side of the road scaffolding defences have been built in front of the grassy area which is now part of the Brooklands Pleasure Park – although whether these would have stopped a determined invader is open to question. Traffic is very light and just one car can be seen but on this occasion the photographer has unfortunately missed any of the six buses per hour between Brighton and Worthing or three per hour on the Lancing circular services!
West Sussex County Council Library Service

There were fears that any invasion would be preceded by heavy bombing including gas attacks and the population were warned to carry their gas masks at all times. Here, a policeman stands in the centre of the road wearing his gas mask and steel helmet during an exercise in High Street, Bognor Regis to test the readiness of the local population to withstand a gas attack. Several onlookers, apparently without masks, are watching from the corner of London Road whilst a Southdown Leyland Titan in the distance is likely to face delays in reaching the Bus Station. As this appears to be in grey livery the date is 1942 or later. *West Sussex County Council Library Service*

invasion. A concrete machine gun post erected outside the old Town Hall in Worthing was disguised to resemble a shop and called 'Hyam Ready' but proved very difficult to remove at the end of hostilities. Access to vulnerable defence areas was restricted and coastal batteries built where holidaymakers would normally be strolling at this time of year. As an example, the whole promenade in Worthing west of Heene Terrace was closed off by barbed wire as more elaborate fortifications were constructed. Road blocks manned by the newly formed LDV force were set up to check Identity Cards and anyone failing to stop was liable to be shot in the tense atmosphere that now prevailed across southern England. To deny the invader fuel supplies, petrol pumps were removed from service stations near the coastal areas and preparations made for the destruction of the few that remained.

On Saturday 20 July, Ironside was replaced by General Alan Brooke who was committed to a more mobile and aggressive form of warfare. The fixed stop line concept was largely abandoned over the following months and replaced by a series of strongly defended 'islands'. Many of the road blocks were removed altogether, as experience had shown they could be as much of an impediment to friends as to foes. The term, Nodal Points, was adopted by spring 1941 to describe these heavily defended locations, usually situated at strategically important road or rail junctions and garrisoned by local Home Guards, along with any available troops stationed in the vicinity. They were intended to restrict, delay or hamper the movement of enemy invaders until reserves and reinforcements could be provided. Category 'A' Nodal Points normally had a garrison of regular troops and were intended to hold out for seven days after invasion without

outside assistance. The market town of Hailsham was one of many prime strategic defence positions in Sussex which, in the event of invasion, would have been designated a Nodal Point. In effect a fortress encircled with barbed wire, concrete anti-tank obstacles known as 'dragon's teeth' and road blocks. Another was situated at Angmering not far from the radar station at Poling while others could be found across the Southdown area at Balcombe, Crawley, Handcross, Turners Hill, Pevensey, Uckfield, Polegate, Stone Cross, East Dean and Friston. All controlled main north-south or east-west road – and sometimes rail – junctions where advancing German troops were to be stopped.

On Wednesday 19 June a leaflet produced in co-operation between the War Office and the

A scene showing Worthing in wartime looking north from South Street towards the old Town Hall. On the right is a concrete above ground air raid shelter for those unfortunate enough to be caught out during an alert. They were not generally well regarded and used only as a last resort. In front of the Town Hall can be seen the 'Hyam Ready' fortress, designed to prevent the advance of German invaders, which was fortunately never put to the test but proved hard to remove at the end of the war!

OMNIBUS PASSENGER REGULATIONS.

1. Every endeavour will be made to keep to the advertised times, but the Company will not be responsible for any delay, failure or alteration, or for loss, or injury arising therefrom.

2. All fares are collected on the buses, and passengers are requested to see that they obtain a new ticket, punched in their presence at the number which corresponds to the stage at which they board d the bus.

3. Tickets must be retained and shown to any official of the Company on request.

4. Persons travelling to or from a place where no fare has been fixed must pay the fare chargeable to or from the place beyond. Passengers are not allowed to stand on the upper deck of an omnibus, and only 8 allowed to stand inside.

5. **CHILDREN** over 3 and under 14 years of age are conveyed at half rates, provided they do not occupy a seat to the exclusion of another passenger.

Adult fare, 1d., 1½d., 2d., 2½d., 3d., 3½d., 4d.

Child's fare, 1d., 1d., 1d., 1½d., 1½d., 2d., 2d., and thereafter half-adult single fare to nearest penny.

6. **RETURN TICKETS** are available to return on any day, except Workmen's or Day Tickets, which are available on day of issue only.

7. **DOGS.**—All dogs must be paid for at quarter single fare, fractions of a 1d. to count as a 1d. The Company reserve the right to refuse to carry any dog if the conductor considers it is likely to be a nuisance or inconvenience to the passengers. In no case is a dog allowed on the seat.

8. **TREES, &c.**—Passengers travelling on the upper deck of an omnibus are cautioned to keep their seats whilst going under bridges, and to beware of overhanging trees. The Company cannot accept any responsibility for damage or injury arising from neglect of this warning.

9. **PASSENGERS' LUGGAGE.** Personal hand luggage will be carried free of charge at Owner's risk if it does not occupy a seat or space to the discomfort of other passengers. When more than two such articles are brought by one passenger, an excess luggage charge will be made for each additional article and it will be carried only if accommodation permits. Trunks and heavy articles weighing more than 56lbs. cannot be accepted.

NOTE.—All luggage should be clearly labelled.

Excess Luggage Charge.

Each article of personal hand luggage in excess of two :—	Up to 1/- Single Fare,		**2d.**
	„ 2/- „	„	**3d.**
	Above 2/- „	„	**4d.**
Folding Chairs up to 2d. Single Fare		...	**1d.**
„ „ „ 4d. „	„	...	**2d.**
„ „ above 4d. „	„	...	**3d.**

For unaccompanied parcel & luggage rates, see inside back cover.

Bicycles will be carried on *single-deck omnibuses only* at the following rates :—Up to 1/6 Single Fare, **6d.**; above 1/6. **1/-**

Despite the grave threat facing Southdown in summer 1940 the company's Omnibus Passenger Regulations make no reference to wartime conditions. But passengers travelling on the upper deck are warned about the danger of overhanging trees! German fighter-bombers will soon pose a more lethal threat!

Ministry of Home Security was sent to all British households. This is included as Appendix 6. Both Houses of Parliament met in secret session on Thursday 20 June to discuss Home Defence and in view of the grave situation, the second London County Council evacuation scheme was completed on Saturday 22 June, but this time 100,000 children were moved to the West Country and Wales.

Operation Sea Lion – The Plan

Following the fall of France, Britain appeared to be beaten and with little hope of waging war alone against the might of the German forces across the Channel. Even Hitler was surprised by the speed of the German military success in Europe although no detailed plans existed for an invasion of Britain. Instead, he was confident that common sense would soon prevail and that eventually Britain must seek to come to terms with Germany, thus avoiding the need for a seaborne invasion across an often difficult English Channel. But, with no sign of such a response from Britain, on 16 July 1940 Hitler issued Directive Number 16 which set out plans for an amphibious operation against England. This was given the codeword 'Sea Lion' and Tuesday 13 August was, rather optimistically, the original date set by Hitler for the invasion to commence.

On 17 July the German Army presented its initial plan for the invasion of Britain. Six divisions were to land between Ramsgate and Bexhill, four would land between Brighton and the Isle of Wight and three on the Dorset coast. Two Airborne divisions would also be deployed, with follow up forces including six Panzer and three Motorised divisions. Planning for the invasion continued throughout August amid great controversy between the Army and Navy chiefs over the size and scope of the operation.

In the eventual plan finalised in the last few days of August the first wave was to comprise nine infantry divisions, with two airborne divisions in direct support. But, it would take no less than eleven days to land the whole of these nine divisions, and thereafter they could expect reinforcements at the rate of only two divisions every four days. D-Day was now to be Saturday 21 September with embarkation starting on the previous day before a night crossing of the Channel and assault of the beaches at dawn. The aim was to capture southern England within the first ten days, London shortly afterwards, and the whole of Britain within a month. The nine divisions in the first wave comprised four divisions of 16 Army embarking at Rotterdam, Antwerp, Ostend, Dunkirk and Calais, two divisions of 9 Army embarking at Boulogne and three divisions of 9 Army embarking at Le Havre. The invading troops landing in Sussex would have the following objectives:

The 7th Division and 1st Mountain Division landing at Camber Sands, Rye and Winchelsea Beach were to head towards Hawkhurst.

The 34th Division and 26th Division landing at Bexhill and Pevensey were to head towards Uckfield.

The 6th Division landing at Cuckmere Haven were to follow the River Cuckmere until past Alfriston then turn west towards Ringmer.

The 8th Division landing at Rottingdean were to head towards Burgess Hill.

In addition airborne forces were to be dropped behind the beaches in the first hours of the attack and capture the high ground north and north west of Folkestone before securing crossings over the Royal Military Canal for the benefit of the seaborne troops coming ashore in that sector. At the same time they were to generally cause as much disruption to the defenders as possible and establish a road block on the

Canterbury to Folkestone road while other airborne troops were provisionally directed to be dropped on the downs behind Brighton. The port of Newhaven would have been used for the unloading of supplies and equipment in the days after the initial invasion if all went according to plan. Thousands of horses had to be conveyed across the English Channel as, surprisingly, they formed the main transport for the invasion army. Assuming the landings were successful the hoped for bridgeheads were to be expanded in 16 Army's sector to the line Canterbury–Ashford–Tenterden–Etchingham, and in 9 Army's sector to a line running from 'the high ground 29 km north and west of Bexhill' through Uckfield to 'the high ground west and south west of Lewes'. From these bridgeheads the two armies planned in due course to break out and secure their first objective, the line Portsmouth–Petersfield–Guildford–Reigate–Gravesend, by which time the whole of the Southdown area would have been under German control. Meanwhile the British defenders were, optimistically, not expected to counter attack in strength until the morning of the fifth day after the landings.

Four German spies were successfully parachuted into Kent on 3 September 1940 but were soon captured. After interrogation they were found to be an advance guard for the invasion, which they claimed, was to take place in the near future. On Tuesday 10 September Hitler decided to postpone 'Operation Sea Lion' until 24 September and on Saturday 14 September he again postponed the operation to start on 27 September, the last day of the month with suitable tides. With the onset of autumn and winter this was the last likely date for a cross channel invasion in 1940. On Tuesday 17 September Hitler postponed Operation Sea Lion until further notice. In fact the whole scheme was, in effect, abandoned and the invasion barges returned to their normal duties but in Britain, fears of invasion were raised again in the Spring of 1941. By then Britain's defences were much improved with many more trained and better equipped men available. After Germany invaded the Soviet Union, on 22 June 1941, it was unlikely that there would be any attempted landing as long as that conflict continued and from July 1941 construction of new anti-invasion fortifications was greatly reduced.

Compulsory Evacuation Schemes

The government was clearly very worried that once any invasion began the defending forces would be seriously hampered by floods of refugees attempting to flee from the threatened areas. Whilst the official response was for the population to 'stay put' it was also realised that large numbers of civilians must not be allowed to fall easily into enemy hands. In September 1940 a scheme was therefore developed in strict secrecy for a 'Compulsory Evacuation Scheme' of 31 specified coastal and inland towns between Great Yarmouth and Newhaven. At this time the towns between Brighton and Littlehampton were specifically excluded from the evacuation although just how it would have been possible to detain people in, say, Peacehaven, when their neighbours in Newhaven and points east had been forcibly evacuated is an interesting matter for speculation!

The plans envisaged that all women and children would be evacuated in two days, and the remainder of the population not required for defence purposes, within another three. Local bus operators such as Southdown would have conveyed the evacuees to designated stations from where special trains, which were to have priority over all but those carrying troops, would depart for safer areas on the southern outskirts of London. Evacuation was to begin 21 days before the enemy's preparations for invasion were considered likely to be completed and detailed schedules were prepared to cover the various moves between railway stations and specially created reception areas.

There was considerable official concern that the presence of such a large civil population in the group of towns west of Brighton and the possibility that refugees blocking the few approach roads through the Downs would prove so great a handicap to the Armed Forces as to prejudice the successful defence of the country. The coastal area between Brighton and Littlehampton had been identified as one of the most vulnerable and dangerous in the country and British surveys had concluded that the beaches were eminently suitable for the enemy landing of tanks, wheeled vehicles and troops. The Prime Minister had also asked for a scheme which covered the evacuation of civilians from all the Coastal areas from the Wash to the Isle of Wight – including the western side of the Southdown area – but this does not seem to have been considered in detail due to the enormous problems associated with adding just the Brighton to Littlehampton area. It was estimated that the additional number of persons to be evacuated from the towns of Brighton, Hove, Portslade, Southwick, Shoreham, Worthing and Littlehampton was approximately 300,000, of whom the great majority must be accommodated in the London area which, because of the available electrified railway lines, was already due to absorb many thousands of those evacuated from the other south eastern towns. At least 260,000 would have to be taken into already devastated parts of central London, unless accommodation could be made available elsewhere, possibly at a time of severe pre-invasion bombing. Given the dire circumstances that might then prevail it was unlikely that the railways could quickly transfer such large numbers of civilians to safer areas whilst under heavy bombardment. There were also major problems in providing adequate shelters from attack and very real fears of a breakdown in civil order.

Brighton in wartime! Access to Brighton's beaches had been closed during the invasion scare in July 1940 and this desolate scene looking west along Brighton seafront is dominated by abandoned boats, Pillboxes, tank traps and barbed wire. Although the threat of a German invasion was past by 1944 dangerous minefields remained concealed beneath the shingle. In the distance can be seen the remains of the West Pier after a gap was cut into the decking in 1940 to deter a landing by invaders.
Brighton & Hove Museums

Despite all these reservations the towns between Brighton and Littlehampton were added to the compulsory evacuation scheme during early 1942 although fortunately the plans were never implemented. The whole civilian population of the area, with the exception of those who were required to remain to assist the military, would be moved north to London and its suburbs. In the Brighton area alone it was planned that 27 trains would depart from Brighton each day over a four day period with an additional 16 from Hove and 7 from both Preston Park and Falmer each day. The total number to be evacuated from Brighton was estimated at 126,400, Hove 51,200, Portslade 10,400 and Southwick 8,800 and buses from Brighton Corporation, Brighton Hove & District and Southdown would all have been involved. Each person would be allocated a designated assembly point and where the evacuees

lived within walking distance of a station, they were expected to make the journey on foot, but buses had to be provided from the majority of assembly points. In the case of Portslade the evacuees were to be taken to the Recreation Ground, but in the event of wet weather, they were to assemble inside Southdown's Portslade Works. Falmer station was to be used for those living in the Moulscombe, Bevendean, Rottingdean and Woodingdean areas where operations would have been mainly carried out by Southdown. Similar evacuations were planned from Shoreham, Lancing, Worthing Central, West Worthing, Goring, Angmering and Littlehampton with all trains to be composed of electric multiple units and therefore limited to the Southern Railway electrified network making them especially vulnerable to any power disruption as a result of enemy action. Most trains were to travel direct to Victoria, London Bridge or Waterloo although some went to south London suburbs such as Barnes, Esher, Malden, Wandsworth Common and Purley and a few even further afield to Chertsey, Dorking North, Leatherhead, Farnham, Guildford, Camberley and Bagshot. In view of the massive operation most of the normal bus and train services would have been suspended or severely curtailed during the evacuation period.

Although Portsmouth was an important military objective the compulsory evacuation plans did not include the city despite the very real possibility of Portsea Island being cut off by an enemy advance from the east. Instead plans were made to keep the bulk of the civilian population within the city and ensure the vital A27 and A3 routes were kept open for the military and free of refugees. By September 1940 a secret plan was evolved under which Portsmouth was divided into four areas each controlled by either the Army, the Royal Navy, the Royal Marines or the Home Guard, who, on the given order, would close all necessary roads with barriers or wooden barricades and stop large numbers of people from leaving. Again, it is fortunate that the plan did not have to be put into action.

What if the invasion had succeeded?

Whilst it is generally accepted that Operation Sea Lion in its final 1940 form would have been disastrous for the German invaders, it is interesting to consider the likely effect on the Southdown area if a landing had been successful. Almost to the last moment Hitler believed that the British Government would capitulate, or be overthrown, before a single German soldier had attempted to land and so little attention had been given to the administration of British territory once occupied. For instance it is not known whether the United Kingdom would be divided, as France had been, into an Occupied and an Unoccupied Zone or what part, if any, might be allotted to the King and to Parliament at the end of fighting. Some of the plans are known and included the internment and despatch to the Continent of all able bodied males between the ages of 17 and 45. The Chief Supply Officer (England) was to be responsible for seizing such stocks of food, petrol, motor transport and horse drawn vehicles as had not already been taken over by the Armies. Oil and petrol supplies were especially important, and all captured stocks were to be made available to the fighting troops. Any surplus was to be allotted to essential industry and only then, after these priorities had been met, any residue could be used for distributing foodstuffs to the civil population. German criminal law and penal regulations were to be introduced and armed insurgents of either sex would be dealt with the utmost severity. Britain would have faced a similar fate to the other conquered countries of Europe but with only the faintest hope of help from afar.

---

21 — SHOREHAM—Buckingham Park—Southlands Hospital—SOUTHWICK — 21
With connections at Southwick to Brighton

	NS	NS	NS	NS	NS		*and daily at the following minutes past each hour*	*until*					
Shoreham *Station S.R.* ...	7 30	8 0	8 20	8 50	9 20	9 50	20 50		5 20	5 50	6 22	6 55	7 28
Shoreham *Erringham Road*...	7 33	8 3	8 23	8 53	9 23	9 53	23 53		5 23	5 53	6 26	6 59	7 32
Shoreham *Bridge Hotel* ...	7 36	8 6	8 26	8 56	9 26	9 56	26 56		5 26	5 56	6 29	7 2	7 35
Shoreham *Station S.R.* ...	7 39	8 9	8 29	8 59	9 29	9 59	29 59		5 29	5 59	6 32	7 5	7 38
Buckingham Park ...	7 41	8 12	8 32	9 2	9 32	10 2	32 2		5 32	6 3	6 36	7 9	7 42
Southlands Hospital ...	7 43	8 14	8 34	9 4	9 34	10 4	34 4		5 34	6 5	6 38	7 11	7 44
Kingston Lane *North End* ...	7 46	8 17	8 37	9 7	9 37	10 7	37 7		5 37	6 8	6 41	7 14	7 47
Southwick *Town Hall* ...	7 51	8 22	8 42	9 12	9 42	1012	42 12		5 42	6 14	6 47	7 20	7 53
Southwick *Schooner Hotel* ...	7 52	8 23	8 43	9 13	9 43	1013	43 13		5 43	6 15	6 48	7 21	7 54
Southwick *Schooner Hotel*	7 58	8 28	8 48	9 18	9 48	1018	48 18		5 48	6 20	6 53	7 26	7 59
Portslade *Station Road* ...	8 2	8 32	8 52	9 22	9 52	1022	52 22		5 52	6 25	6 58	7 31	8 4
Hove *Hove Street* ...	8 7	8 37	8 57	9 27	9 57	1027	57 27		5 57	6 30	7 3	7 36	8 9
Brighton *Pool Valley* ...	8 16	8 46	9 6	9 36	10 6	1036	6 36		6 7	6 40	7 13	7 46	8 19

				★	★
Shoreham *Station S.R.* ...	8 1	8 34	9 7	9 40	1013
Shoreham *Erringham Road*...	8 5	8 38	9 11	9 44	1017
Shoreham *Bridge Hotel* ...	8 8	8 41	9 14	9 47	1020
Shoreham *Station S.R.* ...	8 11	8 44	9 17	9 50	1023
Buckingham Park ...	8 15	8 48	9 21	9 54	1027
Southlands Hospital ...	8 17	8 50	9 23	9 56	1029
Kingston Lane *North End* ...	8 20	8 53	9 26	9 59	1032
Southwick *Town Hall* ...	8 26	8 59	9 32	10 5	1038
Southwick *Schooner Hotel* ...	8 27	9 0	9 33	10 6	1039
Southwick *Schooner Hotel*	8 32	9 5	9 38	10 6	1039
Portslade *Station Road* ...	8 37	9 10	9 43	1011	1044
Hove *Hove Street* ...	8 42	9 15	9 48	1016	1049
Brighton *Pool Valley* ...	8 52	9 25	9 58	1026	1059

NS—Not Sundays. ★—Through buses to Brighton.

SPECIAL HOSPITAL SERVICES

In addition to the above services, on Wednesdays and Sundays only (Hospital Visiting Days) the following special through buses will be run between Brighton and Southlands Hospital—

Brighton *Pool Valley* dep.	2 0	2 20
Hove, *Hove Street* ,,	2 9	2 29
Portslade, *Station Rd* ,,	2 14	2 34
Southwick *Town Hall* ,,	2 19	2 39
Southlands Hospital arr.	2 27	2 47

Return from Southlands Hospital at 4.4 p.m. and 4.20 p.m to Brighton.

The preliminary phase of what has become known as the Battle of Britain began on Wednesday 10 July with German air attacks on English Channel convoys aimed at tempting the RAF into battle. The first raid on Portsmouth late in the afternoon of Thursday 11 July caused some of the worst British civilian casualties of the war so far. Although many bombs fell onto the dockyard, damage was slight but several of the attacking aircraft missed the dockyard and bombed the densely populated areas of North End around Kingston Crescent. Fighter Command HQ had received plenty of warning of the incoming raid but the sirens in the city were not sounded until 1759 just three minutes before the enemy aircraft appeared overhead and as a result many people were caught on the streets in the midst of the falling bombs. At Kingston Cross the Blue Anchor public house was destroyed by a direct hit while another bomb exploded in part of Drayton Road School which

was being used as a first aid post killing eleven people and seriously injuring many more. Damage at Old Portsmouth disrupted Corporation trolleybus services for the first time since the war began and illustrated their vulnerability during raids. In total twenty HE bombs had fallen within the populated areas of the city leaving 19 people dead and 26 seriously injured. Scores of buildings had been destroyed or badly damaged in the attack and large crowds of people flocked to the affected areas to view the shattered buildings and watch the progress of the rescue work attracting a stern rebuke which was published in the pages of the Portsmouth Evening News.

In the early morning of Monday 15 July a single German bomber dropped nine small bombs on the Kemp Town area Brighton causing considerable damage to property in Bennett Road, Bristol Gardens, Henley Road, Prince's Terrace, Rugby Place and Whitehawk Road.

Portsmouth's first bombing raid came late in the afternoon of Thursday 11 July 1940 and this picture shows the scene at Kingston Cross where the Blue Anchor public house was destroyed by a direct hit. The sirens were sounded only a few minutes before the enemy aircraft appeared overhead resulting in many homeward bound workers being caught on the streets as the bombs started to fall. A temporary single storey building was erected and still remains in place. Bus services would have been severely disrupted as this busy junction marked the point where Southdown services via Fratton continued ahead into Kingston Road whilst buses for Theatre Royal turned right into Kingston Crescent to gain Commercial Road.
Portsmouth News

Three people died and four others were seriously injured in this first attack on Brighton.

On Friday 26 July service **21** was withdrawn between Brighton and Southwick and between Shoreham and Shoreham Beach following the closure of the Shoreham Beach area. Fears of German invasion meant this area, known locally as Bungalow Town, had become a further casualty of the war. Amid confusion and criticism the army gave residents 48 hours notice to leave their homes before demolishing about 700 of the houses and leaving a few of the more substantial ones for military use. Guns were moved in and access to the beach was prohibited except to the Army and Observer Corps. The reduced bus service provided a half hourly frequency between SOUTHWICK (SCHOONER HOTEL) and SHOREHAM STATION via normal route to Shoreham High Street then Victoria Road, Mill Lane, Upper Shoreham Road and Buckingham Road. Following these changes the **21A** between Southwick Town Hall and Shoreham Station was probably withdrawn at the same time but no later than close of service on 10 August 1940. In the Eastbourne area the **99** to Hastings via Pevensey Bay and Bexhill and the **98** to Pevensey via Pevensey Bay were suspended on 31 July 1940. It is likely that the famous **97** to Beachy Head operated by the three axle Leyland Tigers 550-3 was suspended at the same time. This left just an hourly service **96** via Stone Cross serving Pevensey and Pevensey Bay – but no services along the coast road – along with the inland

96	EASTBOURNE — PEVENSEY Via STONE CROSS and WESTHAM				96					
		NS	NS							
Eastbourne *Pevensey Road*...		8 0	9 13	1013	then hourly until	513	615	721	827	9 33
Eastbourne *Archery* ...		8 5	9 19	1019		519	621	727	833	9 39
Hide Corner ...		8 11	9 25	1025		525	628	734	840	9 46
Stone Cross ...		8 1	9 28	1028		528	631	737	843	9 49
Westham *Railway Hotel* ...		8 18	9 33	1033		533	637	743	847	9 55
Pevensey *Old Mint House* ...		8 21	9 36	1036		536	640	746	852	9 58
Pevensey Bay *Bay Hotel* ...		8 26	9 41	1041		541	646	752	858	10 4
		NS	NS							
Pevensey Bay *Bay Hotel* ...		8 26	9 43	1043	then hourly until	543	648	754	9 0	10 6
Pevensey *Old Mint House* ...		8 31	9 48	1048		548	653	759	9 5	1011
Westham *Railway Hotel* ...		8 34	9 51	1051		551	657	8 3	9 9	1015
Stone Cross ...		8 39	9 56	1056		556	7 2	8 8	914	1020
Hide Corner ...		8 42	9 59	1059		559	7 5	811	917	1023
Eastbourne *Archery*...		8 48	10 5	11 5		6 6	712	818	924	1030
Eastbourne *Pevensey Road*...		8 55	1011	1111		613	719	825	931	1037

NS—Not Sundays.

hourly service **15** to Hastings via Hailsham. The Home Secretary announced that civilian air raid casualty figures in July were 258 killed and 320 seriously injured.

August

On Tuesday 6 August Goering set 10 August 1940 as 'Eagle Day', the start of the Luftwaffe's major offensive against the RAF and its airfields, but due to poor weather conditions it was delayed until 13 August 1940. Shortly before 1130 on Monday 12 August a force of nearly one hundred and fifty enemy aircraft formed up over France

Although this photograph was almost certainly specially posed for the camera such checks became commonplace as a German invasion seemed a strong possibility in the months following the evacuation from Dunkirk in summer 1940. Passengers' I.D. cards would be checked and after the introduction of the Visitor Bans in some coastal areas anyone not entitled to be travelling in the zone was liable to be removed from the bus and obliged travel home at their own expense.
West Sussex County Council Library Service

and set course for the Sussex coast. Almost at once this huge formation was detected by the radar station at Poling near Littlehampton which monitored its progress. Soon after 1200 some 25 bombers attacked Portsea, Old Portsmouth and parts of Southsea. Some bombs hit the dockyard causing extensive damage although casualties were light with only three dockyard workers killed and seventeen injured. But, as in the first raid on 11 July, the civilian areas suffered the brunt of the bombing, and whilst the Germans could claim the attack was directed at legitimate military targets, almost half of all bombs dropped in the raid fell with devastating effect on the Portsea and Old Portsmouth areas of the city. The flimsy houses in the district proved to be particularly vulnerable to the effects of high explosive bombs. Corporation trolleybus services were again disrupted and the harbour railway station was badly damaged by a large oil filled incendiary bomb which destroyed access to the landing stage, seriously damaged four trains and closed the station. Fires were started in several buildings and at St Georges Square a trench shelter in which 147 people were taking refuge received a direct hit. Despite initial fears of heavy loss of life, most had a miraculous escape with only one small boy killed and eleven other people hurt. Casualties for the raid totalled 29 killed and 126 injured.

From mid August air raid warnings became a common occurrence and although bus services continued to run as closely as possible to the published timetables, the inevitable stops at air raid shelters and route diversions once bombs had fallen, played havoc with schedules. As fears of German paratroopers in various disguises spread across the country, buses were also frequently required to stop at security check points while passengers' ID cards were carefully scrutinised. There remained a great deal of misunderstanding, not only along the south coast, but also in London and the country at large about the restrictions that followed the

naming of West Sussex as part of the Defence Area. Many were under the impression that travel to Brighton, Worthing and Bognor was banned for holidaymakers because they were in a Defence Area but in fact the RTC had, rather surprisingly, placed no restrictions on travel to and from these areas. Steps had been taken to counteract the rumour that Brighton and Hove were out of bounds to visitors and the railway companies had instructed their booking clerks not to make any enquiries of passengers as to the purpose for which they were visiting these towns. There was even pressure from those still involved in attracting tourists to the area that not enough was being done to promote the fact that visitors could still visit the resorts – despite the grim war situation. Eventually the Worthing Publicity Association had to admit that in view of the difficulties which had arisen in connection with the war during recent weeks it had been found necessary to discontinue all publicity and the Regional Transport Commissioner had strongly objected to the efforts being made to induce people to come to Worthing!

Tuesday 13 August was the original date set by Hitler for the invasion of Britain but after many delays it was intended as the first day of the maximum offensive by the Luftwaffe to destroy RAF airfields and gain air supremacy over England in preparation for Operation Sea Lion. The Luftwaffe launched 1,485 sorties, but suffered heavy losses of aircraft and crew. Although 'Eagle Day' was to have been 13 August, Goering decided that due to the poor results, 15 August would instead be known as 'Eagle Day'. The Luftwaffe launched its greatest attacks so far against the RAF's airfields, involving more than 1,000 German planes and 1,786 sorties. On Friday 16 August radar stations along the coast again detected a large formation of enemy aircraft approaching Portsmouth in what appeared to be a repeat of the 12 August attack. At 1250 as the enemy aircraft approached the Nab tower, the sirens sounded across

A sharp reduction in operations on Hayling Island in September 1939 rendered most of the specially built lightweight buses and coaches surplus to requirements. The Tilling-Stevens buses were requisitioned for Military service in 1940 and many of the Leyland Cubs and Cheetahs were stored for periods during the war. Seen outside Emsworth garage in wartime livery and fitted with headlamp cowls is car 9 (DUF 9) a Leyland Cub SKPZ2 with Park Royal rear entrance body. The Cubs were withdrawn in October 1956 soon after the opening of the new Langstone Bridge between Havant and Hayling Island. J F Parke © Omnibus Society

Portsmouth but a few minutes later the formation split up with the majority of the bombers setting course for the RAF Fighter Command aerodrome at Tangmere, east of Chichester which was all but destroyed in the ensuing dive bombing attack. As a 'Sector' station Tangmere became the principal station in one of the seven sectors of No. 11 Group which defended the South and South East of England and was the single most important defence establishment in Sussex during 1940. At 1300 the aerodrome was heavily attacked by a large force of Junkers Ju87 dive bombers which dropped some 20 bombs scoring hits on two hangars and numerous other buildings. Casualties were reported as 12 dead and five injured but even after the destruction Tangmere was never non-operational and continued throughout the remainder of the battle in the forefront of Britain's defence. At 1720 bombs fell in the Hampden Park area of Eastbourne killing three Corporation workmen who were collecting scrap material for Salvage Week. The scale of aerial warfare across most of Sussex on that Friday brought civilian fatalities and destruction to many parts of the Southdown area.

Further heavy raids by the Luftwaffe resumed on an extensive scale on Sunday 18 August with major damage to airfields and establishments at Thorney Island, Gosport, Ford and Poling. The Chain Home Station at RAF Poling which provided low level raid cover for the south coast between Portsmouth and Brighton was heavily bombed at 1445. On Monday 19 August the whole of Britain was declared a Defence Area and the situation regarding the movements of people into Defence Areas in Sussex and Kent was further clarified by the RTC for the South Eastern area. It was stressed that the new Defence Order was a precautionary measure although no fresh restrictions applied on the south coast including West Sussex. People from west of Newhaven were not allowed to visit towns to the east such as Eastbourne except for business purposes although registered residents in the restricted area could travel outside if they wished. On service 12 this meant that Brighton residents could not have a holiday trip to Eastbourne but Eastbourne residents could enjoy a leisure visit Brighton!

Churchill reviewed the progress of the air war in the House of Commons and said "Never in the field of human conflict, was so much owed by so many, to so few". After losing 20 per cent of their Stuka force to the RAF the Luftwaffe withdrew the Ju87 dive bomber from strategic operations against England. Some eleven raids were plotted along the South Coast on Thursday 22 August and bombs were dropped on the Kemp Town area of Brighton only 100 yards from a gun battery which was, fortunately, not put out of action. Further attacks occurred in Newhaven and Seaford without serious damage or loss of life and from this date onwards there followed almost daily occurrences of bombing, machine gunning and aerial battles across the Southdown area.

On Saturday 24 August Portsmouth endured its third heavy raid of the war. A large number of enemy aircraft arrived over the city at 1620 and in the five minutes that it took for the bombers to pass, Portsmouth was subjected to the worst air raid to be suffered by any city, apart from London, for the whole of the Battle of Britain. Some sixty five heavy bombs, including some fitted with delayed action fuses, were dropped quite indiscriminately on shops and houses all across the southern half of Portsmouth and Southsea. As in the previous raids, the time between the warning being sounded and the arrival of the bombers overhead was desperately short, with the result that again many people were caught in the open unable to reach a proper shelter as the bombs came whistling down. The Kings Road area of Southsea suffered severe damage with many houses and shops destroyed. At the Princes Theatre in Lake Road, close to the Commercial Road shopping centre, a 500 kg bomb crashed through the flimsy roof completely wrecking the interior of the cinema. The matinee audience included many local children but fortunately the majority of people in the cinema at the time had reached the rear exit when the bomb exploded. The mine and torpedo base at HMS Vernon was hit for the first time during this raid and several buildings were destroyed or damaged by blast but otherwise destruction in the dockyard itself was relatively light. But, although only nine bombs fell into the dockyard the loss of life was heavy for in one tragic incident near the old Block Mill a bomb pierced the roof of an underground vault used as an air raid shelter and killed or injured some 65 dockyard workers. Across the city there was a great deal of damage to property and in the few minutes the raid lasted nearly 700 people were rendered homeless. The final death toll reached 125 while 300 were injured of which over 100 were seriously hurt.

Portsmouth was bombed again at 1600 on Monday 26 August although, as the lead bombers were constantly being harried by RAF fighters, they over flew the city without releasing their

Car 109 (BUF 209) is a Leyland Titan TD4 with Short Bros lowbridge body new in 1935 seen heading east somewhere on service 22 which at this time ran hourly between Brighton and Petworth with a few journeys extended on to Duncton. It retains full lined out prewar livery but the roof is now dark green. Most of this batch of 39 Titans were included in the postwar rebodying programme but car 109 was instead rebuilt by Southdown in 1946 and then outlasted all others with original bodies surviving until sale in February 1956.
Frank Willis

Before the war Southdown issued timetable books to coincide with the seasonal variations between Summer and Winter schedules and at other times when necessary. The need to continuously update services to meet new demand or withdraw lightly used journeys to conserve fuel meant that it was necessary to announce most changes by means of locally distributed leaflets – few of which have survived – and only produce a new book when absolutely necessary. The onset of 'real' war during the summer of 1940 with the consequent evacuation of many residents from coastal towns lead to the curtailment or complete withdrawal of many services and the issue of Emergency Timetable No 3 as from 29 August 1940. The introduction to this timetable now includes specific references to the Defence Area restrictions but surprisingly no mention of the ban on non essential leisure travel on some of its services. To reduce the need for relief buses at peak times those who do not need to travel at those times are politely requested not to do so.

Southdown Motor Services, Ltd.

In Association with the Southern Railway

EMERGENCY TIME TABLE No. 3

29th AUGUST, 1940, and until further notice

This Time Table Booklet includes all the alterations to Southdown Bus Services which have been made since the issue of Emergency Time Table No. 2, together with minor adjustments to Services 20, 30, 31, 50, 55, 57, and 89, which will have effect as from August 29th, 1940.

Defence Area restrictions, more particularly in the Coastal areas, the regulation of fuel supplies and other circumstances make inevitable constant adjustments of the services to meet the changing conditions. Such alterations will be advertised locally in the areas affected, with as much notice as possible, and the changes will subsequently be included in the next Southdown Time Table.

Passengers who are free to choose their time of travel are asked to avoid making their journeys at peak traffic periods when the accommodation on the buses is required by workpeople. Whilst contributing to the National Effort in this manner, passengers will generally secure greater comfort for themselves.

Table of Contents:

bombs. On reaching Cosham and Farlington the attackers turned and dropped their bombs at random, many falling harmlessly on open ground at Farlington or into Langstone Harbour but one hit the Hilsea gas works causing some small fires. Others fell on the Royal Marine Barracks at Fort Cumberland in which over two hundred Marines were present at the time, but only 14 men were killed or wounded. The last raid on Portsmouth during August took place soon after 2100 on Tuesday 27 August when a small force of enemy bombers dropped several HE bombs and a large number of small incendiary bombs over a wide area around the city. The incendiary bombs fell on and around Fort Nelson and eventually spread east via Southwick to Fort Widley and south into Wymering and along Southampton Road. Compared to previous raids damage was slight with only thirty eight incidents reported, many of which were minor fires caused by the incendiaries.

Emergency timetable No. 3 was issued to include all changes to services up to and including **Thursday 29 August 1940** although some of the alterations to services occurred earlier in July or August as the war situation unfolded. Since the previous issue, bombs had fallen across the coastal towns, there were now well founded fears of a German invasion along the South Coast at any time and the reduced bus services reflected the grave situation now facing the Southdown area. Local school children were being evacuated and many residents who had no

need to stay were encouraged to move away from the coastal towns. The onset of air raids raised the important question of whether bus services should be stopped during the frequent alerts. In Portsmouth, all Corporation vehicles stopped whilst others, including Southdown, continued to run as long as safety permitted leading the Transport Committee to request the Chief Constable to stop all public service vehicles for the period of alerts. No change occurred to the through Henfield journeys on service **27** but short workings to Devil's Dyke were probably withdrawn by this time, if not earlier. At some point in 1940 the Devil's Dyke Hotel was requisitioned by the Army and during their tenure it was gutted by fire in 1945.

Service **45** was again revised to provide

1 journey per hour Theatre Royal – direct – Fareham – Warsash

2 journeys per hour Bradford Road – Fratton – direct – Cornaway Lane, Portchester

2 journeys per hour Theatre Royal – Castle Street – Fareham

2 journeys per hour Theatre Royal – Castle Street – Cornaway Lane, Portchester

3 journeys per hour Theatre Royal – direct – Fareham

With holidaymakers gone from the resort, the local circular service **51** in Bognor Regis had its frequency reduced from 20 minutes to 40 minutes each way daily and so could be worked by one bus. This service was a haunt of the remaining Tilling Stevens saloons in their final days of service with Southdown.

27	BRIGHTON—HENFIELD via Devil's Dyke, Poynings & Edburton					27
						SSO
Brighton *Pool Valley*	9 30	12 30	3 30	6 30		9 30
Seven Dials	9 39	12 39	3 39	6 40		9 40
Tivoli Crescent North	9 44	12 44	3 44	6 46		9 46
Tongdean Lane	9 47	12 47	3 47	6 49		9 49
Saddlescombe Road	9 50	12 50	3 50	6 52		9 52
B'ton & Hove Golf Links	9 52	12 52	3 52	6 55		9 55
Devil's Dyke Hotel	9 58	12 58	3 58	7 1		10 1
Poynings *Church*	10 7	1 7	4 7	7 11		10 11
Edburton *Church*	10 16	1 16	4 16	7 21		10 21
Small Dole	10 25	1 25	4 25	7 31		10 31
Henfield *George*	10 33	1 33	4 33	7 40		10 40
						SSO
Henfield *George*	8 50	10 50	1 50	4 50		8 1
Small Dole	9 0	11 0	2 0	5 0		8 12
Edburton *Church*	9 10	11 10	2 10	5 10		8 23
Poynings *Church*	9 18	11 18	2 18	5 18		8 32
Devil's Dyke Hotel	9 30	11 30	2 30	5 30		8 45
B'ton & Hove Golf Links	9 35	11 35	2 35	5 35		8 51
Saddlescombe Road	9 37	11 37	2 37	5 37		8 53
Tongdean Lane	9 40	11 40	2 40	5 40		8 56
Tivoli Crescent North	9 43	11 43	2 43	5 43		9 0
Seven Dials	9 47	11 47	2 47	5 47		9 4
Brighton *Pool Valley*	9 55	11 55	2 55	5 55		9 13

In favourable weather conditions additional journeys will be run between Brighton (Pool Valley) and Devil's Dyke Hotel.

GO TO IT—

by

SOUTHDOWN

Heavy attacks on south eastern airfields continued during the day on Friday 30 August but without any serious incidents in the Southdown area. A new threat appeared next day as Eastbourne was shelled from the sea, demolishing a house in Hardwick Mews and seriously injuring two women. Fortunately, other shells fell harmlessly in the sea and in open country. Offshore, a German U-boat was seen to submerge and head westward, pursued by two armed trawlers whose crews confirmed that the submarine had fired its deck gun at the town. Later, two more shells were fired at Exceat from off Cuckmere Haven which was a proposed landing beach for the German 6th Mountain Division in the 'Operation Sea Lion' invasion plan. August civilian casualty figures in the UK were announced as 1,075 killed and 1,261 seriously injured.

September

During the first week of September enemy aircraft activity was again centred over south east England during the day with some aircraft reaching as far as the London area. Raids continued with extensive night activity causing air raid alerts to remain in place for many hours although there was little damage within the Southdown area.

Phase 3 of the Battle of Britain began on Saturday 7 September with the start of the London Blitz as, for the first time, the Germans intentionally bombed the capital. Soon after 1700 the enemy started a major attack on industrial and dock property on both sides of the Thames resulting in huge fires, serious damage to property and considerable disruption to rail and road communications in the area. London was now witnessing the attack that had been forecast for the outbreak of war a little over one year earlier. To add to the widespread alarm in southern England the codeword 'Cromwell', which was intended to warn that a German invasion may be imminent, was passed nationwide. This led to Home Guard commanders in different parts of the country calling out their forces under the mistaken belief that the invasion was actually in progress and church bells rang out in some places to warn the population. Nervous officers actually blew up some of the mined bridges including some in East Sussex. The following day, General Brooke made clear that church bells should be rung only if the member of the Home Guard concerned had personally seen more than twenty five paratroops descending, and that the signal 'Cromwell' was not a general callout for the Home Guard, but only applied to specialised units.

For many weeks, day and night attacks continued against London and the south east of England with serious disruption to Southern Railway services. Although London remained the main target of the bombers, many raids crossed the coast between Beachy Head and Selsey Bill

meaning that a large part of the Southdown area was subject to air raid warnings for hours on end. On Tuesday 10 September the Home Office issued a proclamation inviting all those with no official duties to take advantage of a voluntary evacuation scheme and leave coastal towns such as Eastbourne and Hastings clear for the defenders, should an invasion materialise. During the following days many local people accepted the offer and the population of Hastings almost halved overnight from 65,000 to 34,000. Most left on special trains but thousands more made their own arrangements with relatives or friends living in safer places. The town of Eastbourne was attacked by several raiders on Friday 13 September at 1555 as crowds of people taking the opportunity to leave the town for safer areas waited at the railway station. Bombs were dropped in the town centre killing three people and injuring thirty. Some believed that the raid marked the beginning of the preliminary bombardment for the expected invasion and, had German plans been proceeding according to plan, this would indeed have been the eve of 'Operation Sea Lion'.

Saturday 14 September was a grim day across the Southdown area as bombs hit Bognor, Worthing, Brighton, Eastbourne and Hastings. One person died in Worthing's first raid of the war as seven HE bombs fell across the town but it was the bomb that scored a direct hit on the Odeon Cinema in Kemp Town, Brighton during a matinee performance attended mostly by children that caused most outrage. It was estimated that about 300 people were in the cinema at the time the bomb fell at around 1540 causing severe damage. Although initial reports suggested hundreds killed, only four children and two adults in the cinema died and 20 others were injured when the balcony collapsed. Some of those injured later died and in the surrounding area a further 49 people were killed as bombs straddled an area between Edward Street and Upper Rock Gardens. Eight HE bombs fell in Bognor's first raid of the war killing two people. Eastbourne suffered an afternoon of attacks during which seven people died and 56 were injured. Many bombs fell between the seafront and the railway affecting Grove Road, College Road, South Street, Seaside Road, Susans Road and Pevensey Road. Next day the London area was again the chief objective of enemy aircraft during the day, but the Luftwaffe suffered its highest losses since 18 August forcing a serious rethink by the German High Command. In retrospect seen as a turning point in the air war, 15 September is now remembered nationally as Battle of Britain day.

The Prime Minister announced in the Commons that in the first half of September 2,000 civilians had been killed and 8,000 seriously injured in air raids whereas the figure for service casualties for the same period was 250. At 1155 on Friday 20 September HE bombs were dropped near the viaduct on Lewes Road and on terraced houses in Caledonian Road in Brighton. Eleven persons were killed and several injured. As the RAF fighter defences improved, many of the German bombers on daylight raids were driven back from their targets in the London area. There were numerous cases in this period when aircraft that were lost, damaged or under attack by fighters chose to unload their bombs on to the Sussex countryside although fortunately most fell without causing civilian casualties or serious damage to property. Eastbourne was attacked again on Monday 23 September at 1150 as enemy aircraft dropped eight HE bombs in the area around Cavendish Bridge, the railway station and The Avenue and a further 20 between Langney Road/Bourne Street and Avondale Road/Nevill Road. At 1635 hours another eight bombs were dropped around the railway closing the station. There was considerable damage to property and the junction of Bourne Street and Langney Road soon earned the title 'Hell Fire Corner'. A total of 23 people were injured in the day's attacks on Eastbourne. At 1545 on Tuesday 24 September bombs fell on tightly packed working class terraced houses in Albion Hill, Cambridge Street and Ashton Street, Brighton. Two people were killed in the incident and another 50 were injured. As no sirens had been sounded many were caught out in the streets and unable to take shelter.

Thursday 26 September brought further raids to several places in the Southdown area as bombs fell on Eastbourne, Newhaven, Hastings and Bexhill causing widespread destruction and loss of life. On Saturday 28 September Eastbourne suffered another attack including further damage and disruption to the railway as well as serious damage in Cavendish Place, Tideswell Street and Bourne Street. Four died in this attack and 14 others were injured. One of most tragic incidents of the war in Hastings occurred on Monday 30 September when a single HE bomb struck the coping on the roof of the Plaza Cinema and exploded in mid air above the Memorial. People had been out in the street watching the aerial battle raging overhead and as a result fourteen died and twelve were injured.

October

Air raids now became an almost daily occurrence across the Southdown area and the following account includes just a sample of the more serious attacks. On Wednesday 2 October bombs on Hastings, Eastbourne, Ardingly and Worthing caused many injuries and some fatalities along with widespread destruction. Portsmouth suffered again on Monday 7 October when two bombs were dropped in Hawthorn Crescent, Cosham destroying three houses. Later, HE bombs and incendiaries over the southern half of the city caused two major fires which destroyed the Pickford's furniture depository in Swan Street and Government House. Eastbourne and

Horsham were also hit on the same day. Raids on Bexhill, Eastbourne and Hastings occurred on Tuesday 8 October with Eastbourne town centre and the railway damaged again. Further west three low flying aircraft machine gunned Southwick and released twenty four HE bombs onto a residential area killing one person and injuring eight others. Both Shoreham and Ford Aerodromes were attacked with bombs and machine gun fire and aircraft on the ground damaged. At 1905, Park Road in Worthing was hit as two enemy aircraft bombed and machine gunned the town damaging the gas works, demolishing three houses and killing five people.

Daylight raids on Friday 11 October were again mainly confined to the South and South East coasts, where bombs were dropped on several towns including Eastbourne causing damage to residential and business properties. Enemy bombing activity during the day was now on a much smaller scale with only a few minor raids taking place, mainly in Kent and Sussex, but heavy night attacks on London started from around 1900 as raids crossed the Southdown area and sometimes continued until the all clear at 0600. After several planned dates were abandoned at short notice Hitler finally decided to postpone the invasion of Britain until spring 1941 although the local population was, of course, unaware of this fact. Five fatalities were caused in a raid on the Shoreham Shipping Company Wharf on Monday 21 October and next day enemy aircraft returned to Eastbourne dropping eleven bombs on the already devastated Langney Road and Bourne Street area. Three people were killed and 15 injured in this attack. Just after 1700 on Monday 28 October fifteen or more aircraft attacked Newhaven which was first machine gunned and then bombed. Over thirty bombs were dropped on the town striking the Fort, harbour and nearby streets and resulting in one death and six people being injured. On Tuesday 29 October Portsmouth suffered another raid when nine HE bombs hit the city causing over thirty casualties as well as much destruction of property, centred mainly in the Goldsmith Avenue area of Fratton as well as Devonshire Avenue and Suffolk Road in Eastney. The British Air Ministry considered the Battle of Britain was over by Thursday 31 October although what became known as 'The Blitz' was to continue, weather permitting, until May 1941. British civilian casualty figures were announced for October as 6,334 killed and 8,695 seriously injured.

The Blitz : November 1940 – May 1941

Whilst the Battle of Britain may have officially ended on Thursday 31 October, German aircraft continued their attacks on targets throughout the Southdown area. The night time curfews in the coastal areas had proved very unpopular and difficult to enforce. As from Friday 1 November

1940 it was decreed that all would cease but the South Eastern RTC felt strongly that this area was still particularly at risk and therefore some restrictions were maintained. From Thursday 5 December 1940 the curfew applied only between 2230 and 0530 in an area of Kent and East Sussex which extended as far west as the western edge of Newhaven UDC. On the evening of Saturday 2 November enemy aircraft jettisoned twelve HE bombs including two which fell in the path of a Southdown bus working a northbound service 95 at Middle Road, Rushlake Green killing five passengers and the conductor. Further details of this incident can be found in Chapter 8. A serious raid occurred on Sunday 10 November when a number of aircraft approached just east of Eastbourne pier, dropping at least ten bombs from the Albion Hotel to Langney Road and another ten bombs between Langney Road and Dennis Road. Despite the intensity of the raid only two people were killed and five others injured. Later in the day 20 HE bombs and many incendiaries were dropped on the Copnor and North End areas of Portsmouth. The Southern Railway line was hit at Copnor Bridge and widespread damage caused to properties in the two areas. Sixteen casualties resulted from the raid which again struck residential rather than military areas of the city. Eastbourne suffered two attacks on Tuesday 12 November, the first at 1420 when a low flying aircraft machine gunned the Eastbourne streets although no casualties seem to have resulted. At 1930 the Broadwater area of Worthing was hit as bombs fell at Hadley Avenue demolishing four houses, killing four people and injuring a further 15.

Against a general pattern of service reductions an important new service numbered **36** appeared from Thursday 14 November running between BRIGHTON (POOL VALLEY) and HAYWARDS HEATH STATION via Patcham, Pyecombe, Clayton, Stone Pound, Hassocks, Keymer and Burgess Hill. The two-hourly daily

23 36	BRIGHTON — Ditchling — HAYWARDS HEATH BRIGHTON—Burgess Hill—HAYWARDS HEATH	23 36

Route No.	23	36	23	36	23	36	23	36	23	36	23	36	23
Brighton *Pool Valley* ...	8 55	9 55	1055	1155	1255	1 55	2 55	3 55	4 55	5 55	7 1	8 7	9 24
Preston Circus ...	9 0	10 0	11 0	12 0	1 0	2 0	3 0	4 0	5 0	6 0	7 6	8 12	9 29
Patcham *Fountain* ...	9 5	10 9	11 9	12 9	1 9	2 9	3 9	4 9	5 9	6 9	7 16	8 22	9 39
Pyecombe *Downland Cafe* ...	9 16	1016	1116	1216	1 16	2 16	3 16	4 16	5 16	6 18	7 24	8 30	9 §47
Clayton *Post Office* ...	9 20	1020	1120	1220	1 20	2 20	3 20	4 20	5 20	6 22	7 28	8 34	§
Hassocks *Stone Pound* ...	9 23	1023	1123	1223	1 23	2 23	3 23	4 23	5 23	6 26	7 32	8 38	10 5
Keymer *Cross Roads* ...	9 26	1026	1126	1226	1 26	2 26	3 26	4 26	5 26	6 29	7 35	8 41	10 8
Keymer *Church* ...	9 27		1127		1 27		3 27		5 27		7 36		10 9
Ditchling *Church* ...	9 30		1130		1 30		3 30		5 30		7 39		10 12
Folders Lane *East End* ...	9 36		1136		1 36		3 36		5 36		7 45		10 18
Folders Lane *West End* ...		1034		1234		2 34		4 34		6 38		8 50	10 22
Burgess Hill *Hoadleys Corner* ...		1036		1236		2 36		4 36		6 40		8 52	10+24
Worlds End ...		1040		1240		2 40		4 40		6 44		8 56	
Wivelsfield *Ote Hall Chapel* ...	9 41		1141		1 41		3 41		5 41		7 52		
Jeffrey's Green ...	9 44		1144		1 44		3 44		5 44		7 55		
Haywards Heath *Sussex Hotel* ...	9 48	1049	1148	1249	1 48	2 49	3 48	4 49	5 48	6 54	8 0	9 6	
Haywards Heath *Station S.R.* ...	9 53	1054	1153	1254	1 53	2 54	3 53	4 54	5 53	7 0	8 5	9 12	

§ Via Hurstpierpoint.   † To Burgess Hill Station (arr. 10.25 p.m.).

For additional buses between Brighton and Haywards Heath via Hassocks and Burgess Hill see Service 30.

service provided a new link through Keymer and the eastern side of Burgess Hill and supplemented services 23 and 30 between Brighton and Haywards Heath. Although in post war years the 36 became a part of the 30 group half hourly service between Brighton, Haywards Heath and Horsted Keynes it was initially designed to run on the alternate hours to service 23. First departures generally started later than would be expected nowadays but evening services in the country areas continued much later even in the blackout.

The night of Thursday 14 November saw the first major Blitz on a city outside London, when the centre of Coventry was largely destroyed. Throughout that night enemy aircraft bound for Coventry flew over Portsmouth guided by a sophisticated network of radio beams known as the X system. The sirens sounded in the city as early as 1930 and the air raid alert, which lasted for nearly eleven hours, was the longest continuous period under warning up to that date. Some of the passing aircraft took the opportunity to unleash their loads on the city with many HE

Starting on 21 November 1940 Worthing service 3A was diverted inland at Western Place and no bus services ran further west along Marine Parade or West Parade until December 1944. The reason is evident from this scene looking east from the southern end of Grand Avenue across rolls of barbed wire along West Parade. The innocent looking seaside structures on the right are in fact mostly gun emplacements built to defend the coastline against invasion in the summer of 1940. *West Sussex County Council Library Service*

Route No.	31	9	9A	68	31	9A	68A	31	9	68	31	9A	68A	31	9	68	31
	N S	N S	N S	N S		N S	N S		9			N S					
Arundel *Ford Road*	...	...	...	756	...	...	...	...	9 0	...	...	...	...	...	9‡42	...	...
Arundel *Square*	...	...	8 0	...	819	8 34	...	...	9 4	...	9 19	9 34	...	9 49	10 4	...
Arundel *Station S.R.*	...	...	8 2	...	821	8 36	...	...	9 6	...	9 21	9 36	...	9 51	10 6	...
Lyminster *Church Corner*	...	...	...	811	826	8 41	...	...	9 11	...	9 26	9 41	...	9 56	1011	...
Wick *Post Office*	...	...	811	...	830	8 45	...	...	9 15	...	9 30	9 45	...	10 0	1015	...
Littlehampton *East Street*	740	745	757	816	816	835	8 50	8d50	9 5	9 20	9c20	9 35	9 50	9d50	10 5	1020	10c20
Rustington *Church*	751	w	8 36	...	827	846	...	9 1	916	...	9 31	9 46	...	10 1	1016	...	10 31
Angmering *Crundens Corner*	756	759	813	...	832	851	...	9 6	921	...	9 36	9 51	...	10 6	1021	...	10 36
Angmering *Preston Place*	757	...	814	...	833	852	...	9 7	...	...	9 37	9 52	...	10 7	...	...	10 37
Angmering-on-Sea	8 1	...	817	...	...	855	...	...	...	...	...	9 55	...	...	...	...	...
Angmering *Village*	...	8 3	...	...	...	...	...	925	...	...	...	...	...	...	1025	...	...

Route No.	9A	68A	31	9	and the following minutes past each hour	68	31	9A	68A	31	9	until	68	31	9A	65A
Arundel *Ford Road*	...	...	...	10‡42		...	...	...	...	...	‡42		...	...	...	...
Arundel *Square*	1019	1034	...	10 49		4	...	19	34	...	49		5 4	...	5 19	5 34
Arundel *Station S.R.*	1021	1036	...	10 51		6	...	21	36	...	51		5 6	...	5 21	5 36
Lyminster *Church Corner*	1026	1041	...	10 56		11	...	26	41	...	56		5 11	...	5 26	5 41
Wick *Post Office*	1030	1045	...	11 0		15	...	30	45	...	0		5 15	...	5 30	5 45
Littlehampton *East Street*	1035	1050	10d50	11 5		20	c20	35	50	d50	5		5 20	5c20	5 35	5 50
Rustington *Church*	1046	...	11 1	11 16		31	46	...	1	16	...		5 31	5 46	...	...
Angmering *Crundens Corner*	1051	...	11 6	11 21		36	51	...	6	21	...		5 36	5 51	...	...
Angmering *Preston Place*	1052	...	11 7	...		37	52	...	7	...	...		5 37	5 52	...	...
Angmering-on-Sea	1055	...	...	...		...	55	...	...	...	...		...	5 55	...	...
Angmering *Village*	...	...	...	11 25		...	...	...	...	25	...		...	...	...	...

This was the last timetable of the war to show services between Littlehampton and Rustington via the 'COAST' road as buses finally fell victim to the increased anti-invasion defences as from 21 November 1940. The above timetable from 29 August 1940 shows the early part of the daytime service and includes service 9A which only appeared in the summary.

The timetable below shows the late afternoon and evening eastbound service on the 31 towards Brighton after all Southdown routes were terminated short of South Parade Pier at Southsea The Circle. Evening services had already been reduced but further reductions were to follow in January 1943.

bombs falling on the Cosham area killing one boy. Large numbers of incendiaries were also dropped on the Highbury Estate in Cosham as well as parts of Wymering and Paulsgrove although little damage was caused and there were few casualties. As usual, at this time, the raiders also machine gunned the streets as they passed. During the evening of Saturday 16 November two HE bombs fell in Middle Street, Southsea killing five people and injuring nine others. The city was not under air raid warning at the time of the attack leaving many in the streets without shelter.

Emergency timetable No. 4 covered details of changes in services up to and including **Thursday 21 November 1940** together with complete faretables. Following invasion fears many of the roads in the coastal areas were closed or restricted resulting in several diversions to bus services which would often need to be introduced at very short notice. Some of the alterations shown may therefore have been introduced earlier. Service **3A** (formerly Tramocars

31	PORTSMOUTH, CHICHESTER, BOGNOR, LITTLEHAMPTON, WORTHING AND BRIGHTON														31
Southsea *The Circle*	...	...	...	3 55	4 25	4 55	5 25	5 55	6 28	7 1	7 34	8 7	8 40	...	...
Portsmouth *Theatre Royal*	...	4 2	4 32	5 2	5 32	6 3	6 36	7 9	7 42	8 15	8 48	9 30			
Cosham *Railway Bridge*	...	4 18	4 48	5 18	5 48	6 20	6 53	7 26	7 59	8 32	9 5	9 47			
Havant *Church*	...	4 37	5 7	5 37	6 8	6 41	7 14	7 47	8 20	8 53	9 26	10 8			
Emsworth *Square*	...	4 45	5 15	5 45	6 17	6 50	7 23	7 56	8 29	9 2	9 35	1017			
Thorney Corner	...	4 47	5 17	5 47	6 19	6 52	7 25	7 58	8 31	9 4	9 37	1019			
Nutbourne *Bell*	...	4 53	5 23	5 53	6 26	6 59	7 32	8 5	8 38	9 11	9 44	1026			
Bosham *Swan*	...	5 0	5 30	6 0	6 33	7 6	7 39	8 12	8 45	9 18	9 51	1033			
Fishbourne *Post Office*	...	5 7	5 37	6 8	6 41	7 14	7 47	8 20	8 53	9 26	9 59	1041			
Chichester *West Street*	... arr.	5 12	5 42	6 14	6 47	7 20	7 53	8 26	8 59	9 32	10 5	1047			
Chichester *West Street*	... dep.	5 13	5 43	6 15	6 48	7 21	7 54	8 27	9 0	9 33	...	...			
Merston Corner	...	5 23	5 53	6 26	6 59	7 32	8 5	8 38	9 11	9 44	...	...			
North Bersted *Post Office*	...	5 32	6 3	6 36	7 9	7 42	8 15	8 46	9 21	9 52	...	...			
Bognor *Station S.R.*	...	5 39	6 10	6 43	7 16	7 49	8 22	8 55	9 28	10 1	...	...			
Bognor *Bus Station*	... arr.	5 42	6 14	6 47	7 20	7 53	8 26	8 59	9 32	10 5	...	...			
Bognor *Bus Station*	... dep.	5 44	6 16	6 49	7 22	7 55	8 28	9 1	...	10†5	...	...			
Felpham *South Downs Hotel*	...	5 54	6 27	7 0	7 33	8 6	8 39	9 12	...	1016	...	...			
Yapton *Sparks Corner*	...	6 4	6 37	7 10	7 43	8 16	8 49	9 22	...	1026	...	...			
Littlehampton *East Street*	... arr.	6 19	6 52	7 25	7 58	8 31	9 4	9 37	...	1040	...	...			
Littlehampton *East Street*	... dep.	6 22	6 55	7 28	8 1	8 34	9 7	9 40	...	...	...	...			
Rustington *Church*	...	6 35	7 8	7 41	8 14	8 47	9 20	9 53	...						
Angmering *Crunden's Corner*	...	6 40	7 13	7 46	8 19	8 52	9 25	9 58	...						
Ferring *Henty Arms*	...	6 49	7 22	7 55	8 28	9 1	9 34	10 7	...						
Goring *Church*	...	6 57	7 30	8 3	8 36	9 9	9 42	1015	...						
Worthing *Dome*	... arr.	7 10	7 43	8 16	8 49	9 22	9 55	1028	...						
Worthing *Dome*	... dep.	7 12	7 45	8 18	9 0	9 24	10 5	...	...						
Shoreham *Bridge Hotel*	...	7 33	8 6	8 39	9 21	9 45	1026	...	†Between Bognor Bus Station and Felpham this Bus is diverted via Bognor Rly. Stn. & Upper Bognor Road (Service 50 Route)					
Brighton *Pool Valley*	...	8 3	8 36	9 9	9 51	1015	1056	...							

T1) was diverted between Splash Point and Tarring Road to operate via Marine Parade, Western Place, Rowlands Road, Hythe Road, Hastings Road, Winchelsea Gardens, Romney Road, Wallace Avenue, Mill Road and Grand Avenue. This rerouted all buses away from Worthing Sea Front west of Western Place and partly replaced service **5A** which was withdrawn. The frequency was increased to provide a 10 minute service daily except on Sunday mornings when a 15 minute service operated between Splash Point and Wallace Avenue/Goring Road only. Also in Worthing service **7A** was diverted between Broadwater Street East and Upper Brighton Road to operate via Forest Road in both directions.

As a result of the road closures in sensitive coastal areas, some complicated changes in the Angmering, Rustington, Littlehampton and Arundel areas affected services 9, 9A, 31, 68 and 68A. Services 9, 9A and 31 were diverted away from Sea Lane and Sea Road with buses no longer running between Rustington and Littlehampton via the B2140 coast road. Consequently services **9** and **9A** were diverted between Angmering Station and Littlehampton via Station Road, Mill Lane, Worthing Road, Horsham Road and East Street and both services were withdrawn between Littlehampton and Arundel. Service **31** was diverted from Rustington, The Street via Rustington Street, North Lane, Worthing Road, Horsham Road, East Street, Beach Road, New Road, Surrey Street, Broadway and Terminus Road (returning via Terminus Road, Broadway, High Street and East Street). As a result service **68** was withdrawn between Rustington and Littlehampton and revised to operate from LITTLEHAMPTON (NORFOLK ROAD) to ARUNDEL SQUARE via South Terrace, Beach Road, New Road, Clifton Road, High Street and Church Street to East Street and then as previously. The new terminus in Littlehampton served an area near to the sea front that was no longer covered by services 9, 9A and 31. A few journeys extended in Arundel to terminate at Arundel (Ford Road) in place of service 9. A 30 minute service was provided daily although service 68A – which operated in the opposite direction around the Rustington loop – was now withdrawn. Service **11** was curtailed to terminate at FERRING (FERRINGHAM LANE at its junction with CLOVER LANE) and withdrawn in Ferring from Ocean Drive, South Drive and West Drive.

The daytime frequency of service **12** was revised as follows

1 journey per hour Tongdean to Eastbourne

1 journey per hour Tongdean to Seaford

1 journey per hour Tongdean to Peacehaven Rosemary

1 journey per hour Tongdean to Peacehaven Annexe (12A)

1 journey per hour Brighton Station to Saltdean Mount (12B)

This marked a reduction from four to two journeys per hour beyond Peacehaven as far as Seaford. In the Eastbourne area, now suffering from a depleted local population, visitor bans and repeated air attacks, there were further reductions in frequency with services **93**, **94** and **96** all reduced from hourly to two hourly.

In the November 1939 revisions some services to South Parade, Southsea had been reduced and from 21 November 1940 all the remaining Southsea routes were curtailed, someway short of the sea front at The Circle. Situated at the junction of Victoria Road South and Clarendon Road it was a convenient turning point for services via both Theatre Royal and Fratton. Services **31**, **39**, **40** and **42** via Theatre Royal ran as normal route to Palmerston Road and then via Clarendon Road. Service **31A** and **41** via Fratton ran as normal route and were simply curtailed at The Circle. Fratton journeys on service **45** continued to terminate at Bradford Road (Plaza) until 12 June 1941 when they too were extended to terminate at The Circle. It is interesting to note that Portsmouth Corporation trolleybus services had been withdrawn from South Parade Pier as from 5 July 1940 when the sea front was closed to civilian traffic.

At 1410 on Friday 22 November enemy aircraft again visited Eastbourne dropping HE bombs across the town centre from the railway station and Gildredge Hotel in Terminus Road to the Cavendish Hotel in Devonshire Place. Cornfield Road, Seaside Road and Compton Street were also hit and further devastation caused to the already battered town. Fortunately, given the extent of the raid, only one lady was killed and ten people were injured. Three young children were amongst the seven fatal and 16 injured casualties when bombs destroyed houses in Orchard Road in Horsham late on Friday 29 November. Leyland Cub car 19 operating the 2143 journey from Highlands Estate on service 72 is believed to have been damaged in this incident although it is not known whether any bus passengers were injured or killed. British civilian casualty figures for the month of November amounted to 4,588 killed and 6,202 injured, a welcome reduction on the past two months.

The raids on Portsmouth had devastated hundreds of houses leading many to leave the city at night in the hope of finding a safe place to sleep. This in turn led to overloading of Southdown's country services and starting on Monday 2 December two new express services were introduced to strengthen the busy services along the A3 corridor north of the city. These ran between Theatre Royal and Lovedean or Horndean every 30 minutes during the busiest morning and evening hours to provide a bus every 15 minutes between Portsmouth and Cowplain. On Saturdays the express services ran in the midday peak instead of evenings. Buses ran non-stop between North End and Park Lane, Cowplain and it is believed that 1400 class

saloons were normally used. These little known additional journeys did not appear in the Southdown timetables or leaflets but continued after the war until withdrawn on 7 January 1949.

Portsmouth was again attacked starting at around 2000 on Thursday 5 December with a major raid that killed 44 people and injured around 140 others. Some 30 HE bombs hit the Dockyard and HMS Vernon starting major fires and causing serious damage. Residential streets in Fratton were also hit and fires raged in many parts of the city. Four HE bombs on Cosham struck Highbury Buildings, Windsor Road, the Railway Goods Yard and the Carlton Cinema in the High Street where three died and 40 were injured. Next day at 1935 the raiders returned as six HE bombs and numerous incendiaries fell on the western area of the city and dockyard starting 28 fires and fracturing gas and water mains. Bombs also hit Eastern Road, First Avenue and Second Avenue in Farlington with one person killed and 23 injured in the raid. The ban on visitors to the coastal parts of the Southdown area was finally relaxed for the winter as from Saturday 7 December but still applied east of Peacehaven. At 2335 on Wednesday 11 December Newhaven suffered its worst attack of the war as one 500 kg bomb scored a direct hit on three houses in Folly Field, Lewes Road completely demolishing one and seriously damaging two others. Many were buried under the debris and despite the efforts of the rescue squads 12 people died in the incident.

The city of Portsmouth was once again destined to be the focus of German attacks in the run up to Christmas. On Saturday 21 December three HE bombs fell on Victoria Road in Southsea while next day five HE bombs and a number of incendiaries hit the Hard near the Naval barracks. The Post Office on the Hard was

Eastbourne's town centre received more than its fair share of bombs during the war and especially during the 'Hit and Run' attacks. This is the scene in Terminus Road looking north towards the Railway Station on 22 November 1940 after enemy aircraft dropped bombs in a line from the station to the sea front. The shops on the right and the Gildredge Hotel in the background took direct hits but only one person was killed and ten injured. Note the white lines on the trees to assist pedestrians in the blackout. Outside the station stands a Corporation double decker whilst a Southdown Leyland Tiger coach waits to turn right into Gildredge Road probably on diversion due to the closure of Terminus Road. *T R Beckett/Eastbourne Gazette and Herald*

72 72B 73	HIGHLANDS ESTATE — HORSHAM (CARFAX) / HORSHAM (CARFAX) — THE COMMON / ST. LEONARDS — HORSHAM (CARFAX)	72 72B 73

	NS	NS	NS	NS	NS	NS	NS	NS	SO	NS		NS
St. Leonards Hotel	...	...	...	...	...	...	...	...	...	...		...
Highlands Estate	...	...	7 52	8 22	8 42	9 2	9 22	9 42	...	10 2		10 22	10 42
Horsham *Station S.R.*	...	...	7 58	8 28	8 48	9 8	9 28	9 48	...	10 8		10 28	10 48
Horsham *Carfax*	7 25	7 40	8 0	8 30	8 50	9 10	9 30	9 50	9 50	10 10		10 30	10 50
The Common	7 33	7 48	8 8	8 38	8 58	9 18	9 38	9 58	9 58	10 18		10 38	10 58

	★	NS		NS		NS		NS	NST			NST
St. Leonards Hotel	1055					1255						
Highlands Estate	...	1122	1142	12 2	1222	1242	...	1 22	1 42	2 2	2 22	2 42
Horsham *Station S.R.*	11 3	1128	1148	12 8	1228	1248	1 3	1 28	1 48	2 8	2 28	2 48
Horsham *Carfax*	1110	1130	1150	1210	1230	1250	1 10	1 30	1 50	2 10	2 30	2 50
The Common	1118	1138	1158	1218	1238	1258	1 18	1 38	1 58	2 18	2 38	2 58

	★	NST		NST		NST	★	NST		NST		NST		★
St. Leonards Hotel	2 55						4 55							7 1
Highlands Estate	...	3 22	3 42	4 2	4 22	4 42	...	5 22	5 42	6 3	6 25	6 47		
Horsham *Station S.R.*	3 3	3 28	3 48	4 8	4 28	4 48	5 3	5 28	5 48	6 9	6 31	6 53	7 10	
Horsham *Carfax*	3 10	3 30	3 50	4 10	4 30	4 50	5 10	5 30	5 50	6 11	6 33	6 55	7 17	
The Common	3 18	3 38	3 58	4 18	4 38	4 58	5 18	5 38	5 58	6 20	6 42	7 4	7 26	

	NST		NST		NST	★	NST		NST		NST
St. Leonards Hotel						9 13					
Highlands Estate	7 31	7 53	8 15	8 37	8 59	...	9 43	10 5	1020	...	1049
Horsham *Station S.R.*	7 37	7 59	8 21	8 43	9 5	9 22	9 49	1011	1026	...	1055
Horsham *Carfax*	7 39	8 1	8 23	8 45	9 7	9 29	9 51	1013	1028	1040	1057
The Common	7 48	8 10	8 32	8 54	9 16	9 38	10 0	1022	...	1049	

★ Arrives Carfax 11.5 a.m., 1.5, 3.5, 5.5, 7.12 & 9.24 p.m.   NS—Not Sundays.   NST—Not Suns. or Thurs.

1941

The first Portsmouth 'Blitz' occurred on the night of Friday 10/Saturday 11 January lasting for seven hours and leaving 171 people dead and 430 injured. The attack was the main air raid by the German air force on the UK that night, Portsmouth having been selected as the target because much of the country was covered with cloud. Unfortunately, Portsmouth's position on the coast to the north of the Isle of Wight made the city easier for the bombers to locate in the poor conditions. They were guided by two VHF radio beams which intersected over Southsea Common, a method with an accuracy of about one mile at that range. These radio beams were detected in advance, so the authorities had some warning that Portsmouth might be a target. Over 150 German aircraft were involved in the raid, dropping 140 tons of HE bombs and over 40,000 incendiaries. The latter soon caused 28 major fires, as well as 2,314 smaller ones, which proved difficult for the fire services to bring under control as around 60 water mains were wrecked. Most of the death and destruction occurred in the southern parts of the city, centred on Landport, Old Portsmouth, Southsea and Fratton. Incendiary bombs fell on the imposing Guildhall and despite all the combined efforts of the Civil Defence services it proved impossible to extinguish the fires which burned for several hours. The roof collapsed leaving just the outer walls and many valuable paintings, furniture and civic possessions were lost. With the Guildhall wrecked, the city council took over the Royal Beach Hotel on Southsea sea front for its offices. The main shopping centres in

destroyed by a direct hit but otherwise little damage and few casualties resulted from the attack. Far worse was to come at 1850 on Monday 23 December when the Conway Street area of Landport was hit by a massive 2500 kg HE bomb which wrecked whole streets of small houses in a densely populated part of the city. Eighteen people were killed and two hundred and twenty injured including those in the Dockyard. Although this marked the last raid on the city for 1940 the New Year would bring even greater devastation. On Friday 27 December fifteen HE bombs were dropped on the Bersted area of Bognor stretching from the Servite Convent to Hawthorn Road and across Chichester Road and Sherwood Avenue killing one person. British civilian casualty figures for the month of December totalled 3,793 killed and 5,244 injured.

Photographed on layover in Cambridge Road, Portsmouth after the war is car 951 (UF 8851), a Leyland Titan TD2 new in 1933 and rebodied with an austere looking Willowbrook lowbridge body to utility specification in May 1944. Of particular interest is the fact that the destination screen shows it to have operated on one of the limited stop services introduced in December 1940 between Lovedean or Horndean and Theatre Royal and originally covered by 1400 class Tigers.
Alan Lambert collection

The wrecked remains of Handley's department store at the junction of Palmerston Road and Osborne Road in the heart of Southsea's once famous shopping district after the bombing raid on the night of Friday 10/Saturday 11 January 1941. At this time all Southdown buses from Theatre Royal to Southsea had been curtailed at The Circle and operated via the northern (now pedestrianised) section of Palmerston Road to the right of the picture and then turned left into Clarendon Road. With no chance of building a new store until the end of hostilities some temporary gardens were constructed on the site helping to mask the remains of walls and foundations.
Portsmouth News

Palmerston Road, King's Road, and Commercial Road were largely reduced to rubble and other buildings destroyed included six churches, the Eye and Ear Hospital, part of the Royal Hospital, Clarence Pier, the Hippodrome Theatre in Commercial Road along with three cinemas, the Dockyard School, the Connaught Drill Hall in Stanhope Road, Central Hotel in Commercial Road, and Royal Sailors' Rest. The FA Cup – won by Portsmouth in 1939 – had been stored in the vaults of Lloyds Bank in Commercial Road, and was dug out of the rubble after the attack. The Southern Railway was also badly affected with damage to Portsmouth and Southsea, Portsmouth Harbour, Fratton and Gosport stations and disruption on all lines in the area. The girders supporting the already damaged Harbour Station were blown away causing one coach of a train to crash down on to the mud below. The water main was hit and the tide out so no water could be pumped from below to save the burning station which had to be abandoned until after the war. A direct hit on the power station left the Corporation trolleybuses stranded all over the city. There was some further damage at HMS Vernon but most of the worst effects of the raid were felt in the business and residential areas of the city. With many restaurants and around 50 food shops destroyed emergency arrangements had to be made to feed the people.

During the air raids on Portsmouth the Royal Portsmouth Hospital in Landport was hit on three separate occasions. Its location dangerously close to the Naval Dockyards made it especially vulnerable to the inaccurate bombing of the time. Although the patients were safely evacuated several members of staff were killed and on the night of 10/11 January 1941 two of Southdown's fourteen ambulance conversions based at Portsmouth – cars 1089 and 1092 – were totally destroyed whilst parked at the hospital.
Portsmouth News

Open air canteens were set up including one outside the ruins of the Guildhall and a mass funeral was held at Kingston Cemetery on 17 January for some of those killed during the air raid.

Whilst the bombing attacks had so far had little effect on the Naval Dockyards they had already destroyed and damaged many houses in the residential areas of the city. Shopping centres in Southsea and Commercial Road were blitzed and some military establishments and commercial premises had to be relocated causing essential workers to change their travel arrangements. The destruction of homes also led to large numbers of people moving to the apparently safer areas outside the city and beyond the boundary of the Corporation bus and trolleybus services adding pressure on the overworked Southdown bus services along the A3 corridor. In addition the Corporation were concerned about the serious loss of passengers on their services resulting from the exodus from the city and suggested that a simple solution would be to extend some of their bus services beyond Cosham. After a conference in December 1940 between the RTC for the Southern Area and representatives of Portsmouth Corporation and Southdown, it was agreed that the Corporation buses would run along the London Road as far as Cowplain and that it was hoped to start a service as soon as possible. By 8 January 1941 agreement was reached for an extra peak time service from Theatre Royal as far as Waterlooville and the operation of Corporation buses on other Southdown routes out of Portsmouth was also discussed, but no agreement was reached at this time. According to press reports these additional buses commenced on Monday 3 February.

Southdown fares were charged and passengers were specifically asked not to use these extra buses for short rides within the city.

Following the disastrous fire raid on London on 29 December 1940 and the increasing destruction caused by incendiary bombs falling on unoccupied premises, the Government introduced compulsory fire watching duty for most civilians on Monday 20 January. On Friday 31 January Winston Churchill and his wife visited Portsmouth and made an extensive tour of the bombed areas. King George VI and Queen Elizabeth also visited Portsmouth to inspect Civil Defence services on Thursday 6 February as well as seeing the interior of the burnt out Guildhall and touring the city to visit emergency centres, Police and ARP personnel. UK civilian casualty figures for the month of January were announced as 1,500 killed and 2,012 injured whilst those for February fell to 789 killed and 1068 injured.

Some further enhancement of services in Portsmouth occurred from Monday 17 February. To provide extra capacity along the A3 corridor new Southdown Service **37** was introduced between PORTSMOUTH (THEATRE ROYAL) and WATERLOOVILLE (HEROES INN) via Commercial Road, Kingston Crescent, London Road, Northern Road, Spur Road, London Road and Purbrook with a 30 minute service daily until 1800. In addition a new Service **37A** began between PORTSMOUTH (THEATRE ROYAL) and WATERLOOVILLE (HEROES INN) as service 37 to Purbrook Church then via Stakes Road and Stakes Hill Road. This ran every 30 minutes daily until 1800 and replaced service 39 via Stakes during the daytime. These new services only appeared in the

Car 194 (EUF 194) is a Leyland Titan TD5 with Beadle lowbridge body new in June 1938 and seen at Haywards Heath station. It is in the livery adopted from 1943 with allover grey except for apple green below the lower deck windows. The driver is in the process of changing the destination blinds and most potential passengers seem to be Army personnel. As part of the postwar rebodying programme the Beadle body was scrapped in 1949 and a new Park Royal highbridge body fitted. *Southdown Enthusiasts Club – W J Haynes Collection*

Portsmouth–Waterlooville summary timetables. Service **39** was withdrawn between Southsea (The Circle) and Theatre Royal and the daytime service diverted away from Stakes being replaced by new service 37A.

Daytime services along the A3 corridor now amounted to 12 buses per hour as follows:

37   2 journeys per hour Theatre Royal – Main Road – Waterlooville

37A 2 journeys per hour Theatre Royal – Stakes – Waterlooville

39   2 journeys per hour Theatre Royal – Main Road – Waterlooville – Hambledon

40   1 journey per hour Southsea (The Circle) – Theatre Royal – Main Road – Waterlooville – Clanfield – Petersfield

40B 1 journey per hour Theatre Royal – Main Road – Waterlooville – Clanfield Drift Road

41   2 journeys per hour Southsea (The Circle) – Fratton – Main Road – Waterlooville – Horndean

42   1 journey per hour Southsea (The Circle) – Theatre Royal – Main Road – Waterlooville – Horndean – Petersfield

42B 1 journey per hour Theatre Royal – Main Road – Waterlooville – Snells Corner

With the return of spring came the renewed threat of German invasion although Britain's defences were much improved with many better equipped trained men available. During March the public were urged to carry their gas masks at all times and further school children from the coastal areas deemed at most risk were evacuated to towns in the Midlands and North. The authorities had already prepared a top secret plan to compulsorily evacuate all civilians from some of the coastal towns in East Sussex and Kent should the need arise and in March notices were posted in these areas warning of the increased risk of invasion. Residents were advised:

> "Last year all who could be spared from this town were asked to leave, not only for their own safety, but so as to ease the work of the Armed Forces in repelling an invasion. The danger of invasion has increased and the Government requests all who can be spared, and have somewhere to go, to leave without delay.
>
> When invasion is upon us it may be necessary to evacuate the remaining population of this and certain other towns. Evacuation would then be compulsory at short notice, in crowded trains, with scanty luggage, to destinations chosen by the Government. If you are not among the essential workers mentioned above, it is better to go now while the going is good."

Those affected included school children, mothers with young children, aged and infirm persons, persons living on pensions and persons in retirement or without occupation. Essential workers which included members of the Home Guard and Observer Corps, Police, Fire Brigade and ARP and casualty services and all involved in war work were warned they must stay. All employees of transport undertakings such as Southdown were required to remain. Unlike in the 1940 scare the message to those who stayed was very clear and unambiguous. In the meantime further defences were built and from 25 March it was again decreed that no visitors travelling for the purposes of Holidays, Recreation and Pleasure would be permitted to enter the coastal defence zone which in the Southdown area now extended from Hastings to Littlehampton. The remaining residents were registered and permits issued for travel to and from the restricted area although contemporary reports suggest that enforcement was patchy for those entering the area by bus. The threat of a German invasion in the area remained until the Allied landings in Normandy in June 1944 although fortunately the emergency civilian evacuation schemes that were devised never had to be implemented.

During March 1941 the Luftwaffe changed to a policy of repeated air attacks on individual cities which included Portsmouth. Five night raids were made on the city in one week with the heaviest raid on the night of 10/11 March. On Sunday 9 March some 34 HE bombs were dropped across Portsea, Southsea and Fratton and the following day marked the Second 'Blitz' on Portsmouth as 250 HE bombs fell on the southern half of the city in a raid lasting from 2000 until 0200 next day. Over 46,000 incendiaries were dropped starting serious fires in the Dockyard, at the Royal Naval Barracks, at Vosper's shipbuilding works as well as parts of Portsea, Landport, Southsea and North End. Three HE bombs fell on the Eastney depot of Portsmouth Corporation and exploded after falling through the roof and hitting one of the main girders in the east bay of the then bus section. Ten buses were completely destroyed including four double deckers, five single deckers and one of the Guy seafront runabouts which dated from 1924. Fire destroyed some of the stores and slight water damage was caused to machinery with the estimated cost of the damage between £30,000 and £40,000. North End depot also suffered bomb damage during the same air raid but no vehicles were damaged. The electricity supply to the city was cut off and all Corporation trolleybuses were stopped for several days. Bus services were soon restarted only to be curtailed again as unexploded bombs were found. Major disruption was caused by an unexploded bomb at Portsbridge which meant that the only way in and out of the city was over the temporary bridge across Port Creek to the east of Portsbridge. Once again residential areas were badly hit with 93 people killed, 164 seriously injured and 83 slightly injured. It was the 37th raid on the city as well as the 481st alert so far.

FOR SERVICES 37 and 37a . . .

Portsmouth-Waterlooville
via Main Road (37)
or via Stakes (37a)

See Special Summary Pages 24 to 31

To provide extra capacity along the A3 corridor new Services **37** and **37A** were introduced from 10 April 1941 between Portsmouth (Theatre Royal) and Waterlooville (Heroes Inn) with a 30 minute daily service on each route until 1800. The 37A diverted via Stakes and replaced service 39 during the daytime. The service details only appeared in the Portsmouth-Waterlooville summary timetables.

The wartime timetables were smaller than those produced before the war and did not include faretables or timetables for the London Express Services. The first complete edition, numbered Emergency Time Table No 1, was issued for 16 November 1939 and included all the alterations to services up to that date. This format continued until issue No. 9 dated 5 October 1942 but even greater demands for economy lead to the publication of separate 'War Edition' timetables for East Sussex, West Sussex and Hampshire. These appeared as and when necessary starting from 3 January 1943 and continuing until 13 May 1945. A complete system timetable was then issued to normal peacetime standards on 9 December 1945.

SOUTHDOWN
MOTOR SERVICES LIMITED

EMERGENCY
TIME TABLE

No. 5

APRIL 10th, 1941
AND UNTIL FURTHER NOTICE

3 D.

Southdown Motor Services, Ltd.
In association with the Southern Railway.

EMERGENCY TIME TABLE No. 5

10th APRIL, 1941, and until further notice

Since the publication of Emergency Time Table No. 4, alterations have been made to several Southdown Bus Services. These alterations are now included in this booklet, together with minor adjustments to Services 13A, 27, 44 and 69, which will have effect from April 10th, 1941.

Defence Area restrictions, more particularly in the Coastal areas, the regulation of fuel supplies and other circumstances make inevitable constant adjustments of the services to meet the changing conditions. Such alterations will be advertised locally in the areas affected, with as much notice as possible, and the changes will subsequently be included in the next Southdown Time Table.

Under present conditions it is not possible to publish Fare Tables with each issue of the Official Time Table. Complete Fare Tables were, however, published with Emergency Time Table No. 4, dated 21st November, 1940. All fares have since remained unaltered except for slight adjustments in the areas of Brighton and Hove, where halfpenny increases in certain local fares were ordered by the Ministry of Transport, and the introduction of additional Workmen's Fares in the Portsmouth area which were advertised locally by special bus notices.

TABLE OF CONTENTS.

On Tuesday 11 March some 20 HE bombs along with incendiaries fell mainly on the Cosham, Fratton and Southsea districts causing more casualties. HMS Vernon suffered further damage and at the north end of the city Queen Alexandra Hospital and Highbury Estate were both hit.

After a few weeks of comparative peace German aircraft returned to Eastbourne at 2125 on Wednesday 12 March when a single raider dropped eight bombs on the eastern side of town including the workshops of the Corporation Bus Depot in Churchdale Road. During the war there were two direct hits on the Eastbourne Corporation depot, three staff were killed and three buses damaged whilst in service. Four HE bombs were dropped on the Archery area of Eastbourne at 0939 on Friday 28 March, completely demolishing six houses and severely damaging many others. Three people were killed and 25 injured in the raid. With the return of Spring and more extensive air raids British civilian casualties for March increased to 4,259 killed and 5,557 injured.

Seaford suffered a brief but vicious attack early on Tuesday 1 April, when a single enemy aircraft released four bombs across Broad Street, Church Street, West Street and Chatham Place causing widespread devastation. The old Manor House and Kennards Dairy House were wrecked, killing one of the dairy employees, and nine people injured in the incident. Tuesday 8 April was a day of raids across the Southdown area from Portsmouth to Hastings. Some 36 HE bombs fell on Portsmouth causing further

damage in Landport, Fratton, North End and Southsea while HMS Vernon suffered an incendiary raid. To the east, Hastings experienced a heavy raid as aircraft dropped 28 HE bombs and 300 incendiaries across the town hitting the Railway Station, The Royal East Sussex Hospital and Municipal Hospital. Later Brighton suffered one of its worst raids when bombs fell on the residential area of Norfolk Square causing extensive damage to property, killing at least ten people and injuring many more.

Emergency timetable No. 5 contained details of changes in services up to and including **Thursday 10 April 1941** and, unlike the previous issue, faretables were once again excluded. Worthing was one of the towns that saw its civilian population decline in 1941 and as a further wartime necessity the frequency of local service **3A** was reduced from every 10 to 15 minutes during the daytime and 20 minutes evenings and the route finally curtailed at Worthing Pier as the area around Splash Point had been requisitioned by the military authorities. The frequency of local services **5** and **6** were also reduced from every 10 to 12 minutes during the daytime and 20 minutes evenings daily.

Journeys on service **27** were diverted to avoid the Devil's Dyke Hotel now in the hands of the Military authorities. The timing point was redefined as Devil's Dyke Station – which had closed on 31 December 1938! All services passing through Cosham *from* Portsmouth were diverted from the same date and no longer ran via Cosham Station. Journeys on services **31**, **31A**,

31B, **31C** and **43** were diverted to operate via London Road, Northern Road, Spur Road and Havant Road. Journeys on services **38**, **39**, **40**, **40B**, **41**, **42**, **42A** and **42B** were diverted via London Road, Northern Road, Spur Road, London Road and service **45** journeys now operated via London Road, Northern Road and Southampton Road. Service **68** was curtailed to operate between LITTLEHAMPTON (EAST STREET) and ARUNDEL SQUARE although certain journeys continued to and from Arundel (Ford Road). The section of route in Littlehampton between Norfolk Road and East Street was withdrawn but the frequency increased from 30 minutes to 20 minutes daily. In the Haywards Heath area some limited enhancements to services allowed the daytime frequency of Lindfield service **85** to be increased on Weekdays from hourly to 30 minutes although remaining hourly on Sundays and during evenings. An additional hourly service from mid-morning on Weekdays only between Birch Hotel (Lewes Road) and Haywards Heath Station was also provided on Uckfield service **89**.

By this time the direct services to Hellingly Mental Hospital were still running but with some minor reductions. On alternate Tuesdays and Wednesdays and the first Sunday in each month a service ran from Hove Station via Brighton Pool Valley, Lewes and Golden Cross – with connections from East Grinstead by service 92. On alternate Wednesdays and the first Sunday in each month another service ran from Hurstpierpoint via Hassocks and Ditchling to Lewes where it could be linked with the Hove service. On Sundays it was extended to start and finish at Burgess Hill. Finally every Tuesday, alternate Wednesdays and the first Sunday of each month a service ran from Eastbourne to Hellingly with connections by service 12 from Seaford, Polegate (connections with service 25

27	BRIGHTON—HENFIELD via Devil's Dyke, Poynings & Edburton					27
						SSO
						8 † 4
Brighton *Pool Valley* ...	9 30	12 30	3 30	6 30		...
Seven Dials ...	9 39	12 39	3 39	6 40		...
Tivoli Crescent North ...	9 44	12 44	3 44	6 46		...
Tongdean Lane ...	9 47	12 47	3 47	6 49		...
Saddlescombe Road ...	9 50	12 50	3 50	6 52		...
B'ton & Hove Golf Links	9 52	12 52	3 52	6 55		...
Devil's Dyke Station ...	9 56	12 56	3 56	6 59		...
Poynings *Church* ...	10 3	1 3	4 3	7 7		8 45
Edburton *Church* ...	10 12	1 12	4 12	7 17		8 55
Small Dole ...	10 21	1 21	4 21	7 27		9 5
Henfield *George* ...	10 29	1 29	4 29	7 36		9 14
						SSO
Henfield *George* ...	8 50	10 50	1 50	4 50		7 55
Small Dole ...	9 0	11 0	2 0	5 0		8 6
Edburton *Church* ...	9 10	11 10	2 10	5 10		8 17
Poynings *Church* ...	9 18	11 18	2 18	5 18		8‡26
Devil's Dyke Station ...	9 27	11 27	2 27	5 27		...
B'ton & Hove Golf Links	9 31	11 31	2 31	5 31		...
Saddlescombe Road ...	9 33	11 33	2 33	5 33		...
Tongdean Lane ...	9 36	11 36	2 36	5 36		...
Tivoli Crescent North ...	9 39	11 39	2 39	5 39		...
Seven Dials ...	9 43	11 43	2 43	5 43		...
Brighton *Pool Valley* ...	9 51	11 51	2 51	5 51		9 5

† Service 17 bus from Brighton—passengers change to Service 27 bus at Poynings Cross Roads.

‡ Service 27 bus—passengers to Brighton change to Service 17 bus at Poynings Cross Roads.

SSO—Saturdays and Sundays only

GO TO IT—
by
SOUTHDOWN

from Berwick) and Hailsham (connections with service 15 from Hastings).

Good Friday fell on 11 April but death and destruction still occurred in the west of the area. Two Parachute Mines dropped on Second Avenue and Hardy Road in Farlington killed 20 and injured 30 as well as destroying 50 houses, damaging a further 450 and making 200 people homeless. Some 50 HE bombs also landed on Southsea causing damage to properties in Ashburton Road and Portland Road. In Bognor

Car 1482 (GCD 382), a Leyland Tiger TS8 with Harrington body was delivered in December 1939 and is seen here at the Worthing Library terminus of service 3A – which had replaced the former Tramocars service T1. The service was curtailed at the Pier (as shown on the destination) as from 10 April 1941. At this time car 1482 still retains the rear corner windows and normal seating although it was converted to perimeter seating in June 1942. *Alan Lambert collection*

23 HE bombs were dropped around Linden Road and the railway station causing extensive damage to some 50 houses and railway property and three fatalities. Next day Portsmouth was again attacked with HE and incendiary bombs and parachute mines, two of which fell on The Hard side of the railway embankment. Further devastation was caused across Southsea, Fratton, Copnor and Wymering although worse was to come at the end of the month.

With only limited progress in solving overloading on Southdown's country services from Portsmouth the RTC called a further meeting on 21 March 1941 and informed the Corporation and Southdown representatives that if they could not reach an agreement then he would impose one. The commissioner made it quite clear that he was aware of the problems faced by residents as a result of the inadequate service beyond Cosham to Cowplain and that augmentation was required in certain directions. Southdown appeared unable to cope with the extra passengers at peak periods and he considered that the Corporation was the right authority to provide the additional vehicles as it had lost passengers from its services in the city. As a result it was agreed that commencing 31 March 1941 Southdown would employ 10 surplus Corporation double deckers for an experimental period of two months at a guaranteed rate of £3.10s (£3.50) per day per bus for six days per week. Portsmouth Corporation introduced three new peak time services from Monday 14 April to help further strengthen the very busy Southdown country services. The first ran between Theatre Royal, North End and Waterlooville every 10 minutes in the morning peak and every 15 minutes in the evening peak. In addition there were buses at 0602 from Portchester, Cross Roads to Theatre Royal and 0608 from Drayton to Theatre Royal with return workings at 1820 from Theatre Royal to both Portchester and Drayton. These services were registered under Portsmouth Corporation Defence Permits to run daily throughout the year. Passengers were advised not to use these buses for local journeys within Portsea Island and Southdown fares were charged although the extra timings did not appear in Southdown timetables of the period. The hiring arrangement continued for the remainder of the war but it was not to be the end of the problems between the bus operators in Portsmouth.

To further help ease the pressure on the homeward journey from Portsmouth, special limited stop 'Dockyard Specials' started on 12 routes commencing Tuesday 15 April from H.M. Dockyard (Unicorn Gate) at 1815 on Monday to Friday. These ran as follows:

No.	Destination	Runs Non stop to:
1	Purbrook Common	Portsdown, The George
2	Waterlooville, Heroes	Purbrook Church
3	Cowplain, Park Lane	Waterlooville, Jubilee Road
4	Horndean, Ship & Bell	Cowplain, Spotted Cow
5	Snells Corner	Horndean, Good Intent
6	Clanfield	Lovedean, Post Office
7	Portchester Cross Roads	Wymering, Sixth Avenue
8	Portchester Cross Roads	Wymering, Sixth Avenue
9	Cornaway Lane, North	Portchester, White Hart
10	Fareham Bus Station	Portchester, The Fairway
11	Drayton, New Inn	St Colman's Avenue
12	Farlington, Rectory Avenue	Farlington, Waterworks Road

Buses carried the special numbers shown and numbers 1, 2, 3, 4, 7, 8 and 11 were usually worked by Portsmouth Corporation vehicles. Normal Southdown fares were charged with Workmen's return tickets and Southdown season tickets valid on the limited stop services. The 12 extra buses were provided in addition to the usual services and the company advised that 'almost all of the usual relief buses' from Southsea, The Circle, Theatre Royal and Bradford Junction would be maintained. A special leaflet warned passengers that buses would leave before 1815 if fully loaded and that whilst non stop buses could not be provided for everyone the company hoped that these 12 special buses would improve travelling conditions for those using ordinary services. There was no need for inward morning journeys as before 0900 all buses turned off Commercial Road at Fitzherbert Street and ran via Flathouse Street, Unicorn Road and Edinburgh Road to regain normal route at the Portsmouth & Southsea Station stop.

Hospital Service	HOVE — BRIGHTON — LEWES — HELLINGLY With connections from and to Uckfield, East Grinstead, etc.					Hospital Service
	ALTERNATE TUESDAYS AND WEDNESDAYS AND FIRST SUNDAY OF EACH MONTH					
Hove *Station S.R.*	... ...12 30		**Hellingly** *Mental Hospital* 4 15			
Hove *Company's Office*	... ...12 40		**Golden Cross** *Inn* ... ... arr. 4 30			
Brighton *Pool Valley*	... ...12 50		┌ Golden Cross *Inn* ... ... dep. 4 46			
Lewes *Company's Office*	... ... 1 15	Service 92	Uckfield *Bus Station* 5 15			Service 92
┌ East Grinstead *Crown Hotel*	...12 19		Forest Row *Swan Inn* 6 3			
Service 92 { Forest Row *Swan Hotel*	...12 31		└ East Grinstead *Crown Hotel* 6 15			
Uckfield *Bus Station*	... 1 20		**Lewes** *Company's Office* ... ... arr. 5 0			
└ Golden Cross *Inn*	... arr. 1 46		**Brighton** *Pool Valley* 5 25			
Golden Cross *Inn*	... ... dep. 1 46		**Hove** *Company's Office* 5 35			
Hellingly *Mental Hospital*	... ... 2 0		**Hove** *Station S.R.* 5 45			

Hospital Service	BURGESS HILL — HURST — HELLINGLY Via Hassocks, Ditchling and Lewes.		Hospital Service
	ALTERNATE WEDNESDAYS AND FIRST SUNDAY OF EACH MONTH ONLY.		
Burgess Hill *Royal George*	... ...12a25	**Hellingly** *Mental Hospital* 4 15
Hurstpierpoint *Church*	... ...12 40	**Lewes** *Company's Office* 5 0
Hassocks *Stone Pound*	... ...12 44	**Ditchling** *Church* 5 25
Ditchling *Church*	... ...12 50	**Hassocks** *Stone Pound* 5 31
Lewes *Company's Office*	... ... 1 15	**Hurstpierpoint** *Church* 5c35
Hellingly *Mental Hospital*	... ... 2 0	**Burgess Hill** *Royal George* 5b40

a—Runs from Burgess Hill on first Sunday of each month only.
b—On Wednesdays passengers change at Hassocks for Burgess Hill (arr. 5.52 p.m.).
c—On Sundays passengers change at Hassocks for Hurstpierpoint (arr. 5.10 p.m.).

Portsmouth endured its third 'blitz' on Sunday 27 April as HE bombs and parachute mines once more blasted the city. Over 100 were reported dead and a further 275 injured including nine killed when the Casualty Department at the Royal Hospital was hit again. Two mines fell near Portsmouth and Southsea Station causing much damage and several fatal casualties and there was further destruction to the remaining shopping and business centre in Commercial Road. Once again the already damaged residential areas of Landport, Portsea, Fratton and Southsea were worst hit along with the Dockyard.

An interesting event occurred on Monday 28 April when an unexploded bomb to the east of Littlehampton caused the closure of the A259 between North Lane and Cemetery Corner. As the alternative inland route was via Lyminster, Crossbush and Angmering Village the Police suggested that for the convenience of traffic – and particularly buses – application might be made to reopen the B2140 along Sea Lane and Sea Road for a temporary period. The Military authorities agreed to allow daytime traffic along the coastal route but during the hours of blackout the inland diversion must apply. Daytime buses on services 9, 9A and 31 were therefore once again routed via Sea Road and Sea Lane and it was not until Friday 16 May that the bomb was rendered harmless and the A259 reopened. The increased bombing meant that British air raid casualty figures in April jumped to 6,065 killed and 6,926 injured, not far short of the grim totals experienced during the months of September and October 1940.

Portsmouth was hit again on Saturday 3 May as 41 HE bombs landed mostly on residential streets in Southsea although Portsmouth and Southsea station was hit again. From this date until Saturday 9 August 1941 the start of curfew which extended in the Southdown area as far west as the western edge of Newhaven UDC was altered from 2230 to 2300 to take account of the longer summer days. On Sunday 4 May further HE bombs were dropped on the Portsea, Fratton and Cosham areas of the city with some fatalities and it appeared that the feared pace of death and destruction would increase with the more favourable flying conditions. Shoreham aerodrome was badly hit by a raid in the early hours of Friday 9 May as three HE bombs hit the buildings, setting fire to and destroying No.1 hangar but without any casualties. At this time in the war Shoreham was home to RAF Air Sea Rescue aircraft undertaking valuable search and rescue operations over the Channel. A major and sustained attack against London on Saturday 10 May marked the end of 'The Blitz' as the Luftwaffe was then moved east for a new war against the Soviet Union. Fortunately the Southdown area remained virtually unscathed by the night's raid but the wail of sirens kept many awake as the attackers headed to and from London and some aircraft unloaded their bombs short of target. Bognor, Eastbourne and Hilsea Gasworks at Portsmouth were hit by HE bombs but compared to the destruction around London the area had suffered little damage and remarkably few casualties.

Despite the tempting array of genuine military targets on Portsea Island available to German bombers it was usually the residential and business districts that suffered most in the air raids. This scene shows a rubble strewn Commercial Road after parachute mines and H. E. bombs were dropped on the city on 27 April 1941. Next day, commuters make their way to work on foot past shattered shops as buses are again forced to divert along those roads that remained open. Trolleybuses would be suspended until power and overhead wiring was restored by the crew on the Corporation's tower wagon working in the background.
Portsmouth News

After the heavy bombing raids of early May 1941 the German Luftwaffe moved its main forces east in preparation for the attack on the Soviet Union which began on Sunday 22 June 1941. Whilst this virtually brought to an end the large scale attacks on British cities for the next few years the coastal areas were still subject to what became known as 'Hit and Run' raids. These were usually carried out by one or two fighter-bombers approaching the coast at wave level, so avoiding detection by radar, and launching their attack before the warning sirens had been sounded. They frequently included random machine gunning of the streets to add terror to the death and destruction that followed. Towns such as Eastbourne and Seaford which were close to the easily recognisable white cliffs tended to suffer more than their fair share of these raids which continued until the end of manned aircraft attacks in spring 1944. With almost daily raids the following account can only include the principal and most devastating attacks.

Some changes to services in Havant and on Hayling Island were introduced as from Monday 12 May 1941 although, with the holiday camps long since closed, not of the type seen during normal summers. All journeys on service **47** were revised to operate on Hayling direct via the B2149 with Northney journeys replaced by new service **49** running between WATERLOOVILLE (HEROES INN) and STOKE (YEW TREE INN) via London Road, Hulbert Road, B2150, Havant Road, West Street, South Street, Langstone Road, Langstone Bridge, Northney Road, Church Road, Copse Lane and Havant Road. An hourly service ran daily and replaced the Waterlooville to Havant section of service 48. Due to the weight restricted Langstone Bridge the 49 was operated by Leyland Cubs – or Cheetahs no longer required for their intended coaching duties. Following the major raids earlier in the month British civilian casualties for May were announced as 5,394 killed and 5,181 injured. Although Whit Monday 1941, which fell on 2 June, was celebrated as a holiday except for those

A Military exercise in which the Home Guard resist an 'attack' on the pier by regular troops supported by a Universal carrier provides some entertainment for the residents of Worthing who have gathered outside The Arcade at the sea front end of South Street. It is 3 August 1941 and in the background car 1426 (DCD 326) appears to have stopped before the normal bus stop for the remaining bus services that still traversed a short section of sea front west of the Pier. The censor has blanked out the destination screen but it must have been on service 3A which terminated at The Pier and continued as far as Western Place before turning inland. The Harrington bodied Leyland Tiger TS7 still retains its rear glass corner windows – despite almost two years of war – and has gained a dark green roof but no white spot on the rear.
Imperial War Museum

engaged in the munitions industries there was little sign of visitors in the Southdown area following the ban introduced in March. For those residents who chose to remain in the coastal areas there was still the chance to enjoy an occasional coach excursion while the popular tea gardens at High Salvington still attracted many people from Worthing who enjoyed a trip on the number 4 bus.

From Thursday 12 June 1941 the Bradford Junction journeys on service **45** were extended in line with other Fratton routes to terminate at SOUTHSEA (THE CIRCLE) operating via Victoria Road North and Victoria Road South. Journey times were revised and, unusually, only minimal additional running time was allowed during the hours of darkness. The frequency was increased and revised as follows:

1 journey per hour Southsea (The Circle) – Fratton – Castle Street – Fareham

1 journey per hour Southsea (The Circle) – Fratton – direct – Fareham

3 journeys per hour Theatre Royal – direct – Fareham

4 journeys per hour Theatre Royal – Castle Street – Fareham

1 journey per hour Theatre Royal – direct – Warsash

Certain late evening and early morning journeys terminated at Cornaway Lane daily.

Emergency timetable No. 6 included details of changes in services up to and including **Thursday 10 July 1941**. Invasion fears persisted and with many residents now evacuated from coastal towns to safer areas inland the local bus services in Worthing were further reduced in frequency. Cross linked services **3** and **8** had enjoyed a generous 10 minute daytime service daily but were now reduced to 15 minutes on Weekdays and 20 minutes on Sundays. On service **3A** the last departure now left Worthing Pier at 1940 as non essential evening traffic reduced. Buses on service **4** now ran every 15 minutes daily to Durrington with alternate journeys extended to and from High Salvington – previously a 20 minute daily service throughout. The frequency of services **5** and **6** was reduced from 12 minutes daily throughout to a 15 minute service on each route to Thomas A'Becket with alternate journeys extended to and from Offington Corner (service 5) or Ringmer Road (service 6) on Weekdays. A 20 minute service was provided throughout on both services on Sundays. Service **7** was curtailed to operate between WORTHING PIER and LANCING STATION being replaced between Lancing South Street and Worthing via Brighton Road by service 7A. After 1900 daily it was diverted between Broadwater Street East and West Street to operate via Forest Road and Upper Brighton Road and vice versa, no longer serving Southfield Road, Wigmore Road, Kingsland Road and Sompting Road which were now covered by service 7A. Service **7A** was extended from

Lancing via South Street, Brighton Road, Steyne Gardens and Marine Parade to operate as a circular service from WORTHING PIER replacing the withdrawn section of service 7. After 1900 daily all journeys operated via Forest Road, Southfield Road, Wigmore Road, Kingsland Road, Sompting Road and Upper Brighton Road in place of service 7. New Service **7B** was introduced between WORTHING PIER and HILL BARN CORNER via South Street, Chapel Road, Broadwater Road, Broadwater Street East, Forest Road, Kingsland Road, Sompting Road, Upper Brighton Road, West Street, Busticle Lane and Upper Brighton Road with a 30 minute service daily. The route of service **11** in Ferring had been curtailed in November 1940 but was now extended a few yards further along Ferringham Lane to a new terminus at FERRING (CROSSFIELD'S STORES), still some way from the sea front.

During the month of July, only 501 British civilians died in air raids, a welcome reduction from the days of spring and early summer, while the figure of 169 civilian deaths in August was the lowest monthly total since bombing started. The basic ration of fuel for public service vehicles was discontinued on 19 September 1941 having previously been based on a percentage reduction of the mileage operated before the war. In future the issue of fuel for these vehicles would be entirely at the discretion of the RTCs. There was a disaster on the Southern Railway ferry service to the Isle of Wight on Saturday 20 September when the 'SS Portsdown' working the 0400 Mail service from Portsmouth Harbour to Ryde struck a mine and was lost, together with the captain, seven other crew, 11 Servicemen and some civilians. With the end of major bombing attacks,

Short Bros bodied Leyland Titan TD3 car 971 (AUF 671) has been stopped at a road block 'somewhere in Southern England' during an anti-invasion exercise in October 1941 by which time we now know the prospect of a German invasion was very unlikely. Such traffic checks were common throughout the Southdown area between June 1940 and August 1944 whilst the threat of German invaders remained. At this point in the war car 971 is still fitted with its original 10 inch deep destination box and space for the Southdown fleet name below although the censor has blanked out the destination. Full prewar lined out livery has only so far been altered by the addition of a dark green roof.
Portsmouth News

civilian casualties during September as a result of enemy air raids numbered 217 killed and those for October remained low at 262 killed.

Emergency timetable No. 7 included details of changes in services up to and including **Thursday 29 October 1941**. A number of changes occurred to services east of Chichester. Service **57** was rerouted to operate from CHICHESTER (WEST STREET) to BOGNOR BUS STATION via Maudlin, Crockerhill, Norton, Westergate, Woodgate Crossing, Lidsey and Shripney. The hourly frequency provided a part replacement for service **64** which was withdrawn although reintroduced from Wednesday 8 April 1942. All service **66** journeys now operated via Halnaker – previously served by only alternate journeys. In an evening raid on the town of Worthing on Saturday 1 November the Haynes Road area in Tarring was badly hit destroying nine houses and killing eight people. The ban on visitors to the coastal areas between Hastings and Littlehampton was suspended for the winter from Friday 7 November.

To help hard pressed bus companies in clearing the queues the standing passenger regulations were further relaxed from 20 November 1941. The legal restrictions had been eased in the early days of the war by a Ministry of Transport Order which increased the maximum permitted number of standing passengers to one third of the lower deck seating capacity, with an upper limit of eight if the additional passengers were taken up in circumstances in which undue hardship would otherwise be caused. After two years of growing peak hour demand and reduced services, the need for further relaxation was recognised in a further Ministry Order of November 1941 giving RTCs power to grant dispensation in special circumstances to increase the number of standing passengers to twelve, or half the seating capacity of the lower saloon if that was less. Further dispensation was granted from 27 April 1942 allowing the carriage of up to six standing passengers on one man operated buses.

From Thursday 4 December the period of curfew in the coastal zone became 2230 to 0800 in the east of Southdown's area extending as far west as the western boundary of Newhaven. On Sunday 7 December 1941 Japanese forces attacked the U.S. naval base at Pearl Harbour in Hawaii. The following day the USA and Britain and its dominions declared war on Japan. Germany and Italy declared war on the USA on Thursday 11 December 1941 meaning that the war was now a truly global affair and no longer confined to Europe. Civilian casualties as a result of air attacks fell to 34 in December 1941.

1942

In January 1942 the first American soldiers landed in Britain and in the weeks before the D-Day invasion they became a very familiar sight in the Southdown area. Snow fell across much of the Southdown area during January and early February adding to the discomfort caused by blackout and fuel shortages.

From Wednesday 21 January 1942 the **12** group of services was revised to provide:

1 journey per hour Tongdean to Eastbourne
2 journeys per hour Tongdean to Seaford
1 journey per hour Tongdean to Peacehaven Annexe (12A)
1 journey per hour Brighton Station to Saltdean Mount (12B)

One extra journey per hour was extended beyond Peacehaven, Rosemary to Seaford making a total of three buses each hour from Brighton with one continuing beyond to Eastbourne. No Seaford journeys now terminated at Chyngton Gardens.

A sinister incident occurred at around 2000 on a moonless, overcast and dark Wednesday 4 February as two Canadian sentries patrolling near Pevensey Bay village saw shadowy figures hurrying down the beach towards the sea. They opened fire and noticed a light flashing out to sea. Strong reinforcements were quickly mustered and some 6,000 men waited to see if the enemy would make any other landing attempt. Later it was discovered that there had been concentrations of enemy paratroops on the French coast preparing an Easter landing on the Sussex coast for an attack on the RAF station at Pevensey. This was merely a reconnaissance party which had fortunately been detected and, as a result, defences in the coastal areas were increased.

Some HE bombs fell on Peterborough Road, Wymering on Monday 9 March destroying several houses and causing ten fatalities with others wounded. At 1755 on Monday 23 March four aircraft made a low level attack on Newhaven attacking the town with machine gun and cannon fire. The first bomb hit the marine offices at the southern end of the London and Paris Hotel killing three people and injuring six others.

Starting on Sunday 15 March 1942 service **31** was diverted between Climping and Bilsham Corner to operate direct via A259, no longer running via Yapton which was covered by the reintroduction of a revised service **64** running between WESTERGATE (LABOUR-IN-VAIN) and BILSHAM CORNER via Eastergate, Barnham Station and Yapton. An hourly service ran daily connecting with service 31 at Bilsham Corner and the 57 at Westergate.

Good weather over the Easter weekend in early April attracted many Londoners to Eastbourne and other south coast resorts for a spell by the seaside as the ban on visitors had been lifted for the winter period. The resorts, already battered by air attacks, had no extra food and very little accommodation available. Bus services were already carrying record numbers of passengers and no additional transport facilities could be provided. Visitors were

unable to access the beaches and all peacetime tourism facilities had long since closed down. Along with the remaining local residents of Eastbourne they were of course unaware that the Germans had planned an airborne attack on nearby RAF Pevensey. Adjustments in bus services up to and including **Wednesday 8 April 1942** appeared in *Emergency timetable No. 8.*

At 0750 on Thursday 9 April two bombers dropped bombs and machine gunned the streets of Worthing. A bowls pavilion was destroyed, the Hospital damaged again and the nearby gas works hit once more. Two people were killed and six injured in the raid. Queuing became a daily fact of life during the war and waiting to join a bus usually involved joining a queue. The Regulation of Traffic (Formation of Queues) Order, 1942 came into force on 12 April 1942 and required that queues had to be formed, two abreast, where six or more people were waiting. It was taken very seriously at the time and generally well observed with any breaches considered unpatriotic. Many cases of queue jumping were brought to court where they were often dealt with severely. A ban on visitors was reintroduced between Wednesday 15 April and Saturday 24 October 1942 covering the coastal areas of Sussex between Hastings and Littlehampton and extending inland as far as the northern boundaries of the Rural Districts of Battle, Hailsham, Chailey and Chanctonbury including Arundel and Burgess Hill.

An area of the South Downs stretching from Lewes to the River Arun was closed to the public causing service **27** to be diverted away from Devil's Dyke running between Dyke Road and Poynings via Dyke Road Avenue, Mill Road, Patcham, Pyecombe and Poynings Cross Roads from Wednesday 20 May. It did not regain its former route until 31 March 1946. Large tracts of land across the Southdown area such as the South Downs and Ashdown Forest had already been requisitioned for military training early in

the war. Now, with a growing army and the arrival of more foreign troops the War Office demanded a further 140,000 acres of good farming land across southern England despite protests from the Ministry of Agriculture that home food production for 1943 would be severely affected. From early in 1942 thousands of acres of the South Downs were taken over by the military and the public barred from vast stretches of downland even after the end of hostilities. Thousands of troops were billeted in the nearby towns and once isolated and peaceful farms and downland were now pounded day and night by all manner of artillery and small arms fire causing much devastation. Farmers were forced to give up their land, and the hamlet of Stanmer between Lewes and Brighton was completely evacuated along with its 100 inhabitants. The village shop, parish church and 20 cottages were abandoned and much damage was caused during the military occupation. Shell craters, tank firing ranges and military roads littered the area and the noise of gunfire and the clatter of tank tracks became familiar sounds in the adjoining towns and villages. Most of the buildings in the training areas were destroyed beyond repair and it was several years before the public was able to safely access the South Downs. It also became apparent after the Battle of Britain that many more airfields would be required by the RAF as planning commenced for the Allied landings of France. Seven were constructed in Sussex, all satellite stations of Tangmere, but most were returned to agricultural use as soon as possible after the war.

At 1355 on Monday 4 May nine fighter bombers, each carrying a 250 kg HE bomb, swept across Eastbourne with cannon and machine guns blazing. Bombs struck St John's Church, Meads, houses in Willingdon Road, Cavendish Hotel, the railway station and locomotive sheds and a gasholder. Six people were killed and 36 injured. During May a total of 339 civilians had been killed and 425 injured as a result of enemy

Harrington bodied Leyland Tiger TS8 car 1465 (FCD 265) is seen in High Street, East Grinstead about to operate on service 87 which was curtailed at Tyes Cross between November 1939 and June 1944 as large areas of Ashdown Forest were taken over by the Military for training purposes. A long queue is forming and in the background some of the buildings damaged during the devastating raid of 9 July 1943 can be seen. An Emergency Water Supply has been erected to the right of the picture
J F Parke © Omnibus Society

Help Us to Help The National War Effort

Fortunately the photographer of this emergency water reservoir at the side of Findon Road on the outskirts of Worthing waited until a Southdown Leyland Titan came into view! This was one of many put in place during the Second World War in case the mains water supply was disrupted by air raid damage. Following severe reductions in fuel rationing from 1942 non essential traffic virtually disappeared even from main roads such as the A24 London to Worthing route.
West Sussex County Council Library Service

attacks. At the end of May 1942 the Minister of War Transport announced that the extension of the war area made it necessary to achieve further substantial economies in the consumption of motor fuel for civilian purposes, by cutting down travelling facilities not directly connected with the national war effort. As detailed in chapter 7 RTCs were instructed to withhold fuel rations for long distance coaches, except in cases where real hardship would be caused. Special services for families to visit evacuees were allowed to continue once a month, providing there was no suitable alternative. But, special services to take spectators to horse or dog racing or football were no longer allowed, although fuel was to be made available for concert parties travelling in connection with 'Holiday at Home' schemes. In addition the RTCs requested operators to reduce the number of stopping places and convert some compulsory stops to request, with a view to cutting fuel consumption and the wear on tyres which were in short supply. About 40 bus stops were removed in Brighton and some 88 bus stops removed in Worthing during June 1942. Other reductions followed in Portsmouth and most were never reinstated after the war.

On Saturday 6 June Eastbourne's long running battle to secure a local warning system was at last resolved when air raid sirens were modified so that for a purely local alert the two notes which made up the familiar wailing were separated to create a sound like a cuckoo. During June 1942 British unemployment fell below 100,000 and UK civilian casualties for the month numbered 300 killed and 337 injured, a welcome reduction on the previous month. On 10 June 1942 the Portsmouth Corporation Transport Committee considered proposals to once again extend buses to South Parade Pier and Clarence Pier and a limited daytime trolleybus service to South Parade Pier resumed from 21 June until 18 October although the area remained off limits

to Southdown buses until November 1944. At a further meeting on 21 September 1942 a sub-committee suggested that Southdown should withdraw services 37 and 37A between 0900 and 1600 in favour of an extension to Portsmouth Corporation bus services from Cosham. They were also concerned that evening services returning to Portsmouth should be curtailed at Hilsea after 2200. Southdown responded that as the buses were running to Hyde Park Road for garaging, inconvenience would be caused to passengers and no savings made. With the end of petrol allowances for private motoring which was banned after 30 June 1942 most cars were now laid up for the duration and buses and military vehicles predominated on the streets.

On Friday 17 July Littlehampton was attacked with bombs on Pier Road killing eight and injuring nineteen others. British civilian casualties as a result of air raids in July 1942 were 41 killed and 871 injured. A dramatic incident occurred in Worthing late on Sunday 9 August when a German bomber, hit by anti-aircraft fire, crashed into a doctor's surgery on the corner of Lyndhurst Road and Homefield Road just 50 yards from the edge of the already battered Hospital. Four Canadian soldiers who were billeted above the surgery and the bomber crew died as a result of the crash although there were no civilian casualties. Fortunately the bomber had already dropped HE and incendiary bombs before crashing, but four other unexploded bombs were found in the debris. Earlier in the day the town centre of Littlehampton was again machine gunned and bombed but the sirens were not in operation due to a previous electricity failure. Around 200 properties were damaged while casualties amounted to four dead and 27 injured.

Late on Tuesday 11 August enemy bombers attacked the Upperton, Grove Road and Eastbourne College areas of Eastbourne dropping some 57 HE bombs and over 2,000 incendiaries in what proved to be its most severe night raid of the war. The Railway Station and goods yard were again hit along with Terminus Road, Cavendish Place and Seaside Road although the local Southdown premises escaped damage. Three civilians died and six were injured in the raid. The town of Bognor Regis suffered a significant number of casualties in the bombing of the Sudley Road and Sturgess Road area on Friday 14 August with the total death toll for the raid reaching nine. Next day, while the rescuers were still searching for survivors, it was the turn of nearby Littlehampton to suffer death and destruction as two fighter bombers roared in low and fast spraying machine gun bullets across the town as they released two HE bombs. Three people died and 16 were injured in the attack.

The 'hit and run' raids continued on Wednesday 26 August when two German aircraft dropped bombs on Marlow Avenue and the

adjacent Corporation Electricity Generating Station in Eastbourne. Three people were killed and seven people injured although one of the fighter bombers was brought down beside Lottbridge Drove. Luftwaffe attacks on Britain in August, which were mainly limited to coastal areas, resulted in the deaths of 403 civilians and 509 injured.

To combat the increasing pressure on bus services serving important factories the Minister of War Transport made an Order to take effect from 6 September 1942 amending the previous Order, which had come into force on 12 April 1942 relating to queues for passenger vehicles. The new Order permitted a queue to be broken to give effect to any local scheme for priority to workers and prohibited intending passengers from trying to board a vehicle, which was at or approaching a stopping place before those waiting in a queue. The Order also provided that markings on the pavement for regulating the formation of queues should be regarded as though they were barrier rails. Passengers were required to leave a vehicle at terminal points if requested to do so by the driver or conductor.

On Monday 7 September the Chairman of the UK War Damage Commission stated that up to August 1942 some 597,755 claims had been received. Two days later the Chancellor of Exchequer announced that War Expenditure was costing £12,500,000 per day, an unimaginable sum in those days.

The travel restrictions imposed so far had still not achieved sufficient savings and on 11 September 1942 the Ministry of War Transport announced that travel by road and rail would be further restricted in the coming winter to make room for the growing volume of military and other essential traffic, and to save fuel and rubber. Although the alternative rail services had been severely disrupted during the bombing of 1940/1 the situation was now improved and within the Southdown operating area the existing bus services already provided good links between towns and villages. It was therefore surprising that the only new service provided by Southdown did not directly replace any of its London coach services withdrawn after Tuesday 29 September. From Wednesday 30 September a new Limited Stop coach service was introduced between BOGNOR BUS STATION and HORSHAM RAILWAY STATION calling only at Bognor Railway Station, Chichester (West Street), Singleton, Midhurst, Petworth, Wisborough Green, Billingshurst and Horsham Carfax with a journey time of 2 hours 5 minutes. The service, which was included on the Defence Permit for service 59, ran on weekdays only with four through journeys each way plus various short journeys to and from Midhurst and Petworth. Northbound departures from Bognor were at 0835, 1135, 1235 and 1435 to Horsham plus 1635 to Petworth but continuing to Horsham on Saturdays only. In addition there was an earlier

departure at 0835 from Petworth to Horsham. Southbound departures from Horsham were at 1020, 1220, 1420 and 1620 to Bognor, 1720 to Midhurst and 1920 on Saturdays only to Petworth. An earlier journey ran from Midhurst to Bognor at 0900. Premium fares applied on this service. At this distance in time it is difficult to appreciate the need for this service as it covered existing Southdown bus service 59 almost throughout and many of the links were also possible by frequent electric train services. Contemporary reports suggest that it was designed to 'strengthen service 59 on which loadings were already heavy'.

Eastbourne Railway Station was attacked again around midday on Wednesday 16 September when a 500kg bomb fell on Platform One and ricocheted into the passenger dock where it exploded killing six railwaymen. More than thirty people were injured. In Bognor on Thursday 17 September a low flying fighter bomber released a single 500 kg bomb which passed through one of the gas holders at the gas works without exploding and then detonated on a bridge at Shripney Road. This in turn caused landmines to detonate adding to the damage and as a result all through traffic along the main A29 road was stopped until 25 September when a temporary bridge was constructed to the north west of the demolished structure. Hastings was attacked again on Thursday 24 September, when seven fighter bombers hit the town. Warrior Square was particularly badly hit in the attack which left 23 dead and 43 injured. One of the most tragic bombing incidents in the county of Sussex during the war occurred at Petworth on Tuesday 29 September although it did not involve the greatest loss of life in a single raid. Petworth

The pressure on an already fully stretched public transport system intensified in 1942 as further restrictions were applied to private motoring. The Minister of War Transport made an Order effective from 6 September 1942 whereby markings on the pavement intended for regulating the formation of queues should be regarded as though they were barrier rails. In this obviously posed scene in Brighton which even required the attendance of a Police officer the, mostly, lady shoppers are staying on or within the painted box! The order also prohibited intending passengers from trying to board a vehicle, which was at or approaching a stopping place, before those waiting in a queue.
The Argus

Boys School was bombed by a low flying German bomber which resulted in the deaths of 28 school-boys, two teachers and two other civilians. Many others were seriously injured, but the death toll would have been much higher if some twenty other boys had not been at a woodworking class elsewhere in the town. For such a small town it was a severe blow with some families losing more than one child, or having other children injured. German air raids, mostly limited to the south and east coasts of Britain, killed 207 people with 238 injured in September.

Emergency timetable No. 9 included details of changes in services up to and including **Monday 5 October 1942** and was the last complete network publication until 9 December 1945. It reflected the growing need for economies as the war effort consumed more and more manpower and materials. In Worthing the Sunday frequency of service **3A** was reduced to 30 minutes until midday and then 20 minutes for the rest of the day. The complicated saga of route changes within Worthing affecting services **7** and **7A** continued with all Sunday journeys now diverted to follow the same route as applied after 1900 on weekdays. At the same time the **7B** was withdrawn on Sundays. Service **11** was diverted between Goring Way and Ferring Street to operate direct via Goring Way and Sea Lane.

As a sign that invasion was no longer considered a serious threat, authority for signposts to be re-erected in urban areas was given in October 1942 and for rural areas in May 1943.

On Sunday 25 October a single low flying German aircraft began firing its machine guns as it passed over the centre of Seaford. Five bombs were dropped on Broad Street, Sutton Road and Sutton Park Road killing 14 people, injuring 26 and causing damage to 422 properties. Next day it was the turn of Eastbourne to once again suffer the attentions of the enemy. Around lunchtime a single German aircraft crossed the town from west to east with machine guns firing and dropped four HE bombs in the Churchdale Road area. Death and destruction occurred in Seaside and Willoughby Crescent and the driver of an Eastbourne Corporation bus caught in the midst of the strike was killed along with 14 others. In addition 22 others were injured in the attack. Civilian casualties across the UK for the month of October totalled 229 killed and 370 injured.

The Ministry of War Transport had already announced in September 1942 that travel by road and rail was to be further restricted to save fuel and rubber and to make room for the growing volume of military and other essential traffic. At the end of November a curfew was announced on all bus services operating outside the Metropolitan Traffic Area forbidding the operation of any but essential works services after 2100 on all days of the week and before 1300 on Sundays. From Thursday 17 December 1942 last buses now left the main towns at around 2100 and opposite are a few examples with the July 1939 times shown for comparison.

		Dec 1942	July 1939	
1	Worthing to Storrington	2030	2256	
2	Worthing to Horsham	2103	2046	2146 SSu
12	Brighton to Seaford	2130	0011	
12	Eastbourne to Seaford	2045	2200	
13	Brighton to Lewes	2130	2300	2400 SSu
17	Brighton to Henfield	2110	2110	2216 SSu
23	Brighton to Ditchling & Burgess Hill	2124	2310	
30	Brighton to Haywards Heath	2115	2215	
31	Theatre Royal to Havant & Emsworth	2100	2305	
31	Bognor to Littlehampton	2101	2244	
31A	Southsea Circle to Emsworth via Fratton	2054	2257 (from SPP)	
31F	Brighton to Worthing	2120	2305	
38	Theatre Royal to Wickham	2035	2305	
39	Theatre Royal to Hambledon via Stakes	2100	2242	2305 S
40	Theatre Royal to Clanfield via Lovedean	2100	2255	
42b	Theatre Royal to Clanfield via Horndean	2100	2305 (42)	
45	Theatre Royal to Fareham	2100	2305	
47	Theatre Royal to Hayling			
	(by connection at Havant)	2037	2305	
66	Chichester to Arundel	2101	2044	2144 SSu
68	Littlehampton to Arundel	2110	2240 (9A)	
83	Horsham to Haywards Heath	1956	2145	
95	Eastbourne to Hailsham	2115	2300 (92A)	
95	Eastbourne to Heathfield	2115	2135	2300 SSu (91)
96	Eastbourne to Pevensey Bay	2027	2300	

In July 1939 many last buses had waited for the end of theatre and cinema performances such as the departures from Theatre Royal in Portsmouth which were specified as waiting for the conclusion of the second performance at The Hippodrome. Sadly by this time many such venues had been bombed and, with curfews in place, were no longer attracting large audiences for the late journeys. Buses were, however, permitted to complete round trips and arrive back somewhat later, so, whilst the last 31 from Portsmouth to Emsworth left at 2100 it was still possible to travel from Bognor to Chichester at 2142 and Worthing to Brighton at 2122. Southdown's famous connections were also catered for with the last 47 from Havant Station departing at 2118 after meeting the service 43 due from Portsmouth at 2115. The last bus on local service 44 from Emsworth to Westbourne did not leave until 2147 after connecting with the final 31A from Southsea Circle via Fratton and even returned in service from Westbourne at 2155!

Soon after 1230 on Thursday 5 November, a low flying enemy aircraft dropped four HE bombs from a height of just under 200 feet on the town

Car 198 (EUF 198) is a Leyland Titan TD5 with Beadle lowbridge body and seen at Haywards Heath station on service 82 which at this time ran every 2 hours to Crawley via Handcross. The livery shown is one that applied in 1942/3 with all green upper deck and normal apple green and cream for the lower deck. This vehicle enjoyed a very long life with Southdown and after a body rebuild by Beadle it remained in service until May 1957. The body was then scrapped and a breakdown tender body was fitted allowing it to survive until August 1974 and sale for preservation. Incidentally the rearmost side destination screen wrongly states that this runs via Ditchling and Foxhill which was correct for service 23 with which the 82 interworked.
Southdown Enthusiasts Club – W J Haynes Collection

Summary	SOUTHSEA - Farlington - Havant - EMSWORTH	Summary

WEEKDAY SERVICE (for Sunday Service see following pages)

Route No.	43	31	31a	43	31	*and then at the following minutes past each hour*	31a	43	31a	43	31	*until*	31a	43	31	31a	43	31
Southsea *The Circle* ...		9 25	9 37		9 55		7	...	25	37	... 55		5 7	...	5 25	537	...	555
Portsmouth *Theatre Royal*	922	9 32	...	9 52	10 2		...	22	32	...	52 2		...	522	5 32	...	552	6 3
Fratton Bridge ...		...	9 42	...	...		12	...	...	42	... ...		512	...	...	542	...	...
North End *Office* ...	931	9 41	9 51	10 1	1011		21	31	41	51	1 11		521	531	5 41	551	6 2	613
Cosham *Railway Bridge* ...	938	9 48	9 58	10 8	1018		28	38	48	58	8 18		528	538	5 48	558	6 9	620
Drayton *New Inn* ...	944	9 54	10 4	1014	1024		34	44	54	4	14 24		534	544	5 54	6	616	627
Farlington *Rectory Avenue*	947	9 57	10 7	1017	1027		37	47	57	7	17 27		537	547	5 57	6 8	619	630
Bedhampton *Post Office*...	952	10 2	1012	1022	1032		42	52	2	12	22 32		542	552	6 3	614	625	636
Havant *Church* ...	957	10 7	1017	1027	1037		47	57	7	17	27 37		547	557	6 8	619	630	641
Emsworth *Square* ...		1115	1025		1045		55	...	15	25	... 45		555	...	6 17	628	...	650

Route No.	31a	43	31	31a	43	31	31a	43	31	31a	43	31	31a	31	31	31
Southsea *The Circle* ...	6 8	...	628	641	...	7 1	714	...	734	747	...	8 7	820	...	840	854 ...
Portsmouth *Theatre Royal*	...	625	636	...	658	7 9	...	731	742	...	8 4	815	...	837	848	... 9 0 ...
Fratton Bridge ...	614	...	...	647	...	...	720	...	...	753	...	...	826	...	...	9 0 ...
North End *Office* ...	624	635	646	657	7 8	719	730	741	752	8 3	814	825	836	847	858 910	9 10 ...
Cosham *Railway Bridge* ...	631	642	653	7 4	715	726	737	748	759	810	821	832	843	854	9 5	917 9 17 ...
Drayton *New Inn* ...	638	649	7 0	711	722	733	744	755	8 6	817	828	839	850	9 1	912	9 24 ...
Farlington *Rectory Avenue*	641	652	7 3	714	725	736	747	758	8 9	820	831	842	853	9 4	915	9 27 ...
Bedhampton *Post Office*...	647	658	7 9	720	731	742	753	8 4	815	826	837	848	859	910 921	933	9 33 ...
Havant *Church* ...	652	7 3	714	725	736	747	758	8 9	820	831	842	853	9 4	915 926	938	9 38 915 1011
Emsworth *Square* ...	7 1	...	723	734	...	756	8 7	...	829	840	...	9 2	913	... 935	947	9 47 954 1020

Note.—On Weekdays additional buses will run every 10 minutes between Portsmouth Theatre Royal and Farlington during the early evening peak hours.

44	EMSWORTH — WESTBOURNE	44
	With connections from and to Havant and Southsea	

		NS	NS	NS	NS	NS	NS					
Ser. 31a {	Southsea *The Circle* ...	...	7TR2	1137	12 7	1237	1 7	1§37	2§7	2 37	3 7	3 37
	Havant *Church* ...	7 37	1217	1247	1 17	1 47	2 17	2 47	3 17	3 47	4 17
	Emsworth *Square* ...	7 45	1225	1255	1 25	1 55	2 25	2 55	3 25	3 55	4 25
Emsworth *Square* ...	5 45	7 45	1230	1 0	1 30	2 0	2 30	3 0	3 30	4 0	4 30
Westbourne *Square* ...	5 51	7 51	1237	1 7	1 37	2 7	2 37	3 7	3 37	4 7	4 37

Ser. 31a {	Southsea *The Circle* ...	4 7	4 37	5 7	5 37	6 8	6 41	7 14	7 47	8 20	8 54	...
	Havant *Church* ...	4 47	5 17	5 47	6 19	6 52	7 25	7 58	8 31	9 4	9 38	...
	Emsworth *Square* ...	4 55	5 25	5 55	6 28	7 1	7 34	8 7	8 40	9 13	9 47	...
Emsworth *Square* ...	5 0	5 30	6 0	6 33	7 6	7 39	8 12	8 45	9 18	9 47	...
Westbourne *Square* ...	5 7	5 37	6 8	6 41	7 14	7 47	8 20	8 53	9 26	9 55	...

	NS	NS	NS	NS	NS	NS					
Westbourne *Square* ...	5 51	7 51	1247	1 17	1 47	2 17	2 47	3 17	3 47	4 17	4 47
Emsworth *Square* ...	5 57	7 57	1254	1 24	1 54	2 24	2 54	3 24	3 54	4 24	4 54
Ser. 31a { Emsworth *Square* ...	6 1	8 1	1 1	1 31	2 1	2 31	3 1	3 31	4 1	4 31	5 1
Havant *Church* ...	6 9	8 9	1 9	1 39	2 9	2 39	3 9	3 39	4 9	4 39	5 9
Southsea *The Circle* ...	6TR43	8 48	1 48	2 18	2 48	3 18	3 48	4 18	4 48	5 18	5 48

Westbourne *Square* ...	5 17	5 47	6 19	6 52	7 25	7 58	8 31	9 4	9 30	9 55	...
Emsworth *Square* ...	5 24	5 54	6 27	7 0	7 33	8 6	8 39	9 12	9 38	10 3	...
Ser. 31a { Emsworth *Square* ...	5 31	6 2	6 35	7 8	7 41	8 14	8 47	...	...	...	...
Havant *Church* ...	5 39	6 10	6 43	7 16	7 49	8 22	8 55	...	...	...	...
Southsea *The Circle* ...	6 20	6 53	7 26	7 59	8 32	9TR5	9TR33	...	...	...	...

NS.—Not Sundays.

TR—These buses start or finish at Theatre Royal, Portsmouth instead of The Circle, at the times shown.

§ On Sundays these buses start from Fratton Bridge only (at 1.42 p.m. and 2.12 p.m. respectively).

Before the war, last buses from Portsmouth were generally at around 2300 but by the start of 1943 last buses departed two hours earlier at 2100. This shows the daytime and evening summary of services between Southsea and Emsworth with a last 31A journey from Southsea via Fratton and a final 31 from Theatre Royal. But, the new regulations did not stop Southdown maintaining its connecting services and the last 44 was delayed to depart Emsworth at 2147 after the arrival of the 31A! Note that buses did not run on Sunday mornings although service 31 was allowed to operate from Emsworth to Theatre Royal.

of Seaford. The first three bombs all fell on terraced houses in Pelham Road killing five people. The fourth bomb ricocheted off the concrete yard behind Southdown's garage in Dane Road, damaging the council depot building, before exploding at the foot of the railway embankment. Although the frequency and strength of air raids in the Southdown area had fortunately reduced with the onset of winter there was no room for complacency. On Monday 30 November a train on the Horsham to Brighton line was machine gunned by two enemy aircraft at West Grinstead Station and the driver killed. It was announced on Monday 14 December that British unemployment had reached a new low of 81,943.

On Wednesday 16 December a German bomber crashed into Bognor Gas Works. It first struck the tallest gasholder, leaving its wing inside, and then fell into one of the smaller gasholders. Unexploded bombs were scattered around the gasometer, along with wreckage of the aeroplane and the bodies of all four crew. The

loss of an enemy aircraft was always a boost for civilian morale, although this episode resulted in the deaths of two civilians who died when bombs fell on Victoria Drive and Havelock Road. Next day a German mine which had floated close to Worthing Pier was detonated causing damage to windows over a wide area of the town. Such events became more commonplace in the coming months, often caused by dogs wandering onto the still mined beaches.

The shops and streets of Eastbourne town centre were busy with pre-Christmas shoppers at 1200 on Friday 18 December when a German bomber dropped four 500 kg HE bombs on Terminus Road including two direct hits on Marks and Spencer store. Rescue work proved very difficult due to the extent of the damage and a Casualty Detector Unit was employed for the first time in Eastbourne. Eighteen people died and thirty seven were injured by the bombing with an additional nine casualties among the rescuers hit by falling debris. Church bells rang in Britain on Christmas morning as the ban was lifted for three hours. British air raid casualties for December 1942 totalled 109 killed, 201 injured.

1943

From the start of 1943 Southdown's bus time-tables were published in three separate editions covering East Sussex, West Sussex and Hampshire. The page size was the same as previous editions but the title Emergency Time Table was changed to War Edition and the numbering system – which had reached No. 9 in October 1942 – was discontinued. The *East Sussex* edition retained green print for the cover but for *West Sussex* it became brown while *Hampshire* was red. The price was reduced to 2d and each edition was shown as 'from January 3rd 1943 until further notice' with no further issues until 1 January 1944, any alterations being covered by leaflets.

Last Southdown buses had already been advanced by around an hour in November 1942 but from Sunday 3 January morning services on Sundays were withdrawn on the following routes:

1, 2, 3, 4, 5, 6, 7, 7A, 8, 9, 9A, 10, 11, 12, 12A, 12B, 13A, 13C, 13E, 13F, 14, 15, 16, 17, 18, 20, 21, 22, 23, 24, 25, 26, 27, 29, 30, 31F, 31G, 34, 36, 37A, 38, 40B, 42, 44, 48, 49, 50, 50A, 52, 53, 53A, 54, 55, 56, 57, 58, 59, 60, 61, 63, 64, 66, 68, 69, 70, 71, 72, 72B, 73, 75, 78, 80, 81, 82, 83, 84, 85, 86, 86A, 87, 88, 89, 90, 91, 92, 93, 94, 95, 96 and **119**. In practice this included all services apart from those in the Portsmouth area.

The following Sunday morning services were permitted within the Portsmouth area:

31 Hourly service between Emsworth and Portsmouth Theatre Royal with some additional early morning journeys

31A Half hourly service between Havant Church and Fratton Bridge – number applied in this direction only according to Hampshire timetable

31B Half hourly service between Fratton Bridge and Havant Church – number applied in this direction only according to Hampshire timetable

37 One journey each way between Waterlooville and Portsmouth Theatre Royal

39 Hourly service between Hambledon and Portsmouth Theatre Royal via Stakes

40 Hourly service between Clanfield and Portsmouth Theatre Royal

41 Half hourly service between Horndean and Fratton Bridge

42B Hourly service between Snell's Corner and Portsmouth Theatre Royal

43 Hourly service between Westbourne (Cricketers) and Portsmouth Theatre Royal

45 15 minute service between Fareham and Portsmouth Theatre Royal – apart from 7 early morning journeys, all operated direct, not serving Castle Street in Portchester

47 Two hourly service each way round the Hayling loop

The restrictions were not enforced by the Metropolitan RTC and in the border towns of Horsham, Crawley and East Grinstead LPTB Country buses continued as normal in the evenings and on Sunday mornings until 5 May 1943 when they were finally brought into line with other operators. A number of other alterations to Southdown services took effect from Sunday 3 January – mainly involving further minor reductions in service. In the Worthing area the Sunday service on **3A** was withdrawn completely. Service **13B** running between Brighton Pool Valley and North Moulscombe, Coldean Lane was also withdrawn on Sundays. The Sunday operation on service **18** was reduced from four journeys each way to three journeys from Brighton to Hawkhurst and just two journeys from Hawkhurst to Brighton. On service **21** the circular route in Shoreham was reduced to operate on weekdays only with all Sunday journeys terminating at Shoreham High Street. The weekday afternoon frequency of service **52** was increased from hourly to 30 minutes with five Selsey bound and seven Chichester bound journeys running via Donnington. Service **57** was diverted between Maudlin and Crockerhill to operate via Halnaker and Boxgrove replacing the 66 at Halnaker. Service **66** was again revised and now diverted to operate between ARUNDEL SQUARE and LAVANT STATION via Walberton, The Firs, Fontwell, Slindon Common, Fontwell, Tangmere, Maudlin and Chichester. The loop working at Summersdale was withdrawn and all journeys except one were also withdrawn from Halnaker being replaced by the changes to the 57. An hourly service ran daily with the first and last journeys operated to and from Littlehampton. The frequency of service **68** was reduced from 20 to 30 minutes.

'Hit and run' raids continued to affect coastal towns and cities around Britain throughout 1943 and included some of the heaviest air attacks of the war. On Friday 15 January four German fighter bombers dived across the town of Eastbourne, firing their cannon and each dropping one 500 kg bomb. The local warning system known as the Cuckoo had been silenced by a storm so the public was unaware of an impending attack. Bombs hit Green Street, Wilmington Terrace, Devonshire Place and Hartington Place as well as the cleared area of Cross Street and Duke Street which had already been devastated in earlier raids. Many people were buried in the debris and ten died including one man fatally struck by a machine gun bullet while in the street. A further thirty eight people were injured in the raid. Hailsham's good fortune proved an ill wind for Polegate on Saturday 23 January when it suffered an attack meant for Hailsham, four miles to the north. Instead, four fighter bombers dropped their bombs on the Southlands housing estate of Polegate killing three people in Western Avenue. British civilian air raid casualties for the month of January amounted to 328 killed and 507 injured.

The ban on entry to visitors had been lifted during the winter as the threat of invasion receded but from Thursday 1 April 1943, and after much debate between the Civil and Military authorities, a regulated area was set up covering the east and south coasts between the Humber and Penzance to a depth of approximately 10 miles from which visitors _may_ be excluded from time to time. As far as the Southdown area was concerned this included all those parts affected in 1942 but extended west to include the Hampshire operations and north to include all areas south of the Petersfield-Midhurst-Petworth railway line as well as parts of the Rural Districts of Uckfield and Cuckfield. To test the effectiveness of the ban in the run up to planned Allied landings in France it was only formally enforced in the Southdown area during 1943 between Tuesday 17 August and Saturday 18 September. The results showed that a great deal of manpower was required to control entry and that it was impossible to completely prevent people avoiding the checks.

There was widespread damage in Bognor on Friday 5 February as four HE bombs hit Albert Road, Bognor Pavilion, the Merchant Taylors Chapel and various shops around the town centre. Three people were killed in Albert Road and over 60 were injured, some seriously. Four fighter bombers attacked Eastbourne on Sunday 7 February, each carrying a 500 kg bomb. One scored a direct hit on the Central Fire Station in Grove Road, killing six National Fire Service personnel while a second struck Terminus Road causing further damage to the already battered town centre. Eight civilians died and in addition four soldiers were killed and seventy two people injured. Worthing's first raid of 1943 took place on Monday 8 February when the heavily

Seen in Mount Pleasant Road, Tunbridge Wells on a southbound service 119, car 182 (EUF 182) is a Leyland Titan TD5 with Beadle low bridge body new in May 1938. It is shown in the livery adopted from early 1943 with all over grey except apple green below the lower deck windows and dark green mudguards. In October 1945 the appearance of the bus was changed during a major rebuild by J C Beadle of Dartford and it survived in service until the end of lowbridge buses in May 1957 when it was fitted with a breakdown tender body. After sale in 1974 it has remained in preservation to the present time.
J F Parke © Omnibus Society

populated residential districts of Sugden Road, Homefield Road, and Lyndhurst Road all suffered direct hits. After dropping their bombs the aircraft began strafing the town. A total of nine people were killed and there were a considerable number of other casualties making it Worthing's worst single day of the war so far. German aircraft ranged freely across West Sussex on Wednesday 10 February and bombed Bognor, Chichester, Horsham, Hurstpierpoint, Lancing, Littlehampton, Petworth and Midhurst. This proved to be one of the worst air raid incidents for the city of Chichester with HE bombs scattered across the city causing widespread casualties and damage to property. In the city centre Chapel Street, North Street and St. Martins Street were badly hit and at least 17 civilians killed. Midhurst was hit by bombs which fell on Sheepcote in Sheep Lane killing three people and injuring 40 others while in Horsham bombs struck Wimblehurst Road, Richmond Road and Craven Lodge with two houses destroyed and over sixty damaged. Further to the east, bombs hit Cuckfield Road, Hurstpierpoint and killed a four year old girl. The inland towns tended to suffer less from the 'hit and run' attacks and this proved to be the last air raid on Horsham for over a year.

On Sunday 7 March some 15 enemy aircraft attacked Eastbourne dropping their bombs across the town. Fourteen people were killed and more than fifty were injured. Tragedy struck

Hove on Tuesday 9 March when German aircraft hit the town in a fierce attack which left eleven dead and scores injured. On the same day six aircraft bombed and machine gunned Worthing killing six people and injuring many more. Hastings suffered its worst air raid of the war on Thursday 11 March when 25 HE bombs were dropped and the town was machine gunned by several waves of aircraft sweeping in from the north. In the raid 38 persons were killed, 39 seriously injured and 51 injured. Brighton's first major raid of 1943 took place on Monday 29 March when German fighter bombers raided the town dropping bombs over a wide area. Gloucester Place, Grosvenor Street, Circus Street and Sussex Street were badly hit with eighteen people killed, including three young children at the Circus Street Chest Clinic. British civilian casualties during March 1943 amounted to 293 killed and 439 injured. Eastbourne was attacked again at 1145 on Saturday 3 April resulting in the worst casualty figures during a single raid on the town. Ten aircraft dropped twelve bombs causing extensive damage to dozens of houses, two hotels and several shops. A town centre surface shelter in Spencer Road near the junction with South Street received a direct hit by a 250 kg bomb killing all inside. The final death toll reached 33 with a further 99 injured. In Luftwaffe attacks on Britain during April 1943 172 civilians were killed and 205 injured.

From 19 May 1943 a number of minor route changes took place in the Worthing area in connection with the use of producer gas buses which had commenced operation from Worthing garage on 30 January 1943 initially on service 3 between Worthing Ham Hotel and Goring, George V Avenue. In February the one converted bus moved to Lancing services 7 and 7A and was joined by others as they were equipped but in April it was decided to move all the existing gas buses to services 5 and 6. To avoid reversing movements at the outer terminals service **5** was extended via Findon Road to terminate at CISSBURY HOTEL. The frequency now became 30 minutes daily but the short journeys to Thomas A'Becket were transferred to new service **5A** running every 30 minutes daily between WORTHING PIER and NORTH STAR HOTEL via the same roads as service 5 to Rectory Road and then Littlehampton Road. No Sunday morning service was of course permitted. Service **6** was also revised to operate between WORTHING PIER and NORTH STAR HOTEL being extended a few hundred yards along Littlehampton Road to enable producer gas buses towing their trailers to turn in the hotel forecourt instead of reversing into Ringmer Road. Further details of the gas bus operation are included in chapter 8.

It was announced on Thursday 20 May that signposts could now be re-erected in rural Britain as fear of a German invasion was fading. All of the regulations hastily introduced after the fall of France in June 1940 would be gradually lifted although emergency restrictions on the exhibition of place names were not finally cancelled until October 1944. The remaining sandbag fortifications erected around many public buildings at the start of the war were being dismantled, but some of the wartime defences built after Dunkirk proved too difficult to remove and many reminders of the desperate days of summer 1940 still remain in Sussex. A further heavy attack on Hastings was launched around lunchtime on Sunday 23 May by a force of fighter bombers which dropped 25 bombs and machine gunned the streets. The Old Town, Seafront and London Road areas were badly hit and a total of 25 people killed and 85 injured. The timing of the raid was unfortunate as five hotels and pubs were hit, mostly packed with Sunday lunchtime drinkers. As the attackers headed for home they dropped bombs in Westville Road, Bexhill which killed two women.

Two days later the fighter bombers returned to Brighton again as a force of up to 25 aircraft struck the town at around 1220, killing 27 people and injuring 127, of whom 58 were seriously hurt. This was Brighton's worst air attack of the war causing very serious and spectacular damage across the town with Kemp Town, Black Rock and Preston Park being among the worst affected. Railway lines and properties were particularly badly hit causing significant

Now fitted with a temporary top cover, Brush bodied Leyland Titan TD1 car 821 (UF 4821) unloads passengers at Horsham Carfax after arriving on service 69. As this service was normally operated by 1400 class Leyland Tigers it is likely to have run a relief short journey into Horsham. It still retains prewar cream livery between decks and lining below the lower deck windows.
J F Parke © Omnibus Society

The scene of destruction in Terminus Road, Eastbourne looking north from Seaside Road after the attack on 3 April 1943. The central shopping area suffered especially badly in the raids but fortunately many of the local people had been evacuated from the town in 1940/1. Southdown's Pevensey Road Bus Station was just a few hundred yards away from this location and was fortunate to survive intact despite the many raids on the town centre of Eastbourne.
T R Beckett/Eastbourne Gazette and Herald

Car 121 (BUF 221), a Leyland TD4c with Short Bros highbridge body was new in 1935 with petrol engine and Torque Converter and is seen after being converted to run on producer gas in February 1943. Worthing Town Services were chosen for their lack of hills and service 5 was home to these buses for around 18 months from April 1943. The producer gas equipment was removed in November 1944 and the petrol engine replaced by a Leyland 8.6 litre diesel engine although the Torque Converter was not removed until May 1947. It was rebodied by Beadle in February 1950 and sold for scrap in February 1959.
Southdown Enthusiasts Club – Clark/Surfleet Collection

disruption to local train services which required Southdown to provide replacement buses. One bomb which fell in Argyle Road, bounced over houses and exploded against the London Road railway viaduct north of Preston Circus bringing down one entire span whilst leaving the railway track suspended 70 feet above the ground. Another bomb hit the steps at Lovers Walk and ricocheted into the Pullman Car Works causing considerable damage, while a further bomb wrecked two empty trains standing close to the main line and threw debris from the smashed rolling stock high over the chalk cutting into the gardens of bomb damaged houses along Stanford Road. The Southern Railway's Brighton Running Sheds were also severely damaged and both Brighton Gasworks and Hove Gasworks were hit and gas holders set ablaze. The Whitehawk Garage of BH&D suffered blast damage to its doors and windows and three bus drivers were injured and three buses seriously damaged in the explosions in Arundel Road and Chesham Street. Nearby, the already damaged Marine Gate flats at Black Rock received a further four hits and were now in a very sorry state. Hundreds of people were made homeless after some 150 houses were made uninhabitable.

At some unknown date before 26 May 1943 service **43** was extended from Churcher's Corner via the B2147 to Racton Corner where it connected with service **54** which had been diverted between Funtington and Racton Corner

to operate direct via B2146 and no longer serving Churcher's Corner. This was due to the construction of Funtington Advanced Landing Ground alongside the northern edge of Common Road between Funtington and Churcher's Corner and closure of the road to all traffic as security was increased for the coming Normandy landings. Luftwaffe raids on Britain increased during May 1943 with 584 killed and 733 injured.

Enemy fighter bombers made a further attack on Eastbourne on Friday 4 June killing eight civilians and injuring 33. Damage was caused to the Technical Institute and Central Library and other properties in Grove Road, Woodgate Road, Bowood Avenue, Havelock Road, Southbourne Road and St Anthony's Avenue. The hotels Metropole and Glastonbury on Royal Parade were also badly damaged in the raid. Two days later fourteen enemy aircraft made the last major attack of the war on Eastbourne. Severe damage was again caused, seven civilians died along with several military policemen and 43 others were injured. After crossing the coast near Princes Park the aircraft dropped 500 kg HE bombs on the Crumbles, Princes Park near Channel View Road, Beach Road, Caffyn's Garage at the junction of Seaside and Seaside Road, Ashford Road, The Avenue, St Anne's Road, Lushington Road, College Road and Meads Road. Compared to the previous month's figure British civilian casualties during June 1943 were relatively light at 201 killed and 284 injured.

The bombing of the Whitehall Cinema in East Grinstead on Friday 9 July proved to be the worst air raid disaster of the war for the county of Sussex and killed at least 108 people. It was late afternoon and many children had decided to visit the cinema situated on London Road in the town centre. By this time in the war few people paid any heed to an air raid warning during a performance and so many probably ignored the notice flashed on the screen at 1705. Suddenly, a single aircraft, which had become separated from a group of 10 bombers, appeared out of the hazy clouds and circled the town at around 100 feet before dropping eight bombs across London Road and the High Street. Death and destruction followed in the busy town centre as buildings collapsed and fires spread. One of the bombs exploded in the auditorium of the Whitehall Cinema causing walls, girders and the roof dome to collapse onto the packed audience. Further bombs fell in London Road destroying many shops, including an ironmonger where 500 gallons of paraffin was stored in the basement. Not surprisingly this exploded and the resulting blast swept through the parade of shops and caused the rear of the Sainsbury's branch to collapse. At least 108 people were killed and 235 injured in the attack and, in some cases, no trace was ever found of the victims. After dropping its bombs the German plane machine gunned people in Queen's Road, Railway Approach and London Road. Within minutes A.R.P. and local people arrived at the cinema to help rescue those inside and by 1725 the first ambulances started taking injured and dead to the nearby Queen Victoria Hospital. Canadian troops were soon on the scene to help rescue the people remaining inside the Whitehall Cinema and by 1910 the last of the live casualties were brought out. Air raid casualties in the UK during July were 167 killed and 210 injured.

Although there were very few facilities open even for residents to enjoy and leisure travel was strictly discouraged there are contemporary reports of crowds of visitors in Brighton and Worthing during early August although as from Tuesday 17 August the ban on visitors to the South Coast was reintroduced. Whilst checks on ID cards were still being carried out it is clear from reports that many living in outlying areas could easily travel to the coast by Southdown bus and generally escape detection by this time of the war. Things would change in 1944 as much stricter security was imposed in the run up to D Day.

Italy surrendered unconditionally to the Allies on Friday 3 September and declared war on Germany on Wednesday 13 October. British air raid casualties for the month of September 1943 were the lowest since May 1940 at just five killed and 11 injured. After a lull of 93 days during which no enemy bomb had fallen on England in daylight, two bombs were dropped in fields at Groveland's Farm, Hailsham on Sunday 17

October. Despite huge craters there were no casualties and very little damage was caused. British air raid casualties for October 1943 increased to 118 killed and 282 injured.

There were no major incidents in the Southdown area during November 1943 and British civilian air raid casualties during the month totalled 119 killed and 238 injured. Just 10 civilians were killed in UK air raids in December 1943 and 41 injured.

The Little Blitz : January – April 1944
Timetable booklets were issued for *East Sussex, West Sussex* and *Hampshire* including all changes to services up to and including **Saturday 1**

Whilst large scale attacks on most of the major UK cities had reduced, the towns along the South Coast continued to suffer devastating raids. A further attack on Eastbourne on 4 June 1943 killed eight civilians and injured 33 with damage caused to the Technical Institute and Central Library and other properties in Grove Road between Terminus Road and Ivy Terrace. Rescuers are still searching for survivors and a Corporation Leyland bodied Leyland Titan TD1 has been badly damaged.
T R Beckett/Eastbourne Gazette and Herald

The bombs that fell on the Whitehall Cinema in London Road, East Grinstead on 9 July 1943 also caused extensive damage to buildings on the south side of High Street adjacent to the bus stops which feature in other photographs in this book. These show that despite the efforts of the workmen the building in the centre was subsequently demolished although there is no record of damage to buses or injury to waiting passengers as a result of the incident. In terms of casualty numbers it proved to be the worst air raid disaster of the war for the county of Sussex and killed at least 108 people.
West Sussex County Council Library Service

January 1944. Most of the alterations were minor but there were timing changes to the Limited stop service between Horsham and Bognor with the northbound 1135 altered to depart at 1035 and run an hour earlier as far as Petworth before continuing at 1252 onward to Horsham. The first journey towards Horsham was extended back from Petworth to Midhurst starting at 0823 while the first Bognor bound journey was extended back to depart from Petworth at 0813.

Friday 21 January 1944 marked the start of what was to be known as 'The Little Blitz' as the Luftwaffe launched its biggest raid on Britain for some time. Ninety planes were spotted over South East England as night attacks on London were renewed. The raid proved something of a failure as an apparent navigational error led to flare paths being set down across the whole of Chailey Rural District which was then heavily bombed with incendiary and high explosive devices. Thanks to the rural nature of the area there was little damage and no casualties but London had been spared some of the intended death and destruction. The series of heavy air raids on London and other major cities continued until April and although thousands of HE and incendiary bombs fell across the area most landed in open countryside so that civilian injuries were relatively light. Many Allied and enemy

aircraft also crashed at this time and the wreckage along with hundreds of unexploded bombs often led to roads being closed for days and diversions for buses. Civilian casualties in Britain rose to 107 killed and 260 injured in January 1944. The heaviest night raids on London since 1941 occurred on Friday 18 February as the Luftwaffe intensified their 'Little Blitz' and during February 1944 air raid casualties throughout the UK increased to 961 killed and 1,712 injured. On Friday 3 March it was announced that British civilian casualties since the start of the war now amounted to 50,324 dead while military deaths totalled 50,103. To those who had lived and worked in the front line counties of England these statistics probably came as no surprise.

For one week commencing Monday 6 March 1944 service **9** was curtailed from the west at Sussex Pad Hotel and unable to serve Shoreham while service **10** operated via Brighton Road and Norfolk Bridge rather than Sussex Pad. The **7** was extended from Lancing Station to The Three Horseshoes and returned via Penhill Road. This was probably in connection with military activities in the build up to D-Day and such diversions would be repeated across many parts of the Southdown area in the coming weeks. Starting from Thursday 16 March service **87** was once more extended from Tyes Cross to ASHDOWN

FOREST (THE GOAT) returning to the terminus it had before 16 November 1939. There was also a slight increase in frequency with four journeys each way on weekdays and three journeys each way on Sundays through to Ashdown Forest.

The very last air raid of the war on Brighton was early on Wednesday 22 March while the last air raid on the town of Horsham took place on Friday 24 March when a number of incendiary bombs and one unexploded 250 kg bomb fell 30 yards west of the Horsham to Dorking railway line. Soon after midnight on Saturday 25 March a single enemy aircraft released more than eighty incendiary bombs on Newhaven, which fell around the harbour causing serious fires which were soon brought under control. This proved to be the last manned air attack on Newhaven during the war. But, it wasn't only enemy aircraft that dropped lethal weapons from the sky!! Ten unexploded British 500 lb bombs fell at Chilgrove on Wednesday 29 March while a formation of aircraft was passing overhead. Nearby, a 1,000 lb bomb landed without exploding just 25 feet from the main Chichester to Petersfield road near Harting causing the road to be closed until 17 April when the bomb was made safe. The last time that manned enemy aircraft dropped bombs within the boundaries of the County Borough of Eastbourne occurred at 0335 on Friday 31 March when one 250 kg HE bomb fell on the Crumbles near Pevensey Bay

Road and two 500 kg HE bombs fell near Willingdon Golf Course causing slight damage. Although the 'Little Blitz' continued, air raid victims throughout the UK in March 1944 reduced to 279 killed and 633 injured.

At seven minutes past midnight on Wednesday 26 April bombs again caused widespread destruction in the city of Chichester. Four 500 kg HE bombs fell around Armadale Road, Bridge Road and at St. James School in the west of the city. Casualties included seven killed, 17 seriously injured and 13 slightly injured. Nearby, Bognor had a lucky escape when a night raider dropped four HE bombs which fortunately exploded harmlessly in the sea off the Pier. If they had landed just a few hundred yards inland the result would have very different although Selsey was less lucky as 11 HE bombs caused widespread damage to property but, fortunately, only two civilian casualties. Selsey's location at the southern tip of the Manhood Peninsular offered an easy target for German aircraft and it was to suffer the worst bombing of all the towns and villages in West Sussex. Next day Portsmouth was subjected to more attention from the Luftwaffe as bombs fell in Landport, an area of the city already badly scarred by earlier raids. As the Allies gained dominance in the skies over Britain in the run up to D-Day, UK civilian air raid casualties in April 1944 were down to 146 killed and 226 injured.

Car 409 (GUF 69) is a Guy Arab II with Park Royal highbridge body new in March 1944. With a Gardner 6LW engine fitted from new it is seen after the war on a service 12 working as far east as Seaford. Although first entering service in all grey livery it is now painted in the early postwar standard livery adopted from late 1944 of apple green and cream with dark green roof. The condition of these wooden framed bodies soon deteriorated and car 409 was the first of the conversions to open top, being completed in July 1950.
Southdown Enthusiasts Club – W J Haynes Collection

The Allied invasion of Normandy on Tuesday 6 June 1944 was one of the most dramatic events of the Second World War. The story is well documented and this account only considers the major effect of the preparations on the Southdown area in the months leading up to D-Day. On Tuesday 8 February 1944 plans for the invasion of France, code named 'Operation Overlord', were confirmed. A large part of the Southdown area would now be turned into a vast military camp as thousands of troops arrived to begin intensive training in preparation for the landings. It was not just around Portsmouth that things began to change. The 4th Armoured Brigade arrived in Worthing on 12 February and brought with them more than two hundred tanks to line the town's streets. British Commando units established headquarters at Broadwater Road in Worthing and a large mansion at Goring called Courtlands was taken over as headquarters for the Canadian 1st Army. The 15th Scottish Division had its headquarters at the seafront Beach Hotel and dispersed its artillery between Worthing, Lancing and Ashington. As training intensified the sound of gunfire and the screech and clatter of tank tracks became very familiar to those in the surrounding villages as large areas of once peaceful farm land were requisitioned by the War Office. Fields were overflowing with ammunition dumps, Bren gun carriers, armoured vehicles and all kinds of army transport while tanks, trucks and jeeps camouflaged with netting and foliage were parked along the roadside. Some coastal roads in sensitive areas were completely closed to the public again and in Littlehampton and Shoreham numerous landing craft and loaded ammunition barges were being assembled in the two harbours and along the banks of the Rivers Arun and Adur. Amidst much secrecy the area around the Ferry Boat Inn on Hayling Island was used to construct sections of Mulberry harbour, massive floating concrete harbours that were towed across to France as part of the landings. One of the caissons developed a fatal crack and was eventually abandoned on a sandbank in Langstone harbour but later refloated and towed to safety on Sinah Sands where it still remains.

Portsmouth was the headquarters and main departure point for the military and naval units of Assault Force 'S' destined for Sword Beach on the Normandy coast. Some units of this force assembled at Newhaven and Shoreham while Assault Force 'J' departed from Portsmouth destined for Juno beach. By April southern England was already becoming a huge armed camp, as men, vehicles, stores and ammunition moved forward to their marshalling areas. Taking advantage of the natural woodland cover, many troops camped to the north and east of Portsmouth around Horndean, Rowlands Castle, Cowplain, Waterlooville and Emsworth. But, soldiers were also camped further east at Worthing, Findon, Stanmer Park, Ditchling, Plumpton, Seaford, Lewes and Eastbourne.

It is 1944 and the preparations for D-Day are affecting many south coast towns. In this view looking east towards Worthing Pier American military trucks covered with tarpaulins are parked along Marine Parade. The mass of barbed wire remains along the southern side of the promenade which has been out of bounds to pedestrians since June 1940, although Southdown services 3A, 5 and 5A continued to serve this part of the sea front. The band enclosure (later to become the Lido) and the pier pavilion can be seen on the right although the Waldorf Hotel on the left has long since been demolished.
West Sussex County Council Library Service

Tanks were concealed in nearby woodland and residents reminded to keep quiet about all the activity as a large part of the Southdown area became a massive Military encampment. Southwick House, north of Portsmouth, was chosen as the headquarters for the Supreme Allied Commander, General Eisenhower.

As the date for the Allied invasion of Europe moved closer security was essential and on Saturday 1 April a ten mile deep belt of coastline from Land's End to the Wash was declared a Restricted Area and closed to all visitors although surviving records appear to show that full enforcement did not start until 10 April. Only those who lived in this vast area or could prove they had official business were permitted access, and everyone had to carry their identity card at all times. There were many thorough checks at railway and bus stations and on buses and trains, as well as in hotels, guest houses and places of amusement, and anyone found not carrying their card was arrested at once. As early as 17 August 1943, Southsea seafront had been declared a restricted zone with all remaining hotels and guest houses cleared of civilians and from 19 April 1944 it was closed to all civilian traffic including the trolleybus service to Old Portsmouth. The unused trolleybus over-head wires between the Royal Pier Hotel and Clarence Pier had already been removed at the request of the Military authorities in March 1944.

Starting on Thursday 20 April Southdown bus services **10**, **22**, **31**, **31F** and **31G** were diverted away from the main A259 road beside Shoreham Harbour. All services ran from Hove, Kingsway via Hove Street, Sackville Road, Old Shoreham Road and Upper Shoreham Road then services 10 and 22 ran via normal routes while services 31, 31F, 31G continued via Old Shoreham Toll Bridge, Sussex Pad Hotel, North Lancing, Grinstead Lane, Grinstead Avenue, North Road, Lancing Station, South Street and Brighton Road to regain their normal route. Service **21** was extended to run between Shoreham and Brighton Pool Valley. From Wednesday 3 May services **31**, **31F**, **31G** resumed normal routes between Shoreham Norfolk Bridge and Lancing Three Horseshoes and all services had reverted to normal route by 28 August. Other diversions are likely to have occurred in the Portsmouth and Southsea areas and the company warned that Portsmouth area services were liable to be diverted or curtailed without notice. During May 1944 journeys towards East Worthing on service **3** were diverted between Goring Road and Tarring Road to operate direct via Elm Grove instead of The Drive possibly in connection with D-Day preparations.

In May, after considering tides and moonlight, Monday 5 June was chosen as the new target date for the landings to commence. The start of Exercise Fabius on Tuesday 2 May marked the final rehearsal for D-Day and involved the

landing of 25,000 troops at a number of different beaches along the south coast of England. This was the largest training exercise so far and the last before D-Day. The US 1st and 29th Divisions landed at Slapton Sands in Devon, the British 50th Division at Hayling Island, the Canadian 3rd Division at Bracklesham Bay and the British 3rd Division between Felpham and Littlehampton. Beaches that had been prohibited areas, mined and ringed with barbed wire when a German invasion threatened in summer 1940 were now cleared to prepare for the invasion of France. The exercises, which must have caused considerable disruption to normal life in the affected areas, continued until 8 May. In anticipation of heavy casualties on D-Day, contingency plans were made in Worthing with a large field near Southways Avenue and West Street in Sompting equipped with huts and tents to receive wounded allied troops and German POWs.

On Thursday 11 May the crew of a USAAF bomber returning from a raid over Europe, where it had been hit and set on fire, baled out on crossing the coast and the pilot set his aircraft on course to crash into the sea. Unfortunately, the plane turned back and headed for the centre of Chichester where it crashed into The Hornet, spreading wreckage across the Whyke Lane and Green Lane area and damaging a garage, St John's School, Longs Timber Yard and setting fire to the City Electric Laundry. Some 50 women and girls were working at the laundry which was quickly set alight by the aviation fuel. To add to the devastation two 1,000lb bombs exploded in the flaming wreckage. Four people died and 27 others were injured, 14 of them seriously. A total of 704 houses were damaged in the incident, making it one of the most destructive of the war.

By Monday 15 May the troops that would land in Normandy on D-Day and immediately after-wards were in camps all along the south coast of England. Roads were clogged with endless

Compared to Southdown's peacetime standards car 1474 (GCD 374) looks in need of some attention to body damage in this view at Pool Valley, Brighton. It is a Leyland Tiger TS8 with Harrington body delivered in November 1939 and now in the 1943 style livery of grey roof and window surrounds and apple green below with dark green wings and mudguards. Seating was altered to the standee type perimeter arrangement in October 1941 and did not revert to normal until a rebuild by Portsmouth Aviation in December 1947. Close examination shows that the rear corner windows are still in place although most were removed much earlier in the war.
Southdown Enthusiasts Club – W J Haynes Collection

convoys of tanks, trucks, jeeps and other military vehicles as they headed south towards the marshalling areas. Buildings had to be knocked down, roads widened or newly built, bridges strengthened and lay-bys constructed to accommodate the huge amphibious trucks and giant transports. Sometimes unexpected demolition occurred as massive transporters got stuck under road bridges and took corners off buildings. Security for civilians who remained in the coastal towns was also tightened with more frequent random checks on ID cards. The troops were sealed into their camps on Friday 26 May to allow the start of the final briefings and to guard the secret that the landings were imminent.

As the momentous day approached, men began to embark from Gosport, Portsmouth Harbour, Southsea – where temporary piers were added to South Parade Pier, Shoreham and Newhaven along with numerous other points along the south coast. The scale of the landing force meant that the embarkation process had to be spread over five days and starting on Wednesday 31 May the first troops began to load onto the ships and landing craft that would take them to Normandy. Inevitably, serious disruption to Southdown bus services must have occurred during this time.

Bad weather was predicted for D-Day and General Eisenhower was forced to postpone the invasion for 24 hours because of strong winds and rough seas in the English Channel. At 0415 on Monday 5 June the Allied commanders met again and the forecast was good. D-Day was definitely on for the next day. From sealed camps along the south coast the remaining convoys of troops and equipment were driven under security escort to the embarkation points. Along the streets people waved cheerfully as though this was just another routine exercise. In the early morning of Tuesday 6 June the five great assault forces assembled on the south coast of England began their landings on the beaches of Normandy. Over the centuries Portsmouth Harbour had witnessed the preparation and departure of many military and naval expeditions although none on such a scale as this. The people of Portsmouth and many other towns awoke to discover the vast armada of ships had gone. There was a 'strange silence' in the now deserted streets which had been choked for days with military traffic.

The first official news came at 0930 when General Eisenhower issued Communiqué Number One, telling the French that a landing had been made by the Allies in Normandy. The BBC newscaster John Snagge followed this with a description of the successful landings. Despite some heavy casualties, especially by the American forces at Omaha Beach, the German defenders, stunned and surprised by the massive onslaught, were progressively overwhelmed, and most of the allied objectives were reached and secured by nightfall. But this was just the beginning of a long hard battle to defeat Germany which, in spite of optimism that the war might be over by Christmas, would continue until the following May. Within a week a new German terror weapon would strike a farm near Haywards Heath.

Hitler's V Weapons : June 1944 – April 1945

Second editions of the January 1944 timetables for *East Sussex* and *West Sussex* were issued adjusted to include all alterations up to and including **Thursday 1 June 1944** although no significant changes to services occurred from this date. Across the country there was great relief after the successful landings in Normandy

A very heavily loaded car 550 (AUF 850) is about to leave Haywards Heath Railway Station on the busy service 30 to Chelwood Common where it will connect with service 92 for East Grinstead. This Leyland Tiger TS6T with Short Bros 40 seat body was new in 1934 for the popular Eastbourne to Beachy Head service which was suspended in July 1940. After wartime service, car 550 was rebuilt by Southdown losing its rear roof rack and then returned to Eastbourne although postwar winters were spent on relief work in Portsmouth.
Southdown Enthusiasts Club – W J Haynes Collection

on D-Day and a growing expectation that the war would now be over quickly. There had, however, been rumours for some time about Hitler's secret weapons but most civilians did not believe that these posed a serious threat. During June the weather was cold, damp and grey with some of the worst summer storms in memory adding to weariness brought on by nearly five years of war, rationing and shortages. Any hopes that war on the home front was almost finished were soon to be dashed.

After many delays due to concerted Allied air attacks against the launch sites, four V1 flying bombs were launched against southern England early on Tuesday 13 June. The first fell harmlessly on open farmland at Swanscombe in Kent at 0418 causing little damage. At 0427, the second to be launched landed in a field behind Mizbrooks Farm, just to the north west of Whitemans Green near Cuckfield. Surprisingly, it had appeared from the direction of London, circled between Plaw Hatch and Danehill, and then turned south west over Lindfield before turning due west and exploding on impact. There was slight damage and the blast blew open the door of a pig sty in a nearby smallholding allowing the pigs to escape. The third V1 continued to London and fell at Bethnal Green at 0425 causing some casualties and damaging the railway line, while the fourth landed near Borough Green in Kent. It was the start of a deadly campaign for all the people of southern England and one which would see 880 of these weapons falling on East and West Sussex.

By late 1942 the British government was aware that Germany was developing long range rockets and pilot-less flying bombs although it was not considered desirable to alarm the public at that stage. The flying bombs – or V1s – were 25 feet long with a wing span of 16 feet and powered by a pulse-jet motor. When loaded with fuel, they weighed 2 tons and had a potentially devastating warhead of 2000 lbs of explosives. Originally, the V1 had a maximum range of 150 miles but this was later increased to 250 miles to allow for them to be launched from Holland. About 10,500 were launched towards Britain from June 1944 onwards, 8800 using specially built ramps mostly in northern France and the remainder from modified aircraft. After launching they were intended to fly a direct and straight course towards London. On reaching the target area the motor stopped to be followed by an eerie silence for about ten seconds before impact and explosion. Unlike manned aircraft they could be launched at any time of day or night and in almost any weather conditions.

After further setbacks the flying bomb offensive on Britain really began in earnest on Friday 16 June with 95 V1s crossing the coast before 0600 and a total of 244 reaching England during the day. One of the earliest V1s to fall in the Southdown area occurred at 0400 as one exploded at Riversdale Nursery, Marle Green

In the days when few people owned their own transport Southdown offered an efficient cost effective parcel service throughout its area with many local agents acting as collection and delivery points. There was the option of meeting the bus and collecting your parcel from the conductor at a time when buses could be relied upon to reach a stop on schedule!

near Horam. There were no casualties on this occasion but it was just the first of 159 flying bombs to fall in the Hailsham Rural District area causing widespread casualties and extensive damage to property. Another, seriously off target, fell on the same day at Sand Pit Wood, Park Farm, Eartham near Chichester causing slight damage to buildings and blast damage to a tree plantation but no casualties. The only V1 to fall on Worthing fortunately hit allotments at First Avenue, Charmandean on the edge of the downs and north of Upper Brighton Road causing no injuries. Next day at 2220 a flying Bomb exploded just 75 yards from Possingworth Park Hotel, near Waldron causing extensive damage to the hotel and surrounding houses. One person was killed, eight seriously injured and seven slightly injured. Another 146 V1s were destined to fall in the Uckfield Rural District over the next three months.

On Sunday 18 June at 2025 a V1 fell north of Old Town in Eastbourne causing extensive blast damage to property and injuring 41 people. Just before 2300 on Monday 19 June Richmond Road in Bexhill was hit and 20 people injured in the blast. So far no official word had been given to the public about the new weapons but the Air Ministry finally released the first official details of the V1 flying bomb on the same day. AA gunners christened them 'Doodlebugs', a name by which they are most remembered, especially those who suffered during the attacks. Next day V1s fell alongside Butts Lane, Eastbourne, at Herstmonceux slightly injuring 2 people and at

A wartime view of Brighton sea front looking east along a traffic free Grand Junction Road towards Palace Pier and Marine Parade. Unlike in Worthing, pedestrians are still permitted access to the south side of the promenade although the shingle beaches were still mined!! The building on the left is at the corner of Pool Valley so this is the somewhat depressing – or perhaps re-assuring – scene that greeted upper deck travellers departing from Southdown's Brighton terminus.
Brighton & Hove Museums

Southlands Estate in Hailsham injuring 14 people and causing damage to over 250 houses. By now defences were being reorganised to cope with the menace of the flying bombs and on Wednesday 21 June one was shot down by fighters and exploded on the Downs near Eastbourne. Unfortunately some of those shot down were to fall on populated areas causing serious casualties. Although for a period in July the flying bombs were also targeted on Portsmouth and Southampton most inevitably fell to the east of the Southdown area whilst aimed for London. But, on Sunday 25 June Locksway Road in Milton was hit causing serious injury to 14 people while another, which had been shot down by anti-aircraft fire, fell at Lavant, just 60 yards from Yarbrook Cottages damaging six buildings and injuring one person.

Southsea sea front was reopened to traffic on Thursday 15 June and trolleybus services resumed to South Parade Pier although Southdown services remained at The Circle for several more months. Further pressure on Southdown came on Tuesday 27 June when Portsmouth Corporation applied to extend its services C and D to Farlington on Sundays. Southdown opposed the idea and it was later dropped. During June 1944 some 1,935 civilians in the UK died as a result of air raids.

Throughout July V1s fell almost daily across the Southdown area although usually with few casualties. The worst loss of life in Sussex as a result of a V1 explosion occurred at 1820 on Wednesday 5 July when a 'Doodlebug', shot down by a fighter, fell on a Canadian army encampment at Crowborough Golf Course, killing eight soldiers and wounding seventeen. Sunday 9 July brought further incidents with the first at 1050 at Willingdon where the blast injured 9 people and damaged the church, school, Memorial Hall and 50 houses. Crawley was hit on Monday 10 July when a flying bomb exploded at the junction of Oak Road and West Street killing seven people and injuring 44. There was extensive damage with over 1,200 premises damaged and 24 completely destroyed. A little over one year since the tragic bombing of the Whitehall Cinema in East Grinstead a V1 fell, incredibly, on exactly the same spot and exploded in the rubble of the cinema. In the incident at 0725 on Wednesday 12 July three people were killed, 41 injured and over 400 properties damaged including a number of shops which were totally destroyed. Despite German plans, only two V1s actually fell on Portsmouth but the second which landed on Saturday 15 July caused severe damage in the Stamshaw area with 15 killed and 63 injured.

The death and destruction continued across the eastern side of the Southdown area with incidents recorded on most days. By this time RAF fighter patrols to counter the V1 menace had a high success rate, although the cost in both aircraft and crews was significant. On Wednesday 2 August Churchill made a statement to the House of Commons announcing that after seven weeks of non stop V1 attacks, 5,340 had been launched, 4,735 people killed, 14,000 injured and 17,000 houses completely destroyed.

A rather more hopeful sign of better things to come in Worthing was the appearance of electricians replacing the street lighting which had been disused for almost five years. At 1605 on Thursday 3 August a flying bomb fell at Shortgate, on the Ringmer to Halland road, where five people died and two were injured. The sub-post office, several cottages and the Bell Inn were all destroyed or badly damaged. A V1, already on fire, crossed the coast near Holywell on Monday 7 August losing height only gradually until it crashed and exploded near St Elisabeth's Church and Baldwin Avenue in Eastbourne. Sixteen people were injured and there was severe damage over a wide area. Next day another flying bomb exploded over Uckfield at 2305 partly demolishing two houses and seriously damaging 56 houses and shops.

Although the prewar procedures for Public Inquiries were suspended during the war, a special sitting of the South Eastern RTC was held on 2 August 1944 at Chichester to consider an application by B.S. Williams for a new service from Chichester to East Marden via Chilgrove on Wednesdays and Saturdays. Southdown had accepted that whilst a service was required they were unable to provide one on the grounds that they had insufficient vehicles and crews available. On hearing of the Williams application, however, Southdown submitted a competing application for a Wednesday and Saturday service from Chichester to Petersfield via Chilgrove, North Marden and South Harting which was granted – subject to consultation with the RTC for the Southern Region – and the Williams one refused. So, on Saturday 12 August 1944 resources were found and new service **62** commenced between CHICHESTER (WEST STREET) and PETERSFIELD STATION via Chilgrove, North Marden, South Harting and Nursted. Three journeys each way were provided on Wednesdays and Saturdays only

An application by Potter of Stedham who operated a network of bus routes from Midhurst to Bepton, Stedham and to Petersfield via Linch and Hillbrow was considered by the South Eastern RTC in July. Potter now applied to extend this service via Didling, Treyford, Elsted and Iping back to Midhurst on Tuesday mornings and Thursday afternoons. Southdown had repeatedly been asked by the residents of Elsted to reinstate their service 61 from East Harting – curtailed in September 1939 – but had declined to do so. Now, they not only objected to the Potter application but submitted a competing application to extend service 61 via Elsted to Midhurst every two hours, claiming that it would reduce the amount of duplication on service 60 via Rogate. The Commissioner did not notify Potter of this development until two days before the hearing and granted the Southdown application. The revised operation commenced on Sunday 13

62	CHICHESTER—Chilgrove—South Harting—PETERSFIELD				62
	WEDNESDAYS and SATURDAYS ONLY.				
Ser. 59	Bognor *Bus Station* ...	8 8	12 8	5 8	...
	Chichester *West Street* ...	8 39	1239	5 39	...
	Chichester *West Street* ...	8 45	1245	5 45	...
	Lavant *Church* ...	8 55	1255	5 55	...
	Chilgrove *White Horse* ...	9 9	1 9	6 9	...
	East Marden Road ...	9 12	1 12	6 12	...
	North Marden *Church* ...	9 15	1 15	6 15	...
	South Harting ...	9 25	1 25	6 25	...
	Petersfield *Square* ...	9 40	1 40	6 40	...
	Petersfield *Station S.R.* ...	9 42	1 42	6 42	...
Ser. 42	Petersfield *Square*	9 51	1 51	6 51	...
	Waterlooville *Heroes*	1024	2 24	7 24	...
	Cosham *Railway Bridge*	1037	2 37	7 37	...
	Portsmouth *Theatre Royal*	1053	2 53	7 53	...
Ser. 42	Portsmouth *Theatre Royal*	8 22	1222	5 22	...
	Cosham *Railway Bridge*	8 38	1238	5 38	...
	Waterlooville *Heroes*	8 51	1251	5 51	...
	Petersfield *Square*	9 25	1 25	6 25	...
	Petersfield *Station S.R.*	9 45	1 45	6 45	...
	Petersfield *Square*	9 47	1 47	6 47	...
	South Harting ...	10 2	2 2	7 2	...
	North Marden *Church* ...	1012	2 12	7 12	...
	East Marden Road ...	1015	2 15	7 15	...
	Chilgrove *White Horse* ...	1018	2 18	7 18	...
	Lavant *Church* ...	1032	2 32	7 32	...
	Chichester *West Street* ...	1042	2 42	7 42	...
Ser. 31	Chichester *West Street* ...	1043	2 43	7 43	...
	Bognor *Bus Station* ...	1112	3 12	8 12	...

August 1944 when service **61** was extended via Elsted, Iping Common and Stedham Common to Midhurst. A two hourly service ran daily with some buses continuing to and from Petworth as Service 59. As a result of a complaint that RTCs had been granting permits without notifying other operators which might have interests it was stated that there was now no compulsion upon an RTC to make any notification although in special cases this was sometimes done as an act of courtesy.

SOUTHDOWN MOTOR SERVICES, LTD.

COACH SERVICE : BOGNOR—MIDHURST—PETWORTH—HORSHAM

Starting on MONDAY, AUGUST 14th, 1944, the following Revised Time Table will be operated until further notice :—

Coach Service	BOGNOR—Chichester—Midhurst—Petworth—HORSHAM								Coach Service
	WEEKDAYS ONLY.								
Bognor *Bus Station* ...	...	8 35	1035	...	1235	2 35	4 35	...	
Bognor *Station S.R.* ...	...	8 37	1037	...	1237	2 37	4 37	...	
Chichester *West Street* ...	...	8 55	1055	...	1255	2 55	4 55	...	
Singleton *Post Office* ...	...	9 15	1115	...	1 15	3 15	5 15	...	
Midhurst *Grammar School* arr.	...	9 32	1132	...	1 32	3 32	5 32	...	
Midhurst *Grammar School* dep.	...	9 33	...	1233	1 33	3 33	5†33	...	
Petworth *Square* ...	8 42	9 52	...	1252	1 52	3 52	5†52	...	
Wisborough Green ...	9 0	1010	...	1 10	2 10	4 10	6†10	...	
Billingshurst ...	9 8	1018	...	1 18	2 18	4 18	6†18	...	
Toat Hill ...	9 17	1027	...	1 27	2 27	4 27	6†27	...	
Horsham *Carfax* ...	9 28	1038	...	1 38	2 38	4 38	6†38	...	
Horsham *Station S.R.* ...	9 30	1040	...	1 40	2 40	4 40	6†40	...	
								Sats.	
Horsham *Station S.R.* ...	...	1025	1225	2 25	4 25	5 25	7 25	...	
Horsham *Carfax* ...	...	1027	1227	2 27	4 27	5 27	7 27	...	
Toat Hill ...	...	1038	1238	2 38	4 38	5 38	7 38	...	
Billingshurst ...	...	1047	1247	2 47	4 47	5 47	7 47	...	
Wisborough Green ...	...	1055	1255	2 55	4 55	5 55	7 55	...	
Petworth *Square* ...	...	1113	1 13	3 13	5 13	6 13	8 13	...	
Midhurst *Grammar School* arr.	...	1132	1 32	3 32	5 32	6 32	8 32	...	
Midhurst *Grammar School* dep.	8 36	1136	1 36	3 36	5 36	...	...	...	
Singleton *Post Office* ...	8 53	1153	1 53	3 53	5 53	...	...	...	
Chichester *West Street* ...	9 12	1212	2 12	4 12	6 12	...	...	...	
Bognor *Station S.R.* ...	9 30	1230	2 30	4 30	6 30	...	...	...	
Bognor *Bus Station* ...	9 32	1232	2 32	4 32	6 32	...	...	...	

† or Sats.—Saturdays only.
Passengers travelling on the above Coach Service will be charged the special minimum fares shown below

The Southern Publishing Co., Ltd , 130 North Street, Brighton—D4846

By late 1944 soldiers are starting the difficult job of removing the barbed wire along the seafront at Marine Parade, Worthing which was hastily erected as part of anti-invasion defences in June 1940. Framework for the swings at Hewitt's Funfair is visible in the background along with a Southdown Leyland Titan in full wartime livery on service 5. This service (along with the 5A from May 1943) continued to travel the short distance along the sea front from West Buildings to the Pier throughout the war.
West Sussex County Council Library Service

There were further timing changes to the Limited Stop coach service between Horsham and Bognor starting on Monday 14 August which resulted in no vehicles now starting or ending their journeys at Petworth. The last recorded flying bomb to fall within the county borough of Eastbourne occurred on Monday 14 August when one was destroyed by anti-aircraft fire over Meads and property was damaged. Most places in Sussex west of Seaford suffered less flying bomb activity and the majority fell in open country causing little damage and few casualties but one which landed between Shelley Road and Tennyson Road in Bognor on Sunday 27 August caused considerable destruction with 65 people injured and 550 houses damaged in the incident.

The powers to impose curfews had been formally revoked on 30 May 1944 but the restrictions within the South East region remained in place. With the threat of invasion finally removed the ban on entry for visitors to the coastal areas was lifted on 25 August 1944 although contemporary reports suggest that it was not being strictly enforced during August. In late August a section of the beach at Worthing reopened to the public but the deputy town clerk added a sombre warning that people intent on a paddle 'did so at their own risk' because of the danger of mines. It didn't stop several thousand people from taking advantage of the reopening after four long years of not being allowed access to the beach. On Wednesday 30 August the main British and

Canadian advance began from the Seine and within two weeks the whole of the 'Flying Bomb Coast' had been cleared so the threat to the Southdown area from V1s was over at last. The launching of V1s from France finally ceased on Saturday 2 September.

Victory in the 'Battle of London' was proclaimed on Wednesday 6 September after 80 days of V1 bombardment with over 8,000 flying bombs launched and around 2,300 actually reaching London. Once again, it proved to be a somewhat optimistic assessment as two days later the first of the even more deadly V2 rockets hit London and Paris launched from mobile bases in Holland. In addition V1 flying bombs launched from aircraft commenced within days. The V2 was the first successful long range rocket and whereas the V1 could be seen and attacked by guns or aircraft, this new weapon was effectively unstoppable once it had been fired. The first that the intended victims knew about the arrival of a V2, was when it exploded by which time it was too late to take any avoiding action. The rocket was 46 feet in length and weighed 13 tons when fully loaded with fuel and warhead. From launch to reaching the speed of sound took just 30 seconds. During its brief four minute flight from the launch sites in Holland to Britain travelling at a speed of 3000 mph it reached a maximum trajectory height of between 50 to 60 miles. The warhead weighed one ton and was capable of devastating damage over a wide area.

As with the V1 they could be launched day and night and after a faltering start the first fell without warning on Chiswick in west London at 1843 on Friday 8 September killing three people.

A new *West Sussex* timetable was issued for including alterations up to **Monday 11 September 1944**. The frequency of service **54** between Chichester and Compton was increased to a regular two hourly service daily – plus the existing three journeys each way on Saturdays between Chichester and Hambrook. For several weeks the V2 explosions continued but there was no official response or explanation other than references to 'gas main explosions'. Finally on 10 November the Prime Minister admitted that the country was under attack from long range rockets. Over 5,000 V2 rockets were launched but only 1,115 reached any part of Britain, mostly falling in east and south east London and East Anglia. Fortunately very few affected the Southdown area and none are believed to have been targeted deliberately against Sussex or Hampshire. However, at 1316 on Thursday 14 September a massive explosion rocked the Rotherfield and Crowborough areas as a V2 rocket blew up in mid-air above Rumsden Farm south of Crowborough. This was the first V2 in Sussex, and only the thirteenth to reach the UK. The scattered parts proved to be of value to British Intelligence services desperately seeking to discover the secrets and inner workings of these fearsome devices.

At 1520 on Saturday 16 September the people of Eastbourne were shaken by a massive explosion in the sky over Willingdon which came without warning. Another V2 rocket had blown up in mid-air, fortunately causing no serious damage or casualties. Launched from Holland

against London this rocket was way off-track and seems to have been the furthest south that a V2 is recorded as having fallen. With raids by manned enemy aircraft now unlikely the full blackout regulations were partially lifted on Sunday 17 September and replaced by a 'dim-out' although the original rules applied to a five mile deep zone along the south and east coast which remained on alert for possible attacks by German U-boats believed to be still active. In reality this amounted to a less stringent form of blackout but was welcomed at the time although Southdown retained its blackout timetables on most routes until 13 May 1945. A start was also made on dismantling many of the unsightly

By the autumn of 1944 the south side of Marine Parade in Worthing had been reopened to pedestrians allowing bus services to revert to their normal stops although the concrete blocks which were put in place as anti-invasion defences in 1940 still remain. Three Southdown Leyland Titans in full wartime livery can be seen loading at bus stops near The Dome.
West Sussex County Council Library Service

Park Royal bodied Leyland Titan TD5 car 260 (GCD 360) shows off the modified 1943 livery as it sets down passengers on Grand Junction Road in Brighton before terminating at nearby Pool Valley. It is all over grey to the bottom of the lower deck windows except for an apple green band below the upper deck windows with apple green below the lower deck windows and dark green mudguards. Although blackout regulations still applied to a five mile deep belt along the coastal areas, the white markings applied to all buses at the start of the war began to be removed by the end of December 1944 and all road vehicles were now permitted to operate without headlight masks.
Southdown Enthusiasts Club – W J Haynes Collection

This is the scene in late 1944 looking east along the seafront at Splash Point in Worthing, once the terminus for the Tramocars' services. Bus services were finally withdrawn from this point on 10 April 1941 and never reinstated. A gun emplacement now dominates the scene and although the promenade has reopened to pedestrians the concrete war defences hastily constructed at the top of the beach in 1940 remained in place until the early months of 1945. The local council had carefully removed the decorative lighting from the promenade for safe keeping early in the war. *West Sussex County Council Library Service*

barbed wire barricades and fortifications built along the promenades in 1940.

Changes on Hayling Island with effect from Sunday 24 September saw service **47** reinstated via Northney and the Havant–Northney–Stoke section of service **49** withdrawn, the latter being curtailed to operate between WATERLOOVILLE (HEROES INN) and HAVANT CHURCH every 30 minutes on weekdays and hourly on Sunday. On Sundays Northney was only served by the 47 after 1300. From Sunday 8 October 1944 service **21** was extended from Southwick to Brighton and revised at the Shoreham end of route becoming BRIGHTON (POOL VALLEY) to SHOREHAM (BRIDGE HOTEL) although this may have commenced hourly in June. Certain weekday journeys continued via High Street, Victoria Road and Mill Lane to and from Shoreham (Erringham Road). The frequency became 30 minutes daily throughout. To the west of Southdown territory service **38** was diverted commencing on Sunday 15 October between the Bold Forester Inn and the Falcon Inn to operate via Plough Road and Plough Inn. It had been rerouted on 8 August 1940 probably due to Military activities. To assist with heavy loadings some routes were converted from 1400 class saloons to double deck operation. From Sunday 29 October the Worthing allocation on services **9** and **11** was converted to double deckers with TD1s 806/7 appearing on the 9. Littlehampton followed suit from Sunday 5 November replacing its working on the **9** with a double decker and at the same time the **66** was worked by TD1s 803/16.

Some significant improvements to services between Chichester and The Witterings occurred

from Sunday 5 November when the frequency of service **53** was increased from 2 hourly to hourly each way daily. Service **53A** between Chichester and Itchenor was also increased from four journeys each way daily to a two hourly service daily. A new timetable was issued for the *Portsmouth* area (formerly described as Hampshire) with alterations up to **Sunday 19 November 1944**. By this time the tide of war had turned firmly in favour of the Allies and fears of invasion along the South Coast had passed. It was now possible within the limited vehicle and staff resources available to make some modest reinstatement of withdrawn facilities and one of the first brought buses back to the sea front at Southsea. From 19 November services 31, 31A, 40, 41, 42 and 45 were extended to terminate again at South Parade Pier, Southsea from which they had been withdrawn after operation on 20 November 1941. Services **31**, **40** and **42** via Theatre Royal were diverted at Palmerston Road to run via Clarence Parade and South Parade while services **31A**, **41** and **45** via Fratton were diverted from Victoria Road North via Elm Grove, Grove Road South, Palmerston Road, Clarence Parade and South Parade. Four buses per hour now ran between Theatre Royal and Southsea and six per hour between Fratton and Southsea during daytime on weekdays. Sunday morning services remained unchanged at this time but last buses from Theatre Royal on services **31, 39, 40, 42B** and **45** were extended by 30 minutes to 2130. In addition there was a 2121 departure on service **31A** from South Parade Pier via Fratton to Emsworth and a 2122 service **45** to Fareham via Fratton.

With the end of the war in sight and no air raid alerts for some weeks people could now once again sleep peacefully in their beds. But, at about 0500 on Tuesday 22 November one of the largest explosions in England during the whole of the Second World War occurred at Newhaven. A barge loaded with 180 tons of a very high explosive had broken away from its tug during a storm and drifted ashore below the cliffs west of the town. The vessel then struck a land mine and exploded with great force causing damage to almost every house in Newhaven and smashing windows as far away as Lewes and Seaford. In the town many people were blown out of their beds by the blast and there were hundreds of minor injuries but fortunately only seven serious casualties and one fatality; a naval rating killed when a wall fell on him. The blast was felt as far away as Hailsham and heard way beyond that. Had the explosion occurred during the day when more people were out and about in the town the death toll could have been much higher. The cliff face had also helped to deflect the worst effects of the blast which caused around three times more damage in the area than was inflicted by the enemy during almost six years of war. During the autumn of 1944 the young evacuees who had not already returned to their parents came home to the south coast again with the last of those from Brighton arriving from Yorkshire in early December.

On Sunday 10 December 1944 it was the turn of Worthing's local services to benefit from some limited enhancement including later buses until 2130. The Worthing to Findon short journeys on service **1** were introduced on weekday mornings and Sunday afternoons to operate all day weekdays until 1850 and from 1300 till 1850 on Sundays. Alternate journeys on service **3** were extended along Goring Road to its pre-16 November 1939 terminus at Goring Church and the weekday frequency on linked services **3** and **8** increased from every 15 minutes to 10 minutes, not far short of prewar levels. On Sundays the frequency of both improved from 20 minutes to 15 minutes. The extension to Goring Church may have commenced in August. On service **4** the frequency increased on Weekdays from every 15 minutes to every 10 minutes as far as Durrington with alternate journeys extended to and from High Salvington. At this stage Sundays remained a 15 minute service to Durrington with alternate journeys extended to and from High Salvington.

The replacement of the gas buses allowed some timing revisions on services **5**, **5A** and **6**. Service **11** was withdrawn and replaced by a revised service **31F** which was extended from Worthing to Ferring (Beresford's Stores) via Marine Parade, Heene Road, Mill Road, Goring Road, Mulberry Lane, Goring Way, Sea Lane, Ferring Street and Ferringham Lane. An hourly service ran daily restoring a through link between Brighton and Ferring which had been lost in 1939 but also finally marking the end of the once important service 11.

Park Royal bodied Leyland Titan TD5 car 252 (GCD 352) pauses at Marine Parade, Worthing on its way between Brighton and Ferring. The promenade has been cleared of barbed wire and the ornate light fittings returned in this early postar view. Car 252 was repainted in February 1945 with a dark green roof while apple green has been applied up to the bottom of the lower deck windows. The operation of double deckers over the estate roads in Ferring-by-Sea alarmed the residents and Southdown was eventually forced to terminate the through Brighton service at Ferring Memorial until an alternative solution was found.
C F Klapper © Omnibus Society

67	HAVANT—Rowlands Castle—Compton—South and West Harting—PETERSFIELD				67

Wednesdays and Saturdays only

	WS	WS	Weds.	Sats.
Havant *Station S.R.*	9 21	3 21	6 35	6 35
Rowlands Castle *Station S.R.*...	9 33	3 33	6 47	6 47
Deanlane End	9 38	3 38	6 52	6 52
Forestside *Post Office*	9 45	3 45	6 59	6 59
West Marden *Pond*	9 50	3 50	7 4	7 4

Ser. 54	West Marden *Pond* ...	9 51	3 51	7 51	7 51
	Funtington *Fox and Hounds*	10 8	4 8	8 8	8 8
	Chichester *West Street* ...	1027	4 27	8 27	8 27

Compton *Coach and Horses* ...	9 53	3 53	7 7	7 7
South Harting *Ship Inn* ...	10 6	4 6	...	7 20
West Harting *Greyhound* ...	1010	4 10	...	7 24
Sheet *Half Moon*	1026	4 26	...	7 40
Petersfield *Square*	1030	4 30	...	7 44
Petersfield *Station S.R.* ...	1032	4 32	...	7 46

	WS	WS	Wed.	Sats.
Petersfield *Station S.R.* ...	1234	4 34	...	8 34
Petersfield *Square*	1236	4 36	...	8 36
Sheet *Half Moon*	1240	4 40	...	8 40
West Harting *Greyhound* ...	1256	4 56	...	8 56
South Harting *Ship Inn* ...	1 0	5 0	...	9 0
Compton *Coach and Horses* ...	1 13	5 13	7 13	9 13

Ser. 54	Chichester *West Street* ...	1239	4 39	6 39	8 39
	Funtington *Fox and Hounds*	1258	4 58	6 58	9 58
	West Marden *Pond* ...	1 15	5 15	7 15	9 15

West Marden *Pond*	1 16	5 16	7 16	9 16
Forestside *Post Office*	1 21	5 21	7 21	9 21
Deanlane End	1 28	5 28	7 28	9 28
Rowlands Castle *Station S.R.* ...	1 33	5 33	7 33	9 33
Havant *Station S.R.*	1 45	5 45	7 45	9 45

WS—Wednesdays and Saturdays only.
Weds.—Wednesdays only. Sats.—Saturdays only.

Hants & Sussex renewed their application for an Emsworth to Stockheath service in September 1944 and also proposed a revised timetable for a previously refused Emsworth to West Marden service running hourly from 0700 to 2200. Fearful of expansion by Basil Williams, Southdown submitted a competing application for a Wednesday and Saturday service from Havant to Petersfield via Rowlands Castle, West Marden, Compton, South and West Harting and Durford. At the end of September 1944 the RTC advised Hants and Sussex that he had refused their applications and in November sent details of the Southdown application. Hants & Sussex then submitted an identical timetable to that proposed by Southdown but starting from Emsworth instead of Havant. Although Public Hearings remained suspended 'for the duration' a conference was held at Reading on 22 November 1944 to consider the two applications. Hants & Sussex stated that Southdown had been asked to provide a service on this route by Havant & Waterloo UDC in 1931 and had refused unless the Council would guarantee the costs of operation. Reference was also made to the existing Southdown bus services between Havant and Rowlands Castle which were adequate, whilst there was none between Rowlands Castle and Emsworth. Southdown made much of the proposed connections with their other services at Havant, Compton, South Harting and Petersfield as well as with the Southern Railway at the terminals. Once again the Southdown application was granted and the Hants & Sussex one refused although subsequently a service was approved which commenced in October 1947. As a result, starting on Wednesday 13 December, service **67** broke new ground linking HAVANT STATION and PETERSFIELD STATION via Rowlands Castle, Deanlane End, Forestside, West Marden, Compton, South Harting, West Harting, Durford and Sheet.

Britain's Home Guard, formed in May 1940 to defend the country during some of the darkest days of the war when a German invasion seemed

Car 420 (GUF 120) is a Guy Arab II with Northern Counties metal framed highbridge body to utility specification delivered in October 1944. Fitted from new with a Gardner 6LW engine it was therefore deemed suitable for the hilly service 12 between Brighton and Eastbourne. It is seen at the end of the war in the 1943 livery of all grey with apple green below the lower deck windows, an apple green band below the upper deck windows and a dark green roof. In 1957 car 420 was rebuilt by Southdown to open top for summer operations and remained in service until the end of the wartime Guys in June 1964.
Southdown Enthusiasts Club – W J Haynes Collection

Brush bodied Leyland Titan TD1 car 815 (UF 4815) dating from 1929 has been fitted with a temporary top cover at Portslade Works to allow all year round service. Had it not been for the war these buses – in open top form – would have been used for summer services in coastal towns. It is seen at Emsworth on a 31A working which at this time ran half hourly to Southsea (Circle) via Fratton Bridge. *J F Parke © Omnibus Society*

likely, was formally stood down on Sunday 3 December. Worthing was very fortunate to escape serious death and destruction at about 1745 on Sunday 17 December when a Lancaster bomber, outbound for an attack on Munich, crashed into the sea west of the Pier and blew up with great force. The bomb load and petrol tanks exploded causing a shock wave which damaged 233 houses and hotels as well as many shops in the town. The pilot had apparently struggled to control the bomber in order to clear the town and it was clear just how serious the damage and loss of life would have been had it crashed into Worthing. All seven crew were killed in the incident.

Further good news for passengers came on Monday 18 December and it was now the turn of the important 12 group to benefit from increased frequencies. These services had been severely reduced early in the war and the Eastbourne service had remained at one bus per hour throughout the year. The Brighton terminus now became known as Valley Drive rather than Tongdean although there was no change of route or journey times. The frequency of service **12** increased to:

2 journeys per hour between Valley Drive and Eastbourne,

2 journeys per hour between Valley Drive and Seaford and

1 journey per hour between Brighton Station and Cliff Road, Peacehaven.

This represented an increase of one journey per hour from Valley Drive to Eastbourne and one journey per hour from Brighton Station to Cliff Road, Peacehaven. Service **12A** was curtailed to operate between BRIGHTON STATION and PEACEHAVEN ANNEXE the section

to Valley Drive being replaced by an extra service 12 journey. Finally, the frequency of service **12B** was restored to its prewar level of 30 minutes daily, having been reduced to hourly from September 1939. No Sunday morning services were permitted over these important routes at this time.

Of all the towns served by Southdown, Eastbourne had been particularly hard hit with many devastating air raids and the subsequent evacuation of many residents to safer areas. As a result facilities had been much reduced and a small improvement in the fortunes of bus services in the town came with an additional two hourly service between Eastbourne and Polegate Station on service **94**. It had been reduced to two hourly throughout from 21 November 1940. Journeys on service **119** which ran via Maresfield were renumbered 119A with a two hourly frequency on each service. Details were included in a new *East Sussex* timetable book including all changes up to and including **Monday 18 December 1944**.

Towards the end of 1943 Basil Williams had agreed to purchase the business of Cecil Walling of Eastergate, who traded as 'Silver Queen Bus Service', and ran a service from Bognor to Slindon via Shripney and Westergate where the route divided, going either via Eastergate and Walberton or direct via Fontwell Avenue. In January 1944 Williams formed a new company, Silver Queen Motor Services Ltd, and an application was then made to the South Eastern RTC to transfer the permit from C.J. Walling to Silver Queen Motor Services Ltd. Southdown and the Southern Railway both objected to this, the former submitting alternative proposals for serving the area. Southdown's service 57 already operated over the Bognor–Westergate section of road before continuing to Chichester. At the hearing in April 1944 it was explained that Williams had purchased the business and proposed to continue to operate as before. Southdown responded that in the normal way they would not have objected to the renewal of Walling's permit, but, as the business was being sold and they were prepared to purchase, they felt their company would be able to offer improved services to the public. Cecil Walling indicated that if the application was not granted, he would still continue to operate. The Commissioner refused the application and Walling continued to operate until the end of the year when he sold the business to Southdown who introduced two new services commencing on 21 December 1944. Service **65** ran between BOGNOR BUS STATION and SLINDON (NEWBURGH ARMS) via Shripney, Lidsey, Woodgate Crossing, Westergate, Eastergate, Barnham Station, Walberton, Royal Oak and Slindon Common while service **65A** ran between BOGNOR BUS STATION and SLINDON (NEWBURGH ARMS) as service 65 to Eastergate then via Fontwell and Slindon Common. Both services operated every two hours daily with no Sunday morning service. At first 1400 class Leyland Tigers were used but from 7 January 1945 double deckers appeared on the routes.

1945

In January 1945 it was announced that British Empire casualties up to November 1944 were 282,162 killed, 80,580 missing, 386,374 wounded and 294,438 captured. The demolition of wartime fortifications continued although progress was slow and many proved hard to remove. The 'Hyam Ready' fortress in the centre of Worthing proved too difficult for the pneumatic drills! January was another cold month with heavy falls of snow even in the coastal towns. Fuel allowances were eased from early in 1945, although the restriction on Sunday morning operation remained, and Southdown was one of the first companies to introduce new and innovative routes. In the past couple of years its plans had often been forced by ambitious proposals put forward by Hants & Sussex Motor Services Ltd and its associate companies in the west and north west of its territory to which Southdown felt obliged to respond. Not all of the resulting services proved durable beyond the initial post war boom in demand for bus travel. From Sunday 7 January service **63** was diverted between Halnaker and Maudlin to operate via Boxgrove and Tangmere and the frequency increased to a two hourly service daily. The Petworth to Duncton short journeys were now absorbed into the through service.

A new *West Sussex* timetable book was issued

Setting down in Steyning High Street on a short working on service 22 is car 424 (GUF 424), a Guy Arab II with Northern Counties metal framed body delivered in January 1945. It is in apple green and cream livery with dark green roof as became standard on all deliveries and repaints by late 1944. After a rebuild by Southdown in 1950 and conversion to open top in 1957 it went on to serve with the company until sale in June 1964.
C F Klapper © Omnibus Society

containing all alterations up to and including **Monday 15 January 1945**. In the Bognor area an additional 30 minute service was provided on service **50A** on weekdays only between Elmer and Bognor Bus Station, previously hourly throughout. Selsey service **52** gained an improved frequency and was revised in Chichester to start from West Street rather than the Railway Station. The frequency now became hourly via Hunston and hourly via Donnington. Service **58** was extended beyond East Dean to form a lengthy circular service via Pilleygreen Lodges, Goodwood Grandstand, Kennel Corner, Goodwood House, Goodwood Park, Waterbeach, Westerton and Maudlin. The frequency was increased to two hourly throughout plus a two hourly service daily between Chichester and Singleton. At the same time service **66** was withdrawn without replacement between Chichester West Street and Lavant Station. Buses on service **61** now continued beyond Midhurst to Horsham running as Service 59. All journeys on services **78** and **79** were now curtailed at Horsham (Carfax) and no longer continued across town to Slinfold. Although there was no prospect of an early resumption of the London Express Services the frequency of the Bognor to Horsham Limited Stop service introduced back in September 1942 as a partial replacement was now reduced to two journeys each way plus various short workings. Further enhancement in Worthing occurred from Sunday 28 January when service **5** was extended from Offington Corner via Findon

Road, Worthing Road and High Street to FINDON (GUN INN) running every 30 minutes daily except Sunday mornings.

Although the sea fronts were drab and scarred by war with many shops and hotels still closed, crowds began to return to the promenades and beaches as they were reopened to the public. Eastbourne's beaches were open by February and the pier repaired. In Worthing the huge concrete defence blocks that appeared in the tense days of 1940 were finally lifted onto lorries and taken away in time for the Easter holiday although it would be some time before repairs could be undertaken. From Sunday 25 February services **12**, **12A** and **12B** reverted to their normal peacetime route along Marine Parade in Brighton having been diverted away from sea front gun emplacements since 17 June 1940.

A second edition of the *East Sussex* timetable issued on 18 December 1944 was produced including alterations up to and including **Thursday 1 March 1945**. An additional later evening journey on service **90** was introduced each way daily between Eastbourne and Hellingly Hospital by this date. From Sunday 4 March the eastern terminus of service **55** became NORTH BERSTED (TOAD HALL) and Horsham local service **72** was curtailed to terminate in HIGHLANDS ESTATE at the junction of ORCHARD ROAD and HIGHLANDS ROAD being removed from a short section of Orchard Road. The frequency became every 30 minutes daily reduced from every 20 minutes at certain times

Although the one man operated Leyland Cubs were regular performers on the Horsham local services 72 and 73 for several years, car 22 (ECD 522) appears to be operating a relief journey on normally double decked service 2 to Worthing. After gaining a dark green roof at the start of hostilities car 22 is now in the livery that these vehicles retained after the war. To the right of the picture can be seen a brick built surface shelter to be used by waiting passengers in case of an air raid alert.
J F Parke © Omnibus Society

A busy scene at Petworth Square shows car 103 (BUF 203) attracting a lot of interest for its journey on service 63B to the small village of Sutton. It is a Leyland Titan TD4 with Short Bros lowbridge body new in 1935 and one of the batch that was not rebodied in the postwar programme although the side screen boxes were removed in May 1946. Traversing some unlikely bus territory service 63B was introduced in March 1945 to combat Basil Williams expansionist ideas and provided a 3 hourly service on three days per week in winter and daily in summer.
Alan Lambert collection

and one man operated Leyland Cubs were replaced by 1400 class Leyland Tigers on both **72** and **73**. Service **72B** was withdrawn.

During the autumn of 1944 Basil Williams submitted a revised application for a Tuesday, Thursday and Saturday service through unserved roads from Petworth to Bury via Byworth, Stopham Bridge, Barlavington Lane, Sutton, Bignor and West Burton. Subsequently the application was revised to extend the route further south to Slindon where connections were to be made with the Silver Queen service to Bognor Regis. In October 1944 the RTC notified Basil Williams that he considered the road between Sutton and Bury unsuitable but would consider an application for a Petworth to Sutton service. So, yet another application was made, this time for a Monday, Tuesday, Thursday and Friday service from Petworth to Sutton only. In December 1944 the Commissioner advised he did not consider the road via Byworth suitable and so the route was amended to run via Haslingbourne and New Grove. Towards the end of December 1944, Southdown submitted its own application for a Petworth to Sutton service on Tuesdays, Thursdays and Saturdays, together with an application for a Petworth to Graffham service to be worked by the same bus on the same days. The RTC did not notify Basil Williams of the application for the Graffham service but when he gave his decision in January 1945 on the two Sutton applications, he granted the

Southdown one on the grounds that "the larger operator was in a better position to operate by reason of already having buses available at Petworth." As Basil Williams rightly pointed out, if he had been advised of Southdown's Petworth to Graffham proposal he could have renewed his own application before the decision on the Sutton service was reached. He lost no time in renewing his Graffham to Petworth proposal as an extension of the existing service and on this occasion the Commissioner granted the application. New Service **63B** commenced on Tuesday 20 March between PETWORTH SQUARE and SUTTON (WHITE HORSE INN) via Petworth Station, Heathend, Burton Hill, Byworth Cross Road and Sutton End. A three hourly service ran on Tuesdays, Thursdays, and Saturdays with departures from Petworth at 1010, 1310, 1610 and 1910. An additional journey on Saturdays at 2110

63b	PETWORTH — SUTTON via Duncton Common												63b
TUESDAYS, THURSDAYS and SATURDAYS.													
Petworth *Square* ...	...	1010	1	10	4	10	7	10	9	10	...	...	...	...
Petworth *Station S.R.*	...	1016	1	16	4	16	7	16	9	16	...	...	...	...
Duncton Common ...	...	1018	1	18	4	18	7	18	9	18	...	...	...	...
Byworth Cross Roads	...	1023	1	23	4	23	7	23	9‡30		...	...	...	...
Sutton *White Horse Inn*	...	1028	1	28	4	28	7	28	9	35	...	...	...	...
Sutton *White Horse Inn*	...	1030	1	30	4	30	7	30	9	40	...	...	...	...
Byworth Cross Roads	...	1036	1	36	4	36	7	36	9	46	...	...	...	...
Duncton Common ...	...	1041	1	41	4	41	7	41	9	51	...	...	...	...
Petworth *Station S.R.*	...	1043	1	43	4	43	7	43	9	53	...	...	...	...
Petworth *Square* ...	...	1048	1	48	4	48	7	48	9	58	...	...	...	...
‡—Via Duncton *The Cricketer*													

35	PETERSFIELD — FAREHAM Via Clanfield, Hambledon and Southwick	35

MONDAYS, WEDNESDAYS & SATURDAYS ONLY.

				Mons.	WS	WS	
Petersfield *Square*	...	...	...	9 0	9 50	1 50	...
Buriton Cross Roads	...	...	...	9 6	9 56	1 56	...
Hogs Lodge Corner	...	...	...	9 14	10 4	2 4	...
Clanfield *Rising Sun*	...	...	...	9 19	10 9	2 9	...
Hambledon *George Inn*	...		...	9 32	1022	2 22	...
World's End *Chairmaker's Arms*				9 42	1032	2 32	...
Denmead *Bunkers Hill*	...	...	...	9 47	1037	2 37	...
Southwick *Church*	...	...	...	9 56	1046	2 46	...
Fareham *Bus Station*	...	...	...	10 6	11 4	3 4	...
				WS	Mons.	WS	
Fareham *Bus Station*	...	...	...	1140	1240	3 40	...
Southwick *Church*	...	...	...	1158	1258	3 58	...
Denmead *Bunkers Hill*	...		...	12 7	1 7	4 7	...
World's End *Chairmaker's Arms*			...	1212	1 12	4 12	...
Hambledon *George Inn*	...	...	...	1222	1 22	4 22	...
Clanfield *Rising Sun*	...	...	...	**1235**	**1 35**	**4 35**	...
Hogs Lodge Corner	...	...	...	1240	1 40	4 40	...
Buriton Cross Roads	...	...	...	1248	1 48	4 48	...
Petersfield *Square* ...	...	...	...	1254	1 54	4 54	...

Mons.—Mondays only.   WS.—Wednesdays and Saturdays only.

35a	PETERSFIELD — CHALTON with connections to and from Portsmouth	35a

WEDNESDAYS & SATURDAYS ONLY.

Petersfield *Square* ...	...	...	9 0	1 0	5 0	...
Buriton Cross Roads	...	...	9 6	1 6	5 6	...
Hogs Lodge Corner	...	...	9 14	1 14	5 14	...
Chalton Road Corner	...	...	9 16	1 16	5 16	...
Ser. 42 { Portsmouth *Theatre Royal*	..	8 22	1222	4 22	...
Cosham *Railway Bridge*	...	8 38	1232	4 32	...
Chalton Road Corner	...	9 9	1 9	5 9	...
Chalton Road Corner	...	...	9 16	1 16	5 16	...
Chalton *Church*	...	...	9 22	1 22	5 22	...
Chalton *Church*	...	...	9 23	1 23	5 23	...
Chalton Road Corner	...	...	9 29	1 29	5 29	...
Ser. 40 { Chalton Road Corner	...	9 33	1 33	5 33	...
Cosham *Railway Bridge*	...	10 7	2 7	6 7	...
Portsmouth *Theatre Royal*	...	1023	2 23	6 23	...
Chalton Road Corner	...	...	9 29	1 29	5 29	...
Hogs Lodge Corner	...	...	9 31	1 31	5 31	...
Buriton Cross Roads	...	...	9 39	1 39	5 39	...
Petersfield *Square* ...	...	...	9 45	1 45	5 45	...

included a double run to and from Duncton, The Cricketers on its outward journey.

The already battered town of East Grinstead was singled out for the last air attack of the war in the Southdown area when a V1 flying bomb hit Lowdells Lane and Sackville Lane at 0758 on Sunday 25 March. Eight people were injured and some 50 shops and houses were damaged in the

attack which was fortunately east of the town centre on this occasion. At 1654 on Tuesday 27 March the 1,115th and last V2 rocket to reach England landed in Kynaston Road, Orpington. The very last enemy air attack affecting British soil occurred on Thursday 29 March as a flying bomb landed on a sewage farm at Datchworth in Hertfordshire. Shortly after, one last V1 was shot down near Sittingbourne marking the end of the V weapons campaign.

On Tuesday 10 April Churchill revealed the British Empire military casualty figures up to that point as 306,984 killed. Total casualties were 1,126,802 with the merchant navy losing 34,161 dead or captured. The Home Secretary announced on Friday 20 April that 60,585 British civilians had died and 86,175 were seriously injured in air attacks since the outbreak of war. All Blackout restrictions, excluding a five mile deep zone in the coastal areas, were lifted as from Monday 23 April although it would take many months for the authorities to restore normal lighting to the shabby war torn streets.

As the war finally drew to a victorious conclusion two new market day routes providing new links in the far west of the Southdown area were introduced from Wednesday 25 April 1945. Service **35** ran from PETERSFIELD SQUARE to FAREHAM BUS STATION via Buriton Cross Roads, Hogs Lodge Corner, Clanfield, Broadhalfpenny Down, Hambledon, World's End, Southwick Church and Boarhunt. One journey operated each way on Mondays and two journeys each way were provided on Wednesdays and Saturdays. In addition service **35A** operated between PETERSFIELD SQUARE and CHALTON CHURCH via Buriton Cross Roads, Hogs Lodge Corner and Chalton Road Corner with three journeys each way on Wednesdays and Saturdays.

Car 1454 (FCD 254), a Harrington bodied Leyland Tiger TS8 new in 1938 waits at Fareham Railway Station between duties on service 35. This was introduced on 25 April 1945 just a few days before the war ended and provided infrequent new links on three days per week across the north western fringes of the company's territory between Petersfield and Fareham.
Alan Lambert collection

Express Services

As war loomed at the end of August 1939, Southdown's express services were still busy with holiday and day trip traffic between London and the South Coast. With war now inevitable blackout regulations were imposed on Friday 1 September and the evacuation of children and other vulnerable groups began. Inevitably, the immediate effect of the outbreak of hostilities on Sunday 3 September encouraged many to curtail holidays and visits and return home as soon as possible. At the same time those who could afford to move out of the most 'at risk areas' such as London made their own arrangements to stay in the country or beside the sea. With the prospect of devastation in the capital as soon as hostilities commenced and the railway system already overloaded with official evacuees and military traffic many of those who could get away would have chosen to travel by coach on which a seat could be guaranteed once booked.

To accommodate the massive evacuation from the capital, nine routes were made one way outwards from London including – towards the south – Balham High Road, Morden Road and Sutton Bypass; Kings Road, Putney Bridge, Old Portsmouth Road, Kingston Bypass and Great Chertsey Road. Early on the morning of Saturday 2 September all traffic towards London on these roads was stopped as one way traffic waves operated for three days. Official evacuation traffic was joined by a mass of luggage laden cars, but the carefully prepared arrangements ensured that congestion was no worse than on a usual summer weekend. Inevitably, the unparalleled scope of the road closures would have seriously disrupted the London Express services. During these anxious days after the declaration of war the coach services faced the same problems in the blackout as the stage carriage services with all the added difficulties associated with travelling in Central London. There were obviously numerous difficulties of timekeeping in the darkened streets and a startling increase in road accidents as the winter months progressed. Locating waiting passengers, checking validity of tickets and loading luggage on to roof racks without street lighting must have posed many new challenges for staff. When the sirens sounded the official ARP advice was that all traffic should stop. Coach drivers and conductors were then to continue to the nearest air raid shelter and, after shepherding passengers inside, wait there until the 'all clear' sounded. During the following year's blitz this procedure was to be followed many times leading to many delays and eventually drivers began to take upon themselves the responsibility of assessing the nature of the alert and stopping only when in imminent danger.

Whilst most coach services continued normally after the outbreak of war, at least until late September, the famous Green Line limited stop services of the London Passenger Transport

Typical of the coaches that ran the London services in wartime is car 1105 (BUF 405), one of a batch of 36 Leyland Tiger TS7 coaches delivered for the 1935 season. Most were bodied by Harrington but six, including car 1105, had Park Royal bodies to Southdown's standard design of the time although incorporating some detailed differences. Fitted with folding sunroof and roof luggage racks they were used extensively on the London Express Services as seen here. Several were converted for use as ambulances in 1939 whilst others such as car 1105 continued to maintain the dwindling London operations until curtailment in 1942. With the Express services once again restored car 1105 is seen laying over in the Victoria area after completing a run from Bognor Regis via Chichester. Regrettably, no images have come to hand of Southdown coaches employed on the London services during wartime.
Southdown Enthusiasts Club – W J Haynes Collection

The London to Gosport service was an early victim of the outbreak of war being suspended after operation on Monday 4 September 1939.
In prewar days car 1072 (UF 8842), a Leyland Tiger TS4 with Harrington 32 rear entrance body new in 1932, is seen at Victoria Coach Station awaiting its next run to Gosport through the Meon Valley. The coach was also affected by the war and requisitioned by the Military Authorities in June 1940. Although car 1072 did not return to Southdown again it went on to lead a long life after being rebodied by Burlingham in 1946.
Southdown Enthusiasts Club – W J Haynes Collection

Board were withdrawn after operation on Thursday 31 August 1939. The coaches were quickly converted for use as ambulances to deal with the expected mass of casualties. Passengers wishing to travel by road from London to places such as East Grinstead, Crawley and Horsham now had just the rather less frequent Southdown services as their only alternative to rail travel. It is known that at some point Southdown gained permission to carry passengers between Guildford and London although this ceased when Green Line services resumed. When the expected bombing failed to materialise some Green Line services were reinstated starting from 18 October 1939 although it was several months before services to the south of London started to reappear presumably because of the alternative frequent and mostly electric train services.

Some immediate reductions in Southdown's express services were introduced. On Monday 4 September Southdown announced that the South Coast Express service between Bournemouth and Margate would cease after operation on that day. Southdown coaches no longer ran west of Portsmouth with all Portsmouth to Bournemouth journeys provided by Royal Blue. Similarly the Gosport–Fareham–Alton–Aldershot–London service would also be withdrawn with immediate effect. It was also announced that the last coach from Hyde Park Road in Portsmouth to London would be at 1705 and the last coach from London at 1630 although this may have been a short term restriction and not applied to the other London services. A new London to Brighton 'Autumn' timetable – as it was described – began on Monday 11 September 1939 and was basically the same as the summer version except that

SOUTHDOWN
MOTOR SERVICES, LTD.
(In association with the Southern Railway Company)

Express Coach Service
BETWEEN

LONDON
AND

BRIGHTON

"Every Hour at the Hour"

TIME & FARE TABLE

11th SEPTEMBER, 1939 until WHITSUN, 1940

BRIGHTON DEPARTURES FROM
STEINE STREET COACH STATION. Telephone: Brighton 4033

LONDON DEPARTURES FROM
VICTORIA COACH STATION, S.W.1. Telephone: Sloane 0202

A SPECIAL SUNDAY COACH

WILL RUN BETWEEN

LONDON

Brixton, Streatham, Thornton Heath

AND

HORSHAM, FINDON

WORTHING

WITH CONNECTIONS TO

Lancing—Goring—Angmering and Littlehampton

Starting on Sunday, December 3rd, 1939, and UNTIL FURTHER NOTICE.

FROM LONDON READ DOWN	SUNDAYS ONLY			TO LONDON READ UP
8 30	LONDON (Victoria Coach Station)			8 20
8 44	BRIXTON (St. Matthew's Road)			8 4
8 54	STREATHAM COMMON (Chimes Garage)			7 56
7 1	THORNTON HEATH (The Pond)			7 49
9 4	WADDON (Cross Roads)			7 43
9 13	PURLEY (The Fountain)			7 37
9 17	COULSDON (Red Lion)			7 33
9 31	REDHILL (Market Hall)			7 19
9 43	HORLEY (Albert Road Corner)			7 7
10 0	CRAWLEY (Southdown Station)✱			6 50
10 3	CRAWLEY (Imperial Cinema)			6 45
10 25	HORSHAM (Southdown Office, Carfax)			6 25
10 35	SOUTHWATER (The Cock Inn)			6 15
10 40	WEST GRINSTEAD (Buck Barn, Cross Roads)			6 10
10 46	DIAL POST (The Crown Inn)			6 4
10 54	ASHINGTON (The Stores)			5 56
11 0	WASHINGTON (Southdown Office)			5 50
11 18	dep. Washington	Service	arr.	5 50
11 30	arr. Storrington (The Square)	1	dep.	5 40
11 50	dep. Washington	Service	arr.	5 18
12 3	arr. Steyning (White Horse)	22	dep.	5 3
11 7	FINDON (The Gun Inn)			5 43
11 20	WORTHING (Marine Parade)			5 30
11 20	dep. Worthing (The Dome)		arr.	5 16
11 30	arr. Lancing (Three Horse Shoes)	Services	dep.	5 6
11 39	arr. Shoreham (Bridge Hotel)	31 & 31G	dep.	4 57
11 49	dep. Worthing (The Dome)	Service	arr.	4 48
12 15	arr. Ferring-on-Sea (South Drive)	11	dep.	4 22
11 34	dep. Worthing (The Dome)		arr.	5 3
11 46	arr. Goring (The Church)		dep.	4 51
12 0	arr. Angmering (Preston Place)	Service	..	4 37
12 6	arr. Rustington (The Church)	31	..	4 31
12 17	arr. Littlehampton (East Street)		..	4 20

NOTES: ✱ Ten minutes' stop for refreshments   Times shown in light type are of Southdown Omnibus services, which connect with the London Service Coaches.

SEATS MAY BE BOOKED IN ADVANCE

at any SOUTHDOWN or LONDON COASTAL COACHES OFFICE or Agent or by Telephone or Letter to the nearest SOUTHDOWN OFFICE

SOUTHDOWN OFFICES

HORSHAM	CARFAX		Horsham	336
LITTLEHAMPTON	EAST STREET		Littlehampton	37
WASHINGTON	WAITING ROOM		Ashington	262
WORTHING	MARINE PARADE		Worthing	4666

MAIN LONDON AGENTS—LONDON COASTAL COACHES, LTD., VICTORIA COACH STATION
Buckingham Palace Road. S.W.1.   Sloane 0202

For Booking Agents, Fare Table and General Information. See Overleaf

---

journeys from Brighton at 1300, 1600, 1730 and 2100 and from London at 0800, 1300, 1600 and 2000 were marked as not running between 25 September 1939 and Whitsun 1940. Through running to Worthing via Brighton also ceased after 25 September. The leaflet was to full peace time standard and included the booking kiosks at Palace Pier and Kings Road in Brighton for the last time. Rationing of petrol and diesel fuel began on 23 September 1939 and, with most summer timetables due to end on Sunday 24 September, it is likely that leaflets had already been printed and circulated for normal winter schedules to apply from the following Monday. Due to a lack of surviving publicity material and licensing records for this period it is assumed that normal winter services, similar to those applying for 1938/9, were introduced between London and Eastbourne, Worthing, Bognor Regis and Portsmouth from Monday 25 September 1939.

By mid September there had been little sign of hostilities and no air attacks so the government allowed the reopening from 15 September of cinemas and theatres which had been closed at the outbreak of war for fear of mass casualties in the event of a direct hit. Most places of entertainment in London reopened by 17 December 1939 and many people were determined to celebrate one last Christmas before food rationing started to restrict their lives. All of these factors lead to great demand for the London services and much duplication which was limited only by the fuel rationing and availability of staff and vehicles. Although most of the official military traffic travelled by train there were the wives and girlfriends visiting men called up in the Services or the men themselves dashing home for brief visits who found the coach services cheaper and often more convenient.

The transport of parents of the children evacuated from London to the country also brought a significant boost to the coach services each weekend. On a normal Sunday during the quietest prewar winter months the number of journeys operated between London and Brighton was approximately 20 but with the arrival of the evacuees the company had to operate as many as 60 or 70 journeys. Similar increases had to be made for the services between London and Worthing, Eastbourne, Bognor Regis and Portsmouth although not necessarily in the same proportions. Although this extra traffic required the provision of many additional relief coaches it was nevertheless seen by the authorities as valuable in preserving morale at a time when families were being dispersed by the requirements of war. In addition bus connections had to be carefully arranged to take the parents with the least possible delay to the many small villages where their children were billeted. To offer maximum assistance Southdown, East Kent and Maidstone & District jointly produced a comprehensive timetable running to 57 foolscap pages and circulated a copy of this guide to each agent of London Coastal Coaches. Entitled 'Evacuation Facilities' it included full details of bus and coach facilities provided by the three companies to every town and village served in Sussex, Kent, Surrey and Hampshire. A poster advertising the evacuee facilities was also exhibited by each agent. It was therefore possible for a parent visiting their child billeted in one of the smallest and most isolated districts to obtain in the London area full details of fares, where to change, bus connections and times of arrival and return. The services were carefully arranged to ensure that parents did not have to wait an unreasonable time for a connection. The lack of any bombing caused many of those evacuated to Sussex from London to start returning home and this trend continued until Christmas when many parents decided not to send their children back after the holiday. The special service between Hove, Brighton and Robertsbridge, Darvell Hall Sanatorium was reduced to run on the second and fourth Sunday of the month by 16 November 1939.

Some reductions to London services occurred by December 1939 and new style timetable leaflets appeared at the same time. These condensed timetable information to one side of the sheet – usually with 'read up and read down' either side of the timing points – with all the remainder of the fares, conditions and booking information on the reverse. Leaflets were printed throughout in one colour using the familiar colours used in the past although the wartime paper quality meant some were more easily readable than others.

None of the leaflets issued around this time included the London office at 27 Princes Street, Hanover Square, which was presumably closed although it reappeared on leaflets issued in May 1940. Unlike the bus network which had generally introduced special blackout running times from 16 November 1939 no additional time was allowed on the coach services at this time.

Commencing on Friday 1 December coaches departed from Worthing Marine Parade daily at 0905, 1405 and 1705 with the first service running from Littlehampton. From London coaches departed at 0900, 1400 and 1800 with the final service continuing to Littlehampton. All services now ran via Dorking and Kingston although from Sunday 3 December an additional Sunday only service was introduced departing London at 0830 and operating via Redhill and Crawley. This returned from Worthing at 1730 and was designed to cater for the parents of evacuated children staying in the area. A special leaflet printed in purple was issued for this new service which featured all the usual bus connections along the route. Also, from the same date services between Bognor Regis and London were revised with northbound departures via Chichester, Midhurst and Guildford at 0830, 1330 and 1730 returning from London at 0830, 1330 and 1730. The service via Littlehampton, Arundel, Petworth, Dorking and Sutton which had previously run throughout the year had

withdrawn for the duration, probably from late September. On the Portsmouth service northbound journeys departed at 0805 from Hyde Park Road – which then ran via the Harbour Station Approach – and at 1300, 1600 (Sundays only) and 1700 from Clarence Pier. From London coaches departed at 0830, 1330 and 1730 daily although the last service terminated at Hyde Park Road and did not serve Southsea. All journeys ran via Hammersmith and Richmond to Kingston but no services were provided to the usual terminus at 241 Albert Road, Southsea although at this stage of the war no restrictions were in force in the area and no bombing had occurred. The Southdown office at this address is not included on the leaflet and may have closed by this time. Through bookings were still available to the Isle of Wight although particulars had to be obtained from booking offices and agencies. With the Gosport and Hayling Island routes now withdrawn bus connections were included at Cosham for Fareham, Havant, Emsworth and Hayling Island along with the Aldershot & District services at Godalming and Hindhead.

From Sunday 10 December the Eastbourne to London service was reduced to three coaches each way with departures from Royal Parade Garage at 0900, 1400 and 1700 returning from London at 0915, 1415 and 1815. Journey times remained unaltered and no additional time was allowed for blackout. Starting on Sunday 17 December the Brighton service was reduced to six journeys in each direction – a significant reduction on prewar schedules. Coaches now departed Brighton at 0800, 0900, 1000, 1400, 1700 and 1800. The 0900 and 1800 departures from Brighton served Hassocks, Burgess Hill and Cuckfield with others running via Bolney. The 1800 also served Hurstpierpoint and added ten minutes to the schedule. From London coaches departed at 0800, 0900, 1000, 1400, 1700 and 1800. Again, most ran via Bolney, Albourne and diverted via Hurstpierpoint to set down on request but the 0900 and 1700 from London operated via Cuckfield, Burgess Hill and Hassocks. The 0800 from London was a new innovation for winter and had previously been a summer only operation but obviously proved worthwhile and continued until the severe cutbacks in 1942. All coaches had a 10 minute refreshment stop at Crawley and no additional time was allowed for blackout running. The Day Return fare between London and Brighton was now 5/6d (28p). The weather during the winter of 1939/40 proved to be some of the worst on record with many weeks of snow and ice leading to freezing road conditions. Snow began to fall in Southern England on 12 December continuing into early February and leading to major disruption of road and rail services especially when combined with the difficulties of travelling in the blackout.

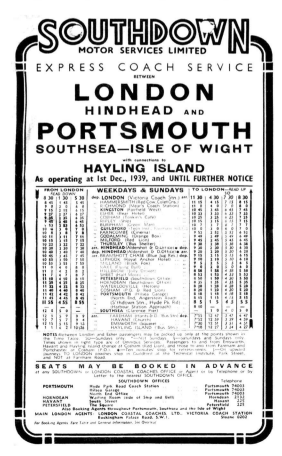

1940

With a return to better weather and little sign of hostilities there were some optimistic expectations of a near normal summer season along the South Coast. Many coach operators were even planning to start up their seasonal express services for the summer of 1940 confident that they could cope with a predicted twenty five per cent cut in fuel. The Minister of War Transport accepted the need for some seasonal increase in coach operations and allowed the fuel ration to be augmented in line with prewar seasonal use, providing total consumption did not go above 75% of that level. Operators in the South of England enjoyed record breaking passenger numbers over the Easter weekend which ran from 22 to 25 March. But, within a few weeks Britain really would be at war and this was the last normal Bank Holiday to be celebrated for over five long years. In April 1940 there was a meeting at Victoria Coach Station of Publicity Officers from the associated companies at which it was decided to mount a special campaign to encourage more midweek traffic and promote day return tickets. The possibility of introducing a standard format for timetables was also discussed although it was to be many years before this became a reality.

Some revisions to coach services occurred from Thursday 21 March mainly affecting afternoon and evening journeys. On the London to Eastbourne service the last coach from the coast was retarded to leave Royal Parade Garage at 1805 and allowed an extra 5 minutes running time between Caterham and Streatham. The Brighton service gained a later Sunday service in each direction, both running via Bolney, departing Brighton at 2000 and London at 2100. The 1800 and 2000 departures from Brighton gained an extra 5 minutes running time between Coulsdon and Streatham and the 2100 from London gained an extra 5 minutes running time between Streatham and Coulsdon. Otherwise the winter timetable continued in operation. The last coach from Worthing to London now departed from Marine Parade an hour later at 1805 and the extra Sunday service via Crawley

and Redhill also ran on Easter Monday 25 March along with an additional 2005 from Worthing via Dorking. An extra 5 minutes running time was allowed on the 1805 journeys from Worthing between Hook and Putney Bridge Station or Coulsdon and Streatham. On the Bognor Regis to London service the 1730 departure became Sunday and Bank Holidays only with an additional departure at 1830 from Bognor Regis. From London the 1730 departure was retarded by an hour to 1830 and a new 2130 journey introduced on Sundays and Bank Holidays. An extra 10 minutes running time was allowed between Esher and Putney Bridge Station on the 1730 and 1830 journeys from Bognor Regis. On the Portsmouth service coaches once more ran through to 241 Albert Road, Southsea although the Southdown office at this address remained closed. Northbound journeys now departed Southsea at 0750 – via the Harbour Station Approach – and at 1250, 1550 (Sundays only) and 1750 via Clarence Pier with a common route from Hyde Park Road. From London the evening coach was retarded to 1830 and a new 2100 introduced on Sundays and Bank Holiday Mondays. Both evening journeys terminated at Hyde Park Road and did not serve Southsea. An extra 10 minutes running time was allowed between Esher and Victoria Coach Station on the 1750 journey from Southsea.

On Monday 8 April Germany invaded Denmark and Norway and the so called phoney war came to an end. On Friday 10 May – the same day that Winston Churchill replaced Neville Chamberlain as Prime Minister – Germany invaded France, Belgium and Holland and within three weeks the British Expeditionary Force had retreated to Dunkirk and the survivors brought back to England. Prospects for the coming holiday season along the South Coast had indeed changed for the worst! Further leaflets were issued dated Saturday 11 May which would normally have marked the start of the Whitsun bank holiday had it not been cancelled at short notice due to the German invasion of the Low Countries. Times for the Eastbourne service remained the same but premium day return fares applied on Saturdays, Sundays and Bank Holidays from 11 May. The 2000 departure from

Brighton and 2100 from London were revised to run daily although the 2100 from London ceased after 9 September. Premium day return fares also applied on this service bringing the London to Brighton day return fare to 6/- (30p) on Saturdays, Sundays and Bank Holidays. The main Worthing service via Dorking remained unchanged but the additional Sunday only operation via Redhill and Crawley became daily departing from London at 0830 and extended to Littlehampton. The return service left Littlehampton at 1800 and Worthing at 1835. Premium day and period return fares applied on this service to Littlehampton (but not Worthing) with the day return fare from London increased from 7/- (35p) to 7/6 (38p) on Saturdays, Sundays and Bank Holidays.

Although there was no change to the main Bognor Regis service two additional journeys were introduced on Saturdays which illustrated the earlier optimistic hopes for a near normal summer season in 1940. These were described as 'through coaches' and departed Victoria at 0945 between 11 May and 7 September calling at all normal stops to Chichester and then either Selsey or Witterings, Bracklesham Bay and Earnley-by-Sea. The return journeys commenced from Earnley-by-Sea at 1420 or Selsey at 1430 and were due to run from 18 May to 14 September. Following the withdrawal from Dunkirk it was announced on Tuesday 4 June that holiday camps were now banned within 10 miles of the east and south coasts of England and the Isle of Wight and so it is likely that these extra services were withdrawn earlier than expected. Premium day and period return fares applied on this service to Bognor Regis (but not Chichester) with the day return fare from London increased to 8/- (40p) on Saturdays, Sundays and Bank Holidays. On the Portsmouth service the 1550 departure from Southsea ran additionally on Saturdays and an extra coach from London was introduced at 1030 on Saturdays and Sundays. Premium single and period return fares applied on Saturdays, Sundays and Bank Holidays from London to all stages, including connecting services, after Waterlooville.

With the German army now occupying the Channel coast of France and Belgium, the Luftwaffe moving on to airfields in Northern France and the German Navy having access to Dutch, Belgian and French ports the outlook for Britain appeared bleak. As described in chapter 2 new Defence Regulation 16A gave the RTCs powers to prohibit visits for the purpose of Holidays, Recreation or Pleasure in designated Defence Areas. The first Defence Area affecting Southdown was imposed on Wednesday 19 June and included the County Borough of Hastings and Borough of Bexhill. The first restrictions on entry to the Southdown area followed on Friday 21 June as journeys for the purposes of Holidays, Recreation and Pleasure were no longer permitted into parts of East Anglia, Kent and East Sussex as far west as Bexhill. By Thursday 4 July the restrictions on visitors were extended to include the resorts of Eastbourne and Seaford which were now effectively closed to holiday visitors. Southern parts of Hampshire including Portsmouth and Southsea followed on Saturday 6 July although it was still possible to buy coach tickets for such journeys. Drivers were now regularly stopped by armed soldiers at check points and all identity cards carefully scrutinised. Any person who was not an existing resident or did not have official business in the restricted area was liable to be turned back without recompense although Southdown timetable leaflets of this period make no reference to the visitor restrictions. Inevitably, there was a significant drop in demand for the coach services.

The first air raids across southern England now began and Hove's first attack came on 30 June. On 2 July 1940 the August Bank holiday – then on the first Monday in August – was officially cancelled. Later on Tuesday 2 July beaches along the South Coast were closed to the public and from Thursday 4 July seafront curfews were imposed which dealt a severe blow to hoteliers and traders in the various resorts. Fears of aiding a German invasion even meant the traditional seaside piers, so much a part of the holiday scene, were sectioned by separating the main pier structure from the promenade.

FREQUENT DAILY COACH SERVICES

FROM VICTORIA COACH STATION ARE RUNNING TO:—

DESTINATION	No. of Daily Departures	First Departure	Last Departure	DESTINATION	No. of Daily Departures	First Departure	Last Departure
Aldershot ...	15	9.15 a.m.	12 md'nt	Hindhead	3	8.30 a.m.	6.30 p.m.
Ascot	5	11.15 a.m.	9.15 p.m.	Horsham	3	8.0 a.m.	6.0 p.m.
Ashford (Kent)	5	8.45 a.m.	6.45 p.m.	Hove	6	8.0 a.m.	6.0 p.m.
Bagshot ...	15	9.15 a.m.	12 md'nt	Hythe	5	8.45 a.m.	6.45 p.m.
Benson	11	8.30 a.m.	9.0 p.m.	Lenham	10	7.0 a.m.	7.0 p.m.
Bexhill	2	9.0 a.m.	5.0 p.m.	Lewes	6	8.0 a.m.	6.0 p.m.
Binfield	5	11.15 a.m.	9.15 p.m.	Littlehampton ...	4	8.30 a.m.	6.0 p.m.
Birchington ...	8	7.0 a.m.	7.0 p.m.	Lyndhurst ...	4	9.0 a.m.	6.45 p.m.
Bognor Regis ...	3	8.30 a.m.	6.30 p.m.	Maidenhead ...	7	9.0 a.m.	9.0 p.m.
Bordon	15	9.15 a.m.	8.15 p.m.	Maidstone ...	9	9.0 a.m.	7.45 p.m.
Borough Green	7	9.0 a.m.	7.0 p.m.	Margate	8	7.0 a.m.	7.0 p.m.
Bournemouth ...	6	8.0 a.m.	6.45 p.m.	Milton Regis ...	8	9.45 a.m.	10.15 p.m.
Bracknell ...	5	11.15 a.m.	9.15 p.m.	Newhaven ...	6	8.0 a.m.	6.0 p.m.
Brighton ...	7	8.0 a.m.	9.0 p.m.	Newington (Kent)	11	9.0 a.m.	6.45 p.m.
Broadstairs ...	8	7.0 a.m.	7.0 p.m.	Oxford	12	9.0 a.m.	9.15 p.m.
Camberley ...	15	9.15 a.m.	12 md'nt	Peacehaven ...	6	8.0 a.m.	6.0 p.m.
Canterbury ...	9	7.0 a.m.	7.0 p.m.	Petersfield... ...	3	8.30 a.m.	6.30 p.m.
Charing ...	8	9.0 a.m.	7.45 p.m.	Platt	—	9.0 a.m.	7.0 p.m.
Chatham ...	12	9.0 a.m.	7.45 p.m.	Portslade ...	6	8.0 a.m.	6.0 p.m.
Christchurch ...	6	8.0 a.m.	6.45 p.m.	Portsmouth ...	3	8.30 a.m.	6.30 p.m.
Cliftonville ...	8	7.0 a.m.	7.0 p.m.	Rainham (Kent)	11	9.0 a.m.	6.45 p.m.
Cobham (Kent)	12	9.0 a.m.	7.45 p.m.	Ramsgate ...	8	7.0 a.m.	7.0 p.m.
Crawley ...	7	8.0 a.m.	9.0 p.m.	Reading ...	5	11.15 a.m.	9.15 p.m.
Dover	5	8.45 a.m.	7.30 p.m.	Rochester ...	12	9.0 a.m.	7.45 p.m.
Eastbourne ...	3	9.15 a.m.	6.15 p.m.	Rottingdean ...	6	8.0 a.m.	6.0 p.m.
Egham	15	9.15 a.m.	12 md'nt	Sandgate ...	5	8.45 a.m.	6.45 p.m.
Embrook	5	11.15 a.m.	9.15 p.m.	Seaford ...	6	8.0 a.m.	6.0 p.m.
Emsworth ...	3	8.30 a.m.	6.30 p.m.	Sheerness ...	3	9.30 a.m.	6.45 p.m.
Fareham	3	8.30 a.m.	6.30 p.m.	Shoreham (Suss.)	6	8.0 a.m.	6.0 p.m.
Farnborough				Sittingbourne ...	11	9.0 a.m.	6.45 p.m.
(Hants) ...	15	9.15 a.m.	12 md'nt	Southampton ...	6	8.0 a.m.	6.45 p.m.
Farnham ...	15	9.15 a.m.	12 md'nt	Southsea ...	3	8.30 a.m.	6.30 p.m.
Faversham ...	8	9.0 a.m.	6.15 p.m.	Strood ...	12	9.0 a.m.	7.45 p.m.
Folkestone ...	5	8.45 a.m.	7.45 p.m.	Sunningdale ...	15	9.15 a.m.	12 md'nt
Frimley ...	15	9.15 a.m.	12 md'nt	Sunninghill ...	5	11.15 a.m.	9.15 p.m.
Gillingham (Kent)	12	9.0 a.m.	7.45 p.m.	Tenterden ...	6	9.0 a.m.	7.45 p.m.
Godalming ...	3	8.30 a.m.	6.30 p.m.	Tollgate ...	12	9.0 a.m.	7.45 p.m.
Grayshott ...	3	8.30 a.m.	6.0 p.m.	Virginia Water	15	9.15 a.m.	12 md'nt
Green Street				Washington ...	4	8.30 a.m.	6.0 p.m.
(Kent) ...	8	9.0 a.m.	6.15 p.m.	Westgate ...	8	7.0 a.m.	7.0 p.m.
Handcross ...	7	8.0 a.m.	9.0 p.m.	West Grinstead	4	8.30 a.m.	6.0 p.m.
Harrietsham ...	10	7.0 a.m.	7.45 p.m.	West Malling ...	7	9.0 a.m.	7.0 p.m.
Haslemere... ...	3	8.30 a.m.	6.30 p.m.	Whitehall ...	15	9.15 a.m.	8.15 p.m.
Hastings ...	2	9.0 a.m.	5.0 p.m.	Winchester ...	6	8.0 a.m.	6.45 p.m.
Havant	3	8.30 a.m.	6.30 p.m.	Winnersh ...	5	11.15 a.m.	9.15 p.m.
Hayling Island ...	3	8.30 a.m.	6.30 p.m.	Wokingham ...	5	11.15 a.m.	9.15 p.m.
Henley	10	9.0 a.m.	9.0 p.m.	Worthing ...	6	8.0 a.m.	6.0 p.m.
High Wycombe	6	9.15 a.m.	9.15 p.m.	Wrotham	7	9.0 a.m...	7.0 p.m.
				Wrotham Heath	9	9.0 a.m.	7.45 p.m.

This table was included in the London Coastal Coaches' Coach Travel brochure for Summer 1940 and illustrates the frequent services from London to destinations across the south of England. Although produced in spring 1940 while the 'Phoney War' still prevailed, the numbers of departures seems to be based on the planned summer frequency and, as far as Southdown was concerned, included many journeys which would in practice involve bus connections. For instance, Worthing did not enjoy six direct departures at any time after the end of the 1939 summer timetable until services resumed in 1946 and the figure must have included bus connections via Brighton. The effect of the blackout has meant that last departures are generally earlier than prewar although Aldershot & District were still offering a midnight departure.

Hopes of a near normal summer season had gone forever.

Many of the air attacks in July had affected Channel convoys and coastal towns but as August progressed the Luftwaffe turned its attention to the destruction of RAF airfields. All Civil Aviation at Croydon Airport had stopped at the outbreak of war as it became a fighter airfield named RAF Croydon which Southdown coaches to Eastbourne, Brighton and Worthing via Crawley passed by along the adjacent Purley Way. At 1905 on Thursday 15 August a bombing attack was made on Croydon Aerodrome which resulted in the destruction of the Rollason Aircraft Works and severe damage to surrounding factories. The airport terminal buildings were partially destroyed but no damage was caused to aircraft or the aerodrome surface although five RAF personnel were killed and a number injured. Hopefully the 1800 coach to Brighton had already passed by safely. Curious crowds of people came from surrounding districts to see the first bomb damage in the London area although the novelty was short lived as Croydon Aerodrome and the nearby factory estates along the A23 road regularly attracted attention from German raiders. At some point by 19 August 1940 Purley Way, south of the Aerodrome Hotel was closed to all traffic and not reopened until July 1945. It is assumed that Southdown coaches

were diverted at Waddon Cross Roads via Denning Avenue, Warham Road and Brighton Road to Purley as this diversion did not affect any boarding or alighting points.

On the night of Saturday 24 August German bombers originally bound for the oil refineries at Thames Haven drifted off course and mistakenly dropped their loads on central London for the first time. It was to become a crucial turning point in the Battle of Britain as attacks on civilian targets had been specifically banned by Hitler who was still hoping Britain would sue for a negotiated peace. Winston Churchill ordered a retaliatory attack against Berlin on Monday 26 August which enraged Hitler who responded by ordering heavy raids on British cities including London. On Saturday 7 September the Luftwaffe launched a huge daylight raid on the East End of London which left 430 dead, over 1600 seriously injured, and thousands more homeless. The bombers were to return to London on 76 consecutive nights missing only 2 November when bad weather prevented their arrival. At first bombs poured down mainly on the dockland areas but the raids on London were soon broadened to cover the West End and the suburbs. Southdown's coaches were now running through some of the worst bombed areas of London with the ever present risk of plunging into a bomb crater in the darkened streets. Some damage was caused from time to time to the glass roof of Victoria Coach Station although considering the amount of destruction in the immediate area the premises were very fortunate in not suffering any major structural damage. During this period Southern train services from the London terminals where many main lines ran on viaducts and embankments were seriously disrupted by bomb damage and unexploded bombs – often for days on end – and the coach services provided a generally reliable alternative.

Invasion fears along the South Coast continued to grow throughout the summer. Local evacuations in Sussex started on Tuesday 10 September following a proclamation from the Home Office inviting all those with no official duties to take advantage of a voluntary evacuation scheme which was designed to leave the South Coast towns clear for the defenders in the event of an invasion. During the following days many decided to take up the offer and move to safer areas inland. Towns such as Hastings and Eastbourne were particularly affected and suffered a major reduction in population. The nightly bombing raids on London obviously made pleasure trips to the capital much less attractive whilst restrictions on visitors travelling to the 'Defence Areas' reduced demand for travel to the coast. As the darker evenings came most people tried to reach their homes or shelters before the sirens sounded and the timings of evening coaches towards London were generally adjusted so that they ran up to two hours earlier than previously. Last coaches from London were also advanced during the winter period to leave between 1730 and 1800 and so hopefully clear the London area before the air raids began in earnest. For several months drivers were faced with ever changing diversionary routes as roads were closed as a result of bomb craters or unexploded bombs. Fortunately there are no surviving records of any serious incidents involving Southdown coaches operating on the London services during this period.

From Monday 7 October the last northbound coach from Bognor Regis was advanced to 1700 while departures from London were revised to 0900, 1300 and 1730. None of the leaflets issued around this time include Southdown's London office at Hanover Square which was presumably closed. From the same date the Portsmouth service was reduced in line with the December 1939 schedule although all services now started from Hyde Park Road and none served Southsea where the sea front areas were now out of bounds to civilians. Northbound departures were at 0805 (via Harbour Station), 1305 and 1705 while services from London were at 0830, 1330 and 1730. An additional journey on Sundays only was introduced between London and Hindhead at 1030 returning at 1730 and these short workings featured in the wartime services up to final withdrawal in 1942. A revised winter timetable was introduced on the London to Eastbourne service from Thursday 17 October. Although the morning departures from each end remained the same the later ones were brought forward to take account of the blackout and the nightly blitz

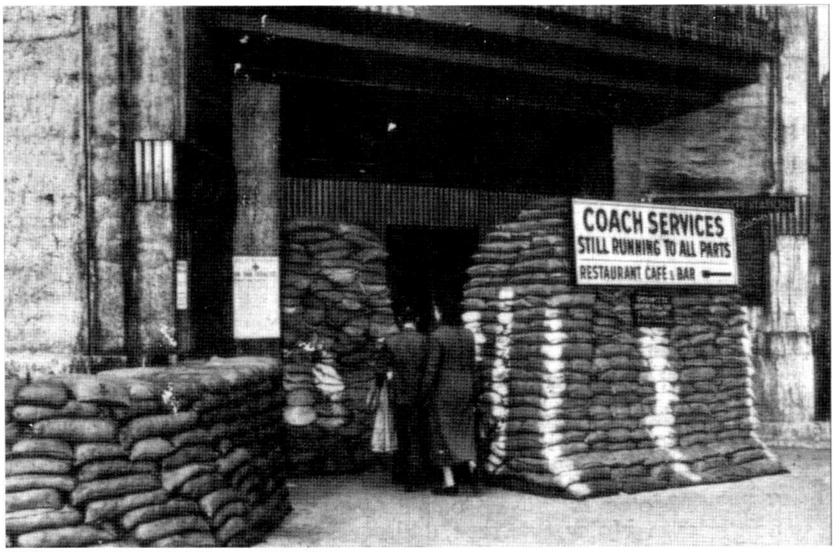

COACH SERVICES
STILL RUNNING TO ALL PARTS
RESTAURANT CAFE & BAR ▶

affecting London. Coaches now left Royal Parade Garage at 0900, 1300 and 1600 and London at 0915, 1315 and 1715. No additional blackout time was allowed except on the last London bound coach which gained an extra 5 minutes between Caterham and Streatham. The Southdown booking offices at 1 Cavendish Place (actually situated at 2A Cavendish Place) and Cavendish Place Coach Station were no longer included on the timetable leaflet and were presumably closed although at this stage of the war coaches still departed from the latter.

The Brighton service winter timetable started on Monday 4 November and was not much changed from the summer service except that coaches tended to run earlier with later journeys being withdrawn. Departures from Brighton were at 0700 (Not Saturdays and Sundays), 0800, 0900, 1000, 1400, 1600, 1700 and 1800 (Saturdays and Sundays). The 0900 and 1700 departures from Brighton ran via Hassocks, Burgess Hill and Cuckfield with others running via Bolney and the 0900 now also served Hurstpierpoint on request. From London coaches departed at 0800, 0900, 1000, 1400, 1600, 1700 and 1800. All ran via Bolney, Albourne and diverted via Hurstpierpoint to set down on request except the 0900 and 1700 from London which served Cuckfield, Burgess Hill and Hassocks. The 0700 from Brighton was a further new innovation for winter and had not previously featured even in summer. It was to continue until the severe cutbacks in August 1942 but did not reappear in 1946. All coaches had a 10 minute refreshment stop at Crawley and only the 1800 from Brighton was allowed an additional 5 minutes for blackout running between Coulsdon and Streatham. To encourage midweek travel the premium fares previously only applied in summer were now extended throughout the year on Saturdays, Sundays and Bank Holidays and this continued until the withdrawal of Southdown coach services in September 1942. The new timetable

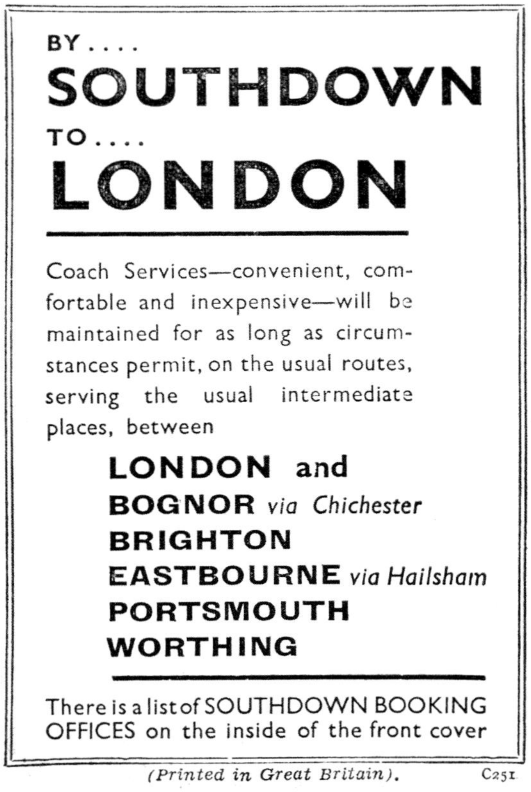

In the autumn of 1940 Southdown coaches on the London services now faced the full fury of the London 'Blitz'. Services were maintained by Leyland Tigers such as car 1099 (BCD 899) new in 1935 and not withdrawn until June 1957 – one of the last prewar Tigers to leave the fleet after serving around double its anticipated life span when new. It is a Harrington bodied Leyland Tiger TS7 fitted with folding sunroof and roof luggage rack for use on the London Express Services and is seen in postwar days near Victoria Coach Station after working a relief duty from Portsmouth.
Southdown Enthusiasts Club – Clark/Surfleet Collection

leaflet now carried a prominent notice – 'To ensure a seat bookings should be made at least 24 hours in advance'.

Another Brighton timetable (below) was issued commencing Thursday 28 November which further reduced the evening service towards London. An additional 1500 coach ran daily from Brighton but the 1700 became Sundays only and the 1800 was withdrawn completely. This meant the last departure from Brighton was at 1600 on Mondays to Saturdays and 1700 on Sundays. The

1600 from Brighton now served Hassocks, Burgess Hill and Cuckfield. No changes were made to the southbound service and all extra time for blackout running was deleted. Worthing services were also revised from the same date with an additional daily journey in each direction, all running via Dorking and Kingston. Coaches now departed Marine Parade at 0805, 0905, 1405 and 1605 and returned from London at 0900, 1400, 1600 and 1800. The 0905 from Worthing and 1600 from London were extended to or from Littlehampton. The extra 5 minutes running time continued on the last northbound service from Worthing. Some small improvements were also introduced on the Portsmouth service. A new journey departed from Hindhead at 0830 on Monday to Saturday and returned from London at 1230 on Saturday and 1630 on Monday to Friday. There was also an extra 1030 journey from London to Hindhead which ran daily except Saturdays. The last daily northbound journey now left Hyde Park Road an hour earlier at 1605 and no additional blackout running time was allowed in the London area.

The ban on holiday visits to many parts of the Southdown coastal area had proved very unpopular and difficult to enforce and was finally relaxed for the winter as from Saturday 7 December. With many people away for the traditional festive period the Luftwaffe launched a major incendiary raid against the City of London on Sunday 29 December destroying or badly damaging many historic buildings in the old part of the city. Firemen from many parts of Sussex were once again called upon to assist their London colleagues.

1941

Although we now know otherwise, the serious prospect of a German invasion along the South Coast seemed to return with the coming of spring and in March 1941 more local school children were sent away to safer areas. Whilst there was no prospect of a normal summer season as had been hoped for a year earlier, some limited improvements to services were introduced on Thursday 20 March. Lighter evenings allowed later last coaches to be provided once more although in most cases they remained significantly earlier than before the war.

On the Eastbourne service an extra departure each way was introduced and coaches now ran from Royal Parade Garage at 0800, 0900, 1400 and 1700 and from London at 0915, 1315, 1715 and 1815. The timing points in Eastbourne were changed and after Royal Parade coaches called at Leaf Hall and Pevensey Road Bus Station. No additional time was allowed on evening journeys and all coaches still called at The Star at Felbridge for a refreshment stop. The northbound afternoon service between Brighton and London was improved with the 1700 departure becoming daily and reinstatement of the 1800 departure on Sundays. The 1500 coach from Brighton introduced in the 28 November 1940 changes was withdrawn at this time. The 1700 service once again ran via Hassocks, Burgess Hill and Cuckfield and the 0700 from Brighton no longer stopped at Crawley for refreshments being timed to arrive at Victoria at 0920. No changes occurred to the southbound service at this time. The last northbound service from Worthing was altered to run one hour later leaving Marine Parade at 1705 and no longer had any allowance for blackout running but otherwise the winter timetable continued unaltered. A new 0730 departure from Bognor Regis was introduced on Mondays only and the afternoon northbound services revised to provide a 1645 on Saturdays and Sundays and a 1730 daily. No additional time for blackout running was allowed

on evening journeys towards London. Coaches departed from London at 0845, 1245 and 1800 daily with an additional journey at 2045 on Sundays. Late afternoon services on the Portsmouth route were revised with the last northbound service retimed to 1705 from Hyde Park Road and a new journey added at 1730 from Hindhead to London on Sundays. The last two journeys from London were run one hour later at 1730 as far as Hindhead and 1830 to Portsmouth although no services continued through to Southsea which had suffered devastating bombing raids by this time.

The ban on visitors to much of the Sussex coast was reintroduced from Tuesday 25 March and in the Southdown area extended from Hastings to Littlehampton. The service between Hove, Brighton and Robertsbridge Darvell Hall Sanatorium was still running on the second and fourth Sundays of each month in April 1941. Although an express service, it offered connections with bus services at Lewes, Cross-in-Hand and Heathfield and, unlike the London services, continued to appear in the bus timetable publications. A heavy bombing raid on Wednesday 16 April resulted in great destruction to the area around Victoria Coach Station in London. Some nineteen Royal Blue coaches were damaged when a shower of incendiary bombs fell close to where they were parked. It is not known if any Southdown vehicles were affected as coaches were normally parked overnight in Samuelsons' garage or in the coach station itself although by this stage of the blitz it seems likely they would have been dispersed in nearby streets to avoid any major concentration of resources.

Although Bognor Regis remained open to holiday visitors throughout the period of the war, whilst the London Express Services were in operation it hardly offered much in the way of normal seaside attractions! In this view at the eastern end of The Esplanade the crew of a light field gun practice take aim at some object out to sea. The remains of the pier can be seen in the background as well as the usual barbed wire intended to defend the town from a German attack – and also to prevent people and dogs wandering on to the mined beaches.
West Sussex County Council Library Service

TRAVEL TO . . .

LONDON

in comfort by . . .

SOUTHDOWN
Express Services

CHEAP DAY return fares are available from all points. Here are a few :

BRIGHTON 5/6*
CHICHESTER 6/6
EASTBOURNE 6/6*
WORTHING 6/6
BOGNOR 7/-†
PORTSMOUTH 7/6

* 6d. extra ⎱ on Saturdays, Sundays
† 1/- extra ⎰ and Bank Holidays

There is a list of SOUTHDOWN BOOKING OFFICES on the inside of the front cover

On Saturday 10 May, the Germans launched a major and sustained attack against London, the heaviest on the capital since the beginning of the Blitz in early September 1940. A third of all streets within Greater London were rendered impassable and some 155,000 families left without gas, water and electricity. Westminster Abbey, the House of Commons, Tower of London and the Royal Mint were all hit. Some 1,436 people were killed and 1,792 seriously wounded. Although not appreciated at the time, it proved to be the last heavy bombing raid on the capital and marked the end of 'The Blitz' on London as most of the Luftwaffe was moved east for the imminent invasion of the Soviet Union. The raids had killed more than 15,000 civilians and destroyed thousands of homes and businesses. Many industrial, residential and commercial districts including the historic heart of the City were in ruins. The end of the bombing raids brought another return of evacuees and the start of reconstruction work in London although building materials were in desperately short supply. In 1944, long after the coach services had been stopped, the V1 flying bombs and V2 rockets were to wreak further havoc and undo much of the rebuilding work that had been completed.

Starting on Thursday 29 May there was some further modest improvement on the Brighton service with the reintroduction of a 1900 departure from London. Northbound departures from Brighton were revised with the 1800 service becoming daily and running via Hurstpierpoint, Hassocks, Burgess Hill and Cuckfield although the 1600 journey was withdrawn. From Thursday 3 July the 1600 journey from London to Brighton was withdrawn on Sundays. Commencing on Sunday 3 August the 1600 from London to Worthing and Littlehampton was withdrawn on Sundays and to provide a replacement service the 1800 was extended through to Littlehampton on Sundays.

Reduced winter timetables commenced on Monday 13 October for what would prove to be the last full winter of operation for 5 years. Although the nightly air raids on London had now virtually ceased the evening departures were once again advanced by at least an hour. The London to Eastbourne service resumed its normal three journeys in each direction with departures now at 0800, 1300 and 1600 from Royal Parade Garage and at 0915, 1315 and 1715 from London. An additional 5 minutes was allowed for the northbound 1600 journey between Caterham and Streatham. The Brighton service winter timetable was similar to that applying from 20 March with last coaches running earlier and later journeys withdrawn. The Sunday only 1800 from Brighton did not appear for the winter. On the Worthing services all through coaches to or from Goring, Rustington and Littlehampton were withdrawn and passengers for these points for the remaining months of operation had to rely entirely on bus connections. Departures from Marine Parade were at 0805, 0905, 1405 and 1605 and from London at 0900, 1400, 1600 (Not Sundays) and 1800. The 1605 from Worthing was again allowed additional running time between Hook and Putney Bridge Station. Coaches from Bognor Regis now departed at 0730 (Mondays only), 0830, 1330 and 1615 with southbound services from London at 0845, 1245 and 1730 daily plus a 2015 journey on Sundays only. The 1615 coach from Bognor Regis was again allowed additional running time between Esher and Putney Bridge Station. On the Portsmouth route northbound journeys were

Express	HOVE—BRIGHTON—ROBERTSBRIDGE Sanatorium Via Lewes — Heathfield For Special Service between Robertsbridge Station and Sanatorium, see foot of opposite page.			Express
	SECOND AND FOURTH SUNDAYS OF EACH MONTH ONLY			
	Hove Station S.R. … … 12 15	**Robertsbridge** Darvell Hall Sanatorium…	**5 0**	
	Hove Seven Dials, Goldsmid Road … 12 20	**Brightling** … … …	**5 8**	
	Brighton Preston Circus, Stanley Road 12 24	**Heathfield** Vines Corner … …	**5 25**	
	Brighton Lewes Road, Bear Road … 12 26	**Cross-in-Hand** … … arr.	**5 30**	
	Lewes County Hall … … arr. 12 43			
	Seaford Clinton Place … 11 24	Cross-in-Hand … …	5 46	
	Newhaven Bridge Street … 11 50	Uckfield Bus Station …	6 11	
	Lewes County Hall … 12 20	East Grinstead Crown …	7 23	
	Haywards Heath Station S.R. … 11 31	**Cross-in-Hand** … … dep.	**5 30**	
	Chailey King's Head … 11 56	**Blackboys** Crown … …	**5 36**	
	Lewes County Hall … 12 31	**Ringmer** Post Office … …	**5 55**	
	Lewes County Hall … dep. 12 43	**Lewes** County Hall … arr.	**6 2**	
	Ringmer Post Office … … 12 50	Lewes County Hall … …	6 26	
	Blackboys Crown … … 1 9	Chailey King's Head …	6 59	
	Cross-in-Hand … … arr. 1 15	Haywards Heath Station S.R. …	7 22	
	East Grinstead Crown … 11 19	Lewes County Hall …	6† 0	
	Uckfield Bus Station … 12 45	Newhaven Bridge Street …	6 33	
	Cross-in-Hand … 1 10	Seaford Clinton Place …	7 0	
	Cross-in-Hand … … dep. 1 25	**Lewes** County Hall … dep.	**6 2**	
	Heathfield Vines Corner … 1 33	**Brighton** Lewes Road, Bear Road …	**6 19**	
	Brightling … … … 1 47	**Brighton** Preston Circus, Stanley Road	**6 21**	
	Robertsbridge Darvell Hall Sanatorium 1 55	**Hove** Seven Dials, Goldsmid Road …	**6 25**	
		Hove Station S.R. … …	**6 30**	
	† Connects at Library Corner with coach from Robertsbridge Sanatorium.			

The closure of the Holiday Camps on Hayling Island at the end of the 1939 season rendered the eleven almost new Leyland Cheetah coaches redundant. Some were stored for periods out of use during the war but, despite their low seating capacity and need for a two person crew, they could often be found on bus duties such as car 501 (EUF 501) seen at Emsworth operating a journey on the local service 44 to Westbourne. They returned to their intended duties after the war and all were withdrawn in 1956 following the opening of the new Langstone Bridge which obviated the need for small lightweight vehicles when crossing to and from Hayling Island.
J F Parke © Omnibus Society

similar to the November 1940 timetable but the 1630 from London to Hindhead did not reappear. The 1605 from Hyde Park Road once more gained an extra 10 minutes running time between Esher and Victoria.

As the war continued the operation of the London express services became increasingly difficult due to a shortage of coaches and staff, fuel rationing and a reduced demand for recreational travel as a bombed and scarred London was no longer the same attraction for visitors. The ban on visitors to the coastal area between Hastings and Littlehampton was suspended from Friday 7 November but several of the south coast towns had been partially evacuated and the continued threat of invasion inevitably led to less demand for long distance travel.

1942

By the early months of 1942 military set backs in the Middle East and the advance of the Japanese in Malaya along with the continuing heavy loss of merchant shipping in the Atlantic were about to have a particularly damaging effect on bus and coach operations. Most long distance coach services had avoided the fate of the Green Line services around London at the outbreak of war when all were withdrawn from 1 September 1939 but later reintroduced in modified form. Many purely seasonal coach services from London to South Coast destinations were even allowed to continue in the summer of 1940 although after July the seaside destinations served were hardly welcoming to visitors. During the 1940/1 blitz,

while the main line railways had experienced great difficulties from air raid damage particularly around London, the coach services often provided a more reliable alternative as road traffic could find a way around almost any bombing incident. But, services from London to Birmingham had already stopped at very short notice on 4 June 1941 at the behest of the RTCs and Coventry to Newcastle services followed on 21 July 1941.

Some minor changes to Southdown services were introduced from Wednesday 1 April with evening services again altered to run later. Timings on the Eastbourne remained as for winter 1941/2 except that the last journeys in each direction were retarded by one hour to 1700 from Eastbourne and 1815 from London. On the Worthing service the last northbound service was altered to run an hour later departing Marine Parade at 1705. The afternoon services from Bognor Regis were revised to depart at 1615 on Saturdays and Sundays and 1730 daily. Services from London remained unaltered except that the last journeys were retarded by 30 minutes to 1745 daily and 2045 on Sundays only. The Portsmouth service reverted to the timetable run from March 1941 but with the addition of a 2100 journey from London on Sundays only. All extra blackout running time was removed from the evening services to London. The ban on visitors covering the coastal areas of Sussex between Hastings and Littlehampton was reintroduced from Wednesday 15 April and continued until after the withdrawal of the coach services.

Southdown leaflets still made no reference to the restrictions but by April 1942 Maidstone & District had added the following warning to its London to Tenterden timetable leaflet.

RESTRICTED AREAS

We would respectfully remind passengers that the Company cannot be held responsible if the authorities do not permit their entry into restricted areas and cannot entertain any claim for refund of fares paid.

Commencing on Monday 11 May the 1600 journey from London to Worthing which ran on Monday to Saturday was withdrawn. No doubt as a wartime economy the remaining stock of April timetable leaflets was overprinted in black to delete this journey. With an urgent need for economies in labour, fuel and tyres the Minister of War Transport announced at the end of May 1942 that the extension of the war area made it necessary to achieve further substantial economies in the consumption of motor fuel for civilian purposes by reducing those travel facilities not directly connected with the national war effort. Travel was now actively discouraged and *"Is Your Journey Really Necessary?"* became one of the best known slogans of the day. Pleasure motoring was banned after 30 June 1942 even where motorists still had petrol coupons issued before the restriction was imposed.

To save scarce paper supplies, remaining copies of the Bognor Regis leaflet originally issued for the 4 July 1942 changes were overprinted for the final 5 August 1942 timetable. The midday journeys have had SATS added over the timing columns and the date of commencement altered.

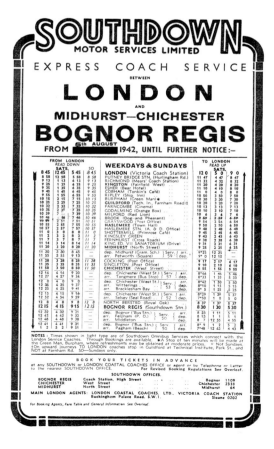

Single and Day Return Tickets may not be booked earlier than three days in advance on the date of travel. **Period Return Tickets** may be booked for travel on any day providing the date of return is not less than three full days after the date of booking. Day and Period Return passengers must state exact time and date of return journey at time of booking, otherwise a ticket cannot be issued. The Company accepts no responsibility in the case of passengers failing to travel at the times so specified

The Regional Transport Commissioners were now instructed under an order issued by the Minister of War Transport to withhold fuel rations for long distance coaches except in cases where real hardship would be caused to outlying districts or to troops in isolated camps. Despite a lack, in many cases, of alternative rail facilities the entire network of coach services from London to East Anglia ceased from 30 June 1942. Further reductions in Southdown coach services were introduced from Saturday 4 July and revised conditions affecting advance bookings started from this time. Previous leaflets had stressed the need for prospective passengers to reserve seats as far in advance as possible but now Single and Day Return Tickets could no longer be booked earlier than *three days in advance* of the date of travel. Period Return Tickets could be booked to travel on any day provided the date of return was not less than three full days after the date of booking. When booking Day or Period Return tickets passengers were required to state exact time and date of return journey at time of booking as open dated return tickets would no longer be allowed. Despite significant reductions since 1939 the Brighton service was, as expected, still the most comprehensive with four daily journeys each way plus additional services on Saturdays and Sundays. Coaches now departed Brighton at 0700 (Not Saturdays and Sundays), 0800, 0900, 1000, 1400 (Saturdays) and 1800 (Daily via Burgess Hill, Sundays only via Bolney). From London there were departures at 0900, 1000 (Sundays), 1400 (Saturdays), 1700, 1800 and 1900. Also from the same date the 0700 (Mondays only) and 1615 (Saturdays and Sundays) from Bognor Regis were withdrawn although southbound services remained unaltered at this time.

Further revised timetables were introduced on Wednesday 5 August and proved to be last before final withdrawal of coach services 'for the duration'. A sign of the changing and difficult times is illustrated by the strap line on the leaflets which changed from 'Seats may be booked in advance' in April 1942 to 'Book your ticket in advance' by August 1942. The Eastbourne service was reduced so that the lunch time journeys at 1300 from Royal Parade Garage and 1315 from

London ran on Saturdays only. On the Brighton service southbound services remained unaltered but the 0700 from Brighton which had run on Mondays to Fridays since November 1940 was withdrawn. The lunch time departures on the Worthing service at 1405 from Worthing and 1400 from London were reduced to run on Saturdays only although other journeys remained unaltered. Similarly, on the Bognor Regis service the 1330 from Bognor Regis and 1245 from London were reduced to operate on Saturdays only. Three daily journeys each way remained between Portsmouth and London plus an extra return trip from Hindhead to London on Monday to Saturday. This service alone among the remaining Southdown London routes retained its daily lunchtime departures in each direction. The Sunday only 1730 from Hindhead to London was withdrawn along with the Monday to Saturday 1030 from London to Hindhead. Although the leaflet still proclaimed services to Southsea and Isle of Wight, coaches had not proceeded further than Hyde Park Road since Summer 1940 and a ban on holiday visitors to the island was in force throughout most of the year.

On 6 September 1942 the Ministry of War Transport announced that travel by road and rail would be further restricted during the coming winter to make room for the growing volume of military and other essential traffic and also to save fuel and rubber. In addition the Green Line coach services of the London Passenger Transport Board would be withdrawn after Tuesday 29 September and replaced where necessary by the strengthening or extension of existing bus services to act as feeders to and from convenient railway stations or other interchange points. Other long distance coach services, including the few still running into London, were also to be discontinued except where portions of the routes could be retained where it was necessary to serve rural areas which would otherwise be isolated. Tuesday 29 September 1942 therefore marked the end for the Southdown express coach services – until a date in the future that few would have dared to predict at this uncertain time. To the very end Southdown had maintained its London outstation with coaches and staff exposed to the nightly bombing raids during the worst of the 1940/1 blitz. Crawley Coach Station closed with the withdrawal of coach services and it is not known for certain what use was made of the premises during the war years although it is likely to have attracted the attention of the Military authorities. It is possible that at some time it was used to store spare seats from the old bodies removed from the TD1s and TD2s which were later used to upgrade the seating in some utility Guys.

Some very limited replacement facilities were provided. One additional morning journey ran from Warninglid to Haywards Heath on bus service 83 serving passengers in the Five Cross

Roads area who previously travelled by coach and a limited stop service commenced between Bognor Regis and Horsham via Chichester, Midhurst and Petworth. This service, on which there were initially four through journeys in each direction, together with one Midhurst–Horsham and one Bognor–Midhurst working, covered part of the former Bognor to London coach service as far as Midhurst and also strengthened bus service 59 on which traffic was already heavy. Full details appear in chapter 5.

It is perhaps surprising that Southdown's London coach services were allowed to continue for as long as they did given that in many cases they paralleled frequent Southern electric train services. Within the company's area the Eastbourne service ran alongside an hourly bus service 92 as far as East Grinstead where rail connections could be made for London – although no attempt was made to extend buses to the railway station after the coaches ceased. The Brighton service also had various parallel bus services which could feed into the rail network at Hassocks, Haywards Heath and Crawley while the Worthing route ran alongside bus service 2 as far as Horsham Station. On the Portsmouth road bus services 40 and 42 ran as far north as Petersfield Station where rail connections could be made onward to Guildford and London. The Bognor and Chichester service was a different proposition as it ran through areas where train services had already been reduced and journeys between, say, Bognor and Guildford involved a

The Express Coach Services have been suspended by order of the Ministry of War Transport and the sandbags have been removed from the front entrance of Victoria Coach Station – to be replaced by a newsvendor – in this post 1942 scene. But, the Coach Station is still fully occupied and the Restaurant and Bar remain open. Surplus office accommodation has been taken over by the National Fire Service and the Enquiry Office transformed into an important information centre for local bus services throughout the country. Note the minimal amount of road traffic and pedestrians at this busy junction.
London Coastal Coaches collection

EXPRESS COACH SERVICES

LONDON

and

THE COAST

By Order of the Ministry of Transport all Southdown London Express Services have been

SUSPENDED

UNTIL FURTHER NOTICE

(Printed in Great Britain).

number of changes whether travelling by road or rail. Given the ability of some operators, including Royal Blue, to persuade the RTCs of the need for replacement limited stop services, such as Portsmouth to Southampton which was already adequately served by rail, it is perhaps odd that no direct replacement link was provided in place of this coach service. Ironically, the ban

on visitors covering the coastal areas of Sussex between Hastings and Littlehampton was eventually lifted on 24 October 1942 just after the London services had been withdrawn for the duration.

In a few cases the RTCs allowed services to continue if truncated at a suitable rail connecting point as happened in the case of Beacon Motor Services of Crowborough which had operated a regular coach service between Crowborough and London via East Grinstead since 1926. The service was suspended between East Grinstead and London and the timetable revised to provide a morning and an evening trip daily from Crowborough to East Grinstead Station via Nutley. The timetable was arranged to connect with trains to and from London Victoria with return departures from East Grinstead delayed when necessary to ensure the connection. After the war this service, now fully restored to London, passed to Southdown along with the local bus services in the Crowborough area in September 1949 with the takeover of Beacon Motor Services.

In November 1942 some 32,000 square feet of the Victoria Coach Station yard was requisitioned by the War Office for allocation to various service units, and the London Coastal Coaches publicity offices, chartroom and other offices on the first and mezzanine floors were taken over by the National Fire Service. Although the coach station itself was quiet the restaurant remained open for business and the Central Enquiry Bureau which had dealt with public enquiries for Express coach services was enlarged in 1942 to provide information on bus services throughout the country. This facility, which was commended by the Press at the time, must have been welcomed by service personnel and those

Following the enforced withdrawal of the London Express Services in September 1942 Southdown introduced a limited stop service between Bognor Regis and Horsham via Chichester, Midhurst and Petworth. Coaches were normally used and at the end of hostilities car 1143 (CCD 743), a Leyland Tiger TS7 with Beadle body, is seen heading north at Petworth Square. The service was reduced in January 1945 and finally ceased in March 1946 shortly after the return of the London services.
C F Klapper © Omnibus Society

members of the public who were often obliged to move to parts of the country previously unknown to them. At a company Board Meeting on Thursday 24 February 1943 it was agreed that Southdown's proportion of the cost for the year commencing 1 January 1943 would be £750 and it was subsequently agreed to renew this for the same sum for 1944. This facility remained open throughout the war and became a permanent feature of London Coastal Coaches range of services when coach operations recommenced. By the time that London faced its next ordeal with the arrival of the V1 flying bombs in June 1944 Southdown's express coaches were no longer a part of the transport scene.

Southdown retained one express service and by late 1944 the journeys each way between Robertsbridge Station and Darvell Hall Sanatorium appear to have been withdrawn. The through service to the Sanatorium from Hove continued to run on the second and fourth Sundays of each month throughout the war.

Tours & Excursions

The outbreak of war in September 1939 and subsequent introduction of fuel rationing brought a drastic reduction in the number of excursions and tours that could be offered although they were not totally banned at this time. With many hotels requisitioned soon after the declaration of war it is likely that Southdown's remaining coach cruise programme for 1939 had to be cancelled although no definite information is to hand. The last departure of the season – a special 12 day autumn tour to Wales, Devon and Cornwall was scheduled to leave on Monday 2 October but may not have survived in the circumstances.

At the start of the war Harvey's Coaches of Eastbourne sold their Excursions & Tours licence to Southdown in September 1939 by which time the prospects for the seaside excursion business looked less than promising. Some local excursions were run as permitted by the availability of drivers, vehicles and fuel and in early 1940 the Minister of Transport accepted the need for a limited seasonal increase in coach operations.

Although it might have been assumed that Southdown's coach cruise programme would have been abandoned soon after the outbreak of war the company had firm plans to operate some holidays in 1940. Although it was unable to offer such variety as in previous years it hoped to run one departure from Brighton each week including

After the withdrawal of the last Express Services from Victoria Coach Station in October 1942 the departure area was used for the parking of Military vehicles as well as coaches employed on contract work in the London area.
As none of the vehicles – including the Samuelson's Leyland Tiger coach – appear to have headlamp masks, this photograph was taken after September 1944 when blackout restrictions began to be relaxed for inland areas. Some temporary repairs to the glass roof are evident but, considering the severe damage inflicted in the vicinity, the Coach Station buildings remain relatively unscathed.
London Coastal Coaches collection

Any wartime activities by Southdown's touring coaches appear to have escaped the camera and it is not known if any were hastily adapted to run the final tours of the 1939 programme. Car 1815 (UF 8829) is a Leyland Lioness LTB1 with Harrington 20 seat bodywork that was extensively modernised in 1937 although the longer Covrad radiator was changed in postwar days
Author's collection

This extract from the London Coastal Coaches' Coach Travel brochure for Summer 1940 suggests that it was not just Southdown who planned to offer coach holidays for the coming season although there is a nice reference to 'coach cruises'. By the time the summer season arrived few among the civilian population would be minded to take holidays or annual outings by the seaside as large swathes of coastline were banned to visitors and hotels closed or requisitioned by evacuated companies and government departments.

OUR TRAVEL SERVICE

BY glancing at our name and address on the front cover, you may recognise us as specialists in coach travel. Based on years of experience, we are in a position not only to book your coach seats, but to give you information and advice on anything pertaining to motor coaching. Despite the inevitable restrictions imposed by the War, our Travel Service is being maintained, features of which are:

COACH SERVICES. We are able to advise you as to times, picking-up points, connections, etc., of services to towns and villages in all parts of the country.

COACH TOURS. The number of coach cruises and inclusive tours will naturally be limited this year, but we should be pleased to give you full details of such delightful holidays. We must urge you, however, to BOOK EARLY.

PRIVATE HIRE. Your firm or your sports club will undoubtedly wish to hold their annual outing, in which case we should be most happy to quote you for one, two, or a fleet of modern luxury coaches, at the lowest rates, consistent with service.

ENTERTAINMENTS. Such an outstanding spectacle as the Tattoo will not take place, but there will be many other entertainments, theatrical shows, sporting events, etc., this year. We can not only book your seat, but in many cases can supply you with your admission ticket.

We, therefore, ask you the favour of keeping this "Coach Travel" booklet for reference, and to kindly note our address on the front cover. A final point—WE CHARGE NO BOOKING FEE FOR ANY COACH TICKET.

For Comfort, Cheapness & Reliability— **TRAVEL BY COACH**

one seven day tour to Devon and Cornwall at an inclusive fare of £13 and one six day tour to North Wales at an inclusive fare of £11. A high standard of comfort, both in the vehicles and accommodation at the hotels was promised and prices were pegged at prewar levels despite the rising cost of fuel and accommodation. Given the perilous position of the country by the early summer of 1940 it seems unlikely that the programme was in fact operated. Unfortunately no copies of the brochure have been located but the tours probably followed similar itineraries to those featured in the 1939 programme subject to availability of hotels. The London office at 27 Princes Street, Hanover Square, W1 was maintained until 24 December 1940 when all prospects of an early return to normal operations had disappeared.

The continued operation of seaside excursions dismayed the Prime Minister when on a visit to the 3rd Division in July 1940 he noted that, whilst the army lacked any vehicles to patrol the 30 miles of coastline for which they were responsible, there were still coaches plying for pleasure trips on nearby Brighton seafront. Despite his comments no attempt was made to curtail such operations at this time although many coaches were being requisitioned for military service. But, in August 1941 the RTCs were instructed to revise the allocation of fuel supplies to operators of coaches which was still based on a percentage reduction of the mileage from before the war. In future supplies would be on a discretionary basis

The availability of coaches for normal 'peacetime' private hires was obviously restricted by fuel rationing which began on 23 September 1939 although adverts for the hire of Southdown coaches appeared in the bus timetables until at least April 1941. A further restriction on fuel supplies for non essential hires was introduced by the RTCs in August 1941 and effectively stopped such activities until after the war.

with operators required to prove they were they were performing a useful and necessary function. The RTCs would now have the power to determine which work was not essential in their opinion and this usually marked the end of leisure excursions and private hire. With visitors banned from many coastal areas and residents moving away to safer areas inland the demand for coach excursions was obviously reduced and it is believed that these had all ceased by the autumn of 1941. Alpha Coaches of Brighton are known to have run their last trip from Brighton to Fletching on Saturday 11 October 1941. Much more stringent controls introduced in 1942, including the withdrawal of all the remaining London express services, would have prevented the use of fuel for such work.

Private Hire & Contracts

The availability of coaches for normal 'peacetime' private hires was obviously restricted by fuel rationing which began on 23 September 1939 although adverts for the hire of Southdown coaches appeared in the bus timetables until at least April 1941. As noted above a further restriction on fuel supplies for non essential hires was introduced by the RTCs in August 1941.

In late August 1939, about a week before the actual declaration of war, Southdown started work on the conversion of 24 Leyland Tiger TS7 coaches for Ambulance work each capable of carrying ten stretchers. Although there are unfortunately no surviving detailed records of the use to which the Southdown ambulances were put it is known that in neighbouring fleets

Private Hire

LATEST LUXURY COACHES AT MODERATE RATES

═══════════

ASK FOR QUOTATION AND ALL OTHER INFORMATION FROM ANY SOUTHDOWN OFFICE OR DIRECT FROM PRIVATE HIRE DEPT., STEINE ST., BRIGHTON.

they were at first used in the evacuation of hospital patients to safer areas outside the danger zones. On 1 September 1939 ten specially converted Ambulance trains were run from London stations to Brighton, Eastbourne and Hastings and it is likely that the coaches assisted in dispersing stretcher patients to local hospitals. As the danger of invasion loomed in September 1940 patients were transferred by ambulance trains from Brighton to Macclesfield, Portsmouth to Leeds and Chichester to Warwick, Preston and Blackburn. In May 1940 they carried soldiers wounded in the fighting around Dunkirk after their return to the UK and later assisted with civilian casualties following serious air raids. Manning was required twenty four hours a day usually on an eight hour shift basis. Some of the converted ambulances were intended exclusively for use by the civilian population in the event of air raids while others were for use by the Military Authorities. Later some of the first casualties to reach this country from the Normandy beaches in 1944 were transferred to hospital in ambulances converted from coaches.

Civilian evacuation began on Friday 1 September 1939 and with Sussex one of the largest reception areas for evacuees there was obviously a busy period providing transport from railway stations to billets. By 1940 local children were being evacuated from the south coast and, whilst most of the longer journeys were undertaken by rail, buses and coaches were usually needed to bring evacuees from assembly points at their schools to the departure station. The period of so called Phoney War during winter 1939/40 allowed Britain to build up its home defences and Southdown coaches were used to transport workmen required for airfield construction often travelling far from their Sussex bases.

Although some 330,000 soldiers were evacuated from the beaches at Dunkirk they were forced to abandon their modern equipment including transport on and around the beaches of Dunkirk. On arrival back in England most of the troops were moved inland by a carefully planned railway operation although in some cases coaches ferried them to the nearest railhead. Air attacks were expected to start at any time and it was essential for the returning Forces to be moved to inland camps and barracks as quickly as possible. Southdown coaches were used as temporary transport for unequipped or newly formed military units often involving the provision of vehicles at all hours of the day and night for troop movements. Following the BEF withdrawal from Dunkirk there was an urgent need to build up the coastal defences with many coaches used every day taking building workers and labourers to the various sites. Vehicles were usually hired by the Ministry of Labour, who were responsible for the labour force, although others were supplied direct to contractors or subcontracted by other operators.

Throughout the war Southdown coaches and buses were often to be found providing emergency substitute services when rail traffic was disrupted by enemy action especially during the blitz period extending from September 1940 to May 1941. Following the severe air raid on Brighton on 25 May 1943 Southdown buses worked between Brighton Station and Hove, Preston Park and Falmer to link with other rail services. Other coaches were engaged on a long term contract for the E.N.S.A. organisation conveying concert parties throughout the country, usually visiting a different military camp or disused theatre each night. Organised from headquarters in the disused Drury Lane Theatre in London, the parties set off by coach for tours of usually two weeks' duration. Southdown coaches were also used to ferry personnel between the various Royal Naval shore establishments.

A top secret project at the time was the Mulberry Harbours construction which took place in Sussex and Hampshire Harbours during 1943/4 in preparation for the D-Day landings and required the transport of thousands of workers to often remote sites. There was a relative lull in large scale enemy bombing raids of Britain's cities after May 1941 which allowed some rebuilding and repairs to damaged housing but the start of the V1 flying bombs campaign in June 1944 caused further widespread destruction to property. Southdown coaches were soon employed in transporting available Sussex building labour to provide first aid repairs in Kent where thousands once again found themselves homeless. In the later stages of the war many Italian and German PoWs were employed for road construction and work on the land with coaches provided to take them from their camps to places of work. Such was the varied work undertaken by Southdown's coaches during the war.

Although normal private hire duties were severely curtailed by summer 1941 there was still plenty of work to occupy Southdown's coach fleet in wartime and car 1220 (FUF 320) still looks in excellent condition in this 1943 view taken at Taunton. It is one of a batch of fourteen Leyland Tiger TS8s with Harrington rear entrance bodywork delivered in summer 1939. This vehicle was converted to a 21 seat Touring Coach in 1949 and remained in the fleet until April 1956.
S L Poole

At the outbreak of war some of the planned 1939 deliveries were still outstanding although at this early stage of the war most orders in hand were completed, albeit with some delays. When it appeared on 31 August 1939 car 249 had the distinction of being the last to be registered for Southdown before the war commenced. Sixteen of the Leyland TD5s on order – cars 250-265 – arrived between October and December 1939 with the last four registered as from 30 December 1939. A further 14 Tiger TS8 buses with

Harrington rear entrance bodywork were still awaited. On these cars – 1472 to 1485 – the front dash panel was flush with the driver's cab giving a neater appearance to the final batch of a very well regarded class of buses. Ten of the batch arrived during November and December 1939 but four – 1480, 1481, 1484 and 1485 – were delayed until 1940 and the final one – car 1485 – was delivered on 15 March 1940. During the war the 1400 class vehicles were subject to a number of modifications as shown later in this chapter.

Car 251 (GCD 351) was one of 12 Leyland Titan TD5s with Park Royal highbridge bodies that entered service in November 1939 after the start of hostilities. Seen at the end of the war, still retaining the dark green roof intended to protect buses from attack by enemy aircraft, it is operating the long standing cross town Bognor Regis local service 55. A nearside fog light was fitted to Southdown buses starting from around 1943 and can usually distinguish a postwar photograph. A new Park Royal body was fitted in March 1950 and car 251 was finally withdrawn from Southdown service in January 1962
Southdown Enthusiasts Club – Clark/Surfleet Collection

What proved to be the final delivery of double deck buses ordered before the outbreak of war included four Leyland Titan TD5s with Park Royal lowbridge bodies which arrived in late December 1939. Seen after the war beside Worthing Garage is car 262 (GCD 362) which was rebodied with a Park Royal highbridge body in April 1950. It was sold to J. Light of Lewes for scrap in March 1961 but remained in their yard for many years.
Southdown Enthusiasts Club – Clark/Surfleet Collection

The final delivery of 1400 class buses comprised 14 Harrington bodied Leyland Tiger TS8 models and all arrived after the start of hostilities. Deliveries began in November 1939 and car 1479 (GCD 379), seen after the war at Hassocks Railway Station, illustrates the detail differences to earlier vehicles with a flush fitting front dash panel resulting in an even more handsome design. Unlike earlier batches which had a cream roof and window surrounds no photographs are known to exist of the late 1939 batch in this livery. As dark green began to be applied to the roofs of all buses at the start of the war, despite no air raids occurring by late 1939, it may be assumed that this was done before these buses entered service.
Southdown Enthusiasts Club – Clark/Surfleet Collection

The Southdown fleet at the outbreak of war consisted of the following vehicles:

237 Double deck buses comprising:
1 Tilling-Stevens Express B10A2 open top new 1929
23 Leyland Titan TD1 open top new 1929
31 Leyland Titan TD1 covered top new 1930-2
16 Leyland Titan TD2 new 1932-3
16 Leyland Titan TD3/TD3c new 1934
51 Leyland Titan TD4/TD4c new 1935-6
99 Leyland Titan TD5 new 1937-9

156 Single deck buses
36 Tilling-Stevens Express B10A2 new 1929-30
6 TSM Express B10A2 for Hayling Island services new 1931
6 TSM Express B39A6 for Hayling Island services new 1933
14 Leyland Cub suitable for one person operation new 1936-7
6 Leyland Cub for Hayling Island services new 1936-7
30 Leyland Tiger TS7 new 1935-6
42 Leyland Tiger TS8 new 1938-9
4 Leyland Tiger TS7T/TS8T for service 97 new 1934-5
10 Shelvoke & Drewry new 1930-8 (ex Tramocars)
2 Dennis Falcon new 1939

313 Coaches
18 Tilling-Stevens B9B new 1926-7 (rebodied in 1935)
18 Tilling-Stevens B10B2 new 1929-30 (rebodied 1934)
46 Leyland Tiger TS2 new 1930-1 (19 rebodied in 1935-6)
24 Leyland Tiger TS4 new 1932-3
3 Leyland Tiger TS6 new 1934
89 Leyland Tiger TS7 new 1935-7 (including 24 converted to ambulances August 1939)
47 Leyland Tiger TS8 new 1937-9
5 Leyland Cub touring coaches new 1933-6
29 Leyland Cub new 1936-8
11 Leyland Cheetah LZ3/LZ4 for Hayling Island services new 1938-9
17 Leyland Lioness LTB1 touring coaches new 1930-3
6 Leyland Tigress RLTB3 touring coaches new 1936

Full details of the Southdown fleet as at 1 September 1939 appear in Appendix 1.

At the company Board Meeting held on Thursday 31 August just days before the start of hostilities it was reported that the following rolling stock had been ordered:

26 Leyland Titan   14 Leyland Tiger
In addition the following additional orders were authorised:
13 single deckers   27 coaches

Since the previous Board Meeting on Thursday 22 June 1939 it was confirmed that the following vehicles had been sold:

28 Leyland TD1/Short Bros
14 Tilling-Stevens Express B10A2/Short Bros
2 Tilling-Stevens Express B10A2/Harrington
4 Tilling-Stevens Express B9B/Harrington
3 Thornycroft (acquired from Tanner, Denmead)

Many passed to Wilts & Dorset, Salisbury and were used in connection with the transport of construction workers to expanding military facilities in the area.

Blackout

On the evening of Friday 1 September 1939, two days before the declaration of war, Britain was plunged into complete darkness as blackout regulations were introduced. Devastating air attacks by enemy night bombers were expected at any time and no light was allowed on the streets. To improve their visibility in the darkened streets all Southdown buses and coaches had white paint applied to the edge of the front wings and at the bottom of the rear panel including the platform area. A large white circular disc was painted on the back, sometimes on the offside corner and similar arrangements were applied to all road vehicles including cycles. At the start of the war most vehicles used during hours of darkness were fitted with a single hooded nearside headlamp to direct a reduced beam downwards. Usually the bulb was removed from the offside headlamp and side and rear lamp glasses were partially masked using the equivalent of two layers of newsprint. Lighting of destination indicators had to be extinguished completely making it very difficult for passengers to identify an oncoming vehicle. The interior lighting of buses and coaches was also drastically reduced so as not to exceed 0.006 candle power at 4ft distance from the lamp – a mere glimmer equal to the light provided by the striking of a match. Often the stairs and platform area of double deckers were unlit making fare collection very difficult for bus conductors. By the middle of October 1939 approved headlight masks that permitted a little more light were becoming available.

BLACK-OUT

YOU can help the Bus-Driver— by hailing the bus boldly, preferably with something white (or light-coloured) in your hand.

YOU can help the Conductor, too—by stating your destination clearly, and by tendering him the exact amount of your fare.

YOU may be sure that both will do their best to help you.

A Gallup poll published in January 1940 claimed that one in every five people had sustained some sort of injury in the blackout since September and for the first months of the war it was more hazardous to be on the roads than in the Armed Forces! It was soon widely agreed by the authorities that some restrictions were in need of modification to try and alleviate the numbers of accidents after dark and from Monday 22 January 1940 the familiar wartime headlight masks were made compulsory for all civilian vehicles. Dipped headlights were now permitted as long as the vehicle had the regulation headlamp covers with three horizontal slits which confined the beam to the ground in front of the vehicle. The new arrangements were generally considered a big improvement. Due to the large number of road accidents it was also decided that from this date the speed limit during blackout hours would be reduced from 30 mph to 20 mph although in practice this had little effect on traffic speeds.

Coaches to Ambulances

When it seemed that war with Germany was imminent, the Government turned its immediate attention to the provision of an adequate number of ambulances. At that time – early in 1939 – the authorities anticipated that, if war did come, there would soon be heavy casualties, not only involving the armed forces, but also among civilians. It was imperative that there should be sufficient large stand by ambulances for the transport of the wounded, the injured and the sick to first aid posts, clearing stations and hospitals as aerial bombardment was expected within hours of the start of hostilities. During the Munich crisis of September 1938, a number of London Transport's Green Line coaches had been prepared for conversion and had proved very suitable for the work. Later the Ministry of Health approached large passenger transport companies throughout the country to determine whether they were willing to place vehicles at the disposal of the Government in a national emergency. In most cases the companies also agreed to provide drivers and maintain and garage the vehicles. Arrangements were completed in March 1939, so that several months before war on Germany was declared, there were hundreds of coaches and single deck buses in regular service with fittings which, at very short notice, would enable them to be converted into stretcher carriers.

In late August, about a week before the actual declaration of war, bus companies such as Southdown received the 'Stand to' order, and garage staffs began work on the conversion of the vehicles. This required the removal of seats and parcel racks, windows made opaque and fitting of supports for ten stretchers plus other equipment to enable them to serve as civilian ambulances. Modifications were also made to the rear of the coach to enable the loading of

Car 1109 (BUF 409) was one of 24 Leyland Tiger TS7 coaches converted for use as ambulances in the final week of peace in August 1939. New in 1935 its Harrington body was reconverted to 32 seat layout in January 1946 in time for the reintroduction of the London Express Services on 22 March 1946. It is seen after the war on a Worthing to London relief working whilst stopped for refreshments at the Holly & Laurel Hotel at Holmwood south of Dorking. Car 1109 survived in service until being sold for scrap in January 1954.
Southdown Enthusiasts Club – Clark/Surfleet Collection

stretchers through the luggage locker which could then be pushed along a special ramp fixed to the floor. Southdown converted 24 Leyland Tiger TS7 coaches for this work – cars 1089 to 1096, 1101, 1102, 1104, 1106 to 1115, 1120, 1123 and 1131 – including examples with Harrington, Park Royal and Beadle bodies. Most companies were able to complete the work within a few days of the outbreak of war although fortunately, after initial evacuation duties, they were not required for civilian use for some months to come.

Whilst parked at the Royal Hospital, Portsmouth two of the fourteen ambulances based at Portsmouth – cars 1089 and 1092 – were totally destroyed during an air raid on the night of 10/11 January 1941. The surviving ambulances were released during 1945/6 and converted for normal coach operation with the first appearing in service during July 1945.

Early Alterations

To make buses less visible to German aircraft the cream roofs on all single and double buses were repainted dark green at the start of the war and this generally remained the standard for single deck buses until about 1960. Use of the three roller blind boxes on the offside of Leyland TS7 cars 1400-29 was discontinued in late 1939, the glass being over painted to show:

'Southdown/(blank)/Services'

in script lettering on a cream background. Where they remained in place these boxes were later painted dark green. It is also thought that the rear corner curved glass windows on most of the 1400 class vehicles were replaced with normal panelling quite early in the war. This may have been to assist in meeting blackout regulations which severely restricted the amount of interior light which was allowed to be visible from

Seen laying over at Haywards Heath Railway Station is a somewhat battle scarred car 1405 (BUF 985), a Leyland Tiger TS7 with Harrington body new in 1935. It has gained what appears to be a grey roof and the offside destination indicators now show Southdown/blank/ Services in script style. This bus was rebuilt by Portsmouth Aviation in 1947 and was one of the last 1400 class Tigers to leave the fleet in June 1957.
Southdown Enthusiasts Club – W J Haynes Collection

outside. There is photographic evidence to show that some may have retained this feature until the bodies were rebuilt in the post war period.

Also, during the early part of the war the company added an 'H' or 'L', as appropriate, in two inch black edged gold lettering beneath the car numbers on the side panels of double deck buses. This was designed to assist operating staff in correctly identifying the height of double deck vehicles during the blackout. Some 70 prewar Titans were fitted with lowbridge bodies for operation on routes where railway over bridges had restricted headroom. In 1939 these were situated at:

Eastbourne, between Stone Cross and Friday Street (B2104) – services 92, 92A and 94

Lewes, Cliffe High Street – services 13, 16, 18, 20, 25 and 119

Shoreham, Old Shoreham Road (A283) – services 9, 10, 22

As the war progressed more double deckers were required to move the heavy wartime loadings and lowbridge buses were used in place of 1400 class saloons at:

Droxford, north of Railway Station (B2150) – service 38

Hassocks, Keymer Road (B2116) near Hassocks Station – service 23

Petersfield, London Road (old A3, now B2070) – services 60, 61

Due to interworking, other services such as the 15, 91 and 93 in Eastbourne regularly featured lowbridge buses although they had no physical restrictions requiring their use. The suffix letters continued after the war whilst lowbridge vehicles remained in the fleet.

To improve their fuel economy Titan TD3c cars 960-3 dating from 1934 had their petrol engines replaced by 8.6 litre diesel engines between late 1939 and summer 1940. Those TD4s delivered with petrol engines were also converted to diesel engines during the early months of the war. Cars 112, 115, 116, 117, 119 and 121 temporarily reverted to petrol engines

in 1943/4 when fitted for producer gas operation and then converted back to diesel at the end of gas operation in 1944. After the major clear out earlier in the summer a few sales of surplus vehicles continued after the outbreak of war. Tilling-Stevens car 647 passed to Worthing Laundry Services on 26 September 1939. Further sales to Wilts & Dorset came on the same date with Titans 891, 894, 899 and 921 passing westwards to be followed on 2 October 1939 by 917 and 919. The well known dealer, Arlington Motor Company of Ponders End, Middlesex took Titan 932 on 24 October along with 868 and 931 on 7 November 1939. Tilling-Stevens saloon 650 moved north to Bradley of Stoke-on-Trent on 7 November 1939 followed by 696 on 16 December 1939. Titan 928 passed to a dealer named Ivor Creek at Southampton on 13 November 1939 as the final batch of TD5s was entering service. Finally car 690 went to Scout of Hastings on 2 December 1939.

At the company Board Meeting on Thursday 30 November 1939 approval was given to purchase the Goodwill of the businesses of H G Bannister (t/a The Blue Bus) of Burgess Hill and Mrs L A Evans (t/a The Red Bus) of Ditchling together with two vehicles for the sum of £300. The vehicles were not used by Southdown and the Chairman & Managing Director were authorised to order additional Rolling Stock if they considered it necessary.

As the demand for transport of workers building the new military bases lessened Wilts & Dorset sold two Titans back to Southdown in late 1939 for the sum of £25 each. The bodies of former cars 881 and 888 were cut down for conversion to breakdown tenders at Portslade Works and renumbered 0881 and 0888. In their new guise they continued in service until November 1957. In February 1940 former 907 was rebuilt in similar fashion at Portslade Works for Wilts & Dorset remaining in use until 1961. During the war years many Southdown vehicles were delicensed and put in store at various times

In summer 1940 the four 3 axle Tigers delivered for Beachy Head service 97 were no longer required for their intended duties and instead moved to provide additional capacity on service 30 between Chelwood Common and Brighton. Car 553 (BUF 553), a Leyland Tiger TS7T with Short Bros 40 seat coach style body new in August 1935 is seen at Haywards Heath Railway Station on a very busy southbound working to Brighton. Standard block style bus fleetnames have replaced the script style coach fleetnames that were carried from new and, despite wartime shortages, side destination boards have been provided. Most of the intending passengers seem to be Army or Navy personnel or perhaps just waiting for the Burrell Arms to open.
Southdown Enthusiasts Club – W J Haynes Collection

although they could still be used in emergency when required by the Military or civilian authorities. These included most of the Leyland Cub coaches, some of the Leyland Cheetahs, all of the Leyland Lioness and Tigress touring coaches, the two Dennis Falcons, the unique open top double deck Tilling-Stevens (car 600) and the open-top Leyland Titan TD1s until they were fitted with temporary canvas tops. In the case of the Cubs and Cheetahs these changed from year to year to even out their mileage.

1940

In the early years of the war the company decided that in order to improve fuel consumption all of the petrol engined 1400 class saloons – cars 1400 to 1429 – should be fitted with diesel engines. Fortunately it was possible to exchange the 8.6 litre diesel engines from coaches laid up as a result of the hostilities. This was completed over a period from 1940 to 1943 and it is thought that the diesel engines came from within the batch of coaches comprising cars 1182 to 1226. Conversely, cars 1441 and 1445 lost their diesel engines in favour of petrol engines for a short time around 1943 possibly due to limited diesel fuel supplies available at or near an outstation. Those buses equipped with the three indicator boxes on the offside had them painted out in the case of 1400 class single deckers or panelled over in the case of highbridge double deckers at the same time.

Former Tramocars S & D Freighters T6-9 were placed in store by 31 December 1939. T6 and T7 were finally sold on 28 April 1941 while T8 was sold on 25 October 1940 to Brighton Corporation and used by the Salvation Army as a mobile canteen. T9 was sold with the later models to the dealer, Arlington Motor Company of Ponders End, Middlesex on 6 July 1942 and saw further service with Worthington Motor Tours of Stafford until the end of 1944. Of the once large fleet of Tilling-Stevens saloons only 689 and 705 were licensed during 1940 and kept as spares but not allocated to regular services. The unique Tilling-Stevens double decker, car 600, was stored at some time during 1940 but later reappeared on tree lopping duties by April 1944. The Acquisition and Disposal of Motor Vehicles Order 1940 was implemented by the Government on 20 July 1940 and from this date application had to be made to the RTC for the purchase and sale of all buses and coaches. The system operated for the remainder of the war and into 1946 and presumably under this approval Titans 869, 870, 900, 908, 914 and 926 were sold to Wintour, a dealer in Walworth, London SE17 on 4 September 1940 subsequently appearing with operators in various parts of the country. On the same date Titans 933-6, 941, 943-5 and 948 passed to Cumberland Motor Services Ltd of Whitehaven.

During 1940 the Lioness and Tigress tourers which were put into store at the start of the war were renumbered as 1801-1823 so that the 3xx

numbers could be used for the twenty Leyland Titans on loan from East Kent Road Car Co. Ltd.

In late July 1940 service 97 between Eastbourne and Beachy Head was suspended for the duration of the war. The petrol engines in the 40 seat three axle Tigers – cars 550 to 553 – had been replaced with 8.6 litre diesel units in late 1939 and from 1 November 1940 they were re-deployed on service 30 between Brighton and Chelwood Common now carrying the standard 'block' style fleetnames.

Buses and Coaches commandeered

In late 1939, the Government conferred powers upon the military authorities enabling them to take over civilian vehicles in cases of emergency. Clearly bus and coach companies now became vulnerable to such action as their rolling stock was readily suitable for use as troop transporters or for conversion to ambulances. A bus company could resist the seizure of any vehicle on the grounds that it was required to provide an essential service for the community, but very rarely were they able to reverse the decision of the War Office. Across the country many buses and coaches were requisitioned in this way during the spring and summer of 1940.

Following the German advances the British Expeditionary Force had lost all its transport in and around Dunkirk resulting in the Emergency Powers (Defence), Acquisition and Disposal of Motor Vehicles Order, 1940, which gave powers for compulsory purchase of civilian vehicles of all types. In June 1940 the military authorities were becoming heavily dependent on civilian vehicles to move troops around the country and embarked on a campaign of compulsory requisitioning of buses and coaches. A representative of CIST (Chief Inspector Supplementary Transport) would usually arrange to inspect vehicles at a specified place and time and operators were sometimes able to influence the disposal of their less desirable vehicles. In particular the military authorities were generally only interested in petrol engined vehicles often sparing the most modern diesel engined buses and coaches in the fleet. Unfortunately a few of Southdown's later Tiger coaches which had already swapped their diesel engines for petrol units from 1400 class saloons were caught in the net in this way. Starting in March 1940 a total of 154 Southdown vehicles were requisitioned by the military authorities in the period to July 1941 – all being single-deck and fitted with petrol engines. Southdown was perhaps fortunate in that many of these were elderly Tilling-Stevens buses and coaches which would have been due for early replacement. They included the twelve special Tilling-Stevens B10A2 and TSM B39A6 light-weight buses used for the Hayling Island services – cars 710 to 721 – which were now largely redundant following the closure of all the holiday camps on the island and subsequent curtailment of services.

39 (DUF 39) is a Leyland Cub KPZ2 with Harrington 20 seat front entrance coach body new in March 1937. Many of these small capacity vehicles were stored for periods during the war and in June 1941 it was requisitioned by the Military Authorities and allocated to the Royal Air Force. Re-acquired by Southdown in November 1945 it was rebuilt by West Nor in July 1946 and is seen at Worthing awaiting custom for an excursion to Alfriston.
A M Wright

The following Southdown vehicles were requisitioned:

7 March 1940
Leyland Tiger coaches – 1041, 1160-76 – allocated to Royal Army Service Corps

28 June 1940
Leyland Tiger coaches – 1062-70, 1072-85 – allocated to Chief Inspector of Supplementary Transport, Eastern Command, Hounslow

4 July 1940
Tilling-Stevens B9B coaches – 402-9, 415/6, 421/4/6-30
   Tilling-Stevens B10A2/B39A6 buses – 640, 665/9-73/5/9, 680/4/6-9, 692-5/9, 700-7/9, 711/4-6/9
   Tilling-Stevens B10B2 coaches – 723-34, 764/6-9
   Leyland Tiger coaches – 1000/7/9, 1030-7, 1040/3-53, 1071
   Allocated to Chief Inspector of Supplementary Transport, Eastern Command, Hounslow

2 August 1940
Tilling-Stevens B10A2/B39A6 buses – 710/2/3/7/8, 720/1 – allocated to Chief Inspector of Supplementary Transport, Eastern Command, Hounslow

19 September 1940
Leyland Tiger coaches – 1193/9, 1200 – allocated to Chief Inspector of Supplementary Transport, Eastern Command, Hounslow

10 October 1940
Leyland Tiger coaches – 1127/9, 1130, 1150 – allocated to Chief Inspector of Supplementary Transport, Eastern Command, Hounslow

17 October 1940
Leyland Tiger coach – 1185 – allocated to Chief Inspector of Supplementary Transport, Eastern Command, Hounslow

31 March 1941
Leyland Tiger coaches – 1184, 1197 – allocated to the Royal Air Force

24 June 1941
Leyland Cub coaches – 37/9, 49 – allocated to the Royal Air Force

30 July 1941
Leyland Cub coach – 46 – allocated to the Royal Air Force

By December 1942 military vehicles were more plentiful and some of the requisitioned buses that were still in a reasonable condition and fit for service were offered for auction through the Ministry of Supply. Southdown would almost certainly not have wanted to reinstate any of the elderly Tilling-Stevens buses and coaches and many ended their days with local War Agricultural Executive Committees around the country. Of the total number taken only Leyland Tigers (cars 1030, 1067, 1068, 1075, 1076, 1079, 1083, 1084, 1085, 1129, 1166, 1168, 1172, 1173, 1174, 1176, 1184, 1193, 1197, 1199 and 1200) and two Leyland Cub coaches (cars 39 and 49) were repurchased by Southdown. In 1946 the company complained to the Ministry of Supply that their vehicles were being sold to other, often competing, operators in London and the south east.

Leyland Titan TD7s diverted

The Ministry of Supply was enabled by the Defence Regulations 1939 to completely control and prioritise all industrial output, with the manufacture of guns, tanks, warships and aeroplanes obviously having top priority. It had the task of ensuring that the country's manufacturing resources and material supplies were conducted as effectively as possible and had powerful authority over all sections of industry. The system which operated for the bus industry was that the Ministry of Supply would procure the manufacture of new vehicles whilst the Ministry of War Transport (MOWT) would allocate them to operators on the basis of greatest need – but only as perceived by the Ministry.

During the early months of the war the supply of new buses continued much as before because most of the component parts had already been made or were in course of production, but as the various manufacturing concerns turned their output increasingly to the war effort, the flow of new buses became ever more erratic and finally ceased completely. In some cases the supply dried up very quickly while in others new buses were built in small numbers right through to the end of 1941. London Transport's last motor bus built to a peace time order, RT 151, was not completed ready for service until January 1942 after over a year's delay waiting for components. Delivery of new buses to most south coast areas ceased quite quickly although Maidstone & District were fortunate to receive a batch of 10 Leyland TD7s in July/August 1940 and the first 20 of an order for 48 new trolleybuses for Hastings in June 1940. Brighton, Hove & District were able to take delivery of 15 Bristol K5G in 1940 although due to the forced evacuation of the Eastern Coach Works factory in May 1940 the fifteen partly finished vehicles were sent down to BH&D, together with all the necessary parts, to enable the bodies to be completed at Holland Road works. For Southdown most of, what was to prove, the final batch of 14 Leyland TS8 buses of the 1400 class arrived in November and December 1939 but delivery slowed considerably and the final one was not delivered until 15 March 1940. Pending decisions by the Ministry of Supply and MOWT as to which operators and areas of the country had the greatest need for new buses, all other outstanding orders were put on hold.

In 1939 as part of its normal replacement programme Southdown had placed an order with Leyland and Park Royal for the supply of 27 Titan TD7 models for delivery in 1940. These would presumably have replaced the remaining closed top TD1s dating from 1930/1 and were due to become:

266-288	GCD 666-688	Leyland TD7
	Park Royal H26/26R	
289-292	GCD 689-692	Leyland TD7
	Park Royal L26/26R	

The fall of France in June 1940 led to much of the company's operating area being declared a Defence Area and later the voluntary evacuation of non-essential residents. Both of these factors were considered at the time likely to have a serious effect on the future revenue earning capacity of Southdown. There was also the fear of German invasion and the possibility of new vehicles falling into the hands of the enemy. As a result the company's already Brighton registered Titan TD7 models were diverted to three other operators well outside the perceived danger area and where the production of war materials had already been expanded.

These vehicles therefore saw no service with Southdown and were instead diverted to:

Western Welsh – GCD 666-9/72/4/5
Crosville – GCD 670/1/3/6-88
Cumberland – GCD 689-92 – the lowbridge models were reregistered before entry into service and the registrations GCD 689-92 were made available for further use by Southdown on Guy Arabs in 1943/4.

According to the company accounts, Southdown had already paid Leyland for the chassis and it is known that in April 1940 the company notified the registration office that they were expecting the completed vehicles. This suggests that it was the sudden deterioration in the war situation from May 1940 onwards that caused the buses to be diverted away from the South Coast. Brighton County Borough Council reserved the appropriate registration marks and it is interesting that a series of handwritten notes survive (still attached to the vehicle registration archives held at the East Sussex Records office in Lewes) recording a number of telephone messages from Southdown to explain that these buses had been diverted elsewhere – in turn to Western Welsh (in October 1940), Crosville (between November 1940 and May 1941) and lastly, to Cumberland (February 1941). Southdown told the registration office that the last four buses had been given Cumberland County Council registrations, but requested that it be allowed to hold over these marks as the plates had already been made up! A pencil note in the archive duly records that Southdown had been told that the four outstanding registration marks would be held over until some new buses were received. The loss of the 27 Leyland Titans to associated companies was finally confirmed at a Board Meeting Thursday 9 January 1941.

Had the war not intervened it is also likely that a further batch of Leyland Tiger TS8s would have been supplied in 1940-1 to complete the replacement of the 36 Tilling-Stevens single deck buses dating from 1929-30. This would have taken the 1400 class to over 100 vehicles but in fact it was to be 1952 before the next full size saloons entered service with Southdown. The twelve shorter and lightweight Tilling-Stevens buses used on Hayling Island services may well have also been replaced by further Dennis Falcons assuming the two purchased in 1939 for

Tramocars work in Worthing proved successful. In the event Hayling Island would have to wait until 1949 to get its new Dennis Falcons.

Given the importance of coaching operations to Southdown it is almost certain that, but for the outbreak of war, a further delivery of 13 Leyland Tiger TS8s would have followed in 1940 and at the company Board Meeting on Thursday 31 August 1939 a further 27 coaches had been authorised. The attractive Harrington body style first seen in 1938 and further improved for the 1939 coaches would probably have graced many further Southdown deliveries over the coming years. In urgent need of replacement were 18 Tilling-Stevens B10B2s new in 1929-30 and rebodied by Harrington in 1934 and a further 18 Tilling-Stevens B9Bs new in 1926-7 and rebodied by Harrington in 1935. Instead all the remaining Tilling-Stevens coaches were commandeered for military use in 1940 and their traditional coaching duties temporarily suspended for the duration. By the time that further new coaches appeared in 1947 almost all of Southdown's prewar coach fleet would have been due for withdrawal under replacement programmes that had applied up to 1939.

'Unfrozen' Buses

As the war continued the Government assumed control over the manufacture of essential goods on the basis of the minimal use of skilled workers and scarce materials. In 1941 the Ministry of Supply first authorised the release by selected manufacturers of any chassis, bodywork or component parts that remained unused from the switch to war work – all these vehicles were referred to as 'unfrozen' buses. Also made available were chassis or complete vehicles ready for export that had been delayed because of the danger of shipping them overseas. Altogether about 530 buses and trolleybuses were produced for domestic operators by these initiatives – some of the export vehicles being to the greater width of 8ft 0ins. Allocation was the responsibility of the Ministry of War Transport and they were distributed to operators between 1941 and 1943, although only one was received locally – ECG 616 a Leyland Titan TD7 with Brush highbridge utility body for Hants & Sussex. None were allocated to Southdown.

Loans from East Kent and Eastbourne Corporation

The loss of the Leyland TD7s to Crosville, Western Welsh and Cumberland left Southdown hard pressed to cope with an unexpected increase in wartime traffic movements. Since the decision to divert the new buses the changing war scene led to a considerably greater demand for transport in the vicinity of the naval base at Portsmouth and around the developing military bases and airfields across Sussex. Southdown had also generously helped other operators in more urgent need of buses with 58 vehicles sold to Wilts and Dorset Motor Services during June and July 1939 – 41 of which were Leyland TD1 and TD2 double deck buses. The company had also sold a further 72 double deck buses between 1938 and 1941.

This loss of older vehicles and non delivery of the expected Leyland TD7s was eventually overcome by loans from other operators in the area. With eastern Kent and the seaside town of Eastbourne particularly vulnerable to enemy attack and with much of the local population evacuated to safer areas, the company was able

Fortunately the photographer has captured one of the loaned East Kent Leyland Titans as it proceeds east on service 4 along Brighton Road, Worthing to the junction with Selden Road before turning left. As most of these buses spent the greater part of their time with Southdown working in a Defence Area where unauthorised photography was banned such photographs are very rare. No other motor vehicles are evident in this view of the main A259 road looking west towards the town centre. Note the white markings on posts to aid pedestrians in the blackout.
West Sussex County Council Library Service

to negotiate the loan of replacement vehicles. At the Board Meeting on Thursday 29 August 1940 it was confirmed that arrangements had been made to hire a number of buses, not exceeding 30, from the East Kent Road Car Company Ltd (EKRCC) at a rental of £2 per day with Southdown to pay for all running costs, servicing and repairs. It was further agreed that Southdown would, if requested, loan to EKRCC a sum not exceeding £30,000, each unit of 10 vehicles hired to the company being considered as security for a loan of £10,000.

The buses included 20 almost new diesel engined Leyland Titan TD5 with Park Royal lowbridge bodies from East Kent which arrived during July and August 1940 and six all Leyland highbridge double deckers from Eastbourne Corporation in December 1940. The loaned vehicles are known to have been allocated to a number of garages including Chichester, Portsmouth and Worthing. Apart from detailing around the driver's cab the East Kent TD5s, AJG 21 to 40 had six bay composite bodywork that was very similar to Southdown cars 262 to 265. Numbered 321 to 330 and 301 to 310 respectively by Southdown, and carrying the 'L' suffix on each side, they were at first operated with Southdown fleet names on cherry red panelling to the waist rail and medium grey above. All were eventually repainted in the full apple green and cream livery with lining out and dark green roofs (while still displaying 'East Kent Road Car Co. Ltd' as legal owner) and they even had the East Kent company radiator plates replaced with the Southdown 'script' style plates. Southdown retained the East Kent destination boxes with a separate route number display which meant that non standard destination and number blinds had to be produced. Initially it is believed they were all allocated to Worthing where they could usually be found on the 3, 4 (full allocation), 5, 6, 7, 7A and 8 and also occasionally on the 10, 31F and 31G, of which only the 10 actually required the use of lowbridge buses. The new destination screens also included services 9, 9A, 22 and 31 so it is possible they appeared on these routes. From 1943 cars 324-6/9 were recorded as transferred from Worthing to Portsmouth and used on the 31. On 9 November 1940 five of these buses (cars 301 to 305, AJG 31 to 35) went for further service with Devon General where they remained until October 1943. The other fifteen buses (cars 306 to 310 and 321 to 330) remained with Southdown until late January 1945 when the first two (AJG 23 and 25) were returned to East Kent. The East Kent radiator plates were taken out of store and refixed a few days before each bus went back to Canterbury – a bus in service with East Kent plates becoming a signal of imminent departure to the local enthusiasts. As more utility Guys entered service the others drifted back over the next twelve months until the last – AJG 26 – reached East Kent on 1 January 1946. At its peak in late 1941 East Kent had some 122

vehicles from its fleet hired to other operators. As the cost of living increased, undoubtedly the rate rose proportionately and by the time of the Board Meeting on Thursday 9 January 1941 the rate had increased from £2 to £3 per day for diesel engined double deck buses.

To cover for the buses sent to Devon General, from mid December 1940, six all Leyland petrol engined highbridge buses were received from Eastbourne Corporation Transport Department, with a total of ten different vehicles of various models being loaned at various times. The four oldest buses were replaced early in 1941 and it is recorded that, of the rest, three were returned in 1942 and three in 1943 – although the exact dates when these last six went back is unknown it is believed they had departed by March 1943 with the last in service, JK 5604, noted on 13 March 1943. Allocated Southdown numbers 400 to 405, and carrying the 'H' suffix on each side all of these buses remained in the ECTD dark blue and primrose livery. The ten vehicles were a rather mixed bag – the oldest four (JK 1237, 1808, 2334 and 2337) had 'piano-fronted' composite six bay bodies, similar to those on Southdown cars 866 to 877 and were allocated to Chichester garage. JK 1237 and 1808 were Titan TD1s new in 1931 and JK 2334 and 2337 were Titan TD2s new in 1932. The other six buses were all fitted with torque converters and were allocated to Worthing garage where they were to be found mainly on the 5/6 services. Four of these (JK 3720, 3724, 5062 and 5063) had metal framed six bay bodies with vee-fronts – JK 3720 and 3724 were Titan TD3c, new in 1934, while JK 5062 and 5063 were Titan TD4c, new in 1935. The last two vehicles (JK 5604 and 5606) were Titan TD4c, new in 1936 and had metal framed five bay bodies to Leyland's classic flat fronted design. Being petrol engined, Southdown paid Eastbourne Corporation at the rate of £2 per day plus all outgoings for each bus.

The 1443 incident
Given the intensity of enemy action throughout the Southdown operating area it is fortunate that so few of its vehicles were seriously damaged. Coaches on the London Express Services continued to ply between the South Coast towns and London throughout the most serious days of the blitz in 1940/1 largely without incident. Specific attacks on buses by enemy aircraft were not unknown and probably the first recorded occurred on 15 August 1940 at Chaldon Cross Roads north of Redhill when a London Transport AEC 4Q4 type on route 449 came under attack. Later, on 31 October 1940, East Kent had two buses attacked in the Canterbury area, both involving loss of life to passengers and staff.

Finally, tragedy struck Southdown at around 1915 on the evening of Saturday 2 November 1940 although not in London or Portsmouth but in a most unlikely rural location. Service 95 was an infrequent 'back' road service between

95	Eastbourne, Rushlake Green Heathfield and Waldron								95

			WO	NWS	WO					
Eastbourne *Pevensey Road*		★	9 25	★	12 53	5 6	6 9	24	...
Stone Cross	...	...	9 40	...	1220	3 20	6 22	9 40	...
Hailsham *Office*	...	8 45	9 55	10 5	1235	3 35	6 39	9 57	...
Cowbeech	...	8 58	10 8	1018	1248	3 48	6 53	10 11	...
Rushlake Green	...	9 7	1017	1027	1257	3 57	7 3	10 21	...
Punnetts Town	...	9 15	1025	1035	1 5	4 5	7 12	10 30	...
Cade Street	...	9 19	1029	1039	1 9	4 9	7 16	10 34	...
Heathfield *Station Road*	...	9 25	1035	1045	1 15	4 15	7 23	10 41	...
Cross-in-Hand	...	...	...	...	1‡20	4‡20	7‡28	...
Waldron *Star Inn*	...	...	...	...	1‡29	4‡29	7‡38	

		NWS	WO	WO						
Waldron *Star Inn*	...	...	...	...	...	1‡30	4‡30	7‡39	...
Cross-in-Hand	...	...	...	...	1	1‡39	4‡39	7‡49	...
Heathfield *Station Road*	...	8 5	8 5	9 25	1045	1 45	4 45	7 56	...
Cade Street	...	8 11	8 11	9 31	1051	1 51	4 51	8 3	...
Punnetts Town	...	8 15	8 15	9 35	1055	1 55	4 55	8 7	...
Rushlake Green	...	8 23	8 23	9 43	11 3	2 3	5 3	8 16	...
Cowbeech	...	8 32	8 32	9 52	1112	2 12	5 12	8 26	...
Hailsham *Office*	...	8 45	8 45	10 5	1125	2 25	5 25	8 40	...
Stone Cross	...	9 0	★	★	1140	2 40	5 40	8 56	...
Eastbourne *Pevensey Road*	...	9 15	...	...	1155	2 55	5 55	9 13	...

WO—Wednesdays only.   NWS—Not Wednesdays or Sundays.
★ **Passengers** to or from Eastbourne change at Hailsham.
‡ Wednesdays and Saturdays only.

Eastbourne, Hailsham and Heathfield which served the villages of Cowbeech, Rushlake Green, Punnetts Town and Cade Street. Leyland Tiger car 1443 operating the 1806 journey from Eastbourne to Waldron had left Rushlake Green and was wending its way peacefully northwards along Middle Road (now Middle Lane) towards Three Cups Corner when twelve HE bombs were jettisoned by enemy aircraft. Ten bombs fell randomly on local farms causing little damage but two dropped on the highway as the bus approached. One of the bombs burst against the nearside rear wheel of the bus causing it to be blown off the road and thrown down a steep embankment into a farm yard and completely wrecked. A first aid party and demolition squads were called but five passengers (four men and a young woman) and the conductor had been killed and three injured passengers detained at the Military Hospital, Hellingly. The time on the official report indicates the bus was running a few minutes late as it should have departed from Rushlake Green at 1903 and given that it was totally dark at the time it seems unlikely that 1443 was deliberately attacked. No other damage or injuries were caused by the bombs and it appears that the late running bus was sadly in the wrong place at the wrong time.

The Harrington bodywork of 1443 was very badly damaged and subsequently scrapped at Portslade Works but the chassis was salvaged by the company. Its diesel engine was removed for further use and a Leyland 7.6 litre petrol engine fitted. The chassis was then fitted with a spare prewar 32 seat centre entrance coach body by Metcalfe although Southdown records show it as having been built by Harrington. The explanation may be that the Metcalfe body was one that had been replaced by a new Harrington body but remained at Harrington's works. The body fitted to 1443 was to a rather odd looking design quite unlike the numerous coach bodies already in service with Southdown although similar to many supplied to coach operators before the war. Behind the sliding entrance door, the last three side windows on both sides were stepped up from the waistline. Because of this there was no room over the windows to place the usual side service details board so a full size single line destination indicator was fitted in a strange three fifths width canopy over the driver's cab. The offside floor level emergency door was in the middle opposite the entrance. Car 1443 had extra chrome beading to form a side flash that swept down from below the waist at the front bulkhead line and over the rear wheel arch to the bottom of the coach in an effort to modernise its

After the body of car 1443 (FCD 243) was scrapped following the serious incident near Rushlake Green in November 1940 the chassis passed to Harrington's of Hove who fitted a rather unusual looking centre entrance coach body by Metcalfe in May 1941. In this form car 1443 became a general purpose coach and is seen in later days after operating a relief working from Brighton to London. *Author's collection*

appearance. Despite being an odd man out it was used as an all purpose coach for its remaining life which ended in 1952 when the body was scrapped and the chassis and running units used in the construction by Beadle of car 876.

The worst bus accident of the war occurred in dense fog at 1030 on 25 November 1940 when a northbound Southdown bus in Preston Road was struck almost head on by Brighton, Hove & District vehicle 6335 travelling in the opposite direction. The collision also involved another BH&D vehicle, 6302, which ran into the back of the Southdown vehicle. All three vehicles were extensively damaged, and 24 people were taken to hospital.

1941

Whilst parked at the Royal Hospital, Portsmouth two of the fourteen ambulances based at Portsmouth – cars 1089 and 1092 – were totally destroyed by enemy action during the devastating air raid on the night of 10/11 January 1941. This brought to three the total number of Southdown buses seriously damaged or destroyed during the war. Most companies in the South Eastern area fared much worse with Portsmouth Corporation losing ten buses in the March 1941 raid.

At the Board Meeting on Wednesday 19 March 1941 the Managing Director was authorised to purchase the following vehicles:

21 double deck omnibuses complete and 3 single deck omnibuses complete.

Given the difficulties with supply it was very unlikely that these orders would be fulfilled for some time to come and 'Utility' designs did not appear until July 1941. In practice the three single deck chassis, presumably intended to replace the vehicles destroyed or seriously damaged by enemy action, did not materialise. The Board also authorised the placing of orders for the post war delivery of:

25 double deck omnibuses complete and 25 single deck omnibuses complete.

This was, indeed, an optimistic statement by the Board as the final outcome of the war at this time was, at best, uncertain for Britain and with the coming of spring, invasion scares were once more the main concern of those who remained on the South Coast. In the event the first postwar deliveries were 25 double deck buses in the shape of cars 266 to 290 delivered in 1946 but, apart from the Dennis Falcon lightweight buses for Hayling Island, no single deck buses were delivered until the Royal Tigers in 1952. The remaining Tramocars, cars T10-12 and 15-17 had all been withdrawn in the summer of 1940 and were placed in store awaiting disposal which was now strictly controlled by the RTCs. T6 and T7 which had been stored since January 1940 were sold to a dealer on 28 April 1941.

1400 class alterations

To cope with growing passenger loads and relieve overcrowding the Minister of War Transport instructed the RTCs in August 1941 to permit single deckers to be adapted to carry the same number of standees as there were seats – up to a maximum of 30 standees – for use on specified services. Southdown adopted the idea with enthusiasm and converted sixty of the 1400 class Leyland Tiger TS7 and TS8 saloons to perimeter seating layout with 30 seats turned to face inwards around the sides of the saloon. This created a large central area for 30 standing passengers thus equalling the total capacity of a

Car 1485 (GCD 385), a Leyland Tiger TS8 with Harrington body was the last of the 1400 class to be delivered on 15 March 1940. It was not registered until 31 May 1940 and then believed to have been first used at Worthing on former Tramocars' services. Seen at Steyning on service 80 at the end of the war it still retains wartime livery with grey roof and window surrounds and light green below with dark green mudguards. The perimeter seating which was fitted in 1942 to many of this class can be clearly seen.
C F Klapper © Omnibus Society

double decker with a full standing load. Previous regulations had not permitted more than eight standing passengers to be carried and the RTC could impose conditions on the use of such 'standee' vehicles.

The first to be converted to standee layout was car 1417 in September 1941. Fourteen others were converted during 1941 including cars 1437, 1440, 1441, 1442, 1445, 1466, 1467, 1468, 1469, 1470, 1471, 1473, 1474 and 1484. A further 27 cars followed in 1942 including cars 1403, 1409, 1411, 1412, 1414, 1416, 1418, 1427, 1428, 1435, 1439, 1444, 1447, 1461, 1463, 1464, 1472, 1475, 1476, 1477, 1478, 1479, 1480, 1481, 1482, 1483 and 1485. Seventeen further conversions during 1943 included cars 1404, 1407, 1413, 1421, 1422, 1426, 1430, 1431, 1434, 1436, 1438, 1448, 1453, 1457, 1458, 1462 and 1465 with the final one, car 1420, converted in January 1944.

The following buses were NOT converted to perimeter seating:

1400-2, 1405/6/8, 1410/5/9, 1423/4/5/9, 1432/3, 1443/6/9, 1450-2/4-6/9, 1460

Buses reverted to 32 or 34 seats in normal 2+2 format between August 1945 and October 1949 often at the same time that the bodies were rebuilt.

The open top TD1s

During the period just before and after the start of the Second World War Southdown had disposed of most of its large fleet of covered top TD1 and TD2 double deckers delivered between 1929 and 1932 mainly to operators such as Wilts & Dorset Motor Services which had greater need due to additional wartime traffic. Following pioneering work by Brighton Hove & District with its sea front service 17, many bus operators working in coastal areas found that open top buses were still popular during the summer months. Southdown therefore decided to retain the rather quaint looking open top Brush bodied TD1s dating from 1929 – cars 801-823 – for seasonal work, rather than replacing them after about 8 years of service in accordance with its normal policy. For the 1937 season they had been repainted with the upper deck panels in cream. But, even in wartime, they were now obviously unsuitable for normal all year round service and when used in emergency to help clear the queues it was found that the public would sooner wait longer in the rain than travel on the open upper decks.

With growing traffic demands and vehicle shortages and little prospect of obtaining additional buses the open top TD1s were taken out of store and fitted with temporary waterproofed stretched canvas top covers between October 1941 and March 1943 so that they could assist with normal services. Quantity production methods were adopted to assemble the metal framework at Portslade Works but with growing shortages of all kinds and reduced manpower available the whole process took many months to complete. Whilst records are not available for the complete batch it is known that the first to appear was car 816 on 14 October 1941 followed by cars 804 and 820 in December 1941. Others followed through 1942 until the last, cars 803 and 812, appeared in March 1943. In this form cars 801-823 were H27/24RO and an 'H' suffix' was added to their fleet numbers.

The covers looked pretty odd and rather flimsy even though they had metal strengthening pieces. Two fixed glass windows were fitted to the front, and five equal length windows fitted on each side. The first forward window on each side had an opening drop glass pane, the other four

After being retained for summer only use the 23 open top Leyland Titans dating from 1929 proved unpopular with passengers when pressed into service during the winter of 1940. Starting in late 1941 they were taken out of store and fitted with ingenious, if rather quaint looking, temporary waterproofed stretched canvas top covers at Portslade allowing them to be used all year on normal services. Car 807 (UF 4807) has been posed for the camera beside the barbed wire defences and shows the white markings and rear spot on the staircase.
C F Klapper © Omnibus Society

windows being fixed. Additional ventilation was available owing to the open staircase design, while louvre ventilators with sliding covers on the inside were provided in the front bulkhead. The interior lighting was ingeniously contrived using old ashtray fittings. The bulb was mounted horizontally with a metal deflector plate above it, so that only reflected light emerged from the ashtray opening. This was directed upwards and diffused over the light brown interior of the rubber cloth. The new top decks proved waterproof and quiet in running and added only 4 cwt 1 qr to the unladen weight. Early publicity pictures apparently showed the canvas tops as being painted dark green with their otherwise predominantly cream livery remaining unchanged. Car 815 received green upper deck panels – probably in October 1942 – but generally as they fell due for repaint the green and grey livery of the period from early 1943 was applied – all grey with the only green being below the lower deck windows. These included 801, 803, 804, 806, 807, 820, 822 and 823. After 1945 the top covers were sometimes painted cream and often a mixture of both green and cream.

These petrol engined buses reverted to their original open top state only gradually between May 1946 and July 1949. Car 810 was noted at Portslade with its top removed in November 1944 but photographic evidence confirms that the temporary top cover was reinstated post war and not finally removed until June 1949. Car 805 was the very last to regain open top form on 4 July 1949 by which time most of these veterans had less than 2 years in service remaining with Southdown. Cars 811 and 823 retained their temporary tops and did not return to public service as open toppers being withdrawn in 1949 and stored at Portslade before sale in 1950. In

addition cars 802 and 822 were converted to tree lopping vehicles and did not return to public service. The H suffixes were removed from fleet numbers when buses were reconverted to open top.

1942
Fleet Liveries

To reduce their visibility to enemy aircraft the roofs of both double deck and single deck buses were painted dark green at the start of the war, but otherwise vehicles continued to be repainted as normal, until supplies of cream paint ran low which is thought to be around 1942. With the greater intervals between repaints, a few vehicles emerged from the war without ever having received grey paint work at all. As wartime paint was also often of poor quality water could find its way to the wooden framing leading to major problems of decay. A new scheme for the distribution of paint for the maintenance of civilian road transport vehicles took effect from 1 January 1943 under which operators of passenger vehicles could purchase permits on application to the Regional Maintenance and Certifying Officer of the Ministry of War Transport. Initially operators did not have their paint allowances reduced because of stocks already held.

Between August 1942 and January 1943 some double deckers were out shopped with the normal green and cream on the lower deck but green above, car 113 being the first to be done. This livery, however, proved short lived and by early 1943 vehicles were being repainted grey with the only green being below the lower deck windows. Single deck buses along with a few coaches were also repainted grey with green below the windows although cars 1219 and 1225 were noted with a separating cream band. In a few

Car 157 (EUF 157) is a Leyland Titan TD5 with Park Royal lowbridge body delivered in February 1938 and seen at Haywards Heath Railway Station on the two hourly service 23 to Brighton via Ditchling. The livery shown is one that was adopted briefly in 1942/3 with all green upper deck and normal apple green and cream for the lower deck. In the postwar rebodying programme the Park Royal body was scrapped in 1950 and a new East Lancs highbridge body fitted allowing it to remain with Southdown until March 1960.
Southdown Enthusiasts Club – W J Haynes Collection

Car 160 (EUF 160) is a Leyland Titan TD5 with Park Royal lowbridge body delivered in February 1938 and seen at East Grinstead High Street before setting out on the hourly service 92. This service took 2 hours and 20 minutes to reach Eastbourne via Uckfield and actually passed under a low bridge at Stone Cross. It is in the livery adopted from 1943 with allover grey except for apple green below the lower deck windows. A new Beadle highbridge body was fitted in 1949 and the bus remained in the fleet until sale in February 1959.
Southdown Enthusiasts Club – W J Haynes Collection

cases the roof was painted black rather than grey although with all these variations dark green mudguards were retained. From the middle of 1943 a green band was added below the upper deck windows on double deckers being repainted, car 236 being the first to be done. With vehicles being repainted at Eastbourne, Portslade or Hilsea it is possible, however, that different versions may have been produced at the same time, depending on paint supplies!

From about April 1944 a very few double deck buses were repainted with a broader green band below the upper deck windows extended down to cover the whole of the upper deck section. Car 118 was the first to be done and others recorded were 106 and 126. With regard to new and rebodied vehicles, Guy Arabs 400, 401, 402, 405, 407, 409 and 421 and the Park Royal utility bodied TD1s entered service in a livery of allover grey but were repainted fairly quickly in grey with green below the lower deck windows as in the early 1943 livery above. Cars 400, 401 and the TD1s, at least, were still in primer. The following deliveries, including the Willowbrook rebodied TD1s, were repainted before entering service, with the exception of cars 416, 417, 427, 442 and 443 which were put into service in all grey livery initially without fleet names. These were subsequently added on a green rectangle until the buses could be returned to Portslade Works in November 1944 (427), December 1944 (417, 442 and 443) and January 1945 (416) for repainting. Cars 436 and 437 were noted when new at Portslade Works in brown primer with the fleet numbers chalked on, but were painted before entering service.

During this period it was noted that some buses were being repainted, or the livery amended, after only a few months. After car 422 entered service on 23 December 1944, all buses

were out shopped in normal apple green and cream livery, but with the green extending to immediately below the windows on both decks, and with a dark green roof. This included the remainder of the East Lancs rebodied TD2s (cars 947, 950, 952, 956 and 958) which were returned during 1945. The honour of being the first vehicle to be repainted in full livery with dark green lining, however, goes to car 150, which was rebuilt by Beadle in November 1944. Subsequent double deck repaints were similarly treated and single deckers appeared in their prewar livery but with dark green roofs, although the Leyland Cub buses gained cream painted window surrounds.

**

At the company Board Meeting on Thursday 25 June 1942 the Managing Director was authorised to purchase the following Rolling Stock if permission could be granted by the Regional Transport Commissioner:

11 new bodies
12 complete vehicles
11 new engines.

The new bodies materialised as six Park Royal and five Willowbrook and were placed on Leyland TD1/2 chassis in 1943/4. A further 10 bodies were also supplied by East Lancs under the same rebodying programme. The complete vehicles eventually arrived as Guy Arabs with utility bodies during 1943/4 and the 11 new engines were presumably the Gardner 5LW models that were temporarily fitted to some rebodied Leyland TD1/2s between 1943 and 1945.

All of the remaining former Tramocars S & D Freighters passed to the dealer Arlington of Ponders End in Middlesex on 6 July 1942. As very non standard vehicles in the fleet they had been in store for some time but several are known to have been sold for further service.

1943

At the company Board Meeting on Thursday 24 February 1943 the Managing Director was authorised to order a further five bodies and one Gardner engine. This comprised the additional East Lancs bodies for the TD2 rebodying programme and a further Gardner engine.

Producer Gas buses

The United Kingdom had traditionally been dependent on the importation of raw materials to produce motor fuels and in the period leading up to the Second World War the Government became increasingly anxious to conserve liquid fuel stocks. It therefore encouraged various experiments using alternative fuels with the Tilling group and London Transport undertaking much development work on a petrol-gas system that enabled buses to be run using home produced anthracite. Known as the producer gas system, various integral conversions were tested – sometimes with disastrous results – before it was decided that it would be safer for buses to tow the gas plant on a separate two wheeled trailer. On producer gas systems the gas did not need to be stored, as it was manufactured to meet the demands of the engine as the vehicle went along. Special legislation had to be rushed through Parliament to enable buses to tow trailers and in October 1939 the Public Service Vehicles (Drawing of Gas Producer Trailers) Order 1939 was introduced. But, the overall response by the industry to the experiments was not enthusiastic. The costs of conversion were substantial – each producer gas trailer cost around £90, which later rose to £106, and availability was patchy for the most appropriate solid fuels for producer gas equipment – coke or anthracite. There were also some who argued that because a producer gas trailer ran on two wheels with rubber tyres, the extensive use of such trailers would greatly increase the demand for tyres and ultimately give rise to further shortages.

During the remainder of 1939 and into 1940, increasing numbers of gas producer units – totalling between 40 and 50 – were put into service with Tilling companies around the country. The first producer gas bus in the local area was Brighton, Hove & District's AEC Regent 6278 in November 1939. It was powered by a converted Gardner diesel engine and equipped with a producer gas plant which was fitted underneath the outside rear staircase thereby dispensing with the need for a trailer. According to contemporary reports, its performance was satisfactory, and it could run one day on 5 cwt of selected small screen Welsh anthracite. Entering service on 20 November 1939, the vehicle was allocated to the flat service 15C route between Old Steine and Patcham, and was found to be able to maintain its schedule without difficulty. Averaging some 80 miles per day, its daily fuel consumption was two gallons of petrol and 2¼ cwt of anthracite. Unfortunately, in November 1940 the gas producer plant exploded while the bus was at the Patcham terminus – depositing the staircase in the road. Later BH&D gas buses towed the more conventional trailer!

Following reluctance by operators to voluntarily convert vehicles to run on gas the Ministry of War Transport was authorised to promote a scheme in April 1942 for the production of up to 10,000 trailer units. This was quickly followed, in May 1942, by a voluntary scheme whereby all bus operators with fleets of over 50 vehicles were

When Southdown finally embarked on converting some Titans to run on Producer Gas the first to appear in January 1943 was car 952 (UF 8852), a Leyland Titan TD2 with Short Bros 50 seat highbridge body. It was then taken from Portslade Works and photographed around the Old Steine in Brighton. Although fitted with Brighton area destination blinds there was no hope of running these buses successfully in such hilly territory and all spent their brief lives running on gas in Worthing where the local town services provided ideal conditions. Conversion back to petrol operation occurred in October 1944.
Alan Lambert collection

On offside view of car 952 (UF 8852) with the destination blinds now changed to service 31. The use of gas buses on such workings only occurred very rarely between Worthing and Brighton and then only on fully loaded reliefs. At this time in January 1943 car 952 is still in full lined out prewar livery although with dark green roof in an attempt to make it less visible to marauding enemy aircraft. The Short Bros body was removed in late 1944 and a new East Lancs body fitted in March 1945.

Alan Lambert collection

'Gearless' buses fitted with a torque converter in place of normal clutch and gearbox were not without their own problems and it is perhaps surprising that these were chosen for conversion.

Whilst publicity photographs were taken of car 952 with its trailer in Old Steine, Brighton complete with destination blinds set for service 31 the gas buses were all based at Worthing for local town services. As gas producer buses performed poorly on gradients and ideally needed to pass close to their home depot in case of the need for attention, the choice of Worthing probably offered the best available. Regular producer gas operation started at Worthing garage on 30 January 1943 by car 952 and trailer running on linked services 3 and 8 between Worthing Pier, Broadwater, East Worthing, Ham Hotel and Goring, George V Avenue. In February it moved to the Lancing services 7/7A, being joined by others as they became available. In April they all moved onto services 5/6 and as further buses were equipped, services 3/8 also received gas buses from August providing a full allocation when available. Local reports confirm that they also made occasional appearances on the 7A and 7B along with service 31 between Worthing and Brighton, but only on fully loaded reliefs. Some alterations to routes became necessary to avoid buses reversing at terminals as shown in chapter 5. Because the trailers could not carry enough fuel for a full day's service the company had 16 producer gas trailers available to cover the service at any one time and these were changed as necessary at the garage. Southdown's experience was much the same as other companies with gas buses struggling to maintain schedules despite their use on the mainly level routes in Worthing.

Supply of producer gas units to bus operators had reached 1,622 by 29 May 1943 although the number of units in regular operation was only 429 despite a much greater enthusiasm among the Tilling Group companies. By 15 October 1943 the total had risen to 739, only a small proportion of the target of 2,500. Against a background of serious manpower shortages the adaptation of vehicles and alterations to premises to house the additional equipment and solid fuel supplies inevitably led to delays especially as most operators were reluctant converts to gas operation. Following experience it was decided that engines converted to run on gas and used on work involving frequent short stops should be kept running so as to maintain the gas supply and to enable the vehicle quickly to start again without the use of petrol. The notice of operators was drawn to the fact that they must make provision to comply with security requirements such as immobilisation in those areas such as Sussex where these still applied. Despite criticism from operators and a slightly improved liquid fuel position the MOWT announced in November 1943 that its policy as regards the use

encouraged to convert 10% to producer gas operation which would have involved the conversion of around 2,500 buses throughout the UK. Incentives to the operators consisted of advice and technical information but no financial assistance was being offered at this stage. Unfortunately reliance on voluntary conversions did not bring the necessary results and, against a background of acute shortages of many kinds, the Ministry issued a directive on 1 October 1942 that all PSV operators with fleets of 150 vehicles or more licensed at 1 May 1942 were required to convert 10% of their total fleet to producer gas operation by July 1943. Despite some promising test results especially within the Tilling Group the response from operators was very patchy and few achieved the target set as producer gas operation was neither cheap nor efficient and it proved difficult to maintain existing schedules.

In order to comply with the October directive Southdown purchased 17 of the producer gas trailers ordered by the Government from the Bristol Tramways & Carriage Ltd. Southdown numbered the trailers GT1 to GT17, although until about September 1943 they appear to have run without visible identification. The first fifteen trailers were delivered between January and May 1943 – the last two arriving later, in March 1944 (GT16) and May 1944 (GT17). It is apparent that some of the trailers were modified after entering service, having an extension fitted to the 'chimney' (exhaust pipe) to avoid poisonous fumes drifting into the bus, and some were rebuilt with three 'scrubbers' (filters) instead of two. Further, between January and November 1943 Southdown converted ten petrol engined double deckers to run on producer gas. Four of the buses were Leyland Titan TD2, new in 1933 (cars 950, 952, 956 and 958) and the other six were Leyland Titan TD4c, new in 1935 (cars 112, 115, 116, 117, 119 and 121). The latter so called of gas producers would not be changed and the scheme to convert 2,500 buses must go ahead. The basis of allocation would be 10% of fleets of 100 or more vehicles and operators could place an immediate order with the Ministry of Labour for any skilled and unskilled personnel they might require to meet their target.

Contemporary reports concerning the operation of gas buses suggest that a very small proportion of staff were really successful in mastering the new techniques. Start up at the beginning of each day was quite a delicate procedure which began by getting the engine running on petrol, then lighting the fire with a coal gas jet and gradually persuading the engine to give up its normal fuel before coaxing it to run on gas. Once the petrol was firmly turned off, the bus could be handed over to the bus driver. The driver's task was always overshadowed by a fear that the engine would stall as, away from the resources and privacy of the garage, restarting was quite tricky. The conductor had to keep an eye on the trailer from time to time and make sure it was not becoming red hot, that the cooling tank was not boiling or that the tyres had not punctured. They also had to make sure careless passengers did not walk into the trailer after they alighted. The smell of producer gas was not pleasant and some conductors with a keen sense of smell found it could become nauseating, especially when a following wind blew onto the platform area. Passengers on a gas bus were probably aware of the smell which wafted around and also had a general impression that the engine was more sluggish than usual. Several cases were reported where people standing in queues or, sometimes, sitting in stationary vehicles, were overcome by fumes and had to receive first aid treatment, although it was not proven that the trailer producers were directly responsible. Anecdotal reports of the era suggest that apart from the high revs and the popping, once the bus was on a level stretch of road in top gear it was actually even quieter than a petrol bus, with a faint hissing noise sounding above the engine. If necessary, bus stops on slight gradients were moved to more level ground when gas bus operation began on a route and schedules sometimes had to be carefully revised to allow for their slower speeds. It was also not unknown for the Police to order them off the road after dark as often the trailers 'glowed' as they travelled along the blacked out streets.

In September 1944 the MOWT decided that in the light of the improved war situation the Government's producer gas scheme could be officially terminated and all ten Southdown buses were 'de-gassed' between September and October 1944. The last gas buses ran on Worthing services 3/8 by 17 August 1944 and on the 5/6 in October 1944 although some were noted on occasional reliefs departing Worthing for Horsham, Bognor and Arundel in September 1944. The first bus to be 'de-gassed' was car 116 in

September 1944 and the last recorded use of the system by Southdown was in the afternoon of 27 October 1944 when car 958 with trailer GT4 left Worthing garage and ran on gas to Portslade Works to be reconverted to petrol operation. Spare trailer GT10 remained at Worthing and was removed on 31 October 1944. The trailers were all sold for scrap on 23 November 1944 and nothing remains of this interesting interlude. Before re-entering service the TD4c's had their petrol engines replaced by Leyland 8.6 litre diesel engines probably reflecting the heavy wear and tear caused by gas operation.

As can seen Southdown – along with most other operators – totally failed to achieve the target of 10% of the fleet running on producer gas. The M.O.W.T. thanked those bus operators who had co-operated in the experiment and although large scale conversion to producer gas had proved unnecessary it stated the experience gained would prove invaluable for the continuance of the national war effort. Given the problems encountered with the relatively small scale conversions it was perhaps fortunate that the fuel supply situation improved before further more drastic measures became necessary.

Before the war only a few Southdown coaches had been fitted with a front spotlight but during the war – believed to be about mid-1943 – Southdown had the whole fleet fitted as standard.

The Utility Guys

Even after the completion and allocation of the 'unfrozen' buses there was clearly an urgent need in the UK for new buses to replace those that had reached the end of their normal operating life and others which had been damaged by enemy action. In early July 1941 plans were announced for the construction of a few makes of chassis to provide 1,600 new buses for use where needed by war workers. The Ministry of Supply had established a working group with manufacturers and bus operators to agree a specification for a standard 'utility' design. In the late summer of 1941 drawings were issued by the National Federation of Vehicle Trades to bus/trolleybus chassis and body builders for both highbridge and lowbridge double deckers and for a large forward control and a small normal control single decker. The design of the bodywork eliminated all curved domes and window surrounds and the interior was most austere – the bodies had only a single 'skin', with no inside panelling. Initially only wooden seating was allowed and on double deck buses the rear upper deck emergency 'window' was unglazed. Only a limited number of opening windows were allowed per bus and just one destination indicator box permitted at the front. As the war continued the authorised standard was progressively relaxed – the rear upper deck emergency exit could be glazed and more opening side windows per bus were allowed. Later, roof domes were rounded off and more comfortable seating was permitted. According to the Ministry of Supply proposals, delivery would commence from late 1941 and continue into the latter part of 1942 although in practice the first complete utility vehicle appeared in the late summer of 1942. Symbolically, the first utility body was built by Park Royal in September 1941 on 'unfrozen' Leyland Titan TD7 chassis 306715, becoming London Transport STD101 – the chassis having been 'borrowed' from an order for the West Riding Automobile Company.

Eventually programmes were drawn up for Leyland and Guy to each construct 500 chassis for double deckers, with Bedford acting as the sole manufacturer of single deck chassis and Sunbeam producing trolleybuses. No doubt many operators would have been happy to take the Leyland built products but eventually it was found that due to military contracts they would be unable to undertake supply of any further bus chassis whilst hostilities continued. As a result the first manufacturer authorised by the government to produce the new utility double deck motor bus chassis was Guy Motors of Wolverhampton who were relatively unknown among most large company fleets. Only Bedford was allowed to build the small normal control single deck chassis – although it produced about 3,200 of its famous OWB model. Of the larger single deck chassis only some 'unfrozen' buses appeared. Although Daimler and Bristol were also subsequently licensed to build utility double deck motor bus chassis, Leyland did not resume the manufacture of bus and coach chassis until after the war had ended.

Sanction for the release of materials to build the utility buses was the responsibility of the Ministry of Supply while allocation of the completed vehicles was arranged by the Ministry of War Transport. The manner in which vehicles were allocated often caused frustration and resentment with a wide range of chassis and body combinations being directed to some operators. In this respect Southdown was relatively lucky to eventually receive a total of 100 Guy Arab double deck buses (cars 400 to 499) between April 1943 and March 1946. Bodywork on these vehicles was shared between Strachan (3 lowbridge, 3 highbridge), Northern Counties (2 lowbridge, 44 highbridge), Park Royal (24 highbridge) and Weymann (2 lowbridge, 22 highbridge). As most utility composite bodies were constructed of poor quality and unseasoned ash many were soon in need of major rebuilds and 33 Guys were subsequently rebuilt and converted to open top for seasonal use. In the case of Northern Counties (and East Lancs which rebodied some prewar Titans for Southdown) the use of steel, rather than timber, for body framing was permitted as these companies had abandoned composite construction before the war and could not easily return to it. Fortunately, almost half of Southdown's utility fleet had metal framed bodywork.

The double deck Arab chassis had been introduced by Guy in 1933 and was the first to enter production with the Gardner LW series diesel engine as standard equipment. The choice of Guy Motors as the major wartime supplier was surprising as by 1937 production of this model had lapsed and it was no longer listed as being available. The strict specification meant that Guy had to redesign the Arab chassis with revised proportions and use more cast iron than aluminium which inevitably led to delays in starting production. The utility specification called for a conventional forward control half cab

Seen in Pool Valley, Brighton on Relief duties is car 401 (GCD 975), a Guy Arab I with Gardner 5LW engine and Northern Counties lowbridge body new in May 1943. Southdown was allocated just two of the original batch of 500 wartime Arabs sanctioned by the Ministry of Supply. The body was removed in 1951 and an East Lancs body new in 1945 was transferred from Leyland Titan car 956. In this form it survived until the end of operation by covered top utility Guys in June 1963.
A B Cross

Car 403 (GCD 689), a Guy Arab II with Strachan lowbridge body delivered in November 1943, looks smart in early postwar livery at Pool Valley, Brighton on the hourly service 16 to Golden Cross via Lewes. Its registration was originally booked for one of the Leyland TD7s which were diverted to Cumberland Motor Services in 1941. The Strachan body was removed and sold for scrap in May 1951 and a metal framed East Lancs body new in November 1944 transferred from Leyland TD2 car 954. It was sold to the Salford dealer Frank Cowley in April 1958.
A B Cross

chassis of normal dimensions (7ft 6ins wide and 26ft 0ins long) suitable for rear entrance double deck bodywork seating 55 passengers (lowbridge) or 56 (highbridge). There is some evidence that the aim was to match the dimensions of the Leyland TD7. Presumably, as at the early stages of the project Guy and Leyland were to be partners as chassis builders, there would have been strong advantages in having directly interchangeable body mounting dimensions.

The wartime Guy Arab retained the Gardner 5LW or 6LW diesel engine as standard and was very similar to the Leyland Titan TD7 except that it had a 'crash' gearbox fitted amidships which was unusual by this time. In operation the four speed sliding mesh gearbox was fairly quiet although the double gate clutch set up a characteristic whistling noise at each change. The Arab also featured flexible engine mountings as standard, although the Gardner 5LW at maximum speed could produce pronounced shivering. Because of the extra weight of the vehicle – nearly a ton heavier than a typical prewar double decker – it was preferable for the 8.4 litre Gardner 6LW engine to be fitted, but these were in very short supply so most of the first 500 chassis were fitted with the 7.0 litre 5LW unit. Chassis with the smaller engine were fitted with a normal length bonnet and short mudguards although those fitted with the larger unit required a longer bonnet with the radiator moved forward slightly and the mudguards swept up at the front edge to match. This produced an overall length of 26ft 5ins which required a dispensation from the Ministry of War Transport.

Guy had previously been manufacturing small military vehicles and it therefore took the company a while to switch over production from this work. Priority was given to operators considered to be in most urgent need and Southdown was allocated just two of the first 500 Guy utility chassis built – subsequently known as the Arab I. Cars 400 and 401 arrived in May 1943 and were fitted with lowbridge Northern Counties 55 seat metal framed five bay bodywork. To denote their lowbridge status they carried the 'L' suffix under the side fleet numbers from new. These bodies had plain front upper deck windows with a very narrow non opening ventilation strip, no side screen box and the mandatory 'lobster' pattern rear dome. The side windows on the upper deck were slightly deeper than those on the lower deck and metal rain strips were only fitted over the side half drop opening windows. On the upper deck the seats were arranged in usual lowbridge format with 4 seats to each row and the offside gangway sunk into the roof of the lower saloon. They were allocated to Brighton from new and contemporary reports indicate their use on local services such as 13B to North Moulscombe but also country services 16 and 25 which required lowbridge buses.

The 501st Guy Arab chassis and all further wartime Arabs had the longer bonnet irrespective of engine size and had the designation Arab II. When delivered most of Southdown's 100 Guy Arab chassis were fitted with the twin plate clutch and sliding mesh gears but during 1948 these were replaced by single plate clutches and the gearboxes converted to constant mesh at Portslade Works. A total of 77 of the Arabs delivered to Southdown had the small 5LW engine with remainder being powered by 6LW units. When new, cars 405-9/16-26/42/3/6/7/63-65 were

The early lowbridge utility bodies were amongst the most angular of all the wartime deliveries as shown by car 404 (GCD 690) at Pool Valley Brighton after the war. It is a Guy Arab II with Gardner 5LW engine and Strachan lowbridge body new in December 1943. The registration had originally been booked for a Leyland TD7 which was diverted to Cumberland Motor Services in 1941. Although sometimes found on the longer Lewes Road country services that required lowbridge buses, car 404 is seen on a local service 13A to North Moulscombe. In August 1951 the Strachan body was scrapped and replaced by an East Lancs high-bridge body originally fitted to Leyland Titan car 940 in 1943. In this form it remained with Southdown until withdrawn in May 1959.
Southdown Enthusiasts Club – Clark/Surfleet Collection

fitted with 6LW engines and where possible, buses with the larger unit were used on the more hilly routes such as service 12 from Brighton to Eastbourne. In later years many engine changes took place, often at the same time as rebuilding or conversion to open-top.

Southdown was authorised for only three more new buses in 1943 which arrived between October and December. Cars 402 to 404 had Guy Arab II chassis fitted with lowbridge Strachan 55 seat composite bodywork and also carried the 'L' suffix from new. The latter two were allocated registrations GCD 689 and 690 which had been reserved for the 1940 Titan TD7s. They had plain front upper deck windows surmounted by small drop in ventilators and the equal depth

Car 410 (GUF 70) a Guy Arab II with Park Royal highbridge body to full utility specification is posed by the Royal Pavilion in Brighton soon after delivery in April 1944. The livery is all grey with apple green below the lower deck windows, an apple green band below the upper deck windows and a dark green roof. This was later selected as one of the first batch of 15 extensively rebuilt by Southdown to open top in 1950-1 for summer use at Brighton, Worthing and Hayling Island. It retained a Gardner 5LW engine throughout its life and was sold for scrap in April 1959.
Roy Marshall

In early postwar days car 415 (GUF 75), a Guy Arab II with Weymann lowbridge body passes through Cosham on a relief working to Bradford Junction via Fratton Bridge although this destination was never included on the Portsmouth screens. It was one of two similar lowbridge examples delivered in late 1944 for use on service 38 which passed under a low railway bridge near Droxford Railway Station. The bodies were removed and sold for scrap in April 1955 and the chassis dismantled at Portslade Works.
Southdown Enthusiasts Club – Clark/Surfleet Collection

side windows had continuous metal rain-strips. All three were allocated to Brighton from new and saw service on the Lewes Road country services where lowbridge buses were required. The five lowbridge buses were refurbished by the company after the war and during 1949 they were reseated using seats from bodies removed from prewar Leylands but as these seats were thicker the seating capacity was reduced. A small metal sun visor was also fitted over the driver's window on all these buses. In 1951 the original utility bodies were removed for scrap and metal framed East Lancs bodies originally on Titan TD1s and TD2s and dating from 1943-5 were fitted.

During 1944 with an improving supply situation Southdown received a further 38 Guy Arabs between March and December. Operators still had to take what was offered and four different styles of five bay 'lobster' domed utility bodywork were fitted to these buses. Cars 405, 406 and 407 had highbridge Strachan 56 seat composite bodies while a further ten (cars 408 to 413 and 442 to 445) had highbridge Park Royal 56 seat composite bodies similar to the six bodies fitted to the rebodied TD1s. Cars 405 and 406 which arrived in May 1944 were allocated registrations GCD 691 and 692 using up those reserved for the TD7s. The Park Royal bodies did not have a drop in glazed ventilator above the nearside lower deck front bulkhead window although the bodies on cars 444 and 445 had radiused bottom corners to the front upper deck windows. During 1951 the Strachan bodies were scrapped and replaced by East Lancs bodies off Titan TD2s. On delivery most Guys were again allocated to Brighton but some were soon transferred to Eastbourne and

Portsmouth while 444 was the first to run at Worthing where the type settled down on town services for many years.

Cars 414 and 415 had lowbridge Weymann 55 seat composite bodies and were the last new side gangway low height buses purchased by the company. They were allocated to Portsmouth and used on service 38 which required lowbridge buses to pass under the low railway bridge near Droxford Station. With a reduced need for lowbridge buses the pair were withdrawn and scrapped in 1955. The other 23 buses – cars 416 to 423 and 427 to 441 – had Northern Counties highbridge 56 seat metal framed bodies which had a rather deeper roof profile than the other double deck buses then in the Southdown fleet making them easily recognisable. They were originally spread between Brighton, Worthing and Portsmouth depots although no Guy utilities were ever allocated to Bognor or Chichester. Cars 405 to 413, 416 to 423 and 427 to 445 carried the 'H' suffix from new. All 38 buses had the separate drop in glazed ventilators above the front upper deck windows and deliveries until at least the end of 1944 had no rear screen boxes fitted. These were added by Southdown at Portslade Works, generally before the buses entered service although, occasionally, as in the case of cars 416, 417, 427, 442 and 443, traffic requirements had to come first and buses were returned to the Works for fitment as the opportunity arose.

All the Arabs delivered to Southdown in 1943 and 1944 arrived fitted with wooden slatted seats and no handrails but these were soon replaced with upholstered squabs using the existing frames. Some, such as cars 400 to 407, 414, 415,

Seen on a westbound service 31 is car 430 (GUF 130), a Guy Arab II with Gardner 5LW engine and Northern Counties highbridge body delivered in August 1944. All of Southdown's 1943/4 Guys were originally fitted with wooden slatted seats although soon replaced with upholstered squabs using existing frames. Hopefully car 430 had already been dealt with given the length of this route! It was rebuilt by Southdown in October 1954 but withdrawn in May 1957 and saw further service with Premier Travel. Note the white blackout markings on the kerb in this early post war photograph.
Southdown Enthusiasts Club – Clark/Surfleet Collection

424 and 425, were completed before entry into service, but others had to await manpower and materials with the last (car 440) being completed in November 1947. Car 423, which was delivered in November 1944, has been recorded as the first utility bus to be delivered with a box for the rear registration number plate – previous deliveries having the number painted on the rear platform window. Soon after the war most of the 38 buses new in 1944 had a small metal sun visor fitted over the driver's cab window and on cars 410 and 412, at least, larger non opening upper deck front windows were fitted.

During 1945 Southdown received a further 52 Guy Arab II chassis fitted with Gardner engines and a variety of 56 seat highbridge bodywork

Car 482 (GUF 182) is a Guy Arab II with Weymann highbridge body delivered in July 1945. It looks very smart when seen in Goring on the busy cross town service 3 between East Worthing (Ham Hotel) and Goring (Aldsworth Avenue) to which it was extended in May 1945. Unfortunately the Weymann bodies suffered the same deterioration as other timber framed utility bodies and many, including car 482, were scrapped in 1955 after just ten years in the fleet.
Southdown Enthusiasts Club – W J Haynes Collection

comprising 21 by Northern Counties, 9 by Park Royal and 22 by Weymann. Delivery of these buses continued throughout 1945 but not in either fleet number or registration number sequence. The Northern Counties metal framed bodies on cars 424 to 426 and 448 to 462 were identical to those buses with highbridge bodies received in 1944. These had the 'lobster' rear dome and were delivered with no side screen box. The last three buses from Northern Counties (cars 463 to 465) were delivered in late August and were built to 'relaxed utility' specification with rear and side destination boxes, a better standard of seating and more rounded rear domes. Fitted with 6LW engines they were allocated to Eastbourne and often found on service 12 alongside some of Brighton's GLW Guys.

The Park Royal composite bodies delivered in 1945 (cars 446, 447 and 466 to 472) were similar to cars 444 and 445 from 1944 except that on these nine vehicles destination displays were fitted at front and rear, and the 'lobster' style rear dome was replaced by a rounded rear dome. The final batch for 1945 consisted of 22 bodies by Weymann. Twenty of these had composite bodywork (cars 473 to 484 and 487 to 494 while two (cars 485 and 486) were metal framed. These buses were similar to the other later utilities, with rear and side destination boxes from new, but the Weymann highbridge bodies had a noticeably softer front profile to the driver's cab and were delivered with plain windows at the front of the upper deck. The two vehicles with metal framed bodies were distinguishable only by the much smaller nearside lower deck front bulkhead window and the rounded window corners on the offside of the driver's cab as compared to the angular corners on the composite bodies. Most of the 1945 deliveries went into service at Worthing and Portsmouth. Soon after the war most of the 52 buses new in 1945 had a small metal sun visor fitted over the driver's window, except that cars 424, 425, 452, 458, 489, 490 and 491, at least, were never fitted with these. Southdown took delivery of the last five of its 100 utility Guy Arab buses in March 1946 – details are included in chapter 10.

As stated earlier the Northern Counties bodies were metal framed whereas most of the others were of composite construction and not expected to have a long life in service with the company. In 1949 it was therefore decided to rebuild the Northern Counties highbridge bodies, a process which continued until 1954 although a few escaped rebuilding and were withdrawn at an earlier date. The rebuild included rounding the front and rear domes and reseating with 54 old seats from bodies being removed from later prewar Titans, or in some cases the seats salvaged from the buses purchased for their diesel engines in 1950/51. A side destination screen box was fitted and the drop in ventilators above the front upper deck windows were removed. After experiments with the conversion

of car 409 to open top in 1950, Southdown completely stripped down and rebuilt a total of 33 bodies for seasonal use. Despite being metal framed and having been rebuilt by Southdown some of the Northern Counties bodied Guys were withdrawn for scrap as early as 1955. The Park Royal bodies on cars 469/70 were removed in August 1951 after less than 6 years service and replaced by East Lancs metal framed bodies removed from TD2s. Of the small 1946 Park Royal batch, the first of those which remained covered top were sold in 1956 and Weymann bodied examples started to go for scrap in 1955. Many former Southdown Guys sold in the late 1950s found new owners and continued in service until the early 1960s.

There was much early scepticism among operators but once some early technical problems were rectified, the utility Guy Arab proved a reliable and economical vehicle. Although soon replaced on the main trunk routes by new Leyland PD2s a few of Southdown's covered top wartime Guy Arabs survived until 1963 albeit in rebuilt or rebodied form with the last withdrawn from local services in Worthing on 30 April in that year. 1963 was also the last full season for the utilities in open top form, although a handful of them ran in early 1964 and some made their final trip to the Derby in June 1964. Southdown was among a number of B.E.T. companies that took Guy Arabs in post war years including a batch of 12 Arab 111s with Northern Counties metal framed bodies in 1948. Further deliveries in 1955/6 added 36 Arab IVs with handsome Park Royal bodies to the predominantly Leyland fleet.

By 1943 some of the coaches that had been requisitioned in 1940 were made available to the company. The following vehicles returned to the fleet during 1943 – 1173 on 28 May, 1030 and 1129 on 8 June, 1079 and 1166 on 12 July and 1197 on 11 August. Car 1030 was probably stored and not used before being sold in June 1947. None of these coaches are believed to have been rebuilt after the war. Two of the stored Leyland Lioness touring coaches, cars 1801 and 1805 were sold to the United States Army on 12 August 1943.

Wartime rebodying programme
During the war years Southdown faced a growing problem of trying to maintain an ageing fleet, many examples of which were over the normal lifespan of around eight to ten years intended when each vehicle was built. With a shortage of skilled manpower and delays in obtaining replacement parts it was inevitable that maintenance of the fleet would be reduced to a minimum and the bodies of most buses suffered as a result. In particular it was the structural condition of timber framed double deck bodies which gave particular cause for alarm. In many parts of the country the replacement of bodies destroyed by enemy action – which seldom wrecked the chassis

– was also important. Fitting new bodywork to existing chassis had been quite common practice from the early days of motor bus operation and Southdown rebodied some early Leyland Tiger coaches in 1936. The reuse of existing chassis was very much in line with general Government policy of avoiding waste and provision was included for specific companies to concentrate on building new bodywork for these older chassis. If this arrangement could also include the many Leyland TD1 and TD2 models with timber framed bodies urgently in need of replacement then a solution to one of Southdown's problems now presented itself. Application was therefore made to the Ministry of War Transport for 21 new bodies to be fitted to earlier Leyland chassis.

Following its considerable support for Wilts & Dorset Motor Services Ltd in its hour of need in 1939/40, Southdown was left in a rather unusual position by the middle of 1942. All 23 of its first Leyland Titan TD1 open-toppers survived – and from October 1941 had been fitted with dark green canvas tops to permit their all year round use. Of the rest of the TD1 fleet, only eight survived in service – cars 871, 874 and 876 with Leyland bodies dating from 1930 and cars 937-940 and 942 with Short Bros bodies dating from 1932. In addition there were thirteen remaining Titan TD2 models – cars 946, 947 and 949 with Short Bros bodies dating from 1932 and cars 950-959 also with Short Bros bodies dating from 1933. It was these vehicles which were now selected for a utility specification rebodying programme undertaken for Southdown between 1943 and 1945 by three companies. Two of these – Willowbrook and East Lancs – had been given the specific task of building on reconditioned rather than

chassis while Park Royal had produced the very first utility double decker to be completed in October 1941.

The complete programme comprised:

Park Royal H30/26R	1943	871, 874, 876, 937, 938, 939
Willowbrook L27/24R	1943	946, 949
East Lancs H26/26R	1944	940, 942, 954, 955, 959
Willowbrook L27/24R	1944	951, 953, 957
East Lancs H26/26R	1945	947, 950, 952, 956, 958

Depending on the coachbuilder involved, the degree of utility in the construction varied. The five lowbridge examples rebodied by Willowbrook represented one of the most austere and least attractive wartime designs while those by East Lancs were to an outline that remained in production almost unchanged through the post war Southdown rebodying programme.

First to appear during early 1943 were the six Park Royal H30/26R utility bodies. These angular five bay bodies were of composite construction built to the strict austerity design defined by the Ministry of Supply and similar to many supplied on both 'unfrozen', reconditioned and wartime chassis. As delivered they had wooden slatted seats although between 1943-5 the seating was reduced to 52 using upholstered seats which had been salvaged from the original bodies. All of the Park Royal bodies were fitted to TD1 chassis – cars 871, 874 and 876 dating from 1930, and cars 937-939 dating from 1932. They entered service in a livery of allover grey primer but were repainted fairly quickly in a grey livery with green below the lower deck windows. Officially only one destination box was allowed at the front but a rear display was fitted at Portslade Works before entering service. The

Passing the old Pier Hotel in Worthing on a Relief working is car 876 (UF 6476), a Leyland Titan TD1 with Park Royal highbridge utility body fitted in 1943. The chassis dated from 1930 and the original Leyland body was scrapped at Portslade Works in 1943. In rebodied form the bus remained in service with Southdown until 1952 completing some 22 years in the fleet. *Southdown Enthusiasts Club – Clark/Surfleet Collection*

rear 'lobster' domes were not rebuilt during their service with Southdown. They were originally fitted with separate ventilators above the front upper deck windows, but on car 938 at least, larger non opening front windows were fitted at a later date. To help offset the lack of opening windows a drop in glazed ventilator was also fitted above the nearside lower deck front bulkhead window. After salvaging the seats the original bodies were scrapped by Southdown at Portslade Works between March and May 1943.

Later in 1943 Leyland TD2 cars 946 and 949 were fitted with new Willowbrook five bay utility lowbridge L27/24R bodies receiving an 'L' suffix

after the fleet number. These were particularly austere looking vehicles of square 'box like' appearance unlike other standard utility designs. They had straight upright fronts, non opening front upper deck windows and a rear dome to the usual 'lobster' pattern. The seating on the upper deck was arranged with 4 seats to each row with the sunken offside gangway intruding into the lower saloon. Between January and May 1944 Leyland TD2 cars 951, 953, 957 were fitted with similar lowbridge bodies by Willowbrook. They entered service in grey livery with a green band below the upper-deck windows and green below the lower-deck windows. After salvaging the

957 (UF 9757) is a Leyland Titan TD2 new in 1933 which was rebodied by Willowbrook with a new lowbridge body to utility specification in January 1944. They were amongst the most angular of all utility bodies produced and usually appear to have been photographed on relief duties but car 957, seen here in Pool Valley, Brighton, is on service 25 which ran to Eastbourne via Lewes. Delivered in grey livery it was repainted by Southdown before entering service and looks quite smart in this scene. Alongside is a Titan still in the 1942/3 livery with all green upper deck. *Southdown Enthusiasts Club – W J Haynes Collection*

seats the original Short Bros bodies were scrapped by Southdown at Portslade Works between October 1943 and July 1944. Not surprisingly these were among the first of the utility bodies to be withdrawn in 1951.

By contrast the 10 five bay bodies by East Lancs were to a more pleasing relaxed utility standard with rounded rear dome. Whilst, officially, the standard wartime bodies were all of composite – wood framed – construction certain manufacturers such as East Lancs and Northern Counties who had already changed over to metal framed bodywork were allowed to continue with this method of production and thereby avoided the worst problems associated with the use of unseasoned timber. In 1944 Leyland TD1 cars 940, 942 and Leyland TD2 cars 954, 955, 959 were fitted with 52 seat highbridge bodies by East Lancs with cars 947, 950, 952, 956 and 958 following in 1945. Delivery was spread over an 18 month period and commenced with car 940 arriving in January 1944 and ending with car 950 in July 1945. They had upholstered seats from new and were fitted with separate ventilators above the front upper deck windows. Eight of these bodies were not originally fitted with a side screen box, but the last two – on cars 950 and 958 – had this feature from new. The original Short Bros bodies were scrapped by Southdown at Portslade Works between April 1944 and October 1946.

Many operators who refurbished their older Titans converted them to diesel engines but all of Southdown's rebodied Titan TD1s and TD2s

retained their smooth running Leyland petrol engines while in service with the company except for cars 871, 874, 876, 937 to 939, 946, 949, 951, 953 and 957 which were temporarily fitted with Gardner 5LW diesel engines in 1943. They reverted to Leyland petrol engines during 1945 and 1946. Whereas many operators also specified a more modern looking and longer 'Covrad' replacement radiator as part of the overhaul exercise, Southdown retained the original squat early 1930s Titan version on these vehicles. After the war many of these 21 rebodied buses had a small metal sun visor fitted over the driver's window. Having completed some 18 to 19 years of service the Titan TD1 and TD2 chassis had reached the end of their extended life but the metal framed East Lancs bodies were considered to be in good enough condition for further use. During 1951 they were therefore fitted to wartime Guy Arab chassis and remained in service with Southdown until 1958-59.

1944
Wartime Rebuilds

In addition to the rebodying programme for the remaining TD1s and TD2s a total of 34 prewar Titans were rebuilt and refurbished during the period between 1944 and 1947. Eighteen Titans dating from 1936-9 were rebuilt by J C Beadle of Dartford during the period 1944-6. Beadle had already supplied many bodies to Southdown in prewar days and was now one of the companies specifically given the task of providing new bodywork for existing chassis. In addition to new bodies built very closely to a distinctive, if somewhat old fashioned, peacetime outline Beadle also rebuilt and refurbished many older bodies for major operators across southern England. Of the six Beadle lowbridge bodied TD4s dating from 1936, three – cars 142, 143 and 144 – were destined to retain their original bodies in the post war rebodying programme and these were thoroughly rebuilt by Beadle in January/ February 1946. The driver's cab was completely refashioned with a narrower door and a much deeper windscreen fitted with a pronounced downward slope to the offside. This became an easily identifiable feature of Beadle bodies and rebuilds of this period. The three roller blind boxes over the nearside lower deck windows were replaced with a screen box over the platform and separate ventilators were fitted over the front upper deck windows – although cars 142 and 144 regained plain windows later and continued in service until 1956. In November 1944 Beadle rebuilt the highbridge body on car 150. This involved removing and panelling over the folding roof as well as the roller blind boxes over the offside lower deck windows.

Fourteen of the Beadle lowbridge bodied TD5s dating from 1938 were rebuilt by Beadle between March 1945 and April 1946 allowing many to continue running in Southdown service until the mid 1950s. All had the three roller blind boxes over the lower deck windows on the nearside replaced with a screen box over the platform. The first to be completed was car 200 which had an experimental narrow side destination box, designed to take a screen from one of the East Kent Titans – without numbers. It was soon realised that if this policy was pursued it would be necessary to design a whole set of separate screens and all the remaining rebuilds were to the standard 41in x 14in size. The first four cars to be rebuilt – 188, 189, 190 and 200 – were virtually unchanged from the original, but the last – car 190 – also incorporated opening ventilators in the front upper deck windows. The remaining ten – cars 181, 182, 184, 185, 191, 192, 195, 196, 197 and 198 – involved major reconstruction, which resulted in the driver's cab being completely refashioned with a narrower door and a much deeper windscreen. Opening ventilators were fitted as on car 190 although most subsequently had the additional ventilators removed. Most of these buses remained in service until the end of lowbridge bus operations in 1956/7 and there is a strong possibility that these were in fact new bodies disguised as rebuilds to circumvent wartime regulations.

Seen at Pool Valley, Brighton after the war on service 23 to Crawley is car 144 (CCD 944), a Leyland Titan TD4 with Beadle lowbridge body new in 1936. In early 1946 Beadle extensively rebuilt the original body – some would suggest effectively a new body was fitted – and car 144 then remained in service until sale in September 1956 by which time Southdown no longer had a requirement for lowbridge buses.
Southdown Enthusiasts Club – W J Haynes Collection

In late 1944 Willowbrook commenced rebuilding four Short Bros bodied Titan TD3 and TD4 models but all retained their original outline. First to be completed was car 974 in December 1944, with car 972 following in January 1945, car 967 in April 1945 and finally car 132 in November 1945.

Commencing in early 1945 Southdown started to undertake some rebuilding work. The amount of rectification work required obviously depended on the particular state of each vehicle although all retained their original outline. Car 962, a Short Bros bodied Titan TD3 dating from 1934 had the front upper deck ventilators and side screen box rebuilt in February 1945. It survived in this form until late 1949 when the body was removed in preparation for a new Beadle body fitted in January 1950. This was followed in May 1945 by car 101, a Short Bros bodied Titan TD4 which continued in service until withdrawn in June 1952 and did not feature in the post war rebodying programme. In June 1945 car 121 had the front upper deck ventilators and side screen box rebuilt surviving in this form until the Short Bros body was removed in late 1949. It was rebodied by Beadle in February 1950. Car 147 had its Beadle body rebuilt with sealed sunroof, front upper deck ventilators and a side screen box over the platform in November 1945. The old body was removed in December 1949 and a new Northern Counties body fitted in March 1950. During December 1945 car 209 had its Park Royal body rebuilt with a side screen box over the platform. The old body was removed in December 1949 and a new Northern Counties body fitted in March 1950. Car 103 had the side screen boxes removed from its Short Bros body

in May 1946 and remained in this form until withdrawn in November 1953. Later rebuilds included car 109 in July 1946, car 107 in December 1946 and car 100 in August 1947 and all remained with original bodies until withdrawal between 1952 and 1956.

Other Titan TD4s were refurbished by contractors who were not previously associated with bus bodywork but, with declining military production, now found themselves with spare capacity and skilled manpower. Car 104 was dealt with by Saunders in December 1946, car 105 by West Nor in February 1947 and car 111 by Portsmouth Aviation in May 1947.

The complete programme consisted of:

Beadle	1944	150
Willowbrook	1944	974
Beadle	1945	181, 182, 188, 189, 190, 196, 198, 200
Southdown	1945	101, 121, 147, 209, 962
Willowbrook	1945	132, 967, 972
Beadle	1946	142, 143, 144, 184, 185, 191, 192, 195, 197
Saunders	1946	104
Southdown	1946	103, 107, 109
Portsmouth Aviation	1947	111
Southdown	1947	100
West Nor	1947	105

With raids by manned enemy aircraft now unlikely, the full Blackout regulations were replaced on Sunday 17 September by the 'dim out' although there was an exception for a five mile deep belt along the coastal areas so

Many of the Beadle bodied Leyland TD5s dating from 1938 had their bodies rebuilt by Beadle during 1945/6. The first few, including car 188 (EUF 188) seen at Pool Valley, Brighton, had the three roller blinds over the nearside windows replaced by a screen box over the platform but otherwise retained their original outline. After its rebuild in May 1945 car 188 survived with Southdown until August 1956 when it was sold for scrap. Service 24 was a long established circular operation running every 2 hours in each direction. *Southdown Enthusiasts Club – Clark/Surfleet Collection*

Laying over at Haywards Heath Railway Station on service 88 is car 143 (CCD 943) a Leyland Titan TD4 with Beadle lowbridge body new in 1936. The original Beadle body was extensively rebuilt to a more modern outline in early 1946 and car 143 then remained in service until sale in October 1953. It is seen after the war in fully lined out early postwar livery with dark green painted radiator. At this time service 88 ran two hourly through to Turners Hill where it connected with LPTB service 434 to Crawley and East Grinstead.
Southdown Enthusiasts Club – W J Haynes Collection

effectively restrictions remained in place for Southdown until the end of the war. In spite of this the white markings added to all buses at the start of the war began to be removed by the end of December. Car 1184 was repurchased from the government on 28 September 1944 for the sum of £175 and rebuilt by Caffyns, Eastbourne in January 1946.

In December 1944 the Minister of Home Security amended the Lighting (Restrictions) Order 1944 to allow a welcome improvement in the standard of lighting for the interior of public service vehicles. Later in the same month the Minister also announced that all road vehicles were now permitted to operate without headlight masks. This relaxation of lighting restrictions was principally to help speed Military vehicles at night but meant that normal conditions now applied for motor vehicles. As prewar standards of street lighting were not yet in operation in most areas, drivers were warned against causing unnecessary dazzle.

Although most of the 1935 Titans were rebodied in the postwar rebodying programme car 109 (BUF 209) was one of those that were given only a body rebuild by Southdown in 1946. It is a Leyland Titan TD4 with Short Bros lowbridge body seen at Pool Valley, Brighton on a clockwise working of the circular service 24 which ran every 2 hours in each direction. It was sold to Hutfield's Coaches, Gosport for further operation in February 1956 after 21 years service!
Southdown Enthusiasts Club – W J Haynes Collection

1945

At the start of 1945 thoughts turned to the resumption of normal postwar production and representatives of both the operating and manufacturing sectors presented a strong case to the Minister of War Transport for important alterations to the Construction and Use Regulations. Whilst a few concessions were made concerning overall height and weight, the principal requests for the overall width limit to be extended to 8 feet and for the overall length of 30 feet already permitted for 3 axle chassis to be allowed for 2 axle chassis were refused. The matter did not rest there but the decision influenced the size of early postwar designs.

In January it was announced that as the wartime restrictions on rear lights on motor vehicles had been relaxed, rear number plates should again be clearly readable at night. Some rear lamps fitted during the war could not be adapted and therefore the requirement was suspended until 29 March 1945. Due to shortages of manpower and parts this was later postponed until 30 June 1945. A further 52 Guy Arabs would be delivered to Southdown during the year helping to ease the problems arising from reduced maintenance of the fleet due to wartime shortages and controls. Many were to a 'relaxed utility' specification announced in January 1945 with the 'lobster' style rear dome replaced by a rounded rear profile. Wooden

slatted type seats would now be replaced by an upholstered pattern to be covered in leather or moquette. In place of the previous four opening windows there could be ten, six in the upper saloon and four in the lower and they could be of the half drop or half sliding type as preferred. Towards the end of the war the folding 'sunshine roof' as fitted to cars 950 to 959, 964 to 975, 122 to 138 and 145 to 150 were sealed in a closed position. As the war drew to an end in May 1945 some elderly Leyland Tiger coaches – cars 1029, 1038, 1039, 1042, 1054 and 1055 were sold to the United States Army.

War damaged vehicles

During the course of the war the company submitted a number of war damage claims covering various incidents in which vehicles sustained damage as a result of enemy action. Some of these, such as the attack on car 1443 on 2 November 1940, are well known but others are more difficult to explain. On 26 September 1940 there is reference to a chassis damaged at Park Royal's works in London and this probably refers to one of the Leyland Titan TD7s which were then in build although by this time the completed vehicles were already destined to be delivered elsewhere. No other Southdown vehicles are likely to have been at Park Royal at this time and no further details are known of this claim.

As is well documented the body of car 1443

A scene at Portslade Works in May 1945 including on the left car 401 (GCD 975) which has just been repainted from grey into the early postwar livery with dark green roof. Next is car 956 (UF 9756) which has just arrived from East Lancs with its new body in allover grey livery while what appears to be car 203 has been repainted in the slightly later version of the livery with cream bands below both upper and lower decks. Ironically the East Lancs body on car 956 was later fitted to car 401 in July 1951!
C F Klapper © Omnibus Society

was destroyed near Rushlake Green on 2 November 1940 and a claim for £607.4s.6d submitted. The destruction of two coaches in use as ambulances at Portsmouth on the night of 10/11 January 1941 is also well documented and the company made a claim for £1064.13s.0d for the loss of these vehicles. Some of the claims which did not involve total losses appear to have been made some time after incidents. For instance on 25 April 1941 it was reported that FCD 387 (incorrect registration) was damaged at Bognor. This is most likely to be a reference to FCD 3**6**7 but no raids are known to have occurred in the area on this day. The nearest report concerning an incident in Bognor was late in the evening of 11 April 1941 after normal bus services had ended. Significant damage occurred in the Railway Station area and, as Southdown had a garage at the corner of Richmond Road and Station Road, it is likely that the vehicle had been parked in the vicinity, possibly on dispersal, when the attack occurred. Also on 25 April 1941 car 188 was reported damaged at Hove although the nearest reference to any known incident in this area is on 28 April 1941. There is an undated claim for damage to a one man operated Leyland Cub – car 19 – at Horsham amounting to £170.18s.5d. Horsham had relatively few air raids but there was a bombing incident in Orchard Road on 29 November 1940 at around 2145. Cubs were used on service 72 and there was a

departure scheduled at 2143 from Highlands Estate (Orchard Road) so it is *likely* that this particular incident can be traced to this specific journey.

Other undated claims are for car 952 damaged at Southsea for which a claim of £153.2s.8d was made and car 160 damaged at some unspecified place for which a claim of £387.11s.3d was submitted. On 3 May 1943 there is a report of damage to car 186 although no bombing incidents have been discovered anywhere in the company area on this day. Cars 1183 and 1207 were reported as suffering damage in Beach Road, Eastbourne on 13 July 1943. No incidents were apparently recorded in Eastbourne on this day although on 6 June 1943 a bomb fell in Beach Road destroying several houses and in view of the proximity of Royal Parade Garage it is possible that these coaches were simply 'dispersed' in the nearby street when the attack occurred. Particularly odd is that cars 1157, 1806 and 1817 were reported damaged on 8 November 1944 although by this time there were no attacks by manned aircraft and no record of V1 or V2 attacks in the Southdown area. As the Lioness coaches had been out of use for several years at this time this may have been a 'catching up' claim as the air war over Britain was coming to an end.

The Southdown fleet as at 8 May 1945 appears in Appendix 3.

The delivery of the utility Guys did not follow the usual ordered pattern and it was not always possible to match fleet and registration numbers. Waiting at Worthing Pier is car 448 (GUF 188) a Guy Arab II with Northern Counties metal framed body delivered new in January 1945 – the same month that service 5 was extended half hourly to Findon. It was hoped that the metal framed bodies would last a full service life and so commencing in 1949 many of the Northern Counties bodied buses, including car 448, were rebuilt by Southdown.
Southdown Enthusiasts Club – W J Haynes Collection

VE Day in Bognor Regis and crowds are gathering in the High Street to celebrate the end of the Second World War in Europe on 8 May 1945. The frontage of Southdown's bus station is visible on the left and wartime surface shelters have been built either side of the entrance and exit. Judging by the numbers gathered in the roadway very little traffic – except buses – is expected. Often diversions to bus services were necessary to avoid the sometimes spontaneous street celebrations. *West Sussex County Council Library Service*

After the successful landings in Normandy in June 1944 there was a sense across the country that the war would soon be over. The civilian population had endured years of hard work, restrictions, blackout, rationing and separation from loved ones and longed for the better days to come after victory was secured. The advent of the V1 and V2 terror weapons had soon put paid to their earlier optimism and many found the final year of the war much more difficult to cope with than even the Blitz of 1940/1. There were fears of a German 'last stand' and the war with Japan was expected to go on for at least another year.

After months of tough fighting German forces in Italy surrendered on Sunday 29 April 1945 and Adolf Hitler committed suicide in his Berlin bunker the following day. Eventually, the German Chief-of-Staff, General Jodl, signed Germany's unconditional surrender to the western allies and Russia at 0241 on Monday 7 May. All operations were to cease at 1 minute after midnight (GMT) on Tuesday 8 May which would be declared VE (Victory in Europe) Day. At short notice a two day national holiday was announced to allow the exhausted population to celebrate victory after almost six long years of war. Despite the dull skies and slight drizzle, crowds flocked to the still bomb scarred towns and city centres and danced and sang in the streets. Many buildings were floodlit for the first time in almost six years while effigies of Hitler were burned, bonfires lit and hastily arranged street parties held across the land. On VE Day a few early morning journeys were cancelled but otherwise Southdown ran normal bus services while on the second day of the holiday, Wednesday 9 May, bus services generally started from 0900 and then ran as normal subject to availability of staff and diversions around special events taking

place. On Thursday 10 May the Prime Minister Winston Churchill announced in the House of Commons that the liquid fuel position would be eased and that subject to labour being available, buses and certain other categories would receive more fuel. More surprisingly, he also announced a small basic ration would be issued within 30 days to owners of private cars and motorcycles.

With victory over Germany now complete the blackout journey times introduced on most bus services on 16 November 1939 were finally abolished although given the sharp reduction in traffic it is surprising that they continued during the summer period at all. Timetable booklets were issued for *East Sussex, West Sussex* and the *Portsmouth area* with all alterations in service up to **Sunday 13 May 1945**. As the war had only ended a few days earlier these timetables must have been formulated under wartime conditions and approved by the RTCs. It was now possible to continue the slow process of restoring services to prewar levels with last buses generally departing from the main centres such as Portsmouth and Brighton at around 2200, although this was still generally an hour earlier than before the war.

In Worthing alternate weekday journeys on service **3** were extended westwards from Goring Church via Mulberry Lane and Goring Way to terminate at GORING (ALDSWORTH AVENUE). At the same time the full service was extended beyond George V Avenue with a 10 minute frequency on weekdays and 15 minutes on Sundays. The route of service **7** was revised (again!) to operate in both directions along Forest Road, Kingsland Road and Sompting Road and the weekday frequency of services **7** and **7A** increased from 30 minutes to 20 minutes although service **7B** was withdrawn. Service **22** was curtailed at PETWORTH SQUARE being replaced between Petworth and Duncton by new service **63A**. An hourly service continued to run daily between Brighton and Petworth.

A new local bus service appeared in Lewes in the shape of service **28** between NEVILL ESTATE (MOUNT HARRY ROAD/CABURN ROAD and LANDPORT ESTATE running via Mount Harry Road, Wendover Crescent, Cross Way, Middle Way, Nevill Crescent, Nevill Road, Spital Road, Western Road, High Street, Fisher Street, Mount Pleasant, White Hill, Offham Road, Kingsley Road, Meridian Road, Baxter Road, Evelyn Road and Fitzroy Road. With a journey time of 13 minutes one bus provided a 30 minute service on weekdays only.

Large parts of Southsea's shopping streets lay in ruins as a result of the 1940/1 blitz and the opportunity was taken to revise the pattern of services in this area. The **31A** was diverted between South Parade and London Road via Clarence Parade, Western Parade, Southsea Terrace, Bellevue Terrace, King's Terrace, Landport Terrace, Hampshire Terrace, Commercial Road and Kingston Crescent instead of via Fratton. To replace the diversion of service 31A via Theatre Royal the **31B** and **43** were revised to operate from South Parade to North End via Clarence Parade, Palmerston Road,

Car 1473 (GCD 373) was delivered in November 1939 after the outbreak of war and is part of the final batch of 1400 class Leyland Tiger TS8s with Harrington bodywork. Seen at Uckfield Bus Station on newly introduced service 32 it is still in wartime livery although the white markings to the front wings have been removed. Along with most of this class car 1473 was converted to perimeter seating during the war which it retained until rebuilt by Portsmouth Aviation in July 1948.
C F Klapper © Omnibus Society

Grove Road South, Elm Grove, Victoria Road North, Fratton Road, Kingston Road, London Road and then as previously. Certain journeys before 0830 continued to operate to and from Theatre Royal via Commercial Road, Greetham Street, Blackfriars Road, Bradford Road and Victoria Road North to normal line of route. The frequency of service **43** remained hourly throughout with an additional hourly service between Southsea and Westbourne (Cricketers) which increased the weekday service between Southsea and Havant via Fratton to four buses per hour in conjunction with the 31B. The Sunday morning service 43 was still restricted to running hourly between Theatre Royal and Westbourne (Cricketers). Service **31C** which ran as far east as Farlington was reduced to operate during early morning periods only.

One of the most significant enhancements to services at this time occurred in the Haywards Heath area. Pressure on the well established service 30 from Brighton to Chelwood Common had been building up steadily and extra capacity was required on the Brighton–Haywards Heath section on which the four Leyland Tiger six wheelers from the peacetime Beachy Head route had been drafted in November 1940. New Service **32** was introduced between BRIGHTON (POOL VALLEY) and UCKFIELD BUS STATION via the same route as service 30 to Danehill and then via Sheffield Green, Splaynes Green, Fletching, Piltdown, Maresfield and Ringles Cross with a two hourly service daily – but still with no Sunday morning journeys. Buses departed Brighton between 0840 and 1840 and Uckfield between 1052 and 2052 with the last bus running only as far as Haywards Heath. In conjunction with services 30 and 36 this increased the combined Brighton-Haywards Heath-HorstedKeynes

frequency to half hourly. New territory was served between Danehill and Fletching and a bus service restored to Sheffield Green, previously on the route of Brighton to East Grinstead service 28. In addition service **36** was extended from Haywards Heath to EAST GRINSTEAD (CROWN HOTEL) via West Common, Lindfield, Stone Cross, Ludwell, Horsted Keynes, Ludwell, Deanlands Farm, Sharpthorne, West Hoathly, Sharpthorne, Tyes Cross, Sainthill, and Dunnings. A two hourly service ran daily throughout. Further new roads for Southdown were served between Horsted Keynes and Sharpthorne, a new direct route provided from Tyes Cross to Sainthill Green and the through link restored between Brighton and East Grinstead although Southdown clearly did not intend to reinstate the prewar direct service 28. This pattern of operation continued largely unchanged until the severe cutbacks of 1971.

Some further improvements were also possible in the Portsmouth and Southsea areas. The weekday service on the **37** was extended by an extra hour to operate until 1827 from Theatre Royal. Service **37A** was extended to operate until 2147 from Theatre Royal daily – previously having ended at 1800. Service **38** was extended from Droxford via Hunt Kennels to its pre-21 September 1939 terminal at MEONSTOKE (BUCKS HEAD). On weekdays a two hourly service ran between Portsmouth and Droxford with four journeys extended to and from Meonstoke. On Sunday afternoons an hourly service ran between Portsmouth and Droxford with four journeys extended to and from Meonstoke. The frequency on weekdays as far as Wickham Square was improved to hourly in conjunction with new service **38A** which ran between PORTSMOUTH (THEATRE ROYAL) and

NEWTOWN (MILES GARAGE) as the 38 to Soberton Heath, Bold Forester then via Plough Inn. Closure of the Meon Valley railway line commencing on 6 February 1955 meant a lengthy extension northwards to ALTON STATION via West Meon, Bailey Green, East Tisted and Chawton. Both services **40B** and **42B** were extended from Theatre Royal to SOUTHSEA (SOUTH PARADE) apart from Sunday mornings when restrictions still applied.

Daytime services along the A3 corridor gave 12 buses per hour as follows:

37   2 journeys per hour Theatre Royal – Main Road – Waterlooville

37A 2 journeys per hour Theatre Royal – Stakes – Waterlooville

39   2 journeys per hour Theatre Royal – Main Road – Waterlooville – Hambledon

40   1 journey per hour Southsea South Parade Pier – Theatre Royal – Main Road – Waterlooville – Clanfield – Petersfield

40B 1 journey per hour Southsea South Parade Pier – Main Road – Waterlooville – Clanfield Drift Road

41   2 journeys per hour Southsea South Parade Pier – Fratton – Main Road – Waterlooville – Horndean

42   1 journey per hour Southsea South Parade Pier – Theatre Royal – Main Road – Waterlooville – Horndean – Petersfield

42B 1 journey per hour Southsea South Parade Pier – Main Road – Waterlooville – Snells Corner

Emsworth local service **44** which had previously not run during mornings – except for some early journeys – was enhanced to run all day (except Sunday mornings) and extended from Westbourne Square to Westbourne Cricketers via North Street and Commonside returning via River Street and North Street. An hourly service continued between Emsworth and Westbourne Square. The frequency of service **47** was increased to provide four buses per hour between Havant and Hayling Island on weekdays and on Sundays after 1300. Half hourly services operated each way around the Hayling loop via Stoke, Manor Corner, Gable Head, Eastoke, Bus Station, Manor Corner and Stoke with an hourly service each way via Northney. A two hourly service was still provided on Sunday morning but no journeys ran via Northney.

Further improvements to services were introduced in the Eastbourne area although no Sunday morning services were yet permitted. The frequency of service **93** to Jevington was increased from two hourly to an hourly service daily. Service **94** was again extended to form a circular service operating from EASTBOURNE (PEVENSEY ROAD) via Pevensey Road, Susans Road, Langney Road, Terminus Road, Upperton Road, Willingdon Road, Eastbourne Road, Polegate High Street, Station Road, Pevensey Road, Dittons Road, Stone Cross, Friday Street, Langney Rise, Seaside and Langney Road. The frequency was significantly enhanced with an hourly service each way throughout daily plus an hourly service via Willingdon to and from Polegate Station and an hourly service via Willingdon to and from Dittons Wood Corner daily. The Heathfield to Waldron section of service **95** was increased from Thursday and Saturday to operate on all weekdays and the frequency of Pevensey Bay service **96** increased from two hourly to an hourly service daily. As a sign that better times were really returning to the area service **99** was reintroduced between EASTBOURNE (PEVENSEY ROAD) and HASTINGS (WELLINGTON SQUARE) with a two hourly service daily. This had been a casualty in the dark days of summer 1940 although the prewar double run to Pevensey, Old Mint House did not reappear.

After limited wartime use car 9 (DUF 9 has returned to its familiar haunts and is seen on service 47 at Havant Station in early postwar livery with dark green roof and cream window surrounds. It was one of six Leyland Cub SKPZ2 models with lightweight Park Royal 26 seat rear entrance bodies new in 1936/7 for use on the Hayling Island services. All survived until 1956 when a new bridge to the mainland was opened allowing normal vehicles to operate the Hayling Island services.
A Duke © Omnibus Society

After complete suspension at the end of July 1940 service 99 reappeared as from 13 May 1945 running between Eastbourne and Hastings via Pevensey Bay. Car 213 (FCD 513) is seen loading passengers on the sea front in Hastings before setting out for its journey to Eastbourne. It is a Leyland Titan TD5 with Park Royal lowbridge body delivered in February 1939 and in this early postwar scene still retains its dark green roof. A new East Lancs body was fitted in June 1949 and car 213 remained in service until sale in January 1962.
C F Klapper © Omnibus Society

On Monday 21 May crowds headed for the seaside to enjoy their first peacetime Whitsun Bank Holiday since the hasty cancellation of the same holiday in May 1940. In resorts such as Brighton most of the shops, cafes, amusements, public houses and hotels were still closed and parts of the beach remained out of bounds because of the danger from mines buried in the shingle back in 1940 when a German invasion loomed. Buckets and spades had to be hired as none had been produced during the war years and promenade shelters presented a shabby unpainted appearance. To make matters worse the weather was wet and windy and there were certainly no coach excursions to nearby attractions. The scene was similar at all the resorts in the Southdown area and it would be another two months before Brighton's beaches were once again safe for bathers, and almost a year before its two piers could reopen to the public. Despite this, the return of peace increased demand for bus travel and by early June it was a common sight to see coaches or single deckers running non stop extras on Southdown's busy trunk routes. To make best use of scarce resources a pavement conductor was often employed to issue tickets before travel as all vehicles used would have had a rear entrance door. From Worthing non stop reliefs were reported operating to Horsham, Storrington, Arundel, Brighton and Littlehampton and even Cheetah 508 was seen running a 2 relief on Thursday 7 June! Starting on 8 June 1945 a non stop coach service began

running 4 times per day in the afternoon between Worthing and Bognor using one coach each from Worthing and Bognor. It only ran on fine days and was subject to vehicle and staff availability. Dennis Falcon car 80 was finally moved from its wartime storage in Worthing garage and noted in use on 31 reliefs on 1 and 2 June 1945.

The first General Election for almost ten years was held on 5 July 1945 but the results were not known for three weeks as counting continued of the Forces still serving overseas. The result brought a landslide victory for the Labour Party with an overall majority of 146 seats. Clement Attlee, who had been Churchill's deputy in the wartime coalition government, became Prime Minister. Among its many manifesto plans was the state ownership of inland transport – road, rail and water – which appeared to mark the end of Southdown as a privately owned company. In fact the BET group, of which Southdown was a part, strongly resisted the compulsory nationalisation of its business and the company was to remain outside direct state control until the formation of the National Bus Company in 1968. Shares held by the Southern Railway passed to the BTC when the main line railways were nationalised on 1 July 1948.

Although fighting continued in the Far East some wartime controls affecting public transport were relaxed during the summer of 1945 and restrictions on evening and Sunday morning services were discontinued in July. Few of the bus stopping places removed in 1942 were, however, subsequently restored. From 8 July 1945 Southdown's first Sunday morning operations outside Portsmouth since January 1943 were restored on services **12** and **13E**. Sunday morning services were restored on the following sections of route from Sunday 15 July 1945: **1, 2, 3, 4** (between Worthing Pier and High Salvington only), **7, 7A, 8, 9A, 10** (between Worthing and Arundel), **14, 15, 16, 17, 20, 22, 23, 30, 31** (between Brighton and Littlehampton), **31G, 63, 68, 81, 83, 84, 85, 86, 86A, 88, 89, 91** (but only 2 hourly frequency), **92, 94** (but on circular journeys only), **95, 96** and **119**. From the same date Worthing services 7 and 7A were again revised. Service **7** now operated LANCING MANOR-SOUTH LANCING-WORTHING-SOUTH LANCING (THREE HORSE SHOES HOTEL) with a 20 minute frequency on Weekdays and 30 minutes on Sundays. The **7A** was curtailed to operate between WORTHING PIER and LANCING MANOR via Sompting with a similar frequency to the 7 and providing a combined 10 minute service between Worthing and Lancing via Sompting. In practice these were advertised as circular services from Worthing with buses changing route number at Lancing Manor.

One of the most ambitious post war enhancements up to this point occurred with the extension of the 13 minute long service **71** (between Storrington and Thakeham) to operate from LITTLEHAMPTON (EAST STREET) to HORSHAM STATION via Crossbush, Arundel Station, Arundel Square, Whiteway's Lodge, Houghton, Amberley, then double run to serve Amberley Post Office, Storrington, Thakeham, Coolham, Brooks Green, Barns Green, Itchingfield, Christ's Hospital and Tower Hill The journey time became 1 hour 53 minutes and a two hourly service was provided daily plus various short journeys between Storrington and Thakeham although no Sunday morning service was included at this time. The section between Storrington and Littlehampton had been covered by service 65 before withdrawal at the start of the war and some new roads for Southdown were served from Thakeham to Coolham. As part of the same programme service **75** was extended from Billingshurst to KINGSFOLD via Billingshurst Station. The frequency was reduced to three journeys each way Saturdays to Thursdays but only two journeys each way on Fridays – when one journey became a 75A to Shipley – plus one journey each way daily to Coneyhurst. All Shipley journeys were now numbered **75A** and ran between HORSHAM STATION and SHIPLEY (PARISH ROOM) via Tower Hill, Christ's Hospital, Itchingfield, Barns Green, Brooks Green, Coolham, Scollier's Corner and Green Street with two journeys each way daily plus one extra each way on Fridays only. In conjunction with the newly extended 71 an hourly frequency was provided between Horsham and Coolham Cross Roads.

There was unprecedented demand for travel in the early weeks of peace and any suitable vehicle could be pressed into service to help move the crowds. Dennis Falcon car 80 (FUF 180), now devoid of its Tramocars fleetnames, was finally moved from its wartime storage in Worthing garage and noted by local enthusiasts in use on 31 reliefs on 1 and 2 June 1945.
C F Klapper © Omnibus Society

Seen at Pool Valley in Brighton is car 408 (GUF 68), a Guy Arab II with Park Royal body which was delivered in March 1944 in all grey livery with apple green just below the lower deck windows. In late 1944 Southdown adopted a revised livery with apple green continuing to the bottom of the upper and lower deck windows, cream window surrounds and a dark green roof and wings as shown here. Alongside are examples of the distinctive heavily rebuilt Beadle bodies belonging to both Southdown (on left with dark green roof on service 119) and Maidstone & District on jointly operated service 18 to Hawkhurst.
C F Klapper © Omnibus Society

The first of the seasonal services to reappear occurred on Sunday 29 July when service **46** commenced operation between HAYLING FERRY and EASTOKE HOUSE having last run in September 1939. An hourly service ran daily although no Sunday morning service was provided at this time. Buses started from Eastoke House at 0925 with the last journey from Hayling Ferry at 2200. In the late 1940s the 46 saw operation by the open top Leyland TD1s as the holiday camps on the island expanded to meet demand. On the same day Sunday morning services were restored on the following sections of route: **10** (restored throughout), **31** (restored throughout), **31A, 50, 50A, 52, 57, 119, 119A**. Service **62** between Chichester and Petersfield had proved successful and was increased to run

on all weekdays from 30 July until 15 September 1946. This was followed on Sunday 12 August by the reintroduction of another prewar seasonal service – the **26A** between SEAFORD (CLINTON PLACE) and EASTBOURNE (PEVENSEY ROAD) via High & Over and Alfriston. This summer only service had last run in 1939 leaving Alfriston to rely throughout the war on the 26 running via Litlington. In prewar days an hourly frequency had run daily starting at 1200 but it now gained a morning operation except on Sundays. Buses departed Eastbourne hourly between 0920 and 2120 and Seaford hourly from 0916 until 2116. From the same date services between Southsea and Havant via Fratton were again revised when **31B** was reduced to an hourly service while in replacement the **48** gained a long extension from Havant over the 31B route via Fratton to Southsea, South Parade. Overall journey time increased from 23 minutes to 1 hour 7 minutes with an hourly service daily although no Sunday morning service was provided at this time.

It was feared that the war in the Far East would continue for many months but American forces dropped an atomic bomb on the Japanese city of Hiroshima on Monday 6 August and a further one on Nagasaki on Thursday 9 August causing massive destruction. Japan surrendered on Tuesday 14 August and VJ Day (Victory in Japan) was celebrated on the following day, Wednesday 15 August with further celebrations marking the final end of the World War.

Commencing Sunday 19 August service **66** was extended from Arundel to Rustington partly replacing service 68 but following the reopened coastal route via Sea Road between Littlehampton and Rustington which had been

12 12a 12b	BRIGHTON (Tongdean) - Newhaven - Seaford - EASTBOURNE BRIGHTON (Station) - Saltdean - PEACEHAVEN (Annexe) BRIGHTON (Station) - Ocean Hotel - SALTDEAN MOUNT	12 12a 12b

LAST BUSES (DAILY).

Tongdean *Valley Drive* ...		8 21	8 36	...	8 51	...	9 6	...	9 21	9 36	...	9 51	10 3	1018	1033	1048
Dyke Road *Tivoli Crescent* ...		7 25	8 40	...	8 55	...	9 10	...	9 25	9 40	...	9 55	10 7	1022	1037	1052
Seven Dials		8 31	8 46	...	9 1	...	9 16	...	9 31	9 46	...	10 1	1013	1028	1043	1058
Brighton *Station S.R.* ...		8 34	8 49	8 56	9 4	...	9 19	9 26	9 34	9 49	9 56	10 4	1016	1031	1046	11 1
Brighton *Clock Tower* ...		8 36	8 51	8 58	9 6	...	9 21	9 28	9 36	9 51	9 58	10 6	1018	1033	1048	11 3
Brighton *Pool Valley* arr.		8 40	8 55	9 2	9 10	...	9 25	9 32	9 40	9 55	10 2	1010	1022	1037	1052	11 7
Brighton *Pool Valley* dep.		8 41	8 56	9 3	9 11	9 18	9 26	9 33	9 41	9 56	10 3	1011	...	...	...	...
Rottingdean *Cross Roads*		8 56	9 11	9 16	9 26	9 33	9 41	9 46	9 56	1011	1016	1026	...	...	...	...
Saltdean *Estate Office* ...		9 0	9 15	9 20	9 30	9 37	9 45	950	10 0	1015	1020	1030	...	...	...	...
Saltdean *Ocean Hotel* ...		...	...	9 21	...	...	...	951	...	1021	...	...	...	...	...	...
Saltdean *Mount Estate* ...		...	...	9 26	...	...	956	...	1026	...	...	...	...	...	...	...
Peacehaven *Hotel* ...		9 6	9 21	...	9 36	9 43	9 51	...	10 6	1021	...	1036	...	...	...	...
Peacehaven *Annexe* ...		...	...	...	...	9 50	...	...	...	...	...	...	...	...	...	...
Peacehaven *Cliff Road* ...		9 10	9 25	...	9 40	...	9 55	...	1010	1025	...	1040	...	...	...	...
Newhaven *Bridge Street* ...		9 17	9 32	...	9 47	...	10 2	...	1017	1032	...	1047	...	...	...	...
Seaford *Clinton Place* arr.		9 30	9 45	...	10 0	...	1015	...	1030	1045	...	11 0	...	...	...	...
Seaford *Clinton Place* dep.		...	...	...	10 0	...	...	...	...	...	...	...	...	...	...	...
Chyngton Gardens ...		...	...	...	10 5	...	...	...	...	...	...	...	...	...	...	...
Exceat Farm		...	...	...	10 9	...	...	...	...	...	...	...	...	...	...	...
Friston Pond		...	...	...	1016	...	...	...	...	...	...	...	...	...	...	...
Eastdean		...	...	...	1018	...	...	...	...	...	...	...	...	...	...	...
Old Town, Eastbourne ...		...	...	...	1029	...	...	...	...	...	...	...	...	...	...	...
Eastbourne *Pevensey Road*		...	...	...	1035	...	...	...	...	...	...	...	...	...	...	...

(vertical note: AS ADVERTISED UNTIL)

Starting Mon. July 2nd 1945

There is no other motor traffic in view in this early postwar view of car 1423 (CCD 33), a Leyland Tiger TS7 with Harrington body new in 1935, as it unloads passengers at Horsham Carfax on newly extended service 71. Although the white blackout markings have been painted out, the bus remains in wartime livery with grey roof and window surrounds and apple green below the windows. It still retains its roof luggage rack and, now disused, offside screen boxes although these will be removed when it is rebuilt by Portsmouth Aviation in 1947.
C F Klapper © Omnibus Society

abandoned in the changes of 21 November 1940. The service now ran between RUSTINGTON CHURCH and CHICHESTER (WEST STREET) via Sea Lane, Sea Road, South Terrace, Beach Road, New Road, Clifton Road, High Street, Church Street, East Street, Beach Road, New Road, Surrey Street, Broadway, Arundel Road, Wick Street, Lyminster Road, Crossbush, Arundel Station, The Causeway, Queen Street, River Road, Arundel Square and as previously. An hourly frequency was provided daily although the Sunday morning service operated between Littlehampton and Arundel only. Additionally, an hourly service operated daily except Sunday morning between Rustington and Arundel. One Chichester bound weekday journey and one Rustington bound daily journey ran via Halnaker. Certain Rustington to Arundel short journeys were extended in Arundel to terminate at Arundel (Ford Road/Priory Road). Service **68** which had served this area since 1927 was withdrawn after operation on 18 August 1945. It was not until 2 June 1946 that service 31 reverted to its prewar route via Sea Road and services 9 and

Car 214 (FCD 514) is a Leyland Titan TD5 with Park Royal lowbridge body and is seen loading at Arundel Square on a service 66 short working to Littlehampton and Rustington. Delivered in March 1939 it was rebodied by Beadle in May 1949 and sold in 1959.
Southdown Enthusiasts Club – Clark/Surfleet Collection

9A continued to follow the inland route formerly covered by services 68 and 68A before the war.

From 16 September 1945 Sunday morning operations were restored on services **59**, **60** and **61**. A permit for the reintroduction of service **97** between EASTBOURNE (ROYAL PARADE) and BEACHY HEAD HOTEL was issued to the company effective from 14 June 1945 although it appears to have only commenced running every hour from Sunday 23 September 1945. Given the improvements in other areas Southdown were no doubt keen to reintroduce this popular service, which had been one of the many casualties of summer 1940, as soon as local circumstances permitted. Service **21A** was reintroduced from Monday 24 September and revised to operate between SOUTHWICK STATION and OLD SHOREHAM (ERRINGHAM ROAD) via Station Road, Albion Street, Kingston Lane, Upper Shoreham Road, Buckingham Road, Brunswick Road, East Street, High Street, Old Shoreham Road and Upper Shoreham Road. A 30 minute frequency was provided on weekdays only and replaced most of the **21** journeys around the northern loop to Erringham Road. Hayling Island service **46** was seasonally withdrawn after close of service on Saturday 28 September although service **26A** remained in operation. From 14 October 1945 Sunday morning services were restored on the following sections of route: **9**, **13A**, **21** (between Southwick (Town Hall) and Shoreham (Bridge Hotel) only), **25**, **26**, **31F** and **36**. A Sunday morning operation was introduced on service **32**.

Further improvements in the Portsmouth area particularly affecting the A3 corridor started on Sunday 28 October. New Service **39A** ran between PORTSMOUTH (THEATRE ROYAL) and WORLD'S END (CHAIRMAKER'S ARMS) as service 39 to Denmead then via Harvest Home Inn. Four journeys at irregular intervals operated each way on Weekdays and two journeys each way on Sundays. This reinstated a service to World's End that had previously been part of the 39 until withdrawal by 16 November 1939. Service **40B** was withdrawn after operation on 27 October 1945 and replaced by additional journeys on service **40** between Southsea and Clanfield. Service **41** was revised to operate daily between Southsea and Horndean being extended from Fratton Bridge to Southsea on Sunday mornings. Early morning service **42A** was completely revised to operate as an hourly all day service daily and extended from Theatre Royal to Southsea, South Parade and also from Horndean to Clanfield replacing service 42B journeys which had run as far as Snells Corner. A wartime arrangement ended when service **43** was curtailed to terminate at CHURCHERS CORNER being withdrawn between Churcher's Corner and Racton Corner to which it had been projected in 1943. It was also extended from

Fratton Bridge to Southsea on Sunday mornings. Service **54** was diverted between Funtington and Racton Corner to once again operate via Churcher's Corner and connections made with the revised service 43. A Sunday morning service was restored at the same time.

From Monday 29 October service **35** was revised and diverted to operate from PETERSFIELD SQUARE or CHALTON CHURCH to FAREHAM BUS STATION. At the same time service **35A** was withdrawn. A very complicated pattern of operation was provided as follows:

Mondays: One journey from Petersfield to Fareham plus one journey from Fareham to Clanfield.

Wednesdays and Saturdays: One journey from Petersfield to Fareham via Chalton, three journeys from Chalton to Fareham and four journeys from Fareham to Chalton. Connections were made at Chalton with service 42 to and from Petersfield.

On Sunday 18 November it was the turn of the Fareham corridor to gain additional facilities as daytime frequencies on service **45** became:

4 journeys per hour Theatre Royal – Castle Street – Fareham

1 journey per hour Theatre Royal – direct – Warsash

2 journeys per hour Southsea – Fratton – Castle Street – Fareham

2 journeys per hour Southsea – direct – Fareham

3 journeys per hour Theatre Royal – direct – Fareham

Both Fratton journeys now ran via Castle Street and the combined service provided buses every 10 minutes direct and every 10 minutes via Castle Street, Portchester. The two journeys per hour running Southsea – direct – Fareham were additional to the ten buses per hour offered in the last prewar timetable.

Bus Services

Since the end of the war leaflets had been issued to cover the many changes to services but a *complete system timetable* was finally published to include all alterations up to **Sunday 9 December 1945**. The layout was similar to the last prewar issues, although without the colourful cover, containing 260 pages at a cover price of 3d. From this date Sunday morning services were restored on the following sections of route: **4** (restored throughout), **5, 6, 38, 52** (Hourly via Hunston only), **53, 66** (Additional Rustington to Arundel journeys operating from 1200) and **93**. As during wartime, some of the alterations shown below may have been introduced at an earlier date. The Worthing and Findon short journeys on service **1** were numbered **1B** with a 30 minute service daily until 1850 although no Sunday morning service was provided at this time. Services **5A** and **6** were revised to terminate at LITTLEHAMPTON ROAD at its junction with RINGMER ROAD instead of the North Star Hotel which had allowed gas producer buses to turn without reversing. A Sunday morning service was introduced on service **5A** for the first time and

Worthing town services now generally continued until 2230.

Service **13A** was renumbered **123** and extended over the **13C** from Newhaven via Bridge Street, Drove Road, Avis Road, Denton Road, Heighton Road, Heighton New Road, New Road and Bridge Street to Lewes. Buses ran every two hours daily plus additional journeys daily each way between Nevill Crescent and County Hall and Saturday journeys each way between County Hall and Southease. A Sunday morning service was also restored at this time. Service **23** was extended from Haywards Heath over the **82** to CRAWLEY (GEORGE HOTEL) via Muster Green, Cuckfield, Whitemans Green, Slough Green, Staplefield, Handcross and Pease Pottage, reverting to its 1 July 1933 route. A two hourly frequency was provided daily and with the development of Crawley New Town during the 1950s it was extended northwards from the town centre to terminate at Northgate, replacing London Transport 483, as from 20 January 1958. Until this round of changes Southdown had avoided numbering routes above 100 (other than the 119) but with the post war expansion chose to renumber some routes rather than use suffix

After running on Producer Gas for a period during the war, car 121 (BUF 221) is now diesel engined but still performing on service 5A and turning at the North Star Hotel to which the route was extended to avoid buses reversing with trailers. Car 121 is a Leyland Titan TD4 with Short Bros highbridge body and originally fitted with a petrol engine and torque converter. Southdown rebuilt the body with front upper deck window vents and a side screen box in June 1945. At this time services 5 and 5A loaded west of Worthing Pier and turned right off Marine Parade at West Buildings.
Southdown Enthusiasts Club – Clark/Surfleet Collection

Starting on 9 December 1945 service 23 was once again extended northwards from Haywards Heath to Crawley in which form it continued for many years. Several of the Beadle bodied Leyland TD5s dating from 1938 had their bodies rebuilt by Beadle during 1945/6. The first few, including car 190 (EUF 190) seen at Pool Valley, Brighton, had the three roller blinds over the nearside windows replaced by a screen box over the platform but otherwise retained their original outline. In addition car 190 gained front upper deck ventilators. Although many of the Beadle rebuilds remained in service until the mid-1950s car 190 received a new Northern Counties body in January 1950 and stayed with Southdown until June 1961.
Southdown Enthusiasts Club – Clark/Surfleet Collection

letters. From this date service **26A**, a summer only route in prewar days, became **126** and in future operated all year round to eventually become the principal route between Seaford and Alfriston.

Service **31A** was extended from EMSWORTH SQUARE via Queen Street, Southbourne, Nutbourne, Bosham and Fishbourne to CHICHESTER, WEST STREET. A 30 minute service ran daily which combined with the 31 to give a 15 minute frequency between Southsea and Chichester via Theatre Royal. Certain

Car 1469 (FCD 369), a Leyland Tiger TS8 with Harrington body, climbs the steep hill to High & Over on all year round service 126 which had replaced the previously summer only service 26A in December 1945. The direct road between Alfriston and Seaford had proved challenging for earlier types but the 1400 class Tigers were more than competent for the task.
C F Klapper © Omnibus Society

Considering the rural nature of much of Southdown's territory, relatively little use was made of the one man operated Leyland Cubs. Starting in December 1945 new local services numbered 68 and 68A provided new facilities in the city of Chichester using one Cub. Park Royal bodied car 17 (CUF 517) is seen on a damp day at the rather basic Railway Station terminus.
C F Klapper © Omnibus Society

journeys on service **39** were extended beyond Hambledon to DROXFORD SQUARE via Race Course Corner and Bushey Down Farm, covered until 21 September 1939 by service **38**. Four journeys each way on weekdays and one each way on Sundays continued through to Droxford.

Two new local services operated by one man Leyland Cubs commenced in Chichester as part of the December changes. Firstly a new CITY OF CHICHESTER CIRCULAR SERVICE numbered **68** was introduced from Chichester Railway Station via Southgate, South Street, Franklin Place, Spitalfields Lane, Adelaide Road, St Pancras, Eastgate Square, The Hornet, Whyke Road, Whyke Lane, Grove Road, Kingsham Road, Basin Road, Canal Wharf and Stockbridge Road with a journey time of 16 minutes. In addition

new service **68A** ran between CHICHESTER RAILWAY STATION and SUMMERSDALE (THE AVENUE) via Southgate, South Street, North Street, Broyle Road and Lavant Road restoring the local service to Summersdale lost in January 1943 when service 66 was rerouted to Lavant. The frequency of both services was 30 minutes on weekdays and hourly on Sunday afternoons and evenings.

Local services in the Haywards Heath area were also improved with the frequency of service **84** increased from hourly each way to every 40 minutes each way daily and service **85** extended hourly daily from Lindfield High Street via Birch Hotel back to Haywards Heath to form a circular service. The frequency now became hourly each way throughout daily plus an hourly service on weekdays between Haywards Heath and Lindfield Post Office via Sunte Avenue. Finally, the hourly Birch Hotel journeys on service **89** were extended via Lewes Road to terminate at Scaynes Hill. The timetable for service **97** now offered a two hourly basic frequency increased to 30 minutes in very fine weather – similar to that operated in winter 1938 – with the first bus departing Royal Parade at 0945 and the last journey from Beachy Head at 1650. The **99** from Eastbourne to Hastings via Pevensey and Bexhill was increased in frequency from two hourly to run every 90 minutes daily. Service **119** was diverted and extended in Tunbridge Wells via Castle Road, Mount Ephraim and Mount Ephraim Road to terminate at TUNBRIDGE WELLS (GREEN LINE COACH STATION). This lasted only until 31 March 1946 and the reintroduction of Green Line services.

As in prewar times Southdown ran no services on Christmas Day but normal Wednesday services were provided from about 0900 on Boxing Day 1945.

CHICHESTER CIRCULAR SERVICE

68 / 68a — Railway Station — North Gate — East Gate — Whyke Road — Railway Station

68a — CHICHESTER Station — SUMMERSDALE The Avenue

CLOCKWISE.

Ser. 68		NS	NS	NS	NS	NS	NS	NS	SO	NS		NS				NS				NS			
	Chichester Station S.R.	...	7 38	8 8	8 38	9 8	9 38	10 8	...	1038	11 8	1138		8	38		7 8	7 38	8 38	9 48
	Chichester Cross	...	7 40	8 10	8 40	9 10	9 40	1010	...	1040	1110	1140		10	40		7 10	7 40	8 40	9 50
	Northgate	...	7 42	8 12	8 42	9 12	9 42	1012	...	1042	1112	1142		12	42		7 12	7 42	8 42	9 52
	Eastgate Square	...	7 46	8 16	8 46	9 16	9 46	1016	...	1046	1116	1146		16	46		7 16	7 46	8 46	9 56
	Rumboldswyke St. Rumbold's Ch.	...	7 50	8 20	8 50	9 20	9 50	1020	...	1050	1120	1150		20	50		7 20	7 50	8 50	10 0
	Chichester Station S.R.	...	7 54	8 24	8 54	9 24	9 54	1024	...	1054	1124	1154		24	54		7 24	7 54	8 54	10 4

Ser. 68a			NS	NS	NS	NS	NS	NS	NS		NS		NS					NS			
	Chichester Station S.R.	...		7 54	8 24	8 54	9 24	9 54	1024	...	1054	1124	1154		24	54		7 24	7 54	8 54	10 4
	Chichester Cross	...	7 26	7 56	8 26	8 56	9 26	9 56	1026	1026	1056	1126	1156		26	56		7 26	7 56	8 56	10 6
	Northgate	...	7 28	7 58	8 28	8 58	9 28	9 58	1028	1028	1058	1128	1158		28	58		7 28	7 58	8 58	10 8
	Summersdale The Avenue	...	7 33	8 3	8 33	9 3	9 33	10 3	1033	1033	11 3	1133	12 3		33	3		7 33	8 3	9 3	1013

ANTI-CLOCKWISE.

Ser. 68a		NS	NS	NS	NS	NS	NS	NS		NS		NS				NS				NS	
	Summersdale The Avenue	...	7 35	8 5	8 35	9 5	9 35	10 5	1035	11 5	1135		5	35		7 5	7 35	8 5	9 5	1015
	Northgate	...	7 40	8 10	8 40	9 10	9 40	1010	1040	1110	1140		10	40		7 10	7 40	8 10	9 10	1020
	Chichester Cross	...	7 12	7 42	8 12	8 42	9 12	9 42	1012	1042	1112	1142		12	42		7 12	7 42	8 12	9 12	1022
	Chichester Station S.R.	...	7 14	7 44	8 14	8 44	9 14	9 44	1014	1044	1114	1144		14	44		7 14	7 44	8 14	9 14	...

Ser. 68		NS	NS	NS	NS	NS	NS	NS		NS		NS				NS				NS	
	Chichester Station S.R.	...	7 14	7 44	8 14	8 44	9 14	9 44	1014	1044	1114	1144		14	44		7 14	7 44	8 14	9 14	...
	Rumboldswyke St. Rumbold's Ch.	...	7 18	7 48	8 18	8 48	9 18	9 48	1018	1048	1118	1148		18	48		7 18	7 48	8 18	9 18	...
	Eastgate Square	...	7 22	7 52	8 22	8 52	9 22	9 52	1022	1052	1122	1152		22	52		7 22	7 52	8 22	9 22	...
	Northgate	...	7 26	7 56	8 26	8 56	9 26	9 56	1026	1056	1126	1156		26	56		7 26	7 56	8 26	9 26	...
	Chichester Cross	...	7 28	7 58	8 28	8 58	9 28	9 58	1028	1058	1128	1158		28	58		7 28	7 58	8 28	9 28	...
	Chichester Station S.R.	...	7 30	8 0	8 30	9 0	9 30	10 0	1030	11 0	1130	12 0		30	0		7 30	8 0	8 30	9 30	...

NS—Not Sundays. SO—Sundays only.

99	EASTBOURNE — Pevensey Bay — Bexhill — HASTINGS This Service is operated jointly by the Southdown Motor Services, Ltd., and Maidstone & District Motor Services, Ltd.	99

					NS											
Eastbourne *Pevensey Road*	...	...	...		7 5	9 30	11 0	1230	2 0	3 30	5 0	6 30	8 30	...	...	...	...
Eastbourne *Archery*	...	...	...		7 10	9 35	11 5	1235	2 5	3 35	5 5	6 35	8 35	...	...	...	...
Coastguard Cottages	...	...	...		7 17	9 42	1112	1242	2 12	3 42	5 12	6 42	8 42	...	...	...	...
Pevensey Bay *Bay Hotel*	...				7 20	9 45	1115	1245	2 15	3 45	5 15	6 45	8 45	...	...	...	...
Barnhorn Lane *Constable's Farm*	...	...			...	9 58	1128	1258	2 28	3 58	5 28	6 58	8 58	...	...	...	...
Little Common *Wheatsheaf*	...	...			...	10 3	1133	1 3	2 33	4 3	5 33	7 3	9 3	...	...	...	...
Sutherland Avenue	...	...			...	10 8	1138	1 8	2 38	4 8	5 38	7 8	9 8	...	...	...	...
Bexhill *Marina*	...	...	...		...	1015	1145	1 15	2 45	4 15	5 45	7 15	9 15	...	...	...	...
Hastings *Wellington Square*	...	...	...		...	1040	1210	1 40	3 10	4 40	6 10	7 40	9 40	...	...	...	...

Hastings *Wellington Square*	...	...	...	9 45	1045	1215	1 45	3 15	4 45	6 15	7 45	...	...	...	...
Bexhill *Marina*	...	...	...	1010	1110	1240	2 10	3 40	5 10	6 40	8 10	...	...	...	...
Sutherland Avenue	...	...		1017	1117	1247	2 17	3 47	5 17	6 47	8 17	...	...	...	...
Little Common *Wheatsheaf*	...	...		1022	1122	1252	2 22	3 52	5 22	6 52	8 22	...	...	...	...
Barnhorn Lane *Constable's Farm*	...	...		1027	1127	1257	2 27	3 57	5 27	6 57	8 27	...	...	...	...
Pevensey Bay *Bay Hotel*	...	...		1040	1140	1 10	2 40	4 10	5 40	7 10	8 40	...	...	...	...
Coastguard Cottages	...	...	...	1043	1143	1 13	2 43	4 13	5 43	7 13	8 43	...	...	...	...
Eastbourne *Archery*	...	...	...	1050	1150	1 20	2 50	4 20	5 50	7 20	8 50	...	...	...	...
Eastbourne *Pevensey Road*	...	...	...	1055	1155	1 25	2 55	4 25	5 55	7 25	8 55	...	...	...	...

NS—Not Sundays.

1946

Since the end of hostilities, demand for bus services had been booming and it was not only the large companies who could see new opportunities. On the north eastern border of Southdown territory Beacon Motor Services of Crowborough increased the days of operation of its service to Uckfield via High Hurstwood from two to three early in 1946 and also introduced a local town service in Crowborough. These were acquired by Southdown in September 1949 becoming **120** and **117/118**. At around the same time Sargent's of East Grinstead increased its service to Edenbridge to daily operation. There was then a major reorganisation two years later with a new Edenbridge – Cowden Cross Roads – Crowborough service connecting with a Cowden Cross Roads to East Grinstead service and also an East Grinstead – Larches – Ashurst Wood route. These all passed to Southdown in March 1951 and then transferred in September of that year to Maidstone & District.

During January service **31A** was extended in Chichester via East Street, The Hornet, Whyke Road, Pound Farm Road and Florence Road to PORTFIELD (THE WHEATSHEAF). The frequency remained at 30 minutes daily. The reason for this short lived extension is unknown but the 31A was diverted to Bognor from 31 March 1946. On 3 February 1946 Sunday morning operations were restored on services **13F, 29, 70, 71, 75, 75A, 78, 79, 80** and **90**. Commencing Sunday 17 February the former Tramocars service 3A was renumbered **11** and a new local service **11A** introduced serving areas to the east of the town centre and then continuing to West Worthing Station. It ran between WORTHING PIER and WEST WORTHING STATION via Marine Parade, Steyne Gardens, Brighton Road, Madeira Avenue, Lyndhurst Road, Homefield Road, Newland Road, Railway Approach, Teville Road and Tarring Road with a 15 minute service daily.

A further *complete system timetable* book was issued including details of revised services up to **Sunday 31 March 1946**. A Sunday morning operation was restored from this date on service **24** while the **27** was diverted between Dyke Road and Poynings to regain its former route via Dyke Road, Dyke Road Avenue, Dyke Road, Devil's Dyke Fork Roads, Saddlescombe and Poynings. A three hourly service operated daily between Henfield and Brighton and the Sunday morning service was restored, although buses did not reach Devils Dyke Hotel again until summer 1949. Service **31A** was again revised, being withdrawn in Chichester between The Hornet and Portfield and extended to BOGNOR BUS STATION via the 31 route. The frequency remained at 30

To meet the heavy demand for travel after the war whilst attempting to catch up on a backlog of maintenance Southdown had to use anything that was available. Car 816 (UF 4816) a Leyland Titan TD1 with Brush body new in 1929 still retains its wartime temporary roof cover when seen laying over in Cambridge Road, Portsmouth. It was converted back to open top form during 1946 but its passenger carrying days were limited and it was transferred to tree lopping duties in the service fleet as number 0816 in November 1948.
Alan Lambert collection

minutes daily providing a combined 15 minute service between Southsea and Bognor with service 31. No Sunday morning service was included at this time. Certain journeys on service **34** were extended to operate between Ditchling and Hurstpierpoint on Sundays but not serving Hassocks Station or Station Approach and at the same time a Sunday morning service was restored.

In the Bognor area services **50** and **50A** were increased from hourly to 30 minutes daily and the complete service 50A extended to operate throughout between Elmer and Pagham providing a combined 15 minute frequency. The Chichester to Selsey via Donnington journeys previously provided as part of the **52** were numbered as a separate service **52A**. An hourly service ran daily and the Sunday morning service via Donnington was restored. Bognor local service **55** was revised to operate between BARRACK LANE (SOUTH END) and NORTH BERSTED (CENTRAL AVENUE) via its existing route to Collyer Avenue then via South Way and Central Avenue to the junction with Greencourt Drive and the Sunday morning service restored. Service **57** was diverted between Crockerhill and Westergate to run via Fontwell and Eastergate, no longer serving Halnaker and Boxgrove which were now covered by revisions to service 66. One journey each way daily on service **63** diverted between Upwaltham and Tangmere serving new roads via Eartham and Crockerhill. Service **64** gained a long extension westward being revised to operate between PARKLANDS ESTATE (WALNUT AVENUE) and BILSHAM CORNER via Chichester, Maudlin, Crockerhill, Norton, Westergate, Eastergate, Barnham Station and Yapton. This provided a

new local facility in Chichester and replaced service 57 via Norton. An hourly frequency was provided daily and the Sunday morning service restored. The former Silver Queen services were revised with the **65** being increased in frequency from two hourly to hourly including on Sunday mornings. Two Slindon bound weekday journeys and one Bognor Regis bound daily journey diverted between Slindon and Eastergate to operate direct via A29 and Fontwell Avenue. In consequence service **65A** was curtailed and diverted to operate between FONTWELL AVENUE (NORTH END) and SLINDON (NEWBURGH ARMS) only via Goodacres, Long's Corner and Slindon Common with a journey time of 8 minutes. Buses ran every two hours daily including on Sunday mornings and connected with service 57 at Fontwell Avenue for Bognor or Chichester. This facility was covered by service 65 layover time at Slindon. Service **66** reverted to its prewar route between Crockerhill and Maudlin operating via Boxgrove and Halnaker and a Sunday morning operation was restored to service **69** at this time.

In the east of the area a full hourly service was restored on Sunday morning to service **91** – previously only two hourly. Service **119** was diverted in Tunbridge Wells to operate via London Road and Church Road to terminate at Church Road returning via Mount Pleasant Road, Vale Road and London Road. The reintroduction of Green Line services on 6 March 1946 presumably meant the Coach Station was no longer available. Finally, with the London Express Services restarting on Friday 22 March 1946 the remnants of the Bognor to Horsham Limited Stop Service were withdrawn completely after operation on 30 March 1946.

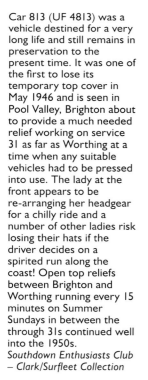

Car 813 (UF 4813) was a vehicle destined for a very long life and still remains in preservation to the present time. It was one of the first to lose its temporary top cover in May 1946 and is seen in Pool Valley, Brighton about to provide a much needed relief working on service 31 as far as Worthing at a time when any suitable vehicles had to be pressed into use. The lady at the front appears to be re-arranging her headgear for a chilly ride and a number of other ladies risk losing their hats if the driver decides on a spirited run along the coast! Open top reliefs between Brighton and Worthing running every 15 minutes on Summer Sundays in between the through 31s continued well into the 1950s.
Southdown Enthusiasts Club – Clark/Surfleet Collection

A new *complete system timetable* book of 312 pages was issued covering all alterations up to **Sunday 2 June 1946**. It included the Express Services, reference to coaches being available for Private Hire and Excursions, but not fares, and the cost had risen to 4d. It is again likely that some of the alterations had been introduced at an earlier date. Many services gained frequency improvements and later buses were introduced in the Brighton and Worthing areas on services **3, 4, 5, 5A, 6, 7, 8, 11, 11A, 12, 12A, 12B, 13, 13B, 13E, 13F** and **31F**.

From 0930 all buses on service **4** were extended to run to High Salvington with a 10 minute frequency throughout on weekdays and a 15 minute frequency on Sundays. Since 10 July 1941 half of the service had terminated at Durrington with only alternate buses continuing to High Salvington. Additional journeys were introduced on service **12** in Seaford between Clinton Place and Chyngton Gardens having been withdrawn from 8 April 1942. The frequency of service **18** was increased from four journeys each way on weekdays and two each way on Sundays to a regular two hourly service daily and the Sunday morning service restored. Service **26** between Seaford, Alfriston and Berwick Station via Litlington was renumbered **98** and extended through new territory for Southdown to GOLDEN CROSS via Coppice Corner, Chalvington, Ripe, Yew Tree Inn and Lime Kiln Farm. Connections were made at Golden Cross with services 16 and 92. A three hourly service ran daily plus one journey each way between Seaford and Berwick Station. The service through Litlington was reduced from the

previous two hourly frequency – hourly until 10 July 1941 – and reflected the fact that the 126 direct via High & Over had become the principal all year hourly service between Seaford, Alfriston and Berwick. As usual with Southdown the new service managed to achieve a remarkable number of connections. Service **27** was further diverted via Poynings Cross Road between Saddlescombe and Poynings Church although still unable to reach Devil's Dyke Hotel. As the area around Devils Dyke had been used for military purposes in wartime and was still out of bounds to the public it was not possible to reintroduce normal summer bus services for the 1946 season but seven additional journeys ran between Pool Valley and Devil's Dyke Fork Roads on fine days.

A further welcome sign of returning normality came with service **31** reverting to its pre-21 November 1940 route between Rustington, The Street and Littlehampton, East Street. It now ran via Sea Lane, Sea Road, Norfolk Road, South Terrace, Beach Road, New Road, Clifton Road, High Street and Church Street. When service **66** was extended to Rustington from 19 August 1945 it had followed its prewar route via Sea Road but as from 2 June 1946 it was diverted between Rustington and Littlehampton, East Street to operate via Rustington Street, North Lane, Worthing Road and Horsham Road being replaced by the diversion of service 31. The frequency was reduced to an hourly service throughout daily with certain journeys still terminating at Arundel, Ford Road. New service **66A** was introduced between RUSTINGTON CHURCH and ARUNDEL SQUARE via The Street, Sea Lane, Sea Road, South Terrace, Beach Road,

New Road, Surrey Street, High Street, Church Street, East Street, Lyminster, Crossbush and Arundel Station. A 30 minute service operated daily which combined with service 31 to provide four buses per hour along Sea Road. This arrangement applied only for summer 1946 – by summer 1947 service 31 was running every 15 minutes throughout. Service **32** which had been introduced on 13 May 1945 was diverted between Fletching and Uckfield to operate via Shortbridge and The Rocks covering yet more roads for the first time.

With the reopening of Holiday Camps and return of visitors to Hayling Island, service **46** was reintroduced between HAYLING FERRY and EASTOKE HOUSE daily until 28 September but with the frequency increased to 30 minutes for the 1946 season. The Sunday afternoon time-table on service **47** now operated all day but with a two hourly diversion via Northney. In addition a new service **47A** commenced between HAVANT STATION and EASTOKE HOUSE via North Street, South Street, Langstone Road, South Hayling Road, Havant Road, Church Road, Elm Grove, Mengham Road, Selsmore Road, Rails Lane and Southwood Road. An hourly service was provided daily although no buses ran on Sunday mornings. The 47A provided additional buses to South Hayling, Southwood Road and Eastoke House at the far south eastern end of the island. Before the war some high summer journeys on service 47 had run between Southsea and Eastoke House.

A complex series of changes affected services 54, 62 and 67 in the Chichester, Havant, Compton and Petersfield areas which had recently featured in territorial battles with Basil Williams. Firstly, service **54** was extended from Compton via South Harting, Nursted and Stanbridge to PETERSFIELD STATION. Between South Harting and Petersfield this partly replaced service 62 via South Harting which was in turn diverted to replace 67 although via a different route. A generous two hourly service was provided daily on service 54. At the same time the Chichester to Hambrook journeys were transferred to a new service **54A**. Between South Harting and Petersfield, The Square service **62** was rerouted to operate via West Harting in place of the **67** which was curtailed to run between HAVANT STATION and COMPTON (COACH & HORSES INN). The frequency of service 62 became four journeys each way daily plus two additional journeys each way on Wednesdays and Saturdays and one late journey each way on Saturdays between Chichester and Chilgrove while the 67 became a 3 or 4 hourly service daily (again) and was diverted at Deanlane End to double run to and from Finchdean. Service **63B** between Petworth and Sutton now ran daily throughout the summer period having previously only operated on Tuesdays, Thursdays and Saturdays since its introduction in March 1945. Service **69** was extended from Arundel Square to Bognor Bus Station and from Horsham Carfax to the Railway Station partly replacing prewar seasonal route 62 but running direct from Yapton via Ford to

Two 1400 class Harrington bodied Leyland Tigers meet at Pulborough Station on route 69 in an early postwar scene whilst the service was still operating to the wartime 90 minute frequency between Arundel and Horsham. Heading south towards Arundel is car 1457 (FCD 257) which appears to be in standard post war livery with dark green roof whilst the following Horsham bound bus is one of the later members of the class dating from 1939/40 and still in wartime grey and green livery.
C F Klapper © Omnibus Society

Arundel. It now became BOGNOR BUS STATION and HORSHAM STATION via Yapton, Ford, Ford Station, Arundel and then as previously. Certain journeys operated between Five Oaks and Broadbridge Heath via Slinfold and the frequency was improved from every 90 minutes to an hourly service daily.

Service **86A** was renumbered **82** and extended from Brook Street to BALCOMBE (HALF MOON HOTEL) having been curtailed at Brook Street on 16 November 1939. A two hourly service ran throughout plus an additional two hourly service between Haywards Heath and Whiteman's Green. Haywards Heath local service **84** was altered from every 40 minutes each way around the loop to an hourly service clockwise daily and two journeys per hour anticlockwise daily. Service **86** was extended over new roads for Southdown from Balcombe to TURNERS HILL via Cowdray Arms Hotel, Worth Priory and Grove House. A two hourly service ran throughout daily plus two weekday journeys each way to Stoney Lane and one journey each way to Balcombe on Saturdays and Sundays. Connections were advertised with LPTB service 434 to East Grinstead. The other Southdown route to Turners Hill, service **88**, also gained an increased frequency and now ran every two hours throughout plus a two hourly service between Haywards Heath and Ardingly (Hapstead Hall) daily. The additional Ardingly journeys added were regular hourly departures from Haywards Heath but a 30/90 minutes frequency from Ardingly.

As already covered in earlier chapters the war had seriously affected the city of Portsmouth and its local transport undertaking. The population of the city dropped by around a third as people were evacuated and often rehoused outside the city boundary. Bus services on Portsea Island had been reduced, especially on routes that could

be served by trolleybuses, and some buses used to augment Southdown peak services which were carrying the displaced people to country districts. New housing was desperately needed and post war plans envisaged new estates being built in areas served exclusively by Southdown buses and outside the existing boundaries of the Corporation bus network. Relations between Southdown and the Portsmouth Corporation transport department were not always cordial and, after peace was finally declared, negotiations began in May 1945 over joint running on various services to reflect the new situation. An agreement was eventually reached which came into force on Monday 1 July 1946 with the operators pooling mileage and receipts in an agreed proportion, originally 57% to the Corporation and 43% to Southdown. The co-ordination area included Portsea Island but also extended northwards to Petersfield, west to Fareham and east as far as Emsworth covering an area of 127 square miles. Under the agreement Corporation buses would run beyond the city boundary and protective fares charged on Southdown buses within the city would be removed. It also enabled each partner to run mileage for the other resulting in Southdown vehicles occasionally appearing on former Corporation routes and vice versa. A new *Portsmouth Joint Services* timetable book dated **Monday 1 July 1946** was issued in similar format to the current Southdown editions for all services within the designated area. Southdown services included all those operating on Portsea Island plus 35, 44, 46, 47, 47A, 49 and 67 although the wartime Portsmouth or Hampshire area timetables had also included 60, 61 and 62. It was not until 6 June 1948 that the protective fares charged by Southdown between North End and South Parade or Clarence Piers were finally removed.

For the first time since August 1940 Bognor

After the war public transport remained under great strain and helping out on a bus service into Portsmouth is car 1095 (BCD 895), a Leyland Tiger TS7 with Harrington coach body new in 1935 for use on the company's Express Services. It was one of 24 Tigers that were converted for use as ambulances in August 1938 and restored to normal seating during 1946. The body was not given a rebuild after the war and car 1095 was sold for scrap in October 1953.
Southdown Enthusiasts Club – W J Haynes Collection

Hastings via Pevensey Bay was increased to run hourly daily, having been every 90 minutes during the previous winter. As from Thursday 1 August service **64** was further extended in Chichester every two hours from Parklands Estate to WEST BROYLE (BUTTERFLY CORNER) via Old Broyle Road, St Paul's Road and Parklands Road although the main service remained hourly between Parklands Estate and Bilsham Corner. Lewes local service **28** was increased to run every 20 minutes on weekdays as from Monday 19 August although no Sunday service was provided.

By September 1946 the RTCs were moving gradually towards a return to the prewar licensing system and some had already held public sittings. With a return to some normality there was less need for short term amendments and the company was able to introduce a *complete system timetable* book for the winter services starting on **Sunday 29 September 1946**. A pleasing new transitional cover design appeared to replace the plain wartime look adopted in November 1939. A double deck bus was shown climbing a hill with downland and sea in the background not unlike the design adopted from June 1947 and continued until 1960. The interior layout also became the standard for post war timetables up to 1965. A very useful detailed summary of alterations was included within the 268 pages for a cover price of 4d. Page size also increased to 108mm by 171mm allowing greater clarity and improved layouts. From this date service **1** was extended from Storrington to PULBOROUGH STATION via Mill Lane, Roundabout Farm, West Chiltington Common Post Office, then a double-run to serve West Chiltington Village, Heath Mill and Marehill replacing service 70. The frequency remained hourly daily but not all journeys diverted via West Chiltington village. Whilst most of the Worthing local services retained their summer frequencies throughout the year, only alternate journeys on service **4** continued beyond Durrington to and from High Salvington as in winter 1945. To better serve Worthing Railway Station service **7A** was diverted between Chapel Road and Broadwater Road to operate via Chapel Road, Railway Approach, Teville Road and Broadwater Road. With service 69 now operating hourly along Ford Road in Arundel most journeys on service **10** were curtailed at Arundel Square with just two early or late journeys on weekdays and one on Sundays remaining.

The Chyngton Gardens journeys on service **12** in Seaford were withdrawn for the winter period. Service **13E** between Brighton and East Moulscombe gained an additional 12 minute service during weekday peak periods – including midday – to provide a 6 minute frequency. The Sunday frequency on service **15** was reduced from 30 minutes to hourly but Weekdays remained at 30 minutes – increased from hourly in winter 1945 and better than prewar summer

local circular service **51** had its frequency increased to every 20 minutes each way on week-days as from Monday 8 July although no Sunday service was provided. It had been reduced to every 40 minutes each way during the war. Further significant enhancements to summer services in the Eastbourne area occurred from Sunday 14 July when the frequency of joint service **15** to Hastings via Hailsham was increased from hourly to 30 minutes daily. In addition service **91** gained an additional hourly service between Eastbourne and Heathfield daily to make this section every 30 minutes for the first time ever. The Beachy Head service **97** was increased to run every 15 minutes on fine days in line with prewar summers. The last bus from Royal Parade departed at 2045 returning from Beachy Head at 2105. Finally, service **99** to services! Service **27** was extended in Henfield via Station Road to terminate at HENFIELD STN.

In the Ferring area new service **31E** commenced between SOUTH FERRING (SOUTH DRIVE) and NORTH FERRING CORNER via South Drive, West Drive, Ferringham Lane, Ferring Street and Sea Lane returning via Sea Lane, Ferring Street, Ferringham Lane and West Drive. One special journey extended weekdays only to Goring Station via Goring Way and another ran weekdays only as far as Ferring (Henty Arms). With a journey time of just 9 minutes a 30 minute frequency was provided daily probably using a Leyland Cub one man bus. In consequence service **31F** was curtailed to operate only between BRIGHTON (POOL VALLEY) and FERRING (WAR MEMORIAL) where connections were made with the 31E. This change is believed to have been as a result of local residents' further concern about the use of large buses running along the private roads in Ferring-by-Sea. Presumably the situation was resolved from 15 June 1947 when the 31F was once again extended to Beresford's Stores using the prewar Dennis Falcons but it was 21 March 1948 before these 'bigger' buses reached South Drive again.

Hayling Island seafront service **46** was withdrawn for the winter after operation on 28 September 1946 and the Sunday frequency on service **49** was seasonally reduced from 30 minutes to hourly. A Sunday service running every 40 minutes each way was finally restored to Bognor circular service **51**. Service **54A** between Chichester and Hambrook was improved to a 2 hourly service of 6 journeys running on Wednesdays and Saturdays. The short journeys on service **60** between Petersfield and Rogate introduced from 2 June 1946 were extended to and from Fyning. The frequency of service **62** was seasonally reduced to just three journeys each way on Wednesdays and Saturdays only, although a daily service was reinstated for summer 1947. Service **63B** was seasonally reduced to run on Tuesdays, Thursdays and Saturdays only as in winter 1945. The frequency of service **66** was increased to hourly daily throughout plus an hourly service between Rustington Church and Arundel Square replacing service 66A although running via the inland route between Rustington and Littlehampton. Service **67** between Havant and Compton was reduced from daily operation to just Wednesdays, Saturdays and Sundays only for the winter period.

The Scaynes Hill journeys on service **89** departing Haywards Heath at 0851, 1151, 1351 and 1751 were extended on Tuesdays and Saturdays along new roads for Southdown to and from Butterbox Corner via Nash Farm. In the postwar boom the 89 was further extended from Haywards Heath to Horsham from 6 June 1948 to form an important and useful cross country link which continued until the April 1971 service reductions.

The frequency of service **90** was increased to a regular three hourly service daily plus a weekday morning journey each way between Heathfield and Hailsham via Hellingly Mental Hospital although the additional hourly journeys on service **91** between Heathfield and Eastbourne were seasonally withdrawn. Recently extended service **98** was revised to provide three through journeys each way plus three journeys each way between Seaford and Berwick Station via Litlington on Sundays to Fridays and four through journeys each way plus four journeys each way between Seaford and Berwick Station on Saturdays. Service **99** was seasonally reduced from hourly to every 90 minutes daily as in winter 1945.

98 — GOLDEN CROSS — Ripe — Berwick — Alfriston — SEAFORD — 98

		NS	SO						NSS	SSO		
Ser. 16	Lewes County Hall ... dep.	9 11	...	1211	...	...	6 11	...	...	9 11	...	...
	Golden Cross Inn ... arr.	9 44	...	1244	...	...	6 44	...	...	9 44	...	...
Ser. 92	Hailsham *Southdown Office* ... dep.	9 25	...	1225	...	...	6 25	...	...	9 25	...	...
	Golden Cross Inn ... arr.	9 46	...	1246	...	...	6 46	...	...	9 46	...	...
	Uckfield Bus Station ... dep.	9 20	...	1220	...	...	6 20	...	...	9 20	...	...
	Golden Cross Inn ... arr.	9 46	...	1246	...	...	6 46	...	...	9 46	...	...
	Golden Cross Inn ... dep.	9 46	...	1246	...	...	6 46	...	...	9 46	...	...
	Chalvington *Church Lane*	9 53	...	1253	...	...	6 53	...	...	9 53	...	...
	Ripe *Lamb Inn*	9 55	...	1255	...	...	6 55	...	...	9 55	...	...
	Chalvington *Church Lane*	9 57	...	1257	...	...	6 57	...	...	9 57	...	...
	Berwick Station S.R.	10 6	1017	1 6	3 17	5 17	7 6	9 17	...	10 6	...	...
	Berwick Cross Roads ... arr.	10 9	1020	1 9	3 20	5 20	7 9	9 20	...	10 9	...	...
Ser. 25	Lewes County Hall ... dep.	9 35	9 35	1235	3 35	5 35	6 35	8 35	9 35	9 35	...	...
	Berwick Cross Roads ... arr.	10 9	10 9	1 9	4 9	5 9	7 9	9 9	10 9	10 9	...	...
	Eastbourne *Pevensey Road* ... dep.	9 50	9 50	1250	2 50	4 50	6 50	8 50	...	9 50	9 50	...
	Berwick Cross Roads ... arr.	1020	1020	1 20	4 20	5 20	7 20	9 20	...	1020	1020	...
	Berwick Cross Roads ... dep.	1020	1020	1 20	3 20	5 20	7 20	9 20	1010	1020	1020	...
	Alfriston *The Cross*	1028	1028	1 28	3 28	5 28	7 28	9 28	1018	1028	1028	...
	Litlington *Plough and Harrow*	1036	1036	1 36	3 36	5 36	7 36	9 36	...	1036	...	...
	Exceat Farm	1043	1043	1 43	3 43	5 43	7 43	9 43	...	1043	...	...
	Seaford *Clinton Place*	1052	1052	1 52	3 52	5 52	7 52	9 52	...	1052	...	...
Ser. 12	Seaford *Clinton Place*	1054	1054	1 54	3 54	5 54	7 54	9 54	...	...	...	...
	Newhaven *Bridge Street*	11 7	11 7	2 7	4 7	6 7	8 7	10 7	...	...	...	...
	Brighton *Old Steine*	1142	1142	2 42	4 42	6 42	8 42	1042	...	...	...	...

NS—Not Sundays.   NSS—Not Saturdays and Sundays.   SO—Sundays only.   SSO—Saturdays and Sundays only.

The direct services to Hellingly Mental Hospital had continued throughout the war years. These now ran on alternate Tuesdays and Wednesdays and the first Sunday in each month from Hove Station via Brighton Pool Valley, Lewes and Golden Cross – with connections from East Grinstead by service 92. On alternate Wednesdays and the first Sunday in each month another service ran from Burgess Hill, Hurstpierpoint, Hassocks and Ditchling to Lewes where it could be linked with the Hove service. Finally every Tuesday, alternate Wednesdays and the first Sunday of each month a service ran from Eastbourne to Hellingly with connections by service 12 from Seaford, Polegate (connections with service 25 from Berwick) and Hailsham (connections with service 15 from Hastings). The services proved to be long lasting. After 1972 the remaining services were numbered 516 from Brighton and 590 from Eastbourne with the Brighton service surviving many cutbacks to remain in operation in the early 1980s.

Whilst staff and vehicle resources were still scarce, enhancements were introduced to meet increased demand for travel. Starting from Sunday 10 November, Bognor gained improved evening services after 2130 on the **50**, **50A** and **55** to Elmer, Pagham and North Bersted.

1947

During the early months of 1947 Britain suffered its most severe and protracted spell of bad weather during the twentieth century causing serious disruption to road and rail travel. Snow began to fall in south east England on Thursday 23 January and the weather remained bitterly cold for many weeks with huge snow drifts bringing transport to a standstill in many parts of Britain. By 28 January temperatures were at freezing throughout the day and on the following night lights went out across the country. Supplies of coal could not be transported to essential industries causing short time working in many factories while the freezing conditions soon led to power cuts which continued until April. All operators suffered a major fall in non essential leisure travel as bus services were disrupted by the snow and ice.

A further *complete system timetable* was issued containing all alterations up to **Sunday 5 January 1947**. The former Tramocars services along the western end of Worthing Sea Front had been severely reduced and diverted during the war as gun emplacements stood ready to repel a German invasion. With normality returning to the promenades it was now time to reintroduce bus services to this part of town although the numbers T1, T2, 3A and 5A were long gone. Service **11** was diverted between Marine Parade and Wallace Avenue via Marine Parade, West Parade and Wallace Avenue regaining the route of the former 3A (and its T1 predecessor) which had been diverted away from the Sea Front on 21 November 1940. A 15 minute frequency was provided on Weekdays and after 1200 on Sundays with a 30 minute service on Sunday mornings. Although service **11A** was a recent introduction it was completely revised to run along many roads previously covered by service 5A (and predecessor T2) until withdrawal on 21 November 1940. It now operated from WORTHING PIER to WORTHING DOME via Marine Parade, Western Place, Rowlands Road, Grand Avenue, Tarring Road, Teville Road, Victoria Road, Railway Approach, Chapel Road,

Car 1461 (FCD 261) is a Leyland Tiger TS7 with Harrington body new in 1938 and seen at the Worthing Pier terminus on one of the rather complex interworked routes that were introduced on 5 January 1947 finally absorbing the old Tramocar services. It was rebuilt by Portsmouth Aviation in 1947 and became one of the last of the prewar Tiger buses to remain in service being sold in January 1957. *Southdown Enthusiasts Club – Clark/Surfleet Collection*

South Street and Marine Parade with a 30 minute service daily except hourly on Sunday mornings. New Service **11B** replaced the 11A on the eastern side of town but on a reduced frequency operating between WORTHING PIER and WORTHING DOME via Marine Parade, Western Place, Rowlands Road, Grand Avenue, Tarring Road, Teville Road, Victoria Road, Railway Approach, Newland Road, Homefield Road, Lyndhurst Road, Madeira Avenue, Brighton Road, Steyne Gardens and Marine Parade. A 30 minute frequency was provided daily except hourly on Sunday mornings.

One of the very few remaining bus services totally within the Southdown area still in the hands of a small private operator was that between Arundel and Burpham operated by Mrs Hay-Will. Southdown acquired the goodwill of the service for £450 on 4 January 1947 and next day introduced new Service **70** between ARUNDEL SQUARE and BURPHAM (GEORGE & DRAGON HOTEL) via Queen Street, The Causeway, Burpham Road, Warningcamp and Wepham with a journey time of 18 minutes. Five journeys ran each way daily and a one man operated Leyland Cub was normally used on the service. Service **97** was again enhanced from Sunday 30 March to provide a basic 2 hourly

70	ARUNDEL—BURPHAM Via Warningcamp Turning and Wepham.											70
			NS	SSO								
Arundel *Square*	... ...	9 15	1115	1215	2 15	5 15	9 15	...				
Ser. ⎰ Worthing Dome ...		8*41	1041	1141	1 41	4 41	8 41	...				
10 ⎱ Burpham Road *South End*		9*16	1116	1216	2 16	5 16	9 16	...				
Burpham Road *South End*	...	9 19	1119	1219	2 19	5 19	9 19	...				
Warningcamp Turning...	...	9 22	1122	1222	2 22	5 22	9 22	...				
Wepham Corner ...	...	9 28	1128	1228	2 28	5 28	9 28	...				
Burpham *George & Dragon*	...	9 33	1133	1233	2 33	5 33	9 33	...				
			NS	SO	SaO							
Burpham *George & Dragon*	...	9 34	1134	1234	1 34	2 34	5 34	9 34	...			
Wepham Corner ...	...	9 39	1139	1239	1 39	2 39	5 39	9 39	...			
Warningcamp Turning...	...	9 45	1145	1245	1 45	2 45	5 45	9 45	...			
Burpham Road *South End*	...	9 48	1148	1248	1 48	2 48	5 48	9 48	...			
Ser. ⎰ Burpham Road *South End*		9 49	1149	1249	1 49	2 49	5 49	9 49	...			
10 ⎱ Worthing Dome ...		1024	1224	1 24	2 24	3 24	6 24	1024	...			
Arundel *Square*	... ...	9 52	1152	1252	1 52	2 52	5 52	9 52	...			

* or NS—Not Sundays.   SaO—Saturdays only.
SSO—Saturdays and Sundays only.   SO—Sundays only.

frequency on wet days increased to every 30 minutes in fine weather with the last bus from Beachy Head departing at 1920. Commencing Sunday 11 May the off peak frequency as far as East Moulscombe on service **13E** was increased to 6 minutes. The peak time service remained every 6 minutes throughout to Higher Bevendean.

Summer services in the Portsmouth area commenced from Sunday 18 May. Journeys from Southsea, South Parade Pier on service **31** were diverted to operate via South Parade, Clarence Parade, Western Parade and Southsea Terrace having previously run via Palmerston Road and Kent Road. Service **31C** between Theatre Royal and Farlington was withdrawn although latterly it had only provided a few early morning journeys on weekdays and a 30 minute service during Sunday mornings. Southdown had enjoyed only a token presence at Clarence Pier in prewar days with service 38 acquired from Blue Motor Services (Boarhunt) Ltd from 16 September 1935 running to Hambledon and Droxford. In one of the first curtailments of the war this was cut back to start from Theatre Royal from 21 September 1939 and, although buses returned to South Parade from 19 November 1944, there was no similar reintroduction of Southdown buses to Clarence Pier as it had been totally destroyed by German bombs on the night of 10/11 January 1941. Despite the loss of the Pier facilities, services **37**, **37A**, **39** and **39A** were all extended beyond Theatre Royal to commence from SOUTHSEA (CLARENCE PIER) running via Pier Road, Bellevue Terrace, Kings Terrace, Landport Terrace, Hampshire Terrace, Commercial Road and then as normal route. The frequency of services **37** and **37A** was improved to every 30 minutes daily although no Sunday morning service was provided at this time. Sunday morning journeys on service **39** were also diverted between Purbrook Church and

A rear view illustration of car 21 (ECD 521), a Leyland Cub KPZ2 with Park Royal 20 seat body, waiting at Burpham on infrequent service 70 to Arundel which was acquired from Mrs Hay-Will on 4 January 1947. The Cubs retained cream window surrounds after the war unlike other single deck buses in the fleet.
Southdown Enthusiasts Club – Clark/Surfleet Collection

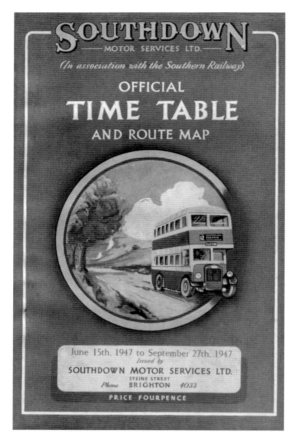

Waterlooville via Park Avenue and Stakes Hill Road. Summer services were also introduced to Hayling Island at this time. Seasonal service **46** was reintroduced between HAYLING FERRY and EASTOKE HOUSE with a 30 minute service daily. The frequency of service **47** was increased to provide an hourly service each way around the Hayling Island loop via Northney plus an hourly service each way direct on weekdays. On Sundays an hourly service ran each way via Northney plus an hourly service each way direct after 1500 meaning that Northney now gained an hourly service all day on Sundays. An hourly Sunday morning operation was also introduced on service **47A**. Finally service **49** between Waterlooville and Havant was increased to run every 30 minutes daily as in summer 1946.

By the end of the war Shoreham Beach was looking forlorn and derelict but, in spite of this, many of the plot holders returned and repaired those properties that were still standing and made plans to rebuild those that were demolished by the military in 1940. A bus service was once again required and from Sunday 25 May service **21** was extended from Shoreham High Street to Shoreham Beach via Norfolk Bridge, Brighton Road, Kings Drive and Beach Road, having been abruptly withdrawn during the invasion scare of summer 1940. An hourly service was provided throughout plus an hourly service between Pool Valley and Shoreham Bridge Hotel daily and the Sunday morning operation was

restored in full. Improved summer frequencies were introduced from Wednesday 11 June 1947 on the Eastbourne to Hastings services operated jointly with Maidstone & District. Inland route **15** was again increased to run every 30 minutes daily as in summer 1946 while the coastal route **99** via Pevensey Bay increased to hourly daily also as summer 1946. The frequency was further increased to 30 minutes from 13 July 1947.

The main *summer timetable* was issued to commence on **Sunday 15 June 1947** and the cover design was that which became standard until 1960. Against a green background a Leyland Titan is depicted on service 12 climbing a hill with downland and sea in the background. Although both staff and vehicle resources were still limited there was a huge demand for travel and the new timetable attempted to provide some of the desired facilities. Alternate journeys on service **1** were now diverted to serve West Chiltington village offering a more regular frequency. On service **4** there was no change in frequency until 1400 and then a 10 minute service ran on weekdays throughout to High Salvington. On Sundays a 15 minute service ran throughout all day although this was not as generous as in summer 1946 when a 10 minute service ran throughout the day on weekdays. Service **9** was extended from Shoreham to Brighton and from Littlehampton to Arundel to operate between BRIGHTON (POOL VALLEY) and ARUNDEL SQUARE as service 10 to Patching then via Angmering Village, Angmering Station, Littlehampton, Wick, Lyminster, Crossbush and Arundel Station. An hourly service ran daily although there was no service between Littlehampton and Arundel on Sunday morning. In addition service **9A** was extended hourly from Littlehampton to ARUNDEL providing a 15 minute daytime frequency between Rustington, Littlehampton and Arundel in conjunction with service 66.

The first housing development in Coldean was the Parkside estate of the late 1930s around Park Road which was completed in 1948 when it was still part of Falmer parish. The rest of the estate, which was then part of Stanmer parish, was developed by Brighton Corporation from 1950 and on 1 April 1952 the whole area of Coldean became part of the County Borough of Brighton. Clearly Southdown saw this as part of their territory and from Sunday 15 June introduced new service **13A** between BRIGHTON (POOL VALLEY) and COLDEAN ESTATE (FOREST ROAD) via Grand Junction Road, Old Steine, Pavilion Parade, Marlborough Place, Gloucester Place, Richmond Place, Richmond Terrace, Lewes Road and Coldean Lane. The new service terminated about half a mile along Coldean Lane and a 30 minute frequency was provided daily.

New roads for Southdown between Cooksbridge and Spithurst were covered by a new service numbered **19** running between LEWES (COUNTY HALL) and SPITHURST (PARK

FARM) via Offham, Cooksbridge, Gallybird Hall, Barcombe Cross and Mount Pleasant. On weekdays four journeys ran each way plus one additional journey each way on Wednesdays and Saturdays, while three journeys were provided each way on Sundays. An additional hourly service was introduced on service **22** between Brighton and Steyning daily, except on Sunday mornings, making this section half hourly. In Newhaven new local service **26** commenced running between GIBBON ROAD and DENTON via Gibbon Road, Fort Road, South Road, Dacre Road, Meeching Road, High Street, Bridge Street, New Road, Avis Road and Denton Road. Buses returned via Heighton Road, Heighton New Road, New Road and Bridge Street and then as outward route reversed. The journey time was 14 minutes and an hourly service was provided daily increased to 30 minutes during weekday peak periods. As a result service **123** was withdrawn between Bridge Street and Denton and diverted to East Side via Railway Road and Norton Road. Denton had been served by service 123 since 9 December 1945 but all services to Gibbon Road had ceased by 3 January 1943 and the new service brought a significant enhancement to local buses in Newhaven.

Additional journeys were added to the basic three hourly all year service **27** but still unable to access the Devil's Dyke Hotel area. Seven extra 'fine days only' journeys ran each way daily between Brighton and Devil's Dyke Fork Roads. With booming demand for bus travel the frequency of service **31** was increased to 15 minutes throughout between Brighton and Southsea daily and service **31A** withdrawn in consequence. The situation in Ferring-by-Sea

19	LEWES — BARCOMBE — SPITHURST via Offham and Cooksbridge.						19
		NS	NS				WSSO
Lewes County Hall		8 55	1155	1 55	4 55		9 30
Lewes Nevill Crescent (North End) ...		8 59	1159	1 59	4 59		9 34
Offham Post Office		9 3	12 3	2 3	5 3		9 38
Cooksbridge Station S.R. ...		9 6	12 6	2 6	5 6		9 41
Barcombe Cross		9 16	1216	2 16	5 16		9 51
Spithurst Church		9 20	12 0	2 20	5 20		9 55
Spithurst Park Farm		9 22	1222	2 22	5 22		9 57
		NS	NS				WSSO
Spithurst Park Farm		9 23	1223	2 23	5 23		9 58
Spithurst Church		9 25	1225	2 25	5 25		10 0
Barcombe Cross		9 29	1229	2 29	5 29		10 4
Cooksbridge Station S.R. ...		9 39	1239	2 39	5 39		1014
Offham Post Office		9 42	1242	2 42	5 42		1017
Lewes Nevill Crescent (North End) ...		9 46	1246	2 46	5 46		1021
Lewes County Hall		9 50	1250	2 50	5 50		1025

NS—Not Sundays.   WSSO—Wednesdays, Saturdays and Sundays.

For additional buses between Lewes and Cooksbridge Station, see Service 20.

For additional buses between Lewes and Offham, see Services 20, 24 and 29.

For additional buses between Lewes and Nevill Crescent, see Services 20, 28 and 123.

reverted to the 1944 pattern with service **31F** being extended again to terminate at Beresford's Stores and the short lived local service **31E** withdrawn after operation on 14 June 1947. The **31F** and **31G** were curtailed to start at WORTHING (DOME) and the route in Worthing was revised between Marine Parade and Goring Road to run via West Parade and George V Avenue while the **31G** was also diverted between Goring Way and Littlehampton Road to run via Sea Lane, Ferring Street and Langbury Lane.

The frequency of service **54A** between Chichester and Hambrook was increased to two hourly daily – previously having run on Wednesdays and Saturdays only while service **58** was doubled to an hourly frequency throughout daily plus various additional journeys daily

After wartime storage the two Dennis Falcons returned to service at Worthing in June 1945 but not on the routes that replaced the former Tramocar operations. Eventually they found a regular home on service 31F between Worthing and South Ferring where their lighter weight found favour with the residents of Ferring who feared damage to the private roads over which the buses ran. Car 80 (FUF 180) is waiting departure at the terminus opposite Worthing Dome and will then follow the sea front as far as George V Avenue. In June 1950 they both transferred to Hayling Island and joined a batch of postwar Dennis Falcons on the services to Havant until withdrawn in 1956.
Southdown Enthusiasts Club – Clark/Surfleet Collection

between Chichester and Singleton although no Sunday morning service was provided. An additional hourly service daily between Bognor Railway Station and Chichester (West Street) was provided on service **59** making this section half hourly. The frequency of service **62** was increased to four journeys each way daily plus two additional journeys each way on Wednesdays and Saturdays and one journey each way on Saturdays between Chichester and Chilgrove as in summer 1946. Service **63B** was again increased to a three hourly service daily as in summer 1946.

Saturday journeys on the recently acquired service **70** between Arundel and Burpham were increased from five to six. Service **75** was curtailed at BILLINGSHURST STATION being withdrawn between there and Kingsfold, a section which was now covered by new service 79 although there was no change to the frequency.

Service **78** was extended on Wednesdays and Saturdays from Handcross via B2110 and Great Coopers Corner Farm to BALCOMBE (HALF MOON) with three journeys each way in place of service **79** which was withdrawn. The number **79** was, however, allocated to a new cross country link between STEYNING (WHITE HORSE) and BILLINGSHURST (INTERNATIONAL STORES) via Wiston Park, Buncton, Hole Street, Ashington, Spear Hill, Goose Green, Danhill Cross Roads, Broadford Bridge, Kingsfold and Billingshurst Station. Most of the roads were new to Southdown buses and appeared somewhat unpromising territory although the new service connected with the 22 at Steyning and the 59 at Billingshurst. A four hourly service ran daily with departures from Billingshurst at 0943, 1343 and 1743 and from Steyning at 1234, 1634 and 2034 although it was progressively reduced until final withdrawal on 5 December

1959. The frequency of service **80** increased from 5 to 9 journeys each way on weekdays and from 4 to 7 journeys each way on Sundays. The service was further augmented in post war days but remained a quiet backwater until the Beeching cuts of the 1960s when the Horsham to Brighton railway line was closed leading to the 80 being extended to Brighton. As with most rail replacement facilities of this era, the improvements were to be short lived.

Service **91** was increased to an hourly service throughout daily plus an hourly service between Eastbourne and Heathfield except at the times when the three hourly service 90 operated. This was similar to summer 1946. The Heathfield to Waldron section of service **95** was reintroduced on Sundays and an hourly basic service ran daily on service **97** to Beachy Head increased to 15 minutes in fine weather similar to prewar summers.

The high summer timetable for service **12** from Sunday 13 July included a significant increase in frequency taking it above anything enjoyed in prewar summers and included:

1 journey per hour Valley Drive to Eastbourne

2 journeys per hour Brighton Station to Eastbourne

1 journey per hour Valley Drive to Seaford

3 journeys per hour Brighton Station to Seaford

2 journeys per hour Valley Drive to Peacehaven Annexe (12A)

2 journeys per hour Brighton Station to Saltdean Mount (12B)

As post war development in the area of Brighton between Dyke Road and London Road continued, so the 12 was extended further to serve the new housing and this remained a Southdown preserve until the establishment of the jointly operated Brighton Area Transport Services (BATS) in 1961.

In addition the frequency of service **99** was increased to 30 minutes daily which marked a big increase over the summer 1939 level of just 8 buses running every 1 or 2 hours.

Express Coach Services

Following the end of hostilities in Europe some wartime controls were relaxed fairly rapidly during the summer of 1945 with many of those affecting public transport being discontinued in June and July. The wartime powers which had enabled RTCs to restrict what they considered to be unnecessary services continued for the present and some restrictions on the use of fuel for licensed services remained in place until 1948. Restricted maintenance, vehicles commandeered for military use and lack of replacement new vehicles during the war meant that the coach fleet was in need of major renovation. At the outbreak of war some 313 of the total Southdown fleet of 705 vehicles had been coaches but 121 had been compulsorily acquired for use by the Military Authorities, mainly following the disastrous loss of transport in the retreat to Dunkirk in 1940. By March 1946 Southdown had been able to reacquire just 10 of the 121 and even these would take some considerable time to prepare for peacetime duties. Staff had also worked under difficult conditions for almost six years and until demobilisation started in earnest it was unlikely for resources to be available for the reintroduction of the London express coach services, still regarded by some in authority as unnecessary competition for the hard pressed railways. In addition the Victoria Coach Station yard remained under military requisition until early in 1946.

A brief sign of better times came during July 1945 when some coach excursions were permitted. Regular long distance coach services, including LPTB's Green Line operations, were still not allowed. At the August Bank Holiday angry scenes were reported outside the Orange Coach Station in Brixton as 2000 people waited to book one of the 256 seats available!! They mobbed the booking office and police were called to disperse the crowd, although it was a hopeful sign of how popular coach travel would be in the post war era. Representations were made to the MOWT on 10 September 1945 concerning the possibility of resuming express coach services. The Minister responded that the labour and

At the outbreak of war the Burlingham bodied Leyland Tiger TS7s all acquired a dark green roof in place of the distinctive cream when delivered in 1936. With the resumption of the London Express Services in March 1946 they were again used extensively for this work mainly based at Portsmouth and Brighton. Here car 1155 (CUF 155) is parked in the streets around Victoria Coach Station after working a service up from Portsmouth.
Southdown Enthusiasts Club – W J Haynes Collection

vehicle position did not make a general restoration of such services practicable at present and that local services used by workers and shoppers must be considered first. He also felt that priority should be given to cross country routes on which alternative facilities, including rail, were lacking for the through journey or for intermediate points. Long distance services running parallel to the main line railways should not be resumed for the present. This seemed to rule out any chance of Southdown restarting their London services in the near future although an encouraging sign was the resumption by Premier Travel of their express coach service between Heydon, Chrishall and London from 9 November 1945. This had been withdrawn along with all services between East Anglia and London in June 1942 and probably marked the post war start of coach operations into London.

In January 1946 it was announced that in view of the improved labour position, the RTCs would be prepared to consider applications for the resumption of any express services as from 1 February 1946 provided that applicants had the necessary vehicles and labour to maintain the proposed services efficiently and without detriment to other essential facilities provided by them. After much debate and lots of effort to restore its prewar Leyland Tiger coaches to the usual Southdown high standards the London Express coach services began again on Friday 22 March 1946. Eight services started on the same day operating between London, Victoria Coach Station and Eastbourne, Brighton, Worthing via Dorking or Crawley, Bognor Regis via Chichester or Littlehampton, Portsmouth & Southsea and Gosport. Unlike some operators who chose a phased reintroduction of their services, Southdown decided on an almost normal express programme with some 30 daily departures from London largely based on the prewar winter timetable. They warned, however, that the number of relief coaches would be considerably below the 1939 level. After consultation within the Regional Fares Committees the fares were fixed at a rate of $16^2/3\%$ above those in force before the services were withdrawn in September 1942 in line with the increase in rail fares since the outbreak of war.

In addition to getting the coaches and staff ready there was the need to prepare and distribute publicity and organise booking and charting facilities for a service that had been closed down for nearly four years. The number of booking agents, particularly in the London area, was significantly reduced as businesses had suffered bombing and several years without any coach services on which to book. Some 150 of London Coastal Coaches' 600 agencies in the London area had closed by summer 1942. A particular loss was the Chimes Garage agency at Streatham which resulted in the postwar boarding point at Streatham, traditionally outside Chimes Garage at 253 High Road, being moved a little south to opposite Natal Road where a new booking agent was appointed. This applied on all services running through Streatham.

The timetable leaflets for the reintroduced services were a big improvement on the wartime versions and the same print colour scheme applied as in force up to 1942. There was no separate front cover as in prewar days and timetables appeared on two sides with Booking Agents, fares and conditions on the reverse but they were much easier to read than the wartime publications. Separate timetables were issued for the two Bognor Regis services although all journeys were shown between the terminal points and the leaflet for the service via Littlehampton, Arundel and Dorking was printed in black. Normal booking and reservation arrangements resumed as applying prior to 4 July 1942. The interavailability of road and rail tickets appears to have lapsed on the London Express Services early in the war and on the leaflets issued in March 1946 there was only a reference advising passengers requiring return by rail to see separate announcements. Full details of a new extended scheme appeared in the Summer 1946 timetable leaflets.

The new Eastbourne timetable introduced on 22 March 1946 closely mirrored that operating in winter 1938/9 with northbound departures from Royal Parade Garage at 0800, 1000, 1400 and 1800. From London, coaches departed at 0915, 1415, 1815 and 2115 – so restoring the late coach that had last run in September 1939. In Eastbourne coaches called at Leaf Hall and Cavendish Place Coach Station and all made a 10 minute refreshment stop at The Star, Felbridge. Bus connections were once more featured and through fares available. A day return ticket between London and Eastbourne now cost 7/6d (38p).

Departures from Brighton were at 0800, 0900, 1000, 1200, 1400, 1500, 1700, 1800, 1900 and 2000 plus the return of the 0830 via Henfield and Cowfold on Wednesdays only after an absence of over 6 years. The 0900 and 1900 coaches ran via Hassocks, Burgess Hill and Cuckfield with all others serving Hurstpierpoint, Albourne and Bolney. Services from London departed at 0900, 1000, 1100, 1200, 1400, 1500, 1700, 1800, 1900 and 2100 plus the Wednesdays 1930 via Henfield. All ran via Bolney, Albourne and diverted to set down on request at Hurstpierpoint except for the 1100 and 1900 services which ran via Cuckfield, Burgess Hill and Hassocks. As in prewar days all services called for refreshments at the newly reopened Crawley Station and the day return fare from London to Brighton had risen to 5/9d (29p). The standard journey time was 2 hours 30 minutes and bus connections with through fares once again appeared as in prewar and wartime leaflets.

The Worthing service started with six

Car 1061 (JK 1266) is a Leyland Tiger TS2 new in 1930 which was acquired with the fleet of Southern Glideway Coaches of Eastbourne in March 1932. The original Duple body was replaced by a new Park Royal coach body to Southdown's standard design and served until 1955 before sale for scrap. With a noticeable lack of other traffic it is seen crossing Mitcham Road into Purley Way, Croydon – long before a roundabout was necessary – on a southbound working from London to Brighton.
Author's collection

journeys each way and restored coaches to Littlehampton as well as the route via Crawley and Redhill. Coaches to London left Marine Parade at 0805, 0905, 1005, 1405, 1805 and 1905 with the 0905 and 1905 running via Crawley and Redhill. Other departures served Dorking and Kingston and the 0905 from Worthing started at Littlehampton at 0835. From London, coaches departed at 0900, 1000, 1200, 1400, 1800 and 1900 similar to the last prewar winter service. All ran via Kingston and Dorking except for the 1000 and 1900 which served Redhill and Crawley. The last journey from London continued via Goring, Ferring and Rustington to Littlehampton. As previously all services made a 10 minute refreshment stop with those via Crawley using the Southdown Coach Station while those via Dorking called at the Holly & Laurel Hotel at Holmwood. Bus connections were included once more and a day return ticket from London to Worthing now cost 7/6d (38p).

Both of the routes between Bognor Regis and London reappeared with coaches on the main route via Chichester departing from Bognor Regis at 0830, 1330 and 1830. Departures from London via Chichester were at 0930, 1430 and 1830 and all coaches made a refreshment stop at Burpham, Green Man just north of Guildford. Bus connections were shown but the through tickets on Aldershot & District buses from Godalming to Chiddingfold, Elstead, Witley and Wormley were no longer featured. In addition to the service via Chichester there was the alternative route via Littlehampton, Arundel, Petworth, Dorking and Sutton which left Bognor Regis daily at 0830 returning from London at 1830. As in prewar days this route stopped for refreshment at Holmwood, Holly & Laurel, south of Dorking and diverted via Pulborough only when required for prebooked passengers. Journey time was 3 hours 30 minutes by either route and the day return fare from London to Littlehampton or Bognor Regis was 8/3d (42p).

Seven journeys each way were provided on the Portsmouth and Southsea service and coaches were once again able to serve Southsea. Unlike in prewar days no journeys continued beyond Victoria to Kings Cross Coach Station. On

1230 (GUF 730) is one of 25 Leyland Tiger PS1/1 models with Eastern Coach Works rear entrance bodywork new in April 1947. Seen at Horsham Carfax on a southbound working from London to Littlehampton via Worthing it still retains the top sliding windows as delivered but has a chromed – rather than dark green painted – radiator. All of the batch were originally allocated to the London Express Services but subsequently demoted to bus work. Car 1230 was one that was simply renumbered 692 without any modification and sold in August 1961.
Southdown Enthusiasts Club – Clark/Surfleet Collection

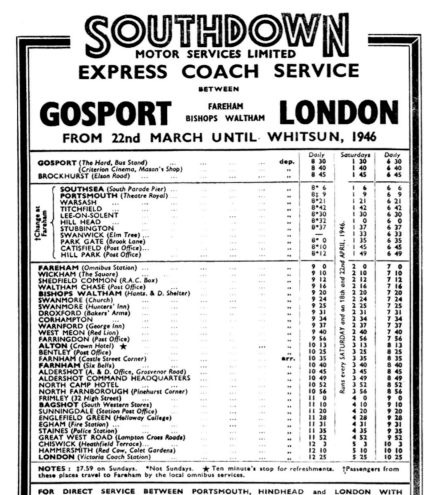

Portsea Island services started at the Southdown Office at 241 Albert Road and then called at a new stop at Morris House, Clarendon Road before joining the prewar route via Portsea Hard, Hyde Park Road, North End and Hilsea. Following severe bombing in 1941 it was no longer necessary to operate via Clarence Pier for Isle of Wight connections. Departures from Southsea were at 0745, 0845, 0945, 1245, 1545, 1745 and 1845 with all running via Putney Bridge Station and Walham Green except the 0845, 1545 and 1845 which served Hammersmith. From London there were departures at 0830, 0930, 1230, 1430, 1630, 1830 and 2100 with all serving Walham Green and Putney Bridge Station except the 0930 and 1630 which ran via Hammersmith. Connections were shown at Cosham with Southdown bus services to Fareham, Havant, Emsworth and Hayling Island but the through tickets on Aldershot & District buses which continued until 1942 were no longer included. A refreshment halt was made at Hindhead although the owners of the Royal Huts Hotel which was used before the war were not anxious to accommodate Southdown any longer and alternative arrangements were sought. The through journey time via Putney was 3 hours 35 minutes, ten minutes longer via Hammersmith, and a day return ticket from London to Portsmouth or Southsea cost 8/9d (44p).

The Gosport route was an early casualty of war having been withdrawn almost immediately on the outbreak of hostilities in September 1939 but it was still included in the grand reintroduction of Southdown's London services. As in prewar days two daily return trips were provided plus an extra lunch time journey on Saturdays. Coaches departed from Gosport, The Hard at 0830, 1330 (Saturdays) and 1830 and returned from London at 0900, 1400 (Saturdays) and 1800.

SOUTH COAST EXPRESS SERVICE

ROYAL BLUE

Bournemouth (Square Station)				8 40	1110	3 25
New Milton				9 15	1145	4 0
Lyndhurst (Hants & Dorset Office)				9 41	1211	4 26
Southampton (Grosvenor Square)				10 5	1235	5 7
Bursledon					1022	
Wickham					1 4	
Fareham (Bus Station, West Street)				1038		5 33
Hilsea (Southdown Station) ★				1051	1 27	5 36
Portsmouth (Hyde Park Road)				11 6	1 42	5 51

		†			
Portsmouth (Hyde Park Road) dep.			11 0	2 0	6 0
Hilsea (Southdown Station)			1115	2 15	6 15
Havant (High Street)			1130	2 30	6 30
Emsworth (The Square)			1137	2 37	6 37
Chichester (West Street)			1155	2 55	6 55
Bognor (Coach Station)			1220	3 20	7 20
Littlehampton (East Street)			1245	3 45	7 45
Arundel (The Square)			A	A	A
Worthing (Marine Parade)			1 15	4 15	8 15
Shoreham (High Street)			1 29	4 29	8 29
Hove (7 St. Aubyns Gardens)			1 40	4 40	8 40
Brighton (Steine Street) arr.			1 45	4 45	8 45

Brighton (Steine Street) dep.			10 0			
Peacehaven (South Coast Road)			1015	2 30	5 30	
Newhaven (Bridge Street)			1025	2 40	5 40	
Seaford (Clinton Place)			1035	2 50	5 50	
Eastbourne (Pevensey Road) arr.			11 4	3 19	6 19	
Eastbourne (Pevensey Road) dep.			1110			
Bexhill (Marina)			1140	3 55		
Hastings (Station Approach) arr.			12 0	4 15		
Winchelsea (New Inn)	9 15	1 0	2 15	4 15	7 15	
Rye (East Kent Office)	9 42	1 27	2 42	4 42	7 42	
New Romney (The Ship)	9 50	1 35	2 50	5035	7 50	
Dymchurch (Bus Station)	1023	2 8	3 23	6 8	8 23	
Hythe (Red Lion Square)	1033	2 18	3 33	6 18	8 33	
Folkestone (109 Sandgate Road)	1048	2 33	3 48	6 33	8 48	
Dover (Pencester Road) arr.	9 0	11 2	2 47	4 2	6 47	9 2
Dover (Pencester Road) dep.	9 20	1122	3 17	4 27	7 17	
Deal (South Street)	9 45	1152	3 42	4 52	7 42	
Sandwich (Cattle Market)	10 3	1210	4 0	5 10	8 0	
Ramsgate (49 Harbour Parade)	1025	1232	4 22	5 32	8 22	
Broadstairs (Pierremont Hall)	1035	1242	4 32	5 42	8 33	
Margate (The Parade) arr.	1048	1255	4 45	5 55	8 45	

ROYAL BLUE

				†		†		
Margate (The Parade) dep.				9 0	1115	1 45	4 45	7 15
Broadstairs (Pierremont Hall)				9 13	1128	1 58	4 58	7 28
Ramsgate (49 Harbour Parade)				9 23	1138	2 8	5 8	7 38
Sandwich (Cattle Market)				9 45	12 0	2 30	5 30	8 0
Deal (South Street)				10 3	1218	2 48	5 48	8 18
Dover (Pencester Road) arr.				1028	1243	3 13	6 13	8 43
Dover (Pencester Road) dep.		9 30		1033	1248	3 18	6 18	8 43
Folkestone (109 Sandgate Road)		9 30		1053	1 8	3 38	6 38	9 3
Hythe (Red Lion Square)		9 44		11 7	1 22	3 52	6 52	
Dymchurch (Bus Station)		9 59		1122	1 37	4 7	7 7	
New Romney (The Ship)		10 9		1132	1 47	4 17	7 17	
Rye (East Kent Office)		1042		12 5	2 20	4 50	7 50	
Winchelsea (New Inn)		1050		1213	2 28	4 58	7 58	
Hastings (Station Approach) arr.		1117		1240	2 55	5 25	8 25	

Bexhill (Marina)			1 35	5 35	
			1 55	6 25	
Eastbourne (Pevensey Road) arr.			2 24	6 54	
Eastbourne (Pevensey Road) dep.	9 25	9 50	2 50	6 55	
Seaford (Clinton Place)		9 50	2 50	7 20	
Newhaven (Bridge Street)		10 0	3 0	7 30	
Peacehaven (South Coast Road)		1010	3 10	7 40	
Brighton (Steine Street) arr.		1025	3 25	7 55	
Brighton (Steine Street) dep.		1035	3 35		
Hove (7 St. Aubyns Gardens)	9 5	1040	3 40		
Shoreham (High Street)	9 16	1055	3 55		
Worthing (Marine Parade)	9 30	11 5	4 5		
Littlehampton (East Street)	10 0	1135	4 35		
Arundel (The Square)			A		
Bognor (Southdown Coach Station)	1025	12 0	5 0		
Chichester (West Street)	1050	1225	5 25		
Emsworth (The Square)	1115	1243	5 43		
Havant (High Street)	1130	1 5	5 50		
Hilsea (Southdown Station)		1115	1250	6 5	
Portsmouth (Hyde Park Road) arr.		1145	1 20	6 20	

Portsmouth (Hyde Park Road)	1115	2 15	6 0	
Hilsea (Southdown Station)	1130	2 30	6 15	
Fareham (Bus Station, West Street)	1143	2 43	6 28	
Wickham	1153			
Bursledon				
Southampton (Grosvenor Square)	1224	2 59	6 44	
Lyndhurst (Hants & Dorset Office)	1246	3 17	7 3	
New Milton	1 12	4 5	7 25	
Bournemouth (Square Stn.) arr.	1 47	4 40	8 26	

NOTES— ★ Change coaches at Hilsea for points beyond Portsmouth. *a* arrives 4.50 p.m. A—Passengers to and from Arundel change at Littlehampton and to and from Southdown Service 66. Times shown in *italics* are the EAST KENT ROAD CAR CO. Service 62. † Passengers to and from points West of Hastings should book their seats at least 24 hours in advance.

No advance bookings will be accepted for journeys wholly between Margate and Hastings on the South Coast Express Service or on the EAST KENT ROAD CAR CO. Service 62.

The Saturday journeys also operated on Maundy Thursday 18 April and Easter Monday 22 April. A refreshment stop was made at the Crown Hotel in Alton and a wide range of Southdown and Hants & Dorset bus connections were made at Fareham. The through journey time was 3 hours 50 minutes southbound and five minutes longer towards London. The day return fare from London to Gosport was 8/9d (44p). Always one of the weaker London services without the duplication associated with the other routes it survived just long enough into the 1970s to became part of the National Travel network. From Thursday 18 April an additional daily journey was introduced each way between London and Bognor Regis via Littlehampton leaving Victoria Coach Station at 0930 and returning from Bognor Regis at 1730.

The South Coast Express reappeared on Saturday 13 May after being suspended at the outbreak of war. Four services a day were offered in each direction as shown below with one through journey each way from Margate to Portsmouth.

Eastbound
1000 Brighton – Margate
1100 Portsmouth – Bognor Regis – Brighton – Margate
1400 Portsmouth – Bognor Regis – Brighton – Eastbourne
1800 Portsmouth – Bognor Regis – Brighton
Westbound
0900 Brighton – Bognor Regis – Portsmouth
0925 Eastbourne – Brighton – Bognor Regis – Portsmouth
0900 Margate – Brighton – Bognor Regis – Portsmouth
1345 Margate – Brighton

In addition to the above, journeys on East Kent bus service 62 between Margate and Hastings were included on the leaflet although no advance bookings were accepted for any journeys on either service wholly between these two points. The timing point at Eastbourne remained Pevensey Road Bus Station as in prewar days but the stop at Hastings was moved to the Station Approach. Connections were made at Hilsea with Royal Blue services to Southampton and Bournemouth although the Associated Motorways network was still to restart. Through journey time was 9 hours 20 minutes westbound and 9 hours 45 minutes eastbound with breaks at Brighton, Eastbourne, Hastings or Dover according to time of day. Fares were significantly higher than prewar with the single fare from Margate to Portsmouth increasing to 16/3d (82p) while a period return from Brighton to Bournemouth now cost 17/6d (87p). Unlike the London services no premium fares were charged at weekends on the South Coast Express.

The service between Hove and Robertsbridge, Darvell Hall Sanatorium was increased to run on all Sundays except the first in the month by 2 June 1946.

Summer timetables were introduced on Friday 7 June 1946 with most coach services returning

to prewar levels of frequency. In some resorts many hotels had been destroyed or damaged and holiday camps were still recovering from their wartime closures so the limited accommodation along the popular South Coast was in great demand. Premium fares applied between London and most coastal destinations on Saturdays, Sundays and Bank Holidays between 8 June and 8 September. Some of the timetable leaflets were to almost full prewar standard with the Brighton cover featuring the familiar nearside view of a Leyland Tiger. Separate timetable leaflets were again issued for the two Bognor Regis services although all journeys on both routes were included between the terminal points. Full details were also included of the interavailability of return road and rail tickets although the supplements were much higher than prewar. For example, on a day return journey from London to Bognor Regis the additional fare to be paid for return by rail was 7/3d (37p) for an adult. Rail passengers could now return by coach but a supplement was still due and in the case of Bognor Regis would have been 1/8d (19p). The scheme was widely advertised in leaflets but the level of supplements must have made it unattractive for most passengers.

On the main London to Eastbourne route via Uckfield extra daily departures were run at 1500 and 1900 from Royal Parade Garage and at 1015

Car 1002 (UF 5742) is a Leyland Tiger TS2 new in 1930 which was rebodied with a new Harrington body to Southdown's standard design in 1935. It was modernised with a Covrad radiator in early post war days and seen in the streets around Victoria Coach Station before operating a relief working to Worthing. It enjoyed a very long life with the company and was sold in October 1951.
A M Wright

and 1515 from London. The route via Seaford was reintroduced between 29 June and 8 September 1946 and followed the same pattern as prewar with northbound departures from Cavendish Place at 0915, 1345 and 1745 and from London at 0945, 1345 and 1845. As in 1939 only the 0945 from London and 1745 from Eastbourne ran daily, the others operating only on Saturdays and Sundays.

With many companies struggling to restore their coach services Southdown somehow managed to reintroduce its full hourly service between London and Brighton. After many difficult years 'Every hour at the hour' once more adorned the front cover of the company's Brighton leaflet. Coaches ran daily from each end hourly between 0800 and 2100. The 0900 and 1900 from Brighton and 1100 and 1900 from London again ran via Burgess Hill. No through coaches ran to or from Worthing via Brighton but the 2100 from London extended to Hove and Portslade as in prewar days. The prewar late coach for theatre-goers at 2350 down from London failed to reappear in the 1946 timetable. Perhaps, more surprising, was the absence of the 0700 from Brighton which had featured in wartime timetables between 4 November 1940 and 4 July 1942. This allowed an arrival in London by 0930 and many onwards connections from Victoria Coach Station but Southdown stuck with a first arrival at 1030. For the main summer period from 7 June to 8 September the day return fare from London to Brighton was increased to 6/6d (33p) on Mondays to Fridays and 7/- (35p) on Saturdays, Sundays and Bank Holidays but reverted to 5/9d (29p) daily from 9 September 1946.

As in summer 1939 there was a choice of route for those travelling between London and Worthing but the prewar summer only extension of the service via Dorking to Kings Cross Coach Station was not restored. Coaches via Dorking departed Worthing at 0805 and every two hours until 2005 while southbound coaches departed from London at 0800 and every two hours until 2000. On the route via Crawley departures from Worthing were at 0905, 1505 and 1905 and from London at 0900, 1500 and 1900. The 0905 from Worthing and 1900 from London were extended to and from Littlehampton via Goring and Rustington. On the Bognor Regis via Chichester route an additional northbound journey was introduced at 1630 while services from London now departed at 0830, 1030, 1430 and 1830 daily plus an extra coach at 2230 on Sundays and Bank Holiday Mondays. The route via Littlehampton was improved to provide three daily journeys in each direction with departures from Bognor Regis at 0830, 1430 and 1830 and from London at 0930, 1330 and 1830.

Three extra journeys were introduced on the Portsmouth and Southsea service making a total of ten daily services in each direction and equal to the last prewar summer. Additional coaches left Southsea at 1345, 1645 and 1945 and London at 1030, 1330 and 1930. The 1345 and 1645 northbound services both served Hammersmith although the 1545 was rerouted via Putney. The 1330 and 1930 from London also ran via Hammersmith. The lunch time journeys on the Gosport route were increased to run daily during the period from 20 July to 25 August 1946 but otherwise the timetable remained unaltered. Premium fares did not apply on this service at summer weekends. With a much depleted fleet and little prospect of new coaches entering service before 1947, demand for seats was soon to exceed supply especially at weekends in June,

This rear view of one of the Duple bodied Leyland Tiger PS1/1 models illustrates Southdown's preference for the rear entrance position which few manufacturers were willing to consider as order books overflowed in the years immediately following the war. Duple, presumably, hoped for significant follow on orders from the company and were successful in the early 1950s. Next to the rear lights is the holder for the Brighton excursion plate which was a requirement of Brighton Council at the time. Car 1316 (HUF 316) was new in July 1947 and is seen at Crawley Station although coaches normally reversed into position outside the refreshment building. *Southdown Enthusiasts Club – Clark/Surfleet Collection*

July and August 1946 as crowds flocked to the seaside once again. Any doubts about the future of long distance coach services were soon dispelled.

The winter 1946/7 timetables for the London services were introduced from Monday 30 September 1946 and ran until Wednesday 21 May 1947. No services were operated on Christmas Day. Some minor changes were made to the Eastbourne winter service although it continued with four coaches a day in each direction. As compared to the 22 March timetable the second service of the day from Eastbourne became 0900 instead of 1000 and the last journey from London was advanced to run an hour earlier at 2000. On the Brighton service the timetable was broadly in line with the last prewar winter with ten northbound journeys and eleven southbound. As compared to the summer 1946 schedule there were no departures from Brighton at 1200, 1300, 1600 or 2100 or from London at 0800, 1200, 1300 or 1600. The same pattern of operation applied to journeys running via Burgess Hill as in the previous summer. The London to Brighton day return fare remained at 5/9d (29p) daily through the winter.

The timetable for the Worthing service was similar to that introduced on 22 March except that the 1200 from London was withdrawn in favour of a 1600 departure which had featured in wartime timetables between 1940 and 1942. The leaflet was overprinted in black notifying

LONDON — PETWORTH — LITTLEHAMPTON — BOGNOR REGIS

LONDON (Victoria Coach Station) dep.	9 30	6 30	...	...	...	Pagham (Beach) ... } Service 50 { dep.	7*52		4 44	...	...	...
CLAPHAM COMMON (Polygon, Old Town)	9 40	6 40	...	...	...	Bognor (Bus Station) arr.	8*13		5 3	...	...	...
SUTTON (Public Hall, Hill Road) ... dep.	10 5	7 5	...	...	...							
EPSOM (Clock Tower) ... ... ,,	10 20	7 20	...	...	...	**BOGNOR REGIS** (Southdown Station) dep.	8 30		5 30	...	...	...
LEATHERHEAD (Church) ... ... ,,	10 30	7 30	...	...	...	FELPHAM (Post Office) ... ... ,,	8 35		5 35	...	...	...
MICKLEHAM (King William IV) ... ,,	10 37	7 37	...	...	...	MIDDLETON (Peter's, Middleton Road) ,,	8 40		5 40	...	...	...
DORKING (White Horse or Bandstand) ,,	10 45	7 45	...	...	...	**LITTLEHAMPTON** (East Street) ,,	8 52		5 52	...	...	...
HOLMWOOD (Holly and Laurel)★ ,,	11 5	8 5	...	...	...	ARUNDEL (Square) ... ... ,,	9 3		6 3	...	...	...
OCKLEY (Pearce's Stores) ... ,,	11 15	8 15	...	...	...	BURY (White Horse) ... ... ,,	9 13		6 13	...	...	...
SLINFOLD (Park Street Corner) ... ,,	11 30	8 30	...	...	...	†PULBOROUGH (The Swan) ... ,,	9 25		6 25	...	...	...
FIVE OAKS (Inn) ... ... ,,	11 35	8 35	...	...	...	FITTLEWORTH (The Fleet) ... ,,	9 22		6 22	...	...	...
BILLINGSHURST (Post Office) ... ,,	11 39	8 39	...	...	...	**PETWORTH** (The Square) ... ,,	9 30		6 30	...	...	...
WISBOROUGH GREEN (Memorial) ,,	11 45	8 45	...	...	...	WISBOROUGH GREEN (Memorial) ,,	9 45		6 45	...	...	...
PETWORTH (The Square) ... ,,	12 0	9 0	...	...	...	BILLINGSHURST (Post Office) ... ,,	9 51		6 51	...	...	...
FITTLEWORTH (The Fleet) ... ,,	12 8	9 8	...	...	...	FIVE OAKS (Inn) ... ... ,,	9 55		6 55	...	...	...
†**PULBOROUGH** (The Swan) ... ,,	12 15	9 15	...	...	...	SLINFOLD (Park Street Corner) ... ,,	10 0		7 0	...	...	...
BURY (White Horse) ... ... ,,	12 17	9 17	...	...	...	OCKLEY (Pearce's Stores) ... ,,	10 15		7 15	...	...	...
ARUNDEL (The Square) ... ,,	12 27	9 27	...	...	...	HOLMWOOD (Holly and Laurel)★ ,,	10 25		7 25	...	...	...
LITTLEHAMPTON (East Street) ,,	12 38	9 38	...	...	...	DORKING (White Horse or Bandstand) ,,	10 45		7 45	...	...	...
MIDDLETON (Peter's, Middleton Road) ,,	12 50	9 50	...	...	...	MICKLEHAM (King William IV) ... ,,	10 53		7 53	...	...	...
FELPHAM (Post Office) ... ,,	12 55	9 55	...	...	...	LEATHERHEAD (Church) ... ,,	11 0		8 0	...	...	...
BOGNOR REGIS (Southdown Station) arr.	1 0	10 0	...	...	...	EPSOM (Clock Tower) ... ,,	11 10		8 10	...	...	...
						SUTTON (Public Hall, Hill Road) ,,	11 25		8 25	...	...	...
Bognor (Bus Station) } Service 50 { dep.	1 11	10 11	...	...	...	CLAPHAM COMMON (Polygon, Old Town) ,,	11 50		8 50	...	...	...
Pagham (Beach) ... arr.	1 30	10 32	...	...	...	**LONDON** (Victoria Coach Station) arr.	12 0		9 0	...	...	...

NO SERVICE ON CHRISTMAS DAY

NOTES : *Not Sundays. †Route via Pulborough only if required to set down or to take up pre-booked passengers at Stopham, Pulborough, Hardham or Coldwaltham.

★A stop of ten minutes for refreshments will be made at Holmwood.

The Eastern Coach Works bodied Leyland Tiger PS1/1 models spent the first years of their life on the London Express Services and here car 1229 (GUF 729) is seen on a Bognor duty in the company of a Windover bodied example probably operating as its relief. After downgrading for bus work in 1957 it was converted for use as a Left Luggage Office at Bognor Bus Station in 1961 where it remained until 1973. A period in store at Portslade Works followed and it finally left the company in 1986 passing into preservation although later broken up to assist in the restoration of car 1249 (HCD 449).
Southdown Enthusiasts Club – Clark/Surfleet Collection

passengers that this 1600 departure does not run on Sundays – either an error or afterthought. Services between Bognor Regis and London were the same as those reintroduced in March with three daily departures each way via Chichester and one return service via Littlehampton. The Portsmouth and Southsea service reverted to the timetable introduced in March with some minor alterations to the northbound service. The 1545 and 1745 journeys became 1445 and 1645 to provide more evenly spaced two hourly departures in the afternoon. The 1445 service from Southsea was altered to run via Hammersmith and the refreshment stop on all journeys was moved from Hindhead to the Green Man at Burpham. On the Gosport route the lunch time journeys were once again reduced to run on Saturdays in each direction but otherwise the timetable remained unaltered.

The winter timetable for the South Coast Express commenced on Monday 14 October and was significantly less than in prewar winters. Just two journeys operated in each direction and no services ran east of Hastings although connections were made with East Kent service 62 for Rye, Folkestone, Dover, Ramsgate and Margate. Timings were as follows:

Eastbound

1100 Portsmouth – Bognor Regis – Brighton – Hastings

1800 Portsmouth – Bognor Regis – Brighton – Eastbourne

Westbound

0925 Eastbourne – Brighton – Bognor Regis – Portsmouth

1335 Hastings – Brighton – Bognor Regis – Portsmouth

Connections were available at Hilsea with Royal Blue services to Southampton and Bournemouth.

1947

A new timetable leaflet was issued for the Bognor Regis to London service dated Sunday 5 January. The only change affected the last northbound service which was revised to run one hour earlier departing at 1730. The very basic level of service offered on the South Coast Express for winter 1946/7 was further reduced from the same date when the 0925 from Eastbourne was altered to start at Brighton and a bus connection by service 12 substituted. In the eastbound direction the

SOUTH COAST EXPRESS SERVICE

ROYAL BLUE	**Bournemouth** (*Square Station*)	...	8 40	3 25
ROYAL BLUE	New Milton	...	9 15	4 0
ROYAL BLUE	Lyndhurst (*Hants and Dorset Office*)	...	9 41	4 26
ROYAL BLUE	Southampton (*Grosvenor Square*)	...	10 5	4 50
ROYAL BLUE	Bursledon	...	1022	5 7
ROYAL BLUE	Fareham (*Bus Station, West Street*)	...	1038	5 23
ROYAL BLUE	Hilsea (*Southdown Station*)★	...	1051	5 36
ROYAL BLUE	**Portsmouth** (*Hyde Park Road*)	...	11 6	5 51
	Portsmouth (*Hyde Park Road*)	dep.	11 0	6 0
	Hilsea (*Southdown Station*)★	...	1115	6 15
	Havant (*High Street*)	...	1130	6 30
	Emsworth (*The Square*)	...	1137	6 37
	Chichester (*West Street*)	...	1155	6 55
	Bognor (*Coach Station*)	...	1220	7 20
	Littlehampton (*East Street*)	...	1245	7 45
	Arundel (*The Square*)	...	A	A
	Worthing (*Marine Parade*)	...	1 15	8 15
	Shoreham (*High Street*)	...	1 29	8 29
	Hove (*7 St. Aubyns Gardens*)	...	1 40	8 40
	Brighton (*Steine Street*)	arr.	1 45	8 45
		dep.	2 15	8†56
	Peacehaven (*South Coast Road*)	...	2 30	9†19
	Newhaven (*Bridge Street*)	...	2 40	9†31
	Seaford (*Clinton Place*)	...	2 50	9†44
	Eastbourne (*Pevensey Road*)	arr.	3 19	10†50
		dep.	3 25	...
	Bexhill (*Marina*)	...	3 55	...
	Hastings (*Station Approach*)	arr.	4 15	...

★Through passengers to points beyond PORTSMOUTH change coaches at SOUTHDOWN COACH STATION HILSEA

A—Passengers to and from Arundel change at Littlehampton to and from Southdown Service 66

The coach arriving Hastings 4.15 p.m. from Portsmouth provides connections with the East Kent Road Car Company's service No. 62 departing Hastings at 5.15 p.m. to Rye, Folkestone, Dover Ramsgate and Margate.

†—Change to Service 12 Bus at Brighton

	Hastings (*Station Approach*)	dep.	...	1 35
	Bexhill (*Marina*)	...	...	1 55
	Eastbourne (*Pevensey Road*)	arr.	...	2 24
		dep.	8†*45	2 25
	Seaford (*Clinton Place*)	...	9† 39	2 50
	Newhaven (*Bridge Street*)	...	9† 52	3 0
	Peacehaven (*South Coast Road*)	...	10† 4	3 10
	Brighton (*Steine Street*)	arr.	10† 27	3 25
		dep.	10 35	3 35
	Hove (*7 St. Aubyns Gardens*)	...	10 40	3 40
	Shoreham (*High Street*)	...	10 55	3 55
	Worthing (*Marine Parade*)	...	11 5	4 5
	Littlehampton (*East Street*)	...	11 35	4 35
	Arundel (*The Square*)	...	A	A
	Bognor (*Southdown Coach Station*)	...	12 0	5 0
	Chichester (*West Street*)	...	12 25	5 25
	Emsworth (*The Square*)	...	12 43	5 43
	Havant (*High Street*)	...	12 50	5 50
	Hilsea (*Southdown Station*)★	...	1 5	6 5
	Portsmouth (*Hyde Park Road*)	arr.	1 20	6 20
ROYAL BLUE	**Portsmouth** (*Hyde Park Road*)	...	2 15	6 0
ROYAL BLUE	**Hilsea** (*Southdown Station*)★	...	2 30	6 15
ROYAL BLUE	Fareham (*Bus Station, West Street*)	...	2 43	6 28
ROYAL BLUE	Burlesdon	...	2 59	6 44
ROYAL BLUE	Southampton (*Grosvenor Square*)	...	3 17	7 3
ROYAL BLUE	Lyndhurst (*Hants and Dorset Office*)	...	3 39	7 25
ROYAL BLUE	New Milton	...	4 5	7 51
ROYAL BLUE	**Bournemout(h** *Square Statioh*)	...	4 40	8 26

★Through passengers to points beyond PORTSMOUTH change coaches at SOUTHDOWN COACH STATION HILSEA

A—Passengers to and from Arundel change at Littlehampton to and from Southdown Service 66

The coach departing Hastings at 1.35 p.m. provides connections with the East Kent Road Car Company's service No. 62 arriving Hastings at 1.5 p.m. from Margate, Ramsgate, Dover, Folkestone and Rye.

***—Not Sundays** **†—Service 12 Bus from Eastbourne to Brighton**

1800 from Portsmouth now terminated at Brighton with passengers for points beyond required to travel by service 12.

On Thursday 23 January, snow began to fall in south east England heralding the start of Britain's most severe and protracted spell of bad weather during the twentieth century, as mentioned earlier, and seriously disrupting road travel for several weeks. Failing supplies of coal – which provided more than 90 per cent of Britain's energy requirements – was already causing short time working in many factories and the freezing conditions soon led to power cuts. By 28 January temperatures were at freezing throughout the day even in London and by the following night all the lights went out across the country. Huge snow drifts brought road and rail transport to a standstill in many parts of Britain leading to a major fall in non-essential leisure travel. The crisis continued into February with rising unemployment and short time working and from Monday 10 February electrical supplies to households were cut from 0900 to 1200 and 1400 to 1600 daily. The weather remained bitterly cold into March with two snowstorms affecting southern England on 4 and 5 March. Power supplies to industry were gradually restored and most of the temporarily unemployed returned to work but the restriction on domestic use of electricity remained in force until the end of April.

From Thursday 3 April an additional daily journey was reintroduced each way between London and Bognor Regis via Littlehampton leaving Victoria Coach Station at 0930 and returning from Bognor Regis at 1730. This service did not run during winter 1947/8 being replaced by an additional Worthing journey extended to Littlehampton. The South Coast Express summer timetable was introduced from Monday 19 May and continued until 11 October.

Services were increased from the 1946 level but not to prewar frequencies. Coaches ran daily as follows:

Eastbound
0930 Brighton – Folkestone
0830 Portsmouth – Bognor Regis – Brighton – Margate
0820 Bournemouth – Portsmouth – Bognor Regis – Brighton *connecting with the*
1450 Brighton – Margate
1330 Portsmouth – Bognor Regis – Brighton – Folkestone
1500 Portsmouth – Bognor Regis – Brighton – Hastings
1450 Bournemouth – Portsmouth – Bognor Regis – Brighton
1845 Portsmouth – Bognor Regis – Brighton

Westbound
0815 Brighton – Bognor Regis – Portsmouth – Bournemouth
0930 Brighton – Bognor Regis – Portsmouth
0840 Hastings – Brighton – Bognor Regis – Portsmouth
0830 Folkestone – Brighton – Bognor Regis – Portsmouth
0800 Margate – Brighton *connecting with the*
1500 Brighton – Bognor Regis – Portsmouth – Bournemouth
1045 Margate – Brighton – Bognor Regis – Portsmouth
1554 Folkestone – Brighton

The new timetable established the daily operation of through coaches between Brighton and Bournemouth with the Southdown coach from Brighton able to connect in both directions with the principal Royal Blue services to and from the West of England at Bournemouth. The Royal Blue coach from Bournemouth connected at Brighton with the East Kent coach from Margate and offered more efficient vehicle and driver operation, introducing a pattern of service that

LONDON — GUILDFORD — HASLEMERE — MIDHURST — CHICHESTER — BOGNOR REGIS

NOTES: Times shown in light type are of Southdown Omnibus Services which connect with the London Service Coaches. Through Bookings are available. ★ A stop of ten minutes will be made at the Green Man, Burpham. *Not Sundays. † Sundays depart 12.43 p.m.

Park Royal supplied the first 12 of an order for 25 rear entrance coach bodies during 1947. Car 1256 (HCD 856), a Leyland Tiger PS1/1 new in May 1947 is seen on an eastbound South Coast Express duty. This design was developed for East Kent Road Car Co. and only slightly modified to suit Southdown's requirements. All of the 1947 batch were withdrawn and sold in spring 1958.
S L Poole

continued for many years. Coaches now departed from Cavendish Place Coach Station in Eastbourne and refreshment halts occurred at Hythe (RH&D Light Railway Station), Hastings, Eastbourne or Brighton according to time of day. At Hilsea Coach Station connections were made with Royal Blue services to Bournemouth with onward facilities to Exeter, Torquay and Plymouth, Yeovil, Taunton and Ilfracombe. Also at Hilsea connections were made with the Associated Motorways service to Salisbury, Bath and Bristol.

The summer timetables for London services introduced on Thursday 22 May were generally in line with those provided in the previous year.

In contrast to the severe winter, the summer of 1947 proved to be one of the warmest on record and the booming demand for holidays and travel led to full coaches on many services for weeks on end. Fortunately Southdown had finally taken delivery of its first new postwar coaches starting in February and although fitted with Eastern Coach Works bus style bodies they were allocated to the London Express Services for most of their time whilst used as coaches.

On the principal route between London and Eastbourne via Uckfield there were departures from Royal Parade at 0800, 0900, 1000 (Saturdays), 1400, 1700, 1800 and 1900 and from London at 0915, 1015 1315, 1415, 1815 and 2115.

Car 1146 (CCD 746) departs from Bognor Regis Bus Station on a service to London via Chichester. It is a Leyland Tiger TS7 with Harrington rear entrance coach body delivered in June 1936 and modernised in 1939 with folding sunroof and glass cove panels. It remained with the company until sale In June 1956 and ended its days with a farmer in Norfolk.
Southdown Enthusiasts Club – Clark/Surfleet Collection

A brand new innovation was the diversion of the 0800 from Eastbourne and 1815 from London to run via Heathfield adding 15 minutes to the overall running time. Between Hailsham and Uckfield coaches served Horam, Maynards Green, Heathfield, Cross-in-Hand, Blackboys and Framfield which normally only enjoyed connections by bus service 91. On the two journeys via Heathfield passengers for Golden Cross and East Hoathly were obliged to travel by bus service 92 connecting at Uckfield. The extra summer route via Seaford and Lewes ran between 28 June and 28 September and followed the same pattern as 1946 but with departures from Cavendish Place at 0915, 1345 and 1745 and from London at 0845, 1345 and 1830. As in 1946 only the first coach from London and last from Eastbourne ran daily, the others only operating on Saturdays and Sundays. Bus connections were now included on this route at Danehill for Horsted Keynes and Lindfield, at Chailey for Newick and at Lewes for Ringmer, Firle and Berwick. Premium fares applied on Saturdays, Sundays and Bank Holidays between 22 May and 14 September although the London to Eastbourne day return fare remained at 8/3d (42p) as in 1946. On the Brighton road the service once again ran hourly between 0800 and 2100 from each end with the usual additional Wednesday service via Henfield. Journeys via Burgess Hill were now standardised throughout the year as the 0900 and 1900 from Brighton and 1100 and 1900 from London with all others running via Bolney. Premium fares applied between 22 May and 14 September although the day return fare from London to Brighton remained at 6/6d (32p) on Mondays to Fridays and 7/- (35p) on Saturdays, Sundays and Bank Holidays as in 1946.

A very comprehensive service was provided between London and Worthing with coaches to London leaving Marine Parade at 0810, 0910, 1010, 1210, 1410, 1510 (Saturdays), 1610, 1810, 1910 and 2010. The 0910, 1510 and 1910 ran via Crawley and Redhill with other departures serving Dorking and Kingston and the 0910 from Worthing starting at Littlehampton at 0840. From London coaches departed at 0800, 0900, 1000, 1200, 1400, 1500 (Saturdays), 1600, 1800, 1900 and 2000. All ran via Kingston and Dorking except for the 1000, 1500 and 1900 which served Redhill and Crawley. The 1900 journey from London continued via Goring, Ferring and Rustington to Littlehampton. The Bognor Regis via Littlehampton service now departed from Bognor at 0830, 1430 (on Saturdays and Sundays) and 1830. Southbound journeys from London were at 0930, 1330 (on Saturdays and Sundays) and 1830. This marked a small reduction from summer 1946 when three coaches daily had been provided. The service via Chichester was increased to four daily departing from Bognor at 0830, 1330, 1630 and 1830 and leaving London at 0830, 1030, 1430 and 1830 with an extra journey at 2230 on Sundays. On Saturdays direct coaches were run between Selsey, Bracklesham Bay and London with northbound journeys at 0930 returning from London at 1400.

On the Portsmouth and Southsea route the summer timetable was similar to that run in 1946 except that the 1330 from London and 1945 from Southsea did not reappear. The 1230 from London now ran via Hammersmith instead of Putney and the 1445 from Southsea continued in place of the 1545 as during the past winter. With no through services yet to Hayling Island passengers wishing to travel from London by coach were obliged to travel via Cosham and the 47 bus service from Havant. There were some minor timing changes on the Gosport route with the last northbound service advanced by 30 minutes to leave The Hard at 1800. On journeys from London coaches now departed at 0830, 1330 (Saturdays) and 1800. The lunchtime journeys were extended to run daily from 5 July to 27 September. From Sunday 15 June the special service to Robertsbridge, Darvell Hall Sanatorium was once again increased to run every Sunday as in 1939 and from winter 1947 it also operated on alternate Wednesdays. The service continued operating until winter 1962/3 but with the dramatic reduction in TB patients the Sanatorium finally closed in 1970.

Tours & Excursions

When peace returned there was soon great pressure on the authorities for some resumption of leisure services and on 6 July 1945 the MOWT announced that operators may provide some limited facilities without the prior sanction of the RTC. These included excursions and tours where the total mileage from and to the garage did not exceed 50. All tours operations were subject to the condition that they must not interfere with the full operation of stage carriage and other essential services and with many coaches still being used for 'war work' the demand for seats massively exceeded the supply available. Contemporary reports indicate that beginning Sunday 8 July Southdown promptly restarted their tour programmes and began operating excursions from Worthing to such local places as Arundel Castle, Bramber Castle, Steyning and Coombes, Bognor and Castle Goring. These ran daily except Saturdays as and when coaches were available after covering relief bus journeys and, presumably, other areas of Southdown followed suit. Evening trips started running from Worthing on Sunday 19 August with cars 1216 and 1224 used on this day. At the Board Meeting on 22 August 1945 the Managing Director was authorised to purchase the business of French & Sons of Seaford, which had a licence for Excursions and Tours, at a price not exceeding £2,000. On 24 September 1945 it was acquired for £1,800.

Any remaining restrictions on the operation of excursions and tours were lifted in time for the 1946 season and demand very soon outstripped

As peace returned to the South Coast there was a huge demand for travel of all sorts and coach excursions proved to be very popular with visitors and locals alike. It took some time for new deliveries of postwar coaches to materialise and in the meantime the handsome 1939 Harrington bodied Leyland Tiger TS8s were among Southdown's front line coach fleet. Car 1226 (FUF 326) is seen on Kings Road, Brighton awaiting custom for an excursion to Bognor although after eleven years service it was upgraded to Touring Coach specification with 21 luxurious seats for use on the company's Coach Cruise programme.
Southdown Enthusiasts Club – Clark/Surfleet Collection

supply. Southdown brought its beautifully written blackboards out of wartime storage to tempt the crowds strolling along the promenades. In the first few summers of peace many thousands of day trippers headed each day to the South Coast resorts and an afternoon coach excursion often featured in their visit. But, in 1946, staff and suitable vehicles were still in short supply and although Southdown had placed an order for 125 new Leyland Tiger PS1 coaches none arrived until 1947. To cater for demand the 1946 programme of excursions was expanded well in excess of prewar days resulting in the use of some vehicles that Southdown would not normally have found acceptable for such coaching

duties. In particular the 1400 class Tiger saloons were to be seen on occasional excursion duties for several postwar seasons. The delivery of new coaches and refurbishment of many prewar coaches allowed for expansion of the 1947 programme of excursions and tours.

At the end of the war thoughts soon turned to the reintroduction of the company's famous coach cruise programme. Given the many problems facing Southdown it was realised that it could be some years before it was possible to replace the prewar Leyland Lioness and Tigress touring coaches which had been mostly stored during the war. There were also problems in finding suitable hotels – partly due to

Car 1265 (HUF 5) is a Leyland Tiger PS1/1 with Harrington front entrance coach body modified with full width canopy to Southdown's specification. Delivered in May 1947 it is seen in Kingsway, Hove with a chalked board advertising excursions which can be booked at Southdown's nearby booking office. Along with other remaining half cab coaches it was sold in 1959.
Southdown Enthusiasts Club – Clark/Surfleet Collection

Southdown reintroduced its Coach Cruises after the war in 1947 and car 1818 (CUF 318) is seen near Victoria Coach Station before setting out on a tour to the Scottish Highlands. It is a Leyland Tigress RLTB3 with Burlingham touring coach body seating just 20 passengers in a 2 + 1 layout dating from 1936 although stored during the war. Progress was at a leisurely pace in the days of a 30 mph speed limit and long before by-passes and Motorways!
Author's collection

Government requisitioning – so that Southdown could not restart their extended tours until the 1947 season using cars 1807 – 1823. The first postwar tour departed fully loaded for Devon and Cornwall on 1 May 1947 with the new programme soon proving very popular. The company decided to rebuild all of the remaining older Leyland Lioness tourers to centre entrance format – as C20C. This was designed to improve their appearance and to standardise the seating plan for booking purposes.

Southdown's London office did not reopen in post war days, the company preferring to rely instead on London Coastal Coaches and its agency network.

Private Hire & Contracts

With a return to peace in May 1945 the coach fleet was in a run down condition by Southdown standards but at the beginning of July the Ministry of War Transport announced that the operation of private hires could be resumed subject to the sanction of Regional Traffic Commissioners. The maximum return mileage was restricted to 70 miles and despite some easing in the shortage of manpower the restrictions continued into 1946. In the immediate postwar period resources were obviously in great demand but the bus timetable of Sunday 2 June 1946 included a reference to coaches now being available for Private Hire.

Whilst most of the coaches originally delivered in the 1930s with folding canvas roof were rebuilt to modernise their appearance, the first two Cubs dating from 1933 remained in original condition throughout their 20 year lives with Southdown. Although looking rather dated car 1 (ACD 101) still appears very smartly turned out in this postwar scene outside the Southdown office at Horsham Carfax. Delivered as 14 seat luxury touring coaches both were converted to 20 seat layout in 1949 and remained with the company until being sold for scrap in June 1953.
V C Jones

THE SOUTHDOWN FLEET

1945

Although the war in Europe came to an end in May there was no chance of any immediate improvement in vehicle supplies and wartime specification buses could be seen entering service across Britain for another year. With reduced maintenance and much tougher operating conditions during the war the composite bodies of most buses in the Southdown fleet suffered as a result. To make matters worse there would be no chance of renewing the badly depleted coach fleet in time to meet the expected demand for travel once restrictions were lifted. A number of differing solutions were evolved which in some cases meant the rebuilding of existing bodies or fitting new bodies to others. Most of the single deck fleet of 1400 class Tigers had their bodies rebuilt along with several Tiger and Cub coaches, while 153 prewar Titans received new bodies over the period 1946 to 1950.

Although the full Blackout regulations had been replaced in September 1944 by the 'dim out' this did not apply in Southdown's coastal areas where some restrictions remained until Monday 23 April 1945. It was now finally possible to remove the headlamp cowls from buses and take down the blackout material from the company offices and works. A prewar standard of interior lighting was soon restored to buses and coaches and the reduced blackout speed limits lifted.

Further Utility Guy Arabs were delivered to Southdown after the end of hostilities. These arrived as cars 463 to 494 with bodywork by Northern Counties, Park Royal and Weymann. Most were to 'relaxed utility' specification with the last three buses carrying Northern Counties metal framed bodies (cars 463 to 465) delivered in late August built with rear and side destination boxes, a better standard of seating and more rounded rear domes. Full details of these vehicles and their subsequent open top roles with the company appear in chapter 8. Immediately after the war three of the 1939 TD5s – cars 212, 245 and 248 – had the three roller blind boxes over the lower deck windows on the nearside replaced with a screen box over the platform.

With the Hayling Island Holiday Camps closed at the outbreak of war and taken over by the Military Authorities the Leyland Cheetah coaches dating from 1938/9 were soon relegated to local bus service work in the area or delicensed and stored during the war years. Along with several Cub coaches they were now taken from storage and prepared for normal duties on Hayling Island. The lightweight Cheetahs remained in service until being made redundant by the opening of the new Langstone Bridge at the end of the 1956 season.

A late 1940s view in Pool Valley, Brighton includes car 212 (FCD 512), a Leyland Titan TD5 with Park Royal lowbridge body delivered in January 1939. Southdown removed the three nearside screen boxes and replaced them with a single screen over the platform in December 1945 but otherwise it survived in original form until rebodied by East Lancs in January 1950. Service 17 linking Brighton and Horsham has survived – with some temporary renumbering and route modifications – to the present day.
Southdown Enthusiasts Club – Clark/Surfleet Collection

Rebuilding the 1400 class

By 1945 the earliest batch of 1400 class saloons would, in normal circumstances, have been nearing the end of their lives with Southdown but it was realised that after full refurbishment these versatile vehicles could provide reliable service for some years to come. Starting in 1945 five companies – as well as Southdown themselves – participated in the rebuilding programme for this class. They included Portsmouth Aviation, Lancashire Aircraft, Air Dispatch and Saunders – who also built complete new bodies

for the company – and local motor dealers Caffyns. In most cases these were companies that had been undertaking military contracts, often in aircraft construction and repair, and who now found themselves with a skilled workforce but no further contracts. The rebuilding of worn out bus bodies proved to be a lifeline for several such businesses in the early postwar period.

The 60 buses that had been converted to perimeter seating during the war reverted to 32 or 34 seats in normal 2+2 format between

After the war the holiday camps on Hayling Island became very popular and Southdown's bus and coach services struggled to cope with demand given the restriction on the weight of buses crossing Langstone Bridge from the mainland. Until some postwar Dennis Falcons arrived in 1948/9 the prewar forward control Leyland Cubs soldiered on including car 9 (DUF 9) dating from 1937. In this scene at Beachlands Bus Station it is carrying the final postwar livery for these buses with broad cream waist band.
Southdown Enthusiasts Club – Clark/Surfleet Collection

A rear view of car 1423 (CCD 33) in Arundel Square on the newly extended service 71. This Harrington bodied Leyland Tiger TS7 is still in wartime livery with grey roof and window surrounds and apple green below the windows along with a white spot to aid other drivers in the blackout. The rear corner windows have been blanked off but it still retains its roof luggage rack and, now disused, offside screen boxes.
C F Klapper © Omnibus Society

August 1945 and October 1949 although contemporary timetable booklets indicate that the number of standees allowed in vehicles with perimeter seating was reduced from 30 to 12 very soon after the end of the war. A notice displayed in Worthing garage on 6 January 1946 stated "a maximum of 12 standing passengers instead of 20 except on certain busy routes or journeys" which were not specified. It added "All were to be converted back to normal seating as soon as possible" although this proved to be a long process. Four were completed in 1945, 23 in 1946, 15 in 1947, 16 in 1948 with the final two – cars 1414 and 1416 – in 1949. In most cases this work was completed at the same time that vehicles were rebuilt although there were several examples where Southdown restored the vehicle to 2+2 seating a year or two before a rebuild occurred. These included 1404 (9/46), 1409 (4/46), 1411 (4/46), 1414 (9/46), 1416 (8/46), 1418 (6/46), 1421 (7/46), 1422 (10/45), 1431 (1/46), 1434 (4/46), 1437 (2/48), 1438 (2/47), 1439 (9/46), 1441 (8/45), 1442 (10/47), 1444 (8/45), 1453 (12/45), 1458 (12/46), 1472 (12/46), 1478 (6/47), 1479 (6/47), 1481 (9/47), 1483 (2/46) and 1485 (5/47). In addition car 1428 was rebuilt to 2+2 seating by Leyland Motors 4/46 but retained offside screen boxes.

The amount of rebuilding work required obviously varied according to the condition of the vehicle. Those members of the class that survived the war with the rear corner windows intact were panelled over as part of the rebuilding programme. All but one of the 1935 batch were rebuilt and this included removal of the rear luggage locker, offside blind boxes, roof luggage rack and ladder and sealing shut the Walman sliding roof. Car 1408 had its sliding roof sealed and roof luggage rack removed by Southdown in 1946 but was not rebuilt until June 1950. Car 1421 did not get a full rebuild although its roof luggage rack was removed by Southdown in 1948 and cars 1421, 1425 and 1429 were notable in retaining their offside screen boxes throughout their service with Southdown although no longer used as originally intended. It is thought that three of the six saloons delivered in 1936 – cars 1424, 1426 and 1427 – were refurbished involving removal of the offside blind boxes and sealing shut the Walman sliding roof. Some 27 of the saloons delivered in 1938 were rebuilt and in the course of this work the Walman sliding roof was sealed up on those buses that were so fitted. This effectively brought the specification of the earlier buses in line with the last batch which had not been fitted with sliding roofs when new. Of the 1939-40 deliveries all except 1483 were included in the programme.

The full 1400 class Rebuilding Programme was:

CAFFYNS	1945	1424, 1454
SOUTHDOWN	1945	1440
CAFFYNS	1946	1445*, 1446, 1447*, 1448*, 1464*
LANCASHIRE AIRCRAFT	1946	1427*, 1435*, 1436*, 1452, 1469*, 1470*
PORTSMOUTH AVIATION	1946	1434, 1456, 1466*, 1467*
SAUNDERS	1946	1419
PORTSMOUTH AVIATION	1947	1402, 1405, 1410, 1423, 1439, 1449, 1461*, 1465*, 1468*, 1471*, 1474*, 1475*, 1476*, 1480*, 1482*
SOUTHDOWN	1947	1462*
AIR DISPATCH	1948	1403*, 1430*
PORTSMOUTH AVIATION	1948	1400, 1407*, 1411, 1412*, 1413*, 1415, 1417*, 1418, 1420*, 1422, 1426*, 1441, 1443, 1457*, 1458, 1463*, 1473*, 1477*, 1479, 1484*
PORTSMOUTH AVIATION	1949	1401, 1404, 1409, 1416, 1472, 1478,
SOUTHDOWN	1949	1406, 1414, 1485
SOUTHDOWN	1950	1408, 1481
SOUTHDOWN	1951	1437

Those marked * were converted to 2 + 2 seating at the same time rebuilding took place.

The following 17 vehicles were not rebuilt during the post war programme – 1421, 1425, 1428, 1429, 1431, 1432, 1433, 1438, 1442, 1444, 1450, 1451, 1453, 1455, 1459, 1460 and 1483. Following refurbishment the class was to be found in the late 1940s on a wide variety of duties ranging from service and relief journeys on both single and double deck stage carriage routes to frequent appearances on the London express services and, in particular, the South Coast

Express, as well as their occasional work on excursion duties. The Chichester and Bognor Area even continued to use 1400 class buses on express and excursion duties during the 1952 summer season. The arrival of the Royal Tiger buses in 1952-3 led to their demise from many of the important single deck services that had been operated by the prewar Tigers for fifteen or more years and the introduction of one man operated Tiger Cubs on many country services in 1954 further reduced their ranks. During the period between 1952 and 1954 twenty nine were converted by Southdown and J.C. Beadle to form 'semi-chassisless' coaches using the original engine and other units of the chassis. The last of the popular 1400 class was sold in 1957 with some having completed 22 years in Southdown service but sadly none survived into the preservation era.

Return of the requisitioned coaches
Between March 1940 and July 1941 some 154 single deck buses and coaches had been commandeered for military service. Many of these were Tilling-Stevens buses and coaches due for early withdrawal but the total also included some late model Leyland Tiger coaches which the company no doubt hoped to return to use as quickly as possible once hostilities ended. As early as 1943 some of the Tigers that had been requisitioned in 1940 were repurchased by Southdown from the Ministry of Supply and almost all required extensive body rebuilds before re-entering coach

service. On some an attempt was made to modernise the rather old fashioned horizontal styling and bring them in line with the last of the prewar coaches. Chrome beading was added to form a side flash that swept down from the waist at the front bulkhead over the rear wheel arch to the bottom corner of the coach.

On 15 November 1945 cars 39 and 1068 were returned to Southdown. The Cub was one of four that had seen service with the RAF since 1941 and it was rebuilt by West-Nor in July 1946, remaining in service until sale in October 1956. Car 1068 dating from 1932 was rebuilt by Caffyns in 1947 and withdrawn in 1951. Despite the end of hostilities the return of the commandeered coaches proceeded at a slow pace and during 1946 Southdown complained to the Ministry of Supply that their vehicles were being sold to other – and in some cases, competing – operators. A further five reached the company in 1946 starting on 4 February with car 1083 which was rebuilt by West-Nor in August 1946. Car 1075 returned on 6 August and was rebuilt by Southdown around August 1947 with a high straight canopy line and fitted with a fixed sun visor above the driver's front windscreen. On 3 September car 1200 rejoined the company and was rebuilt in March 1947 gaining a half length sliding roof in place of its folding roof at the same time. It passed to Samuelson New Transport in the same month. Car 1067 returned on 30 September but the body was removed during 1947 and a new lorry body built at Portslade

In the postwar rebuilding programme the earlier members of the 1400 class Leyland Tigers had their offside appearance significantly altered by the removal of the side destination screens and roof luggage rack. In this scene at Marine Parade in Worthing car 1410 (BUF 990) shows off its final form after being rebuilt by Portsmouth Aviation in October 1947. It is operating a postwar local circular service 11B introduced in January 1947 to replace parts of the old Tramocars' services and provide new links within Worthing. Buses on the 11 group were still referred to as 'Tramocars' by the locals well into the 50s. Note the smartly attired tourists of the era!
Southdown Enthusiasts Club – Clark/Surfleet Collection

Only two prewar coaches – cars 1172 and 1174 – received new bodies in the post war period. Car 1174 (DUF 174) started life as a Leyland Tiger TS7 with Harrington rear entrance body in 1937 but attracted the attention of the Military Authorities in March 1940. It was then requisitioned for use by the Royal Army Service Corps and finally re-acquired by Southdown in December 1948. The Harrington body was removed at Portslade Works in May 1949 and subsequently scrapped and a new Beadle body fitted in August 1949. It is seen at Worthing garage after operating a relief journey from London and survived with Southdown until sale in March 1958.
Southdown Enthusiasts Club – Clark/Surfleet Collection

before it was renumbered to L2. Finally in 1946 car 1176 arrived on 30 November although it was destined not to receive a body rebuild.

Car 1076 arrived back on 4 June 1947 and was rebuilt by Portsmouth Aviation in April 1948 retaining a full length luggage rack and original dropped front canopy. Exactly eight years since the outbreak of war car 1168 returned to the company on 3 September 1947 and was rebuilt by Portsmouth Aviation with a full length roof luggage rack for band instruments in July 1948. Only two of the four Cubs loaned to the RAF were returned to Southdown and the second, car 49, appeared on 15 October 1947. It was rebuilt by Portsmouth Aviation in April 1948 and survived until summer 1956. A further three Tigers were returned in 1948 with car 1084 arriving on 9 June. It was rebuilt by Portsmouth Aviation in December 1948 with a high straight canopy line and fitted with a fixed sun visor above the driver's front windscreen. It remained with Southdown until March 1957.

Cars 1172 and 1174 returned to Southdown on 8 October 1948 and 4 December 1948 respectively. Their bodies were removed at Portslade in May 1949 and new Beadle C32R bodies, of the same design as fitted to the new PS1s, were fitted in August 1949. They were destined to be the only prewar Tiger coaches to be fully rebodied in the post war period. The last of the requisitioned coaches to return were car 1085 on 30 April 1949 and cars 1193 and 1199 on 23 August 1949. All three were rebuilt by Southdown in May 1950. Car 1085 gained a high straight canopy line and

was fitted with a fixed sun visor above the driver's front windscreen, but lost its roof luggage rack, whilst cars 1193 and 1199 were rebuilt with half length sliding sunroofs in place of folding roofs.

Coach Rebuilds

Although some of the coach fleet had not endured such hard work during the war many of the same problems of body decay applied to the prewar coaches as the 1400 class saloons. In the ordinary course of events many were now long overdue for replacement and in order to extend their lives the company embarked on a programme of body rebuilds using many of the same firms – including Portsmouth Aviation, Lancashire Aircraft and Caffyns – that were engaged on the 1400 class work. Towards the end of the programme a significant amount of rebuilding work was also undertaken at Southdown's Portslade Works. In the period between 1945 and 1951 several Leyland Tigers and two Cubs were rebuilt, generally without modification although in some cases, and to modernise their appearance, chrome beading was added to form a side flash that swept down from the waist at the front bulkhead over the rear wheel arch to the bottom corner of the coach. It is thought that a few others also gained this embellishment even though they were not rebuilt at the same time. The programme of refurbishment extended the lives of many prewar Tiger coaches to the end of the 1956 season with final sales taking place in August 1957.

The complete programme is believed to have included:

SOUTHDOWN	1945	1107
CAFFYNS	1946	1184
LANCASHIRE AIRCRAFT	1946	1139
WEST-NOR	1946	39, 1083
WINDOVER	1946	1003
CAFFYNS	1947	1068
PORTSMOUTH AVIATION	1947	1093, 1157, 1159
SOUTHDOWN	1947	1075
??	1947	1200
PORTSMOUTH AVIATION	1948	49, 1061, 1076, 1084, 1088, 1113, 1121, 1134, 1142, 1143, 1152, 1158, 1168
VICKERS	1948	1182
WILLOWBROOK	1948	1136, 1144
BEADLE C32R (new bodies)	1949	1172, 1174
WILLOWBROOK	1949	1153
SOUTHDOWN	1950	1085, 1099, 1100, 1118, 1122, 1141, 1193, 1199
SOUTHDOWN	1951	1114

In addition cars 1145/6 and 1177/8 had their seating capacity increased from 26 to 32 after the war.

Car 1075 (UF 9775) is one of 12 Leyland Tiger TS4 with Harrington 32 rear entrance coach bodies supplied in 1933. All were requisitioned by the Military Authorities in 1940 although the company was able to reacquire six of them including car 1075. It was rebuilt and modernised by Southdown and fitted with a Covrad radiator after the war and seen here at West Street in Chichester operating on the London to Bognor Regis via Chichester service. After a very long life with the company it was sold in January 1956 after completing 23 years service.
Southdown Enthusiasts Club – Clark/Surfleet Collection

1946

In March 1946 Southdown took delivery of the last five of its 100 utility Guy Arab buses – cars 495 to 499. These had highbridge Park Royal composite five bay 'relaxed utility' 56 seat bodies identical to the nine delivered in 1945. Full details of these vehicles and their subsequent open top roles appear in chapter 8.

Sometime after the Second World War it is thought that all the remaining Leyland Tiger TS4 coaches and most of the Lioness coaches delivered in 1933 had their original short Leyland radiator replaced with the longer Coventry Radiator Co. conversion radiator – known as the Covrad. It is certain, however, that

car 1817 retained its short radiator throughout its service with Southdown, and it is possible that car 1816 ran in service with the short radiator post war, but all the others were fitted with the 'Covrad'. Cars 550 to 553 were rebuilt during 1946, losing one seat to become B39C. As with those members of the 1400 class so fitted, all had the folding sunroof sealed shut and the roof luggage rack removed. Until 1952 they were then used again at Eastbourne on Beachy Head service 97 during the summer months but spent their postwar winters on relief work at Portsmouth.

Although many operators had quickly abandoned the torque converters fitted to some prewar Leylands Southdown persevered with theirs until after the war. Between April 1946 and May 1947 cars 960 to 963, 112 to 121 and 145 to 150 were all converted to conventional transmission. Between January 1947 and May 1948 Leyland Cub 17 ran with only 14 seats on service 70 due to a restriction on the road between Arundel and Burpham.

Orders for new buses

As the war came to an end there was some delay before manufacturers were able to switch their production from military to civilian products and it was some time before materials could be released to allow the construction of the new vehicles that operators urgently needed. Southdown's preferred supplier, Leyland Motors announced in November 1944 that they hoped to be able to resume the production of bus and coach chassis around September 1945. Despite initial plans for utility buses in 1941 Leyland had not built any bus chassis since completing the unfrozen Titans and Tigers in 1942. During the war its production consisted entirely of tanks, military vehicles and incendiaries but by December 1945 it had delivered its first postwar double deck Titan PD1 chassis to Charles H. Roe at Leeds for bodying. Because of the urgent need for double deck chassis the first of the equivalent single deck chassis – the Tiger PS1 – was not produced until mid summer 1946 and none entered service with Southdown until 1947.

In December 1945 the Minister of War Transport announced that, in view of the increased production anticipated in 1946, he had decided to discontinue the system of licences to acquire all types of new motor vehicles from the end of the year. At the same time the Minister also removed the control on the sale of used public service vehicles which would no longer require a licence from the RTCs. Manufacturers had undertaken to supply new vehicles to holders of licences to acquire already issued before meeting the orders of other customers. As a result of the delays in restarting production most operators were forced to compromise and in 1946 Southdown took delivery of 25 new Leyland Titan PD1 chassis fitted with composite Park Royal 54 seat highbridge bodies to a transitional five bay design based on the so called 'relaxed utility' style of bodywork. They were allocated the fleet numbers 266 to 290 which were to have been carried by the Leyland TD7s in 1940.

The Titan PD1 was regarded by some as a stop gap chassis, lacking the sophistication of the prewar designs, pending the introduction by Leyland of a larger engine. The new model had a new 7.4 litre direct injection engine designated the 'E181' which developed slightly more power (100 bhp at 1800 rpm) and enjoyed a more favourable fuel consumption than the prewar 8.6 litre engine. The engine had been developed from a smaller experimental unit fitted to some Tiger TS8s delivered to Ribble Motor Services in 1939 and subsequently used in the Leyland Matilda tank. The prewar 8.6 litre diesel engine was renowned for its quiet running but the more efficient 7.4 litre unit was much noisier. A new four speed gearbox was fitted to the PD1, with constant mesh helical gears for second and third speeds, and sliding spur gears for first and reverse. The design reverted to TD5 practice with the reintroduction of the Marles cam and roller steering (in place of worm and nut), and the use of bolted on extensions to support the rear platform of the body. The frontal appearance of the PD1 was also different from the prewar models as the radiator was much wider,

In summer 1946 Southdown took delivery of 25 new Leyland Titan PD1s with Park Royal bodies to a relaxed utility style. Car 272 (GUF 672), in original livery with dark green roof, waits outside Bognor Bus Station on an eastbound service 50A journey to Elmer. In this early postwar scene the wartime temporary air raid shelters built either side of the vehicle entrance/exits have been removed. The wooden framework of these buses soon deteriorated in similar fashion to the earlier utility buses and starting in 1952 all had to be extensively rebuilt by Southdown. Car 272 remained in service until April 1961 and was then sold to J. Light of Lewes for scrap.
Southdown Enthusiasts Club – W J Haynes Collection

Seen in Pool Valley, Brighton on service 122 to Tunbridge Wells is car 266 (GUF 666), a Leyland Titan PD1 with Park Royal body new in June 1946. Originally delivered with a dark green roof and painted radiator it has gained a cream roof. The livery was later modified with cream applied in a straight line around the front dash panel and below the lower deck front window. Poor quality unseasoned timber used for the framework soon led to problems and all were rebuilt by the company starting in 1952. *Southdown Enthusiasts Club – W J Haynes Collection*

with a sheet metal shell instead of a cast aluminium one and external filler cap, offset to the nearside. As delivered, the radiator shell was painted dark green but later on Southdown had the shell chromed on all these buses, which much enhanced their appearance. When new these buses had the dark green roof introduced in wartime to help camouflage buses from enemy aircraft.

Supplies of seasoned wood were exhausted by about 1943 and normal supplies of teak used for the best quality composite bodies were unobtainable with the result that most utility and early post war bodies were constructed of poor quality and unseasoned ash. The condition of the Park Royal composite framed bodies fitted to cars 266 to 290 soon started to show signs of deterioration often caused by rotting of the body framing and Southdown had to completely strip down and reconstruct all vehicles in this batch during 1953/4. Withdrawal started in 1959 but most continued in service until 1963.

Post war rebodying programme

Although Southdown was able to take delivery in 1946 of 25 new double deckers from its preferred supplier, Leyland Motors Ltd, it was obvious that the prewar Titans, whose bodies were approaching the end of their normal life span, would need to continue in service for many years to come. Whilst at the end of the war Southdown opted to rebuild the existing bodies on many of its single deck buses and coaches – usually to the original outline – it chose new bodies for the majority of its older double deck buses in order to prolong the life of the chassis. As a result many of the prewar Titans were to outlive their single deck counterparts and continue in service until

1958-1962 with some chassis completing 25 years of service.

As noted in chapter 8 some of the prewar Titans had been refurbished in 1944/5 but it was clear the condition of many of the composite construction bodies from the 1930s would demand complete replacement if the chassis were to continue in service. Following the 21 new bodies fitted to the Titan TD1/TD2s in 1943-5 this further programme covered most of the remaining prewar fleet of TD3/TD4/TD5s and ran through from February 1946 to June 1950. By that time 153 buses had received new high-bridge bodywork – the other 29 prewar double deck buses being refurbished for further service. Southdown also took the opportunity to reduce the ratio of offside gangway lowbridge buses in the fleet. At the end of the rebodying programme only 23 remained in service whereas in late 1939 the company had 74 such vehicles. In particular, the lowering of the road under the railway bridge at Lewes reduced the requirement and allowed normal highbridge double deckers on all trunk routes through the town whilst similar schemes near Stone Cross and at Shoreham in the postwar years further reduced the need for these unpopular buses.

The postwar rebodying programme involved bodies from five different manufacturers including East Lancs (59 bodies), Park Royal (35), Beadle (32), Northern Counties (17) and Saunders (10). Whilst both Park Royal and Beadle had already supplied many new bodies to Southdown before the war, East Lancs and Northern Counties had only become represented within the fleet as a result of wartime requirements. Nearly all of these new highbridge bodies were to the same basic specification with 54

Among the very first of the buses to reappear in service under the postwar rebodying scheme was car 124 (BUF 224) which was delivered from East Lancs on 2 February 1946. It seen here at Worthing on busy service 10 which for many years ran between Brighton and Arundel via Worthing and the A27. In the postwar travel boom destinations such as Arundel proved very popular on fine days. Car 124 was sold in April 1960 to the Salford based dealer Frank Cowley to which almost all of Southdown's roadworthy fleet passed at this time.
Southdown Enthusiasts Club – Clark/Surfleet Collection

seats, five bay construction, fixed window panes at the front of the upper deck and half drop opening side windows. A small metal sun visor was provided over the driver's windscreen on all these vehicles and many were also fitted with bulkhead heaters in both saloons. Exceptions to this specification were the East Lancs bodies built between 1946 and 1948 which were fitted with separate ventilators above the front upper deck windows – although many were later replaced with plain glass – and their first 25 bodies had only 52 seats. The first 12 bodies from Beadle delivered in 1947/8 also had a rather dated six bay design which was most unusual for

new bodies built after the War. The Beadle body-work fitted in 1949/50 was to a revised design based on a 5 bay structure.

The first prewar Titan to be rebodied in the new programme was car 122 which appeared in February 1946 having had its original Short Bros body removed and scrapped at Portslade in November 1945. This was one of 25 with East Lancs 52 seat highbridge bodies built to a relaxed utility standard and similar in appearance to those fitted to cars 950 and 958 in 1945. They had a rounded rear dome and a prominent feature were the three ventilators inset into the bodywork above the first, third and fifth lower

Car 116 (BUF 216) is a Leyland Titan TD4c new in May 1935. Its original Short Bros highbridge body was scrapped and replaced by a new East Lancs body in March 1947. It was originally petrol engined and was converted to run on Producer Gas between February 1943 and September 1944. After rebodying it led a long life with Southdown and was finally withdrawn from service in January 1961.
Southdown Enthusiasts Club – Clark/Surfleet Collection

Car 128 (BUF 228) shows off the pleasing lines of its new Saunders body which was fitted in July 1947. It is a Leyland Titan TD4 new in 1935 with a Short Bros highbridge body and is seen on layover at the rear of Bognor Regis bus station while on relief duties on the cross town service 55.
Southdown Enthusiasts Club – Clark/Surfleet Collection

deck window on each side. The bodies were mounted randomly on Titan TD3, TD4 and TD5 chassis new between 1934 and 1938, presumably dictated by the condition of the original body. In the early postwar period there were still severe shortages of materials and manpower and delivery continued spasmodically until the arrival of car 170 on 24 January 1948. Withdrawal of these buses commenced with TD3 car 969 in May 1958 followed by car 970 in June 1958, although others lingered on to lead very long lives with Southdown. Car 123 was sold in June 1961 by which time the chassis was 26 years old and the body almost 15 years old and

the very last – car 170 – survived almost until the end of the prewar Titans being sold in January 1962!

The next, and most surprising, supplier was Saunders which delivered car 183 in June 1947. Based on the Isle of Anglesey the company had been busy during the war with contracts for the Admiralty and Ministries of Supply and Aircraft Production and was now anxious to obtain new work for its skilled production staff although it had until now little experience of bus body manufacture. They became most famous for supplying 300 bodies for London Transport's RT class to an almost standard design. The bodies for

Car 172 (EUF 172) is a Leyland Titan TD5 delivered in April 1938 but fitted with a new Beadle 6 bay highbridge body in 1948. It is seen at South Parade Pier, Southsea at the start of the long run on service 31 to Brighton which was scheduled to last 3 hours 59 minutes. Starting on 15 June 1947 a 15 minute frequency operated throughout the route in summer. Car 172 was withdrawn and sold for further service in March 1958.
Southdown Enthusiasts Club – Clark/Surfleet Collection

After a 12 month gap in deliveries East Lancs resumed their share of the rebodying programme in January 1949. The second batch had a distinctly more rounded front dome as shown by car 151 (DUF 151), a Leyland Titan TD5 seen at Fareham Bus Station on a working to Southsea via Fratton. The new body was fitted in June 1949 and car 151 survived in Southdown service until March 1961 when it was sold to J. Light of Lewes for scrap.
Southdown Enthusiasts Club –
Clark/Surfleet Collection

Leyland Titan TD5 car 216 (FCD 516) received its new Beadle 5 bay body in December 1949. It was originally fitted with a Park Royal lowbridge body when delivered in February 1939 and is seen at Pool Valley, Brighton on service 14 to Haywards Heath which for many years ran two hourly via Hurstpierpoint, Bolney and Cuckfield. Along with many other Beadle rebodied Titans it was sold in 1959 to the Salford based dealer Frank Cowley.
Southdown Enthusiasts Club –
Clark/Surfleet Collection

On 1 January 1949 Leyland Titan TD5 car 205 (EUF 205) suffered extensive damage after it was blown off the Old Shoreham Toll Bridge and into the River Adur. The original Park Royal body new in July 1938 was scrapped and a new Park Royal body fitted in May 1949. It is seen here at Worthing Dome after arriving from Angmering-on-Sea on the hourly service 31G and survived with Southdown until sale in April 1961.
Author's collection

Southdown were built using the manufacturer's patented cruciform shaped pillar system with a gently curved rake to the front of the upper deck. Unlike the protracted East Lancs production all were delivered during June and July 1947 before Saunders commenced work on bodies for the RT class. The first of the Saunders bodied Titans to be withdrawn were cars 183 and 186 in December 1958 and the last in service was car 199 which was sold in April 1961.

In August 1947 Beadle completed the first of its batch of 12 six bay bodies with the delivery of car 110. These were more reminiscent of the prewar bodies already supplied to the company and in common with many bodies built by Beadle on prewar Leyland chassis after the war the first and sixth bays were noticeably shorter than the middle four bays. Deliveries on Titan TD3, TD4 and TD5 chassis continued until July 1948 with the arrival of car 172. The six bay Beadle bodies were among the first to be withdrawn and car 138 was scrapped in February 1958. Car 158 was the last of the type to depart in June 1959. In contrast some of the Beadle lowbridge bodies dating from 1938, many of which were extensively rebuilt by Beadle in 1945/6, remained in service with Southdown until the end of lowbridge operations in 1956/7.

East Lancs started a new batch of 34 bodies in January 1949 with the delivery of cars 102, 202, 208, 220 and 244. These bodies – with 54 seats – were very similar to those supplied previously except that they had plain glass in the front upper deck windows and a more pleasing front profile was achieved by turning the rain strips above the upper deck windows down the outside front window pillars. All were fitted to Titan TD4 and TD5 chassis and delivery was completed in June 1950 at the very end of the rebodying programme. An early withdrawal was car 102 in June 1959 but others continued in service for another three years with cars 244 and 246 finally leaving the fleet in July 1962 by which time the chassis were 23 years old.

Beadle commenced production of a further batch of 20 vehicles in March 1949 and whilst very similar to the previous batch these bodies had five equal width windows between the bulkheads. Most were fitted to Titan TD5 chassis but three were mounted on TD4s and five on TD3s. It is notable that three were built on TD3 chassis at the end of the programme in January 1950 when the original Short Bros were over 15 years old. After just 9 to 10 years in service the year 1959 proved to be a bad one for the Beadle bodied vehicles with all but one withdrawn between January and the end of May. Only car 227 which had been fitted with triple route number boxes in December 1956 survived until sale in March 1960 marking the end of this distinctive, if old fashioned, body style with Southdown.

Some of the worst postwar shortages had been overcome by the time that Park Royal joined the rebodying programme and their production of 35

vehicles was completed between May 1949 and April 1950. The first to appear was car 165 and a total of 25 were delivered up to July 1949 with a further ten during March-April 1950. They were fitted with Park Royal's first standard post war body with gently curved front and rear profiles and a distinct improvement on that fitted to the PD1s in 1946. Unlike the other batches all Park Royal bodies were fitted to later Titan TD5 chassis and, apart from the sale of car 159 in February 1960, they remained complete until February 1961. Further significant withdrawals took place in March and April 1961 but 12 remained in stock at the start of 1962. The last Park Royal to depart from the fleet was car 256 in June 1962 although by this time and, despite major rebuilds, several of the 1946 PD1s had left the fleet.

No doubt impressed by the utility products of Northern Counties this manufacturer supplied 17 bodies to Southdown during 1950. These had a number of easily recognisable features including the flared skirts, rounded edges to the front upper deck windows and elegant curved valance from the nearside canopy front to the rear of the front nearside mudguard. Delivery took place between January and April 1950 and, with the exception of three TD4s, all were fitted to TD5 chassis. The first of this batch to be sold was car 148 in June 1959 but most remained in service until late 1961 and six continued into 1962. Finally, the last of the prewar Titans to be sold was car 257 in October 1962 some 23 years after its delivery in the early months of the war.

Ironically the last vehicle to be completed in the rebodying programme was a TD4, car 118 dating from 1935, which was delivered from East Lancs on 3 June 1950. It had taken four and a half years for East Lancs to complete production of a total of 59 bodies and gain the honour of supplying both the first and last!

The fifth company to join the postwar rebodying programme was Northern Counties which had already supplied many utility bodies to Southdown and had been favoured with a batch of 12 Guy Arabs in 1948/9. Starting in January 1950 Northern Counties supplied 17 bodies to an easily recognisable design mostly on later Titan TD5s. An offside view shows Leyland Titan TD5 car 252 (GCD 352) on service 38 outside the Southdown garage at Hilsea when traffic levels permitted such photography! Delivered new in October 1939 with a Park Royal body it was fitted with a new Northern Counties body in February 1950 and remained in service until sale in June 1962.
Southdown Enthusiasts Club – Clark/Surfleet Collection

The following buses were rebodied:

EAST LANCS H26/26R	1946	119, 122-125, 127, 131, 133, 969, 970	
BEADLE (6 bays) H28/26R	1947	106, 110, 112, 120, 126, 138, 965	
EAST LANCS H26/26R	1947	113, 114, 116, 130, 134, 136, 137, 166, 171, 963, 968	
SAUNDERS H28/26R	1947	115, 117, 128, 135, 145, 183, 186, 199, 960, 961	
BEADLE (6 bays) H28/26R	1948	153, 155, 158, 163, 172	
EAST LANCS H26/26R	1948	168, 170, 173, 203	
BEADLE (5 bays) H28/26R	1949	141, 146, 156, 160, 187, 214, 216, 222, 226, 227, 236, 247, 964, 966, 975	
EAST LANCS H28/26R	1949	102, 108, 129, 151, 202, 206-208, 213, 220, 225, 228, 238, 244	
PARK ROYAL H28/26R	1949	152, 164, 165 167, 169, 174, 175, 178-180, 194, 204, 205, 217-219, 223, 224, 235, 239, 242, 249, 250, 256, 264	
BEADLE (5 bays) H28/26R	1950	121, 243, 962, 971, 973	
EAST LANCS H28/26R	1950	118, 140, 149, 157, 161, 162, 177, 193, 201, 210, 212, 215, 221, 229, 230, 237, 245, 246, 261, 265	
NORTHERN COUNTIES H28/26R	1950	139, 147, 148, 154, 190, 209, 211, 234, 241, 252-255, 257, 259, 260, 263	
PARK ROYAL H28/26R	1950	159, 176, 231-233, 240, 248, 251, 258, 262	

The old bodies were removed at Portslade and whilst many were dismantled and scrapped by Southdown others were sold for further use such as store sheds on farms. A few passed to showmen for conversion to caravans but the most unusual were the three that had their top decks placed on houseboats on the River Adur at Shoreham-by-Sea. These were formerly Park Royal highbridge bodied cars 207, 208 and 220 dating from 1939. As the post war bodies were heavier than those they replaced it was necessary to fit the prewar Titan chassis with new heavy duty springs to take the added weight of the body, seats and passengers. As delivered the new bodies all had a standard size destination box fitted over the platform although towards the end of their lives many were removed or painted over.

Unlike many other operators, including neighbouring Maidstone & District, Southdown did not continue its rebodying programme to include wartime or early postwar deliveries although many needed significant attention by the early 1950s. In spite of this the last covered top utility buses remained in service with Southdown until 1963. Four of the five coachbuilders used in the rebodying programme – Northern Counties, Park Royal, Beadle and East Lancs – were destined to supply bodies to Southdown on Leyland PD2/12 chassis during the 1950s. Northern Counties became the sole supplier to Southdown for double deck bodies between 1958 and 1967.

1947

Southdown restarted their programme of extended tours in 1947 using cars 1807 – 1823 which dated from 1930-6. The tours quickly proved very popular, so the company decided to rebuild all the surviving older Lioness touring coaches to centre entrance format (as C20C). The first to be completed was car 1817 which was rebuilt by the company at Portslade Works late in 1947. Of the other 1933 Lioness tourers, cars 1812 – 1814/1816 (which had been rebuilt by Harrington with electrically operated folding sunroof and cove windows in 1937) were similarly rebuilt by Windover in time for the 1948 season – car 1815 was also rebuilt by Windover at the end of that summer. In particular, on this batch, the straight moulding at waist level was unchanged but the long standing weakness in the windscreen pillars was eliminated. Apart from providing a sliding door forward of the rear axle very little other work was required. From the 1930 batch, cars 1803/4/7-11 were rebuilt by Portsmouth Aviation during early 1948 while 1802 and 1806 are believed to have been rebuilt by Southdown in 1949. To augment the ageing Lioness and Tigress touring fleet, nine of the last batch of prewar Tigers – cars 1218 to 1226 – were reseated to C21R at Portslade Works during 1949/50 partly using seats from the 14 seat touring Cubs, cars 1 to 4. They were required to operate a new programme of European luxury tours as well as tours of the U.K. with most retaining 21 seats until withdrawal in 1956.

During 1946 Southdown had only managed to obtain 30 new double-deck vehicles all of which were fitted with what was described as 'relaxed utility' style bodywork by Park Royal but which hardly looked any better than the wartime deliveries. The year 1947 saw a dramatic improvement in supply and included the first new coaches since summer 1939. Following the loss of 125 coaches for military use during the early years of the war Southdown urgently needed to rebuild its much reduced coach fleet and placed an order with Leyland for 125 Tiger PS1/1 models. Materials and labour were still in short supply and it proved difficult to obtain delivery of bodywork to the specification required by Southdown. The company therefore decided that quicker delivery could be obtained if it relaxed its previous rigid prewar specification and also if the order was split between a number of body suppliers. In the event delivery was spread over three years with bodies supplied by six companies to very differing styles although the majority had 32 seats and rear entrances.

Once the Titan PD1 began to enter service in numbers, Leyland turned its attention to its single deck equivalent, the Tiger PS1. It featured the same 7.4 litre E181 direct injection engine coupled with the new four-speed gearbox, Marles cam and roller steering and the wider radiator with the offset filler cap. The prewar dimensions

(27ft 6in long and 7ft 6 in wide, with a wheelbase of 17ft 6in) were also continued. The PS1 was intended as a bus chassis and had a straight rear frame, although body builders or operators often rebuilt these to provide a dropped rear locker for coach work. Subsequently, Leyland offered the PS1/1 variant with a dropped rear frame. The first 25 coaches began delivery in February 1947 and were unlike any previous Southdown coaches. Cars 1227 to 1251 were fitted with 31 seat rear entrance bodies by Eastern Coach Works based on the standard Tilling group service bus body usually matched to a Bristol L chassis. As fitted to the Tiger chassis they had a smaller windscreen than normal with straight bottom edge but were otherwise identical to the standard bus version, with a hand operated externally hung sliding entrance door, fixed roof, straight waistline and, at first, fitted with top sliding vents to side windows. All had script fleet names, a single line destination screen box, with the Southdown block fleet name in a separate glass above, and long wooden detachable express service boards as they were to be used on the London Express Services. At this time the sliding vents were not considered acceptable by Southdown and all were replaced by half drop windows with polished metal surrounds during 1948. Later glass louvres were fitted over all the side windows in 1950. Starting in November

Southdown was able to reintroduce its Coach Cruise programme for summer 1947 using its prewar fleet of 'normal control' Lionesses, Tigresses and Cubs. The surviving 1930 built coaches were all extensively modernised for postwar service and 1808 (UF 6508), a Leyland Lioness LTB1 with Harrington 20 seat Touring coach body, is seen in Bournemouth on a Devon and Cornwall holiday. With the arrival of the new underfloor engined Royal Tigers all of the surviving prewar Lioness and Tigress touring coaches were withdrawn in 1952.
A B Cross

Car 1219 (FUF 319) was one of nine prewar Harrington bodied Tigers to be converted to 21 seat Touring coach format with 2+1 seating layout in 1949/50. They appeared on Southdown's Coach Cruise programme including a new Grand Tour of Britain lasting 18 days as well as European tours when these were able to recommence. It is seen here carrying a board for Frames Tours who used Southdown's licensed tours for their clients at this time.
Author's collection

1954 the company began a programme to downgrade these 25 vehicles for bus work renumbering them in the series 675 to 699 in the chronological order of reclassification. Most survived in their new role until 1961 and two have been saved for preservation.

During May Southdown took delivery of cars 1252 to 1263, further PS1/1s which were fitted with 32 seat rear entrance bodywork by Park Royal to a design developed for East Kent Road Car and similar to that company's prewar standard. Although they had a completely straight waist and roof line, the flared skirt and curved roof beading above the detachable express service boards appeared to soften their appearance compared to the Eastern Coach Works design. As on some of Southdown's 'modernised' prewar coaches, there were dark green painted side flashes edged with polished beading that swept down from just below the waistline over the rear wheel arch to the rear of the coach. They featured an internally hung sliding entrance door and half length sliding sunroof, being withdrawn at the start of the 1958 season. When just two months old car 1255 (HCD 855) was involved in a serious accident in Horsham.

Car 1227 (GUF 727) was numerically the first new postwar coach to join the fleet arriving in April 1947. Lacking the distinctive style of Southdown's prewar coaches it is an Eastern Coach Works bodied Leyland Tiger PS1/1 and has stopped for refreshment at the Holly & Laurel Hotel at Holmwood whilst working a southbound service from London to Worthing. Half drop windows have replaced the original top sliding windows as delivered and the radiator is painted dark green in this late 1940s view. In 1955 car 1227 was modified for bus work and after sale in 1960 it eventually passed into preservation.
Alan Lambert collection

Park Royal supplied a further batch of rear entrance coaches on Leyland Tiger PS1/1 chassis during 1948 similar to the previous year's deliveries. Car 1305 (HUF 305) is taking a break at The Star at Felbridge whilst working a relief journey on the London to Eastbourne Express Service. Half cab coaches appeared as very dated to the public by the late 1950s and all of those remaining with Southdown were withdrawn by early 1959.
S L Poole

The Park Royal body was repaired before the chassis and was therefore fitted to a later chassis. To keep the body in the correct batch the resulting vehicle took the same car number and became 1255 (HUF 285). After the original chassis was repaired it was fitted in February 1948 with a new Beadle body and became 1285 (HCD 855).

Also in May came the first of a small batch of six coaches for use on excursions and fitted with elegant 32 seat front entrance bodywork by local builder Harrington to that company's attractive postwar standard design although without the distinctive rear dorsal fin. Cars 1264 to 1267 arrived during 1947 with 1268 and 1269 following on in 1948. They featured an externally hung sliding entrance door, gently curved waistline, deep flared skirts and a small curved window in the nearside valance. Car 1264 had a traditional half cab without a full width canopy as standard on current bodies from Harrington and was the first such vehicle delivered new to Southdown with that design. Cars 1265 to 1269 were similar but specially modified for Southdown with full width canopies incorporating the usual single line destination display

Full order books in the early postwar years meant that operators had sometimes to take what was available and car 1264 (HUF 4) remained unique for Southdown in that it was built to Harrington's standard front entrance design of the time and without a full width canopy. It is a Leyland Tiger PS1/1 delivered in April 1947 and remained to the end of half cab coaches in the fleet in March 1959. Southdown somehow persuaded Harrington to fit a full width canopy to the remaining five coaches in the batch.
Author's collection

In late 1947 Southdown took delivery of six Leyland Tiger PS1/1 with distinctive 32 seat front entrance bodies built by Windover to their standard design. Car 1275 (HUF 275) is seen at the rear of Bognor Regis bus station where the batch spent their time on excursion, express relief and private hire work in the Bognor and Chichester areas. All were sold in March/April 1958 to dealer Frank Cowley of Salford.
Southdown Enthusiasts Club – Clark/Surfleet Collection

Car 1293 (HUF 293) is one of 23 Leyland Tiger PS1/1 models to be bodied by Beadle with rear entrance coach bodies closer to Southdown's prewar designs than others being supplied at the time. Delivery commenced December 1947 but Beadle was very busy rebuilding and rebodying prewar chassis for many large operators in the south of England and the last did not arrive until July 1949. In 1954/5 the complete batch were 'modernised' by Beadle with full fronts and, although it is debatable whether the end result was very successful, it extended their lives until the end of the 1959 season
Southdown Enthusiasts Club – Clark/Surfleet Collection

Duple finally completed its batch of 40 rear entrance coach bodies on Leyland Tiger PS1/1 chassis in November 1949. Car 1348 (HUF 948) shows off the graceful lines of these final half cab coaches to enter the Southdown fleet as it approaches Victoria Coach Station before operating a London to Eastbourne Express Service. In 1955 it was rebuilt by Beadle with a full front remaining in the Southdown fleet until sale in May 1961
Author's collection

and red block lettered fleet name in a separate glass above. They were all withdrawn in early 1959.

Arriving later in 1947 and generally placed in store until 1948, cars 1270 to 1275 were a batch of six excursion coaches with distinctive 32 seat front entrance bodies built by Windover to their standard design. They had a normal half cab without full width canopy, gently sloping window line and featured an externally hung sliding door and twin leaf sliding sunroof. They spent their whole life on excursion, express relief and private hire work in the Bognor Regis and Chichester areas and were among the first PS1s to be sold, departing at the start of 1958. Beadle was to remain a major supplier of bodywork to Southdown and built 23 rear entrance coach bodies which were closer to Southdown's prewar standard than the other makes, with a straight top and curved bottom to the side windows. Cars 1277 and 1278 were delivered at the end of 1947 but did not enter service until the following spring, the remainder arriving in 1948 and 1949.

Starting in June came the first 20 of a batch of 40 coaches with attractive 32 seat rear entrance vehicles by Duple of Hendon but unlike that manufacturer's postwar standard design. Numbered 1312 to 1331 these all purpose coaches were similar to the Beadle bodies and fitted well with the more traditional Southdown image although neither design quite managed to

achieve the graceful lines of the 1939 Harrington bodied Tigers. They had an internally hung sliding entrance door, curved bottom to the side windows, a flared skirt and, importantly, the small metal sun visor over the driver's windscreen. In an attempt to modernise their appearance all of the Beadle and Duple bodied PS1s were sent to J.C. Beadle at Dartford and fitted with a fully enclosed front end during the spring of 1954 and winter of 1954/55. The resulting appearance was not particularly attractive and the removal of the front bulkhead significantly increased engine noise in the coach. Despite this, the company obtained a further six or seven years use from these all purpose coaches with the last remaining in service until 1962, long after the last of the half cab PS1s had departed.

The first of Southdown's truly postwar double deckers started delivery in May with arrival of the first of a batch of 25 Leyland PD1A fitted with Leyland's newly reintroduced handsome five bay metal framed highbridge bodywork. The PD1A chassis was to a very similar specification as cars 266 to 290 but fitted with Metalastik rubber bushes on the spring shackle pins. Cars 291 to 315 had 54 seats (rather than the normal 56 in this body), five half drop windows on each side and fixed glass in the upper deck front windows. Whilst bearing a strong resemblance to the prewar design, the 1946 version had a

Southdown's first double deckers to full peacetime standard started to appear in May 1947 in the shape of 25 Leyland Titan PD1A models with Leyland metal framed highbridge bodywork. Car 306 (HCD 906) is seen opposite Worthing Dome on service 10 to Arundel. It is in full lined out livery with dark green painted radiator and remained in service until July 1964. Heading towards Brighton is car 405 showing off the very angular rear dome of its Strachan highbridge body.
Author's collection

number of improvements including a double skin roof on the upper deck as standard. Southdown's usual destination displays were fitted on the front, rear and nearside above the entrance on each bus although all later had the nearside screen box removed or painted over. For some reason, they, along with other Leyland bodies, were never fitted with metal sun visors over the driver's windscreen. Unlike the Park Royal bodied examples of 1946 these buses led a full 17 year life with Southdown before being withdrawn in 1964, which seems to dispel any initial doubts expressed in some quarters when the PD1 model first appeared.

Until mid-summer 1948 the radiator shell and mesh on all Leyland PD1 and PS1 models was painted dark green when delivered and all entered service in this form. Southdown later had the shell chromed on all these vehicles which much enhanced their appearance. Coaches were initially in the traditional apple green and dark green coach livery with a cream waistband or flash and script fleet names. The Leyland bodied PD1s were in all over apple green, with a cream band below the windows, cream window surrounds and roof (except for the centre section which was dark green). Six horizontal dark green lines were provided, three separating the green from the cream and one immediately below the windows on each deck and one above the upper deck windows.

Postscript

The summer of 1947 marks the end of this story. After the severe wartime cutbacks Southdown had quickly and successfully restored its network of bus and coach services and was carrying record numbers of passengers. Most bus services ran 7 days a week and the full daytime frequency usually continued up to the last bus with just slightly later starting times on Sunday mornings. Ambitious new links such as the 32 and 71 had already been introduced with the shape of the postwar network remaining virtually unchanged through the 1950s and even 1960s. There were still some important developments to come such as the extension of part of the 119 northward to Gravesend as new service 122 in June 1948 to form one of the longest bus routes in Britain.

Demand for seats on the coach services grew dramatically as a war weary public escaped once more to their favourite seaside resorts. With a serious shortage of most goods and services, fuel rationing and many now enjoying secure full time employment the opportunity to enjoy holidays by the sea and days out by coach was one of the few 'luxuries' available in the early post war years. Coach travel was certainly here to stay and any doubts in 1942 that the express services would ever return and develop in the post war world quickly disappeared. The Coach Cruise programme continued to prosper and in 1949 some of the 1939 Tigers were converted to 21

seat Touring coaches to operate a new programme of European luxury tours and to augment the Lionesses and Tigresses on the UK tours. According to the seating plan in the 1950 brochure the Tigers were used on the 18 day Tour of Britain and 13 day Central Highlands of Scotland departures. In 1950 Southdown started its first overseas tours with a 17 day tour to France and Switzerland operated by Leyland Tiger car 1223. This coach was transferred to Northern Ireland in 1951 where it became the first to operate a programme of Irish tours for the company.

Southdown's fleet was already being transformed by new postwar deliveries and a major rebodying programme for prewar Titans. In 1948 the company took delivery of 80 of the new Leyland PD2 chassis with all metal Leyland bodies and continued to choose Leyland bodies on later 8 foot wide PD2/12 chassis until 1954 when production stopped. As a result the all-Leyland buses in familiar green and cream livery soon became a familiar sight throughout Southdown's territory.

Rationing and controls imposed during the Second World War remained in place throughout the immediate post war period and did not finally end until June 1954. The fragile economy required careful management to ensure that the country recovered from the high cost of nearly six years of total war. Demand for goods and services was high as blitzed towns and cities had to be rebuilt and run down factories refurbished with new and more efficient plant. There was a desperate shortage of housing stock especially in those areas that had borne the brunt of German air attacks. Many thousands of properties in Portsmouth had suffered damage, some two, three or even four times. Around 6,625 properties in the city were totally destroyed and another 6,549 seriously damaged. The Guildhall had been burnt out, Clarence Pier wrecked, a hospital destroyed and four cinemas and a theatre lost. Large areas of the city where people once lived, shopped and worked remained as open spaces simply cleared of wreckage. Serious damage had also been inflicted in Eastbourne and Brighton. Due to shortages of materials, the building of new homes, shops and factories was subject to official approval and it would be many years before the scars of wartime finally disappeared.

Unfortunately, the postwar boom in bus and coach travel was to suffer two major setbacks at the turn of the decade. In the autumn of 1947 the basic petrol ration was relaxed but all fuel rationing for private motoring ended in May 1950 allowing many who had 'suffered' overcrowded public transport to become independent. This combined with a decline in evening cinema and theatre visits, as television became more popular in homes, began a downward spiral in overall bus patronage. Even by 1949 Southdown reported a reduced profit despite a substantial increase in gross revenue and warned that some

Before the war Southdown buses did not display a route number on inbound services towards Portsmouth. In 1945 new screens were introduced for the Portsmouth area and those for the London Road and Havant Road routes included service numbers for all journeys. Despite variations within Portchester and some journeys via Fratton Bridge new screens for the 45 did not include numbers. Car 258 (GCD 358), seen passing through Cosham, is a Leyland Titan TD5 with Park Royal highbridge body new in November 1939 and nicely shows the curved window edges featured on the 1939 deliveries.
Southdown Enthusiasts Club – Clark/Surfleet Collection

of the improved facilities that had been introduced would have to be reconsidered if the number of stage carriage journeys continued to fall. But, Southdown's summer loadings remained healthy for many years as more and more people were able to enjoy holidays by the sea. The ambitious Heathfield scheme jointly with Maidstone & District in June 1957 came, arguably, too late although relief buses on the more important country routes were still a frequent sight throughout the Southdown area for many years to come. Away from the coastal areas much of the company's territory remained rural and many of those who lived in the area were relatively wealthy and able to run their own car. Whether some more pruning should have occurred earlier is a matter for debate but the severe cutbacks of 1971 saw large parts of the familiar stage carriage network disappear overnight, including many which could be traced right back to the 1930s.

Seen at the Rustington terminus of service 66 is car 294 (HCD 894), a Leyland bodied Leyland Titan PD1A delivered in May 1947. Since the war ended this service had already undergone many changes in this area as a result of the reopening of the coast road between Rustington and Littlehampton in August 1945 although by the time car 294 entered service the 66 had already been diverted via the inland route and replaced by an enhanced service 31.
Southdown Enthusiasts Club – Clark/Surfleet Collection

A busy scene at Pevensey Road Bus Station in Eastbourne in 1945. There is a sizeable queue for car 175 (EUF 175), a Leyland Titan TD5 with Park Royal lowbridge body which still retains white markings on the nearside front wing. It is operating an anti-clockwise working on newly reintroduced Circular service 94 which passed under a low bridge at Stone Cross and actually required the use of lowbridge buses. Also present is a Maidstone & District AEC Regal operating on the newly restored joint service 99 to Hastings via Pevensey Bay. There was devastating bomb damage in the close vicinity but Southdown's luck held and the bus station survived unscathed.
C F Klapper © Omnibus Society

As was to be expected Southdown had built many fine garages and small but practical 'dormy' sheds in the 1920s as the fleet expanded and this continued during the 1930s. It was less keen on providing off street bus stations and for many years the Head Office at 5 Steine Street in Brighton was, perhaps, less than prepossessing. A central overhaul works had been built in Victoria Road, Portslade and opened in 1928. The 1930s saw further improvements and expansion. To cater for passengers on the London to Brighton and Worthing via Crawley express services Southdown decided in 1931 to open their own refreshment facilities at County Oak one mile north of Crawley. The company's association with East Grinstead began in July 1933 and a new garage at Chequer Road was opened for business on 9 January 1934 with an enquiry office in the High Street following on 2 December 1937. Expansion in the Portsmouth area demanded a large new garage and coach station which was opened at Hilsea on the northern edge of Portsea Island in 1934 followed by an impressive new bus and coach station in High Street, Bognor Regis in September 1934. To cater for growing seasonal demand a garage was opened in Elm Grove, Hayling Island in September 1935. A new garage at Bedford Row in Worthing with accommodation for a further 50 buses and modern offices for staff was finally opened in

May 1940 and proved to be the last major work built on Southdown's behalf until the 1950s.

Given the many air raids across the company's area – particularly in Portsmouth, Brighton and Eastbourne it is very surprising that none of its properties sustained serious damage as a result of enemy bombing. Much of the area around the Hyde Park Road premises was destroyed during the many heavy bombing raids on Portsmouth in 1941. By the end of the war Eastbourne had been designated the most raided town in the South East Region and yet Southdown's three main properties were all relatively unscathed. Much of Eastbourne's central shopping area was damaged or destroyed and the railway station attacked on several occasions. Many bombs fell at the eastern end of Pevensey Road and in Terminus Road but fortunately none are known to have affected the bus station. The junction of Bourne Street and Langney Road was hit so many times that it became known as Hell Fire Corner and yet the nearby Cavendish Place garage and coach station survived intact. Even the Royal Parade garage was close to bombs that fell on the foreshore or in nearby Beach Road.

Southdown did indeed appear to enjoy a 'charmed' existence through the war.

A list of garages, bus stations and offices in use on 1st September 1939 will be found in Appendix 7.

Whatever the problems caused by the Blackout in the home, most businesses faced even greater difficulties following its introduction on Friday 1 September 1939. At first, no light whatsoever was permitted on the streets and it became illegal to allow any light to show from a building after sunset. Many factories and buildings such as Southdown's Central Works at Portslade had glass roofs which had to be covered or painted black meaning that workers were obliged to work day and night under the glare of artificial lights. As well as darkening their windows most shops, offices, restaurants and places of entertainment had the added dilemma of how customers could enter or leave their premises after dark without any light escaping.

This problem would clearly have affected Southdown's many enquiry offices spread throughout the company area as well as the enclosed bus and coach stations such as at High Street in Bognor Regis, Steine Street in Brighton and Pevensey Road in Eastbourne. The solution for shops and offices usually meant a double door (or heavy curtain) where people entering would open one door and shut it behind them before opening the main door.

At a company Board Meeting on 31 August 1939 it was announced that the BET Federation proposed to make use of the Company's property at 29 Freshfield Road in Brighton during the present emergency. The Managing Director also reported that he had agreed to purchase a plot of land at Elm Grove, Hayling Island for the sum of £574 and at the Board Meeting on Thursday 19 October 1939 the Managing Director reported that he had agreed to purchase freehold land and cottages in High Street, Bognor Regis for £4,500. The wartime conditions had closed down many businesses in the seaside towns leaving many empty properties and several acquisitions were made by Southdown in the following years. Although not its own property, Southdown assumed responsibility for all bus and coach services from Fareham Bus Station in October 1939 when the country's division into Emergency Transport Regions brought Fareham into Portsmouth (Area 6B). Southdown Inspector Vaughan was appointed to act as controller from a Southdown kiosk. The system continued for many years after the war until control was handed back to Hants & Dorset from 8 April 1956.

This is the scene looking east at the corner of Russell Street and Hyde Park Road after the raid on 10 March 1941 which marked the second 'Blitz' on Portsmouth. Southdown's garage in Hyde Park Road, which apparently survived without damage, was situated about 150 yards behind where the photographer was standing to take this image. Another very lucky escape for the company!
Portsmouth News

Southdown's garage in Dane Road, Seaford was very fortunate to survive an attack by a low flying enemy aircraft on 5 November 1942. In this scene after the war Leyland Cub car 20 (ECD520) rests in more peaceful times alongside a vintage Austin car. The garage was closed in 1957 and replaced by larger premises in Claremont Road.
Glynn Kraemer-Johnson

In November 1939 the government agreed that shop windows could be dimly lit while restaurants, cinemas and theatres, and other places of entertainment could once again display an illuminated sign but these had to be extinguished when the air raid sirens sounded. In an attempt to help solve the issue of pedestrian and road accidents the government also gave permission for local authorities to introduce low density street lighting whereby a circle of diffused lighting of very low intensity was directed from street lights on to the ground – providing local councils were prepared to spend money to modify their lighting. These appeared in London in December 1939 and other areas soon followed but no night time lighting of any description was allowed within 12 miles of the south east coast thus excluding a large part of the Southdown operating area.

With a deteriorating war situation and danger of invasion along the South Coast it is not surprising that the offices used mainly for excursion bookings were closed during 1940. It is likely that some were used over the Easter holiday period when it was still possible for visitors to travel to the coastal towns and it is known that the Portsmouth Beach Committee agreed to existing tenants opening their Southsea booking offices at Easter. The following offices were affected:

BRIGHTON	Aquarium Kiosk, Palace Pier – reopened in 1946
	West Street Kiosk, Kings Road
EASTBOURNE	Kiosk, Pier Gates Claremont Hotel, Cavendish Place
LITTLEHAMPTON	Kiosk, The Parade
SOUTHSEA	South Parade Pier Kiosk – reopened in 1946
	No 5 Kiosk near Canoe Lake – reopened in 1946
WORTHING	2 New Broadway, Tarring Road
	45 Marine Parade – reopened in 1946

In addition the office at Elmer Bus Stand at Bognor Regis was probably closed at the same time as it is not included in the August 1940 bus timetable. The office at 241 Albert Road in Southsea also probably closed early in the war and is not included in the London express leaflet for 1 December 1939. In postwar days Southdown often used coaches as roadside booking offices in and around some of the above locations which were not reopened.

At the Board Meeting on Thursday 14 March 1940 the Managing Director reported he had agreed to purchase the freehold property at 11, 11a & 12 Manchester Street, Brighton for the sum of £2,100. This marked the first of a number of wartime acquisitions in this area and at a Board Meeting on Wednesday 19 March 1941 the Managing Director reported agreement to purchase the property No 2 Manchester Street, Brighton for the sum of £1,750. The garage at Elm Grove on Hayling Island was requisitioned by the Ministry of Supply and leased to Airspeed Ltd from 18 October 1940 and was returned to Southdown use in 1946.

With the threat of a German invasion in summer 1940 the company's properties, especially in the coastal towns, had to be closely guarded at all times. All unattended motor vehicles had to be immobilised and stocks of fuel were reduced in vulnerable areas to avoid these aiding an invasion force. A number of overnight parking places are believed to have been used during the war although actual dates of use are uncertain. They were almost certainly rented sites designed to disperse the fleet away from the danger of air raids as well as saving unnecessary dead mileage and included:

COMPTON	Farm barn adjacent to The Square
EAST HOATHLY	Routh & Stevens yard
LOWER DICKER	Hellingly Garage
SINGLETON	Location unknown

The Traffic Regulators Kiosk at South Parade, Southsea was closed on 20 November 1940 as all bus services had been curtailed at The Circle and was reopened from 19 November 1944 when services returned to South Parade Pier again. To promote its 'coach cruise' programme and London express services Southdown had maintained an office in the capital for many years. With little prospect of a return to normality it was decided at a Board Meeting on Thursday 29 August 1940 to give notice to terminate the lease of the office at 27 Princes Street, Hanover Square, London W1 as from the 25 December 1940. It is possible that the office effectively closed for normal business somewhat earlier in 1940 and after the war the company relied on the London Coastal Coaches network of agents in the London area.

In addition to the onerous tasks associated with maintaining an ageing fleet in wartime, Portslade Works was required to carry out Munitions work on behalf of government departments and at a Board Meeting on Thursday 9 January 1941 it was recorded that work had been carried out to the value of £1,723. Also in January 1941 the company made a tax free loan to the government of £50,000 followed in April 1941 by a War Weapons Week donation of £26,000 which was subscribed by management and employees.

Southdown had no overnight parking in Fareham until 1941 but from July three double deckers were outstationed in the town. Following the severe bombing of Portsmouth overnight, vehicle dispersal was now a priority and in 1944 Southdown established its own garage for four double deckers on the east side of the Southern

Car 146 (CCD 946) is a Leyland Titan TD4c seen passing the impressive frontage of Southdown's Hilsea depot which was opened in 1934. After the war it is heading to Southsea via Commercial Road after being rebodied by Beadle with a new 5 bay highbridge body in April 1949. The offside advertising is for Handleys of Southsea, one of many important stores which were destroyed in the bombing raid on the night of 10/11 January 1941 but now open for business again.
Southdown Enthusiasts Club – Clark/Surfleet Collection

Railway's station approach. For similar reasons and to cope with increasing demand in the area, Southdown used a farm barn in East Street, Portchester from around July 1941 until 1949.

In September 1942 the interests of Tilling and BET in the holding company Tilling & British Automobile Traction Co Ltd were divided into separate Tilling and BET groupings. Southdown returned to the BET group and was therefore able to pursue its own independent vehicle purchasing policy unlike those companies which came under Tilling control. With the loss of the London express services the Licensed Restaurant and Bar at London Road, County Oak, Crawley closed after service on Tuesday 29 September 1942. It reopened on 22 March 1946 with the reintroduction of the London services.

Probably the luckiest escape of all for Southdown came soon after 1230 on Thursday 5 November 1942 during a raid on Seaford. A single German aircraft, flying at a height of just under 200 feet, crossed the coastline about a quarter of a mile west of Seaford College and discharged its load of four 500 kg HE bombs on to the town. The fourth bomb ricocheted off the concrete yard behind the Southdown Garage in Dane Road, damaging the council depot building before exploding at the foot of the railway embankment. The distance from the bus garage to the point where the bomb exploded was 148 feet and it made a crater approximately twelve feet in diameter and about six feet deep. No damage was recorded to the Southdown premises!

At the Board Meeting on Thursday 9 December 1943 the Managing Director reported the purchase of the Old Vicarage, North Street, Midhurst for £1,300 and that the Company had entered into an agreement with the Southern Railway Company to rent a piece of land at Fareham Station Goods Yard for the erection of a Garage at an annual rental of £50. At the Board Meeting on Friday 25 February 1944 he reported acceptance of the tender of Messrs Frank J Pridett Ltd for £1,600 for erection of a garage on the land rented from the Southern Railway at Fareham Goods Yard. In addition he reported the purchase by public auction of the freehold property at 2 St Vincent Street, Southsea for the sum of £250. Increasing passenger traffic in the Heathfield area prompted the company to open an enquiry office at Langston's Café in the High Street on Thursday 10 February 1944.

At the Board Meeting on Wednesday 30 August 1944 it was reported that agreement had been reached to purchase the freehold property at 23 Carfax in Horsham for the sum of £2,300. This was next door to the existing office and ideally placed close to the bus and coach stops. It opened on 18 February 1947 and became Southdown's busy enquiry, booking and parcels office in the town for many years to come. It was also reported that the company had agreed to purchase six freehold cottages in Palmers Road,

Emsworth for £1,250. The Managing Director reported agreement at the Board Meeting on Thursday 21 December 1944 to purchase the Goodwill, Assets, and Premises of Mr C G Walling of Eastergate, near Chichester who provided a service of motor buses under the title of Silver Queen Motor Bus Service for the sum of £13,000. Southdown acquired the Silver Queen services between Slindon and Bognor Regis along with the garage at Fontwell Avenue, Eastergate. The company continued to acquire property in the Manchester Street area of Brighton adjacent to its Head Office in Steine Street. At the Board Meeting held on Tuesday 26 June 1945 agreement was reported to purchase 4 Manchester Street in Brighton for £5,000 and further acquisitions were reported at the Board Meeting on Tuesday 16 October 1945. A Garage and Land at East Wittering was acquired for £800 and an office at 2 Cantelupe Road, East Grinstead for £700. The latter was adjacent to the existing office at 33 High Street and allowed for an enlargement of the premises.

From early 1946 an enquiry and booking office was opened at the Heroes of Waterloo Hotel at Waterlooville but only survived for around five years. In September 1946 a yard on the west side of London Road at Horndean was concreted over and from 28 April 1947 became known as Horndean Bus Stand serving the main A3 bus routes as well as the London express service. The former waiting room at the Ship & Bell was closed from 25 March 1947 and moved to Hayling Island where it served as a summer only enquiry office. The gravel surfaced Beachlands parking area gained a tarmac surface and became Beachlands Bus Station in June 1947. Finally, a new garage was opened in North Street, Midhurst in April 1947.

Southdown Staff at War

A full time all year round job with Southdown in the 1930s was something to be valued and many staff served with the company for many years. One of the many problems to beset Southdown at the outbreak of war was the sudden loss of experienced members of the staff – including many reservists – for service with the forces. The seasonal nature of Southdown's traffic along with a sharp reduction in non essential travel such as tours and excursions in the early weeks of the war probably enabled the company to maintain its services to the usual high standard. The fifty 'dual purpose' employees who worked on overhauls at Portslade during the winter but in summer transferred to the depots as drivers, conductors or tradesmen could be redeployed and other seasonal staff given the chance of permanent employment as vacancies occurred. Those who remained with Southdown, and others that could be recruited and trained, carried on gallantly with drivers and conductors forced to cope with all the difficulties of blackout conditions.

Before the outbreak of war the Air Ministry had forecast that Britain could be exposed to sudden air attacks by enemy night bombers causing high civilian casualties and mass destruction. To counter this threat it was widely agreed that if all man made lights visible from the air could be extinguished then the enemy bombers would find it difficult to navigate and pinpoint their targets. In July 1939, Public Information Leaflet No 2 warned civilians that everybody would need to play their part in ensuring that the regulations were properly enforced during the specified blackout periods. All windows, skylights, glazed doors or other openings would have to be screened with dark blinds or brown paper on the glass so that no light was visible from outside. They were advised to obtain any materials they may need for this purpose although no financial assistance was offered at this time.

Kerbs and bollards had been painted white when war threatened at the time of the Munich crisis in September 1938 and on Friday 1 September 1939, two days before the declaration of war, Britain was plunged into complete darkness as the sun set. At first, no light whatsoever was allowed on the streets. All street lighting was switched off and it became illegal to allow any light to show from a building after sunset. Even the red glow from a cigarette was banned, and a man who struck a match to look for his false teeth was fined ten shillings (50p)! Kerb edges were painted white. Pavement obstructions such as trees and lamp posts gained horizontal white stripes and traffic lights were fitted with blackout shields allowing only a small cross of light to be seen instead of the usual full circle. It was forbidden for vehicles to park facing the oncoming traffic at night and pedestrians were reminded that they should always walk facing the traffic and carry or wear something white.

From the very first day the blackout and reduced vehicle lighting gave rise to many problems for Southdown road staff. Despite a dramatic reduction in road traffic bus and coach drivers still had to manage for several hours each winter evening without street lighting and the illumination from familiar landmarks. The special headlight masks fitted from October 1939 only faintly illuminated passengers waiting on the pavement at bus stops. Apart from all the obvious hazards, such as other vehicles and pedestrians, there now appeared brick air raid shelters and military installations erected alongside many roads and drivers were expected to familiarise themselves with all these new obstructions. Particular difficulties must have been experienced by the driver/conductors of the few one man operated buses then in service. Conductors fared little better with the interior lighting of buses and coaches drastically reduced and often the stairs and platform area of double deckers unlit. This made fare collection very

difficult as conductors wrestled with the problems of identifying tickets and coins often aided only by low powered torches. It was inevitable that many costly mistakes would be made and, eventually, operators fitted masks to some bulbs while others were painted blue.

One official historian observed that the blackout 'transformed conditions of life more thoroughly than any other single feature of the war'. Putting in place blackout material every evening and removing it in the morning proved more time consuming than was first imagined and quickly became a tedious chore for most families and for transport workers, often working shifts including long hours of darkness, it was one more burden to be faced. The regulations were stringently enforced and there were harsh punishments for people who did not adhere to the rules. Anyone allowing a chink of light to be visible from the street would soon encounter an air raid warden or policeman knocking at their door leading in some cases to an appearance in court and a hefty fine. In 1940 300,000 people nationwide were taken to court for blackout offences and, although individuals might feel exasperated when reported for allowing a gleam of light, there was plenty of evidence that the general public felt that one person who failed to cover up a source of light was risking the safety of all by, in effect, shining a beacon for the expected German raiders. In the first days of the war it was even forbidden to use a torch during blackout hours but after 13 September this was allowed if it was masked by a double layer of tissue paper and with the weak beam aimed at the ground. Soon torch batteries were in short supply everywhere but if you were lucky enough to have them the torch could be used to hail a bus during the blackout and the Ministry of Information offered the following instructions:

'Shine your torch in a downwards direction so that the beam lights up your feet. As the bus approaches, switch the light of the torch on and off twice. Never shine the torch into the face of the bus driver. Do not shine your torch up at the destination board.'

In October 1939 the British government announced that all men aged between 18 and 41 who were not working in 'reserved occupations' could be called to join the armed services if required. As in the previous war bus drivers and conductors were not considered among the essential occupations, presenting Southdown with ongoing recruitment problems as the war developed. Conscription was by age and on Monday 1 October men aged between 20 and 23 were required to register to serve in one of the armed forces. As the war continued men from the other registered age groups received their 'call-up' papers requiring them to serve in the armed forces. Official government policy stubbornly refused to recognise the importance of public transport and to make it a 'reserved occupation', which would have meant the exemption from

Queuing became a fact of life in wartime Britain and strict regulations covering the formation of bus queues were introduced from April 1942. In this scene in Chapel Road, Worthing several men and women wait patiently at the bus stop on the left. I wonder if busy conductors always strictly enforced the law in such situations? On the right are the remains of Caffyns Garage damaged during a bombing raid on 14 September 1940 along with a concrete above ground shelter intended for anyone caught out in the street during alerts.
West Sussex County Council Library Service

war service of bus drivers, engineers and other essential employees. Eventually, in January 1941, after much pressure and a growing recognition of the essential role being played by the bus industry, the Ministry of Labour announced that all men with current permits or licences to drive public service vehicles, and who were available to act as drivers as and when required, would now be placed in the Schedule of Reserved Occupations. This brought with it additional responsibilities and in some parts of the country bus drivers were brought before the courts for excessive absenteeism and fined or even sent to prison.

It was reported at the Board Meeting on Thursday 30 November 1939 that the company had received a request from the employees for an increase in wages and a bonus to compensate for the increased cost of living arising out of the War. It was decided that no increase should be granted but that a bonus of 2/- per week be paid

towards the increased cost of living. But, by January 1940 employees were awarded an increase in wages of 4s a week following national negotiations between the TGWU and representatives of the employers. As a result of a ballot of the employees it was decided at a Board Meeting on Tuesday 9 September 1941 that the Company should enter into an agreement with the Transport & General Workers Union (TGWU) as to rates of pay and conditions of employment of drivers and conductors. It was reported at the Board Meeting on Thursday 22 January 1942 that the agreement between the Company and the TGWU had been signed.

There was plenty to occupy the depleted Southdown staff and one of the first tasks was to handle the distribution of thousands of child evacuees sent mainly from London to the safety of the Sussex towns and villages. Their stay proved to be short lived and in July 1940 the London evacuees were transferred elsewhere followed by large numbers of local children, mothers and old people as the South Coast itself prepared to face the enemy. As the war developed many new challenges faced Southdown's staff. Some drivers manned the coaches specially converted to ambulances which were used in dispersing the sick and wounded at the time of the Dunkirk evacuation. After Dunkirk the large number of Service personnel stationed in the Southdown area required the provision of vehicles at all hours of the day and night for troop movements as well as others to cater for recreational facilities for the camps. This work called for the willing co-operation of drivers and conductors which was readily forthcoming. Following the Portsmouth blitz many extra journeys had to be provided each day to disperse essential workers to dormitory areas outside the city and away from the danger of bombing. From the Battle of Britain until the end of the 'Hit and Run' raids Southdown buses were liable to attacks from enemy aircraft and it must have been a scary experience working a slow moving bus on service 12 up the hill from Exceat Bridge towards Friston while German fighter-bombers roamed the skies above.

To help beat the growing queues Southdown converted sixty 1400 class Leyland Tiger saloons to perimeter seating allowing 30 standing passengers which must have proved challenging for conductors especially in blackout conditions. Coaches were engaged on long term contract to the E.N.S.A. organisation conveying concert parties from camp to camp throughout the country and often being away for weeks at a time. Later drivers had to cope with the vagaries of handling buses towing the producer gas units designed to help save dwindling supplies of liquid fuel. To meet fuel rationing service frequencies were reduced but with private motoring restricted and eventually banned completely, passenger loadings soon rose rapidly. Mileage decreased from 22 million miles in 1939 to less than 16 million in 1944 despite an increase in passengers from 60 million to 90 million over the same period. But despite frequent air raids in towns such as Eastbourne and Brighton, the blitz suffered by Portsmouth, and with the Battle of Britain fought partly over the skies of Sussex, the casualties to Southdown vehicles, property and staff were remarkably light. As recounted in chapter 8 the worst single incident occurred on the evening of 2 November 1940 when Leyland Tiger car 1443 was blown up near Rushlake Green killing five passengers and the conductor.

Douglas Mackenzie who had been a member of the Southdown board since 1915 died in December 1944. He had been Traffic Manager between 1915 and 1938 and had strongly influenced the development of the company throughout his long period in office.

Of those members of the staff who served with the Forces – 987 out of a prewar total of 2,500 – 27 were killed or missing and 16 taken prisoner with the majority of those who survived returning to the company's service after demobilisation. The end of hostilities marked the start of a very hectic period for Southdown. With houses, televisions, cars and most other consumer goods in short supply for years to come, conditions were ideal for transport companies. The South Coast resorts once again attracted many thousands of day trippers and holidaymakers keen to visit the seaside after almost six long years of war. British demobilisation began on 18 June 1945 and wartime controls on labour finally ended on 20 December 1945. As vehicles and staff became available bus and coach services were rapidly expanded and by 1948 passenger traffic reached an all time peak of 142 million – more than double the prewar level of 60 million. At the same time the mileage operated had advanced from the wartime level of 1944 but by less than 50% above the 1939 figure.

Conductresses

Given the severe manpower problems arising from the loss of so many experienced staff, the employment of women came surprisingly slowly and it was not until 1942 that Southdown began the recruitment of conductresses. The Industrial Court had issued guidelines for their employment in April 1940, just seven months after the war had started. Women conductors had to be aged over 18 and could earn 90% of the male wage, until they were 21 when they were to

Car 307 (AJG 37) is a diesel engined Leyland Titan TD5 with Park Royal lowbridge body new to East Kent in March 1939 which arrived on loan to Southdown on 3 July 1940 at a particularly dark period of the war. It appears to be in fully lined green and cream livery and has gained a Southdown nameplate on the radiator. Note the radiator cap with temperature gauge which was a feature of some East Kent vehicles. For most of their stay with Southdown the East Kent Titans were based in Worthing and, due to strict Defence Regulations, photography was very rare. Seen at the East Worthing terminus of service 4, the smiling conductress is equipped with a TIM ticket machine which was Southdown's standard at the time. Even in wartime a bus ride up to the tea gardens at High Salvington was a popular choice for those who remained in Worthing. With the evacuated residents returning to Kent AJG 37 finally returned home on 4 September 1945.
Southdown Enthusiasts Club – Clark/Surfleet Collection

receive the same pay as men – an early example of equal pay. Their guaranteed week could be 40 hours compared with the standard then of 48, so in many cases it was unequal pay biased in favour of women. Portsmouth Corporation trained women to drive trolleybuses as well as employing 120 as conductresses starting from as early as June 1940. By November 1941 some 40 women were employed by Brighton, Hove and District as conductresses. During 1941 single women aged between 20 and 30 were conscripted and, although women did not take part in the fighting they were required to take up work in reserved occupations – especially factories and farming – which enabled men to be drafted into the services.

By 1943 nearly 90 out of every 100 men previously employed as bus conductors had been replaced by women, who now represented over one third of the total personnel of the bus companies compared to less than 10% in 1939. Although it is accepted that women successfully filled many jobs previously undertaken by men, contemporary reports suggest that in some areas of the country there were high levels of absenteeism among conductresses. Cuts to off peak services due to fuel and rubber shortages meant that a much greater proportion of 'spreadover' shifts were required by 1942. Trying to provide the best possible service despite blackout conditions, air raids, depleted staffs and a limited supply of ageing vehicles, meant that bus work was not very attractive in war conditions. The rewards were already beginning to fall behind the level of wages that could now be earned in industry and as a result transport workers were never to regain the position of importance in the employment league which they had enjoyed before the war. Wage rises were strictly controlled and described as 'War Bonus', this amount always being shown separately from the basic prewar wage. In February 1943, the Minister of Labour announced that 'mobile' women acting as conductors – those with no domestic ties who could move around the country – would be liable to be called up for factory work. Although transport was classed as vital war work, the demands of war factories had to be met before young women were allowed to take work as conductresses.

Home Guard

The Local Defence Volunteer organisation, formed on Tuesday 14 May 1940, was an attempt to bolster the defence of the British Isles against the threatened German invasion from the continent. Consisting of those too old or too young to fight with the Regular Armed Forces, the Home Guard is nowadays often seen as a farcical episode in British history thanks to the popular television comedy series 'Dad's Army' but in the dark days of 1940 the situation appeared desperate, and the threat from across the English Channel, very real. The first recorded patrols were sent out by what later became the Worthing Battalion of the Sussex Home Guard just twenty four hours after the appeal for volunteers was broadcast by Secretary of State for War, Anthony Eden. This no doubt provided the inspiration for Southdown's traffic manager to approach the Local Defence Volunteer Commander and suggest setting up within the Company a separate unit composed of employees and Southdown vehicles. As a result, the traffic manager became Lt Col Alexander H. Burman, officer commanding the 12th Sussex (Southdown Motor Transport) Battalion which eventually attracted over 1,000 employees.

Although the protection of the company's properties and vehicles was obviously of great importance Lt Col Burman realised that Southdown was in a position to be able to provide transport for regular troops in an emergency. He therefore approached the LDV Commanders in East and West Sussex for permission to establish a separate Motorised Transport Battalion although sanction was not given until January 1941. Until then Southdown's LDV/Home Guard carried out the same duties as those units raised in towns and villages across the country. On 31 July 1940 the name of the new force was officially changed to 'Home Guard' on the instructions of Winston Churchill who felt that the original name was uninspiring. In the early days uniforms and equipment were scarce and 'Uniform' often consisted of just an armband with 'LDV' or 'Home Guard' on it, a steel helmet and military respirator – if there were enough to go round. Obsolete military rifles gradually replaced privately owned shotguns, pitchforks, and 'pikes' – a long bayonet welded onto the end of a steel pipe. Eventually proper battledress uniforms and military style equipment was introduced as and when they became available.

Among the duties allocated to Southdown men was a night duty from about 2000 until about 0600 at each garage and where possible this was arranged to coincide with an early bus duty followed by a rest day. With the essential additional work there were many occasions, however, when a day on the buses followed a night on Home Guard duty. On quiet nights it was often possible to get a few hours sleep but air raid warnings could last for several hours and on these occasions any prospect of sleep was forgotten as the garage doors had to be opened up in case of bombs. As in 'Dad's Army', senior officers or NCOs were often working closely during the daytime with colleagues they commanded in the LDV/Home Guard. Whatever relationships existed at work, military protocol was strictly applied when on Home Guard duty. To encourage public interest in Southdown's Home Guard the Battalion held 'Home Guard Sundays' when members of the unit dressed in full Home Guard uniform were allowed to operate the buses.

With the Southdown Battalion spread over

such a large area it was rarely possible to get all the men together at any one time although training exercises were occasionally held at Company level and exercises were also held with regular troops as well as with other local Home Guard units. Throughout the darkest days of the war as many as 35 Southdown coaches were put at the disposal of numerous other Home Guard units during military manoeuvres. Although never relinquishing its duty to protect Southdown property the role of the company's Home Guard was to change somewhat once sanction had been given for the unit to become a Motorised Transport Battalion. In early 1942 the Battalion was placed under direct Army control with operational orders received directly from South Eastern Command. Members of the Battalion were liable to travel far from their Sussex homes on troop carrying duties and expected to take over from Companies of the RASC (Royal Army Service Corps) in the event of an emergency. By the beginning of 1943, the Battalion was able to call on more and more vehicles as local haulage firms offered their services to the Home Guard. As their more mobile role developed the Battalion was reorganised and in 1943 was designated as a Transport Column. Twenty six such Home Guard Transport Columns were formed in Britain, the

Sussex Column comprising five Companies based at the main Southdown garages at Eastbourne, Brighton, Worthing, Bognor and Hilsea (which is of course in Hampshire). Training was now adapted to more specifically meet the unit's developing role with instructors from the RASC being attached in May 1943. Members of the Sussex Column potentially had to operate many miles from Sussex and training also had to include such areas as cooking, static and mobile defence and anti-aircraft work as well as the more usual Home Guard duties. The work of troop carrying and transportation of ammunition and supplies became even more significant as D-Day approached although once the successful landings had taken place in June 1944 the need for Transport Columns began to decline as fears of a German invasion in Southern England were finally ended. The Sussex Transport Column was stood down at the end of 1944 with men from the Column taking part in the Stand Down parade in Brighton on 3 December 1944. In recognition of his work Lt Col Burman was awarded an OBE in January 1943.

Whatever their role, it is clear that for those engaged on essential work – including Southdown staff – 'staying on the Home Front' was not a very safe option.

And finally, a nice view of car 1472 (GCD 372) looking very smart in the sunshine beside Worthing garage. It was delivered in November 1939 as part of what proved to be the final batch of 1400 class Leyland Tiger buses for the company and survived until 1955 after having been rebuilt by Portsmouth Aviation in February 1949. What a pity none of these much admired buses survived into preservation!
Southdown Enthusiasts Club – Clark/Surfleet Collection

++ Denotes a coach converted for use as an Ambulance 8/39

1-2	ACD 101-2	LEYLAND CUB KP2	HARRINGTON C14F	1933
3-5	CUF 403-5	LEYLAND CUB KPZ1	HARRINGTON C14F	1936
7-9	DUF 7-9	LEYLAND CUB SKPZ2	PARK ROYAL B26R	1937
10-12	CUF 410-12	LEYLAND CUB SKPZ2	PARK ROYAL B26R	1936
13-15	CUF 313-5	LEYLAND CUB KP3A	PARK ROYAL B20F	1936
16-18	CUF 516-8	LEYLAND CUB KPZ2	PARK ROYAL B20F	1936
19-24	ECD 519-24	LEYLAND CUB KPZ2	PARK ROYAL B20F	1937
25-26	ECD 525-6	LEYLAND CUB KPZ2	PARK ROYAL B20F	1938
30-35	CCD 700-5	LEYLAND CUB KP3A	HARRINGTON C20F	1936
36-37	CUF 436-7	LEYLAND CUB KPZ2	HARRINGTON C20F	1936
38-54	DUF 38-54	LEYLAND CUB KPZ2	HARRINGTON C20F	1937
55-58	EUF 555-8	LEYLAND CUB KPZ4	HARRINGTON C20F	1938
80-81	FUF 180-1	DENNIS FALCON	HARRINGTON B30C	1939
100-111	BUF 200-11	LEYLAND TITAN TD4	SHORT L26/26R	1935
112-121	BUF 212-21	LEYLAND TITAN TD4c	SHORT H26/24R	1935
122-138	BUF 222-38	LEYLAND TITAN TD4	SHORT H26/24R	1935
139-144	CCD 939-44	LEYLAND TITAN TD4	BEADLE L26/26R	1936
145-150	CCD 945-50	LEYLAND TITAN TD4c	BEADLE H28/24R	1936
151-154	DUF 151-4	LEYLAND TITAN TD5	PARK ROYAL H26/26R	1937
155-180	EUF 155-80	LEYLAND TITAN TD5	PARK ROYAL L26/26R	1938
181-200	EUF 181-200	LEYLAND TITAN TD5	BEADLE L26/26R	1938
201-205	EUF 201-5	LEYLAND TITAN TD5	PARK ROYAL H26/26R	1938
206-211	FCD 506-11	LEYLAND TITAN TD5	PARK ROYAL H26/26R	1939
212-217	FCD 512-7	LEYLAND TITAN TD5	PARK ROYAL L26/26R	1939
218-227	FUF 218-27	LEYLAND TITAN TD5	PARK ROYAL H26/26R	1939
228-239	FUF 228-39	LEYLAND TITAN TD5	BEADLE H26/26R	1939
240-249	GCD 40-9	LEYLAND TITAN TD5	PARK ROYAL H26/26R	1939
301-306	UF 5849-54	LEYLAND LIONESS LTB1	HARRINGTON C20R	1930
307-311	UF 6507-11	LEYLAND LIONESS LTB1	HARRINGTON C20R	1930
312-317	UF 8826-31	LEYLAND LIONESS LTB1	HARRINGTON C20R	1933
318-323	CUF 318-23	LEYLAND TIGRESS RLTB3	BURLINGHAM C20C	1936
401-409	UF 1001-9	TILLING STEVENS B9B	HARRINGTON C30R (1935)	1926
415-416	UF 2015-6	TILLING STEVENS B9B	HARRINGTON C30R (1935)	1927
421/4	UF 2021/4	TILLING STEVENS B9B	HARRINGTON C30R (1935)	1927
426-430	UF 2026-30	TILLING STEVENS B9B	HARRINGTON C30R (1935)	1927
500-504	EUF 500-4	LEYLAND CHEETAH LZ3	PARK ROYAL C24C	1938
505-510	FUF 505-10	LEYLAND CHEETAH LZ4	PARK ROYAL C24C	1939
550-551	AUF 850-1	LEYLAND TIGER TS6T	SHORT B40C	1934
552-553	BUF 552-3	LEYLAND TIGER TS7T	SHORT B40C	1935
600	UF 4300	TILLING STEVENS B10A2	SHORT O24/24RO	1929
640	UF 4240	TILLING STEVENS B10A2	HARRINGTON B30R	1929
647	UF 4647	TILLING STEVENS B10A2	SHORT B31R	1929
650	UF 4650	TILLING STEVENS B10A2	SHORT B31R	1929
663	UF 4663	TILLING STEVENS B10A2	SHORT B31R	1929
665	UF 5065	TILLING STEVENS B10A2	SHORT B31R	1929
669-671	UF 5069-71	TILLING STEVENS B10A2	SHORT B31R	1929
672-673	UF 5072-3	TILLING STEVENS B10A2	HARRINGTON B31R	1929
675	UF 5075	TILLING STEVENS B10A2	HARRINGTON B31R	1929
679	UF 5679	TILLING STEVENS B10A2	SHORT B31R	1929
680	UF 5680	TILLING STEVENS B10A2	HARRINGTON B31R	1930
683-685	UF 5683-5	TILLING STEVENS B10A2	SHORT B31R	1929
686-688	UF 5686-8	TILLING STEVENS B10A2	HARRINGTON B31R	1930
689	UF 5689	TILLING STEVENS B10A2	SHORT B31R	1929
690	UF 6590	TILLING STEVENS B10A2	SHORT B31R	1930
692-696	UF 6592-6	TILLING STEVENS B10A2	SHORT B31R	1930
699-701	UF 6599-6601	TILLING STEVENS B10A2	SHORT B31R	1930
702-707	UF 6802-7	TILLING STEVENS B10A2	SHORT B31R	1930
709	UF 6809	TILLING STEVENS B10A2	SHORT B31R	1930

710-715	UF 7310-5	TSM B10A2	SHORT B26R	1931
716-721	ACD 116-21	TSM B39A6	SHORT B26R	1933
723	UF 5423	TILLING STEVENS B10B2	HARRINGTON C30R (1934)	1929
724-726	UF 5827-9	TILLING STEVENS B10B2	HARRINGTON C30R (1934)	1930
727-732	UF 5830-5	TILLING STEVENS B10B2	HARRINGTON C30R (1934)	1929
733	UF 5836	TILLING STEVENS B10B2	HARRINGTON C30R (1934)	1930
734	UF 5734	TILLING STEVENS B10B2	HARRINGTON C30R (1934)	1929
764-769	UF 6664-9	TILLING STEVENS B10B2	HARRINGTON C30R (1934)	1930
801-823	UF 4801-23	LEYLAND TITAN TD1	BRUSH O27/24R	1929
868-872	UF 6468-72	LEYLAND TITAN TD1	LEYLAND H24/24R	1930
874/6	UF 6474/6	LEYLAND TITAN TD1	LEYLAND H24/24R	1930
891/4/9	UF 7391/4/9	LEYLAND TITAN TD1	SHORT H26/24R	1931
900/8	UF 7400/8	LEYLAND TITAN TD1	SHORT H26/24R	1931
914/7/9	UF 7414/7/9	LEYLAND TITAN TD1	SHORT H26/24R	1931
921/6/8	UF 7421/6/8	LEYLAND TITAN TD1	SHORT H26/24R	1931
931-932	UF 7431-2	LEYLAND TITAN TD1	SHORT H26/24R	1931
933-943	UF 8373-83	LEYLAND TITAN TD1	SHORT H26/24R	1932
944-949	UF 8844-9	LEYLAND TITAN TD2	SHORT H26/24R	1932
950-959	UF 8850-9	LEYLAND TITAN TD2	SHORT H26/24R	1933
960-963	AUF 660-3	LEYLAND TITAN TD3c	SHORT H26/24R	1934
964-975	AUF 664-75	LEYLAND TITAN TD3	SHORT H26/24R	1934
1000	JK 1098	LEYLAND TIGER TS2	PARK ROYAL C32R (1935)	1930
1001-1002	UF 5741-2	LEYLAND TIGER TS2	HARRINGTON C32R (1935)	1930
1003-1005	UF 5803-5	LEYLAND TIGER TS2	HARRINGTON C32R (1935)	1930
1007-1008	UF 5807-8	LEYLAND TIGER TS2	HARRINGTON C32R (1936)	1930
1009	UF 5809	LEYLAND TIGER TS2	HARRINGTON C32R (1935)	1930
1010-1011	UF 5810-1	LEYLAND TIGER TS2	HARRINGTON C32R (1936)	1930
1016-1019	UF 6616-9	LEYLAND TIGER TS2	HARRINGTON C32R (1936)	1930
1021	UF 6621	LEYLAND TIGER TS2	HARRINGTON C32R (1936)	1930
1024	UF 6924	LEYLAND TIGER TS2	HARRINGTON C32R (1936)	1930
1026	UF 6926	LEYLAND TIGER TS2	HARRINGTON C32R (1936)	1930
1029	UF 7329	LEYLAND TIGER TS2	HARRINGTON C32R	1931
1030	UF 7330	LEYLAND TIGER TS2	HOYAL C32R	1931
1031-1033	UF 7331-3	LEYLAND TIGER TS2	HARRINGTON C32R	1931
1034	UF 7334	LEYLAND TIGER TS2	HOYAL C32R	1931
1035-1036	UF 7335-6	LEYLAND TIGER TS2	HARRINGTON C32R	1931
1037-1041	UF 7337-41	LEYLAND TIGER TS2	HOYAL C32R	1931
1042-1055	UF 7342-55	LEYLAND TIGER TS2	HARRINGTON C32R	1931
1061	JK 1266	LEYLAND TIGER TS2	PARK ROYAL C32R (1935)	1930
1062-1073	UF 8832-43	LEYLAND TIGER TS4	HARRINGTON C32R	1932
1074-1085	UF 9774-85	LEYLAND TIGER TS4	HARRINGTON C32R	1933
1086-1088	AUF 786-8	LEYLAND TIGER TS6	HARRINGTON C32R	1934
1089-1096	BCD 889-896	LEYLAND TIGER TS7	HARRINGTON C++R	1935
1097-1100	BCD 897-900	LEYLAND TIGER TS7	HARRINGTON C32R	1935
1101-1102	BUF 401-2	LEYLAND TIGER TS7	PARK ROYAL C++R	1935
1103	BUF 403	LEYLAND TIGER TS7	PARK ROYAL C32R	1935
1104	BUF 404	LEYLAND TIGER TS7	PARK ROYAL C++R	1935
1105	BUF 405	LEYLAND TIGER TS7	PARK ROYAL C32R	1935
1106	BUF 406	LEYLAND TIGER TS7	PARK ROYAL C++R	1935
1107-1112	BUF 407-12	LEYLAND TIGER TS7	HARRINGTON C++R	1935
1113-1115	CCD 713-5	LEYLAND TIGER TS7	HARRINGTON C++R	1935
1118-1119	CCD 718-9	LEYLAND TIGER TS7	HARRINGTON C32R	1935
1120	CCD 720	LEYLAND TIGER TS7	HARRINGTON C++R	1935
1121-1122	CCD 721-2	LEYLAND TIGER TS7	HARRINGTON C32R	1935
1123	CCD 723	LEYLAND TIGER TS7	HARRINGTON C++R	1935
1124	CCD 724	LEYLAND TIGER TS7	HARRINGTON C32R	1935
1125-1130	CCD 725-30	LEYLAND TIGER TS7	HARRINGTON C32R	1936
1131	CCD 731	LEYLAND TIGER TS7	BEADLE C++R	1936
1132-1133	CCD 732-3	LEYLAND TIGER TS7	HARRINGTON C32R	1936
1134-1144	CCD 734-44	LEYLAND TIGER TS7	BEADLE C32R	1936
1145-1146	CCD 745-6	LEYLAND TIGER TS7	HARRINGTON C26R	1936
1147-1150	CCD 747-50	LEYLAND TIGER TS7	HARRINGTON C32R	1936
1151-1159	CUF 151-9	LEYLAND TIGER TS7	BURLINGHAM C32R	1936
1160-1162	DUF 160-2	LEYLAND TIGER TS7	HARRINGTON C32R	1936

1163-1176	DUF 163-76	LEYLAND TIGER TS7	HARRINGTON C32R	1937
1177-1178	DUF 177-8	LEYLAND TIGER TS7	HARRINGTON C26R	1937
1179	DUF 179	LEYLAND TIGER TS7	HARRINGTON C32R	1937
1180-1181	DUF 180-1	LEYLAND TIGER TS8	HARRINGTON C32R	1937
1182-1205	EUF 82-105	LEYLAND TIGER TS8	HARRINGTON C32R	1938
1206-1210	EUF 106-10	LEYLAND TIGER TS8	PARK ROYAL C32R	1938
1211-1212	EUF 511-2	LEYLAND TIGER TS8	HARRINGTON C32R	1938
1213-1226	FUF 313-26	LEYLAND TIGER TS8	HARRINGTON C32R	1939
1400-1419	BUF 980-99	LEYLAND TIGER TS7	HARRINGTON DP32R	1935
1420-1423	CCD 30-3	LEYLAND TIGER TS7	HARRINGTON DP32R	1935
1424-1429	DCD 324-9	LEYLAND TIGER TS7	HARRINGTON DP32R	1936
1430-1441	FCD 30-41	LEYLAND TIGER TS8	HARRINGTON B32R	1938
1442-1465	FCD 242-65	LEYLAND TIGER TS8	HARRINGTON B32R	1938
1466-1467	FCD 366-7	LEYLAND TIGER TS8	HARRINGTON B34R	1938
1468-1469	FCD 368-9	LEYLAND TIGER TS8	HARRINGTON B34R	1939
1470	FCD 370	LEYLAND TIGER TS8	HARRINGTON B34R	1938
1471	FCD 371	LEYLAND TIGER TS8	HARRINGTON B34R	1939
T6	PO 1626	SHELVOKE & DREWRY	HICKMAN B20R	1930
T7	PO 1748	SHELVOKE & DREWRY	HICKMAN B20R	1930
T8	PO 1780	SHELVOKE & DREWRY	HARRINGTON B20R	1930
T9	PO 7706	SHELVOKE & DREWRY	HARRINGTON B26R	1933
T10	PO 8014	SHELVOKE & DREWRY	HARRINGTON B26R	1933
T11	PO 9665	SHELVOKE & DREWRY	HARRINGTON B26R	1934
T12	PO 9890	SHELVOKE & DREWRY	HARRINGTON B26R	1934
T15	APX 237	SHELVOKE & DREWRY	HARRINGTON B26R	1935
T16-17	FCD 16-7	SHELVOKE & DREWRY	HARRINGTON B26C	1938

DELIVERED AFTER 3 SEPTEMBER 1939

250	GCD 350	LEYLAND TITAN TD5	PARK ROYAL H26/26R	10/39
251	GCD 351	LEYLAND TITAN TD5	PARK ROYAL H26/26R	11/39
252	GCD 352	LEYLAND TITAN TD5	PARK ROYAL H26/26R	10/39
253	GCD 353	LEYLAND TITAN TD5	PARK ROYAL H26/26R	10/39
254	GCD 354	LEYLAND TITAN TD5	PARK ROYAL H26/26R	11/39
255	GCD 355	LEYLAND TITAN TD5	PARK ROYAL H26/26R	10/39
256	GCD 356	LEYLAND TITAN TD5	PARK ROYAL H26/26R	11/39
257	GCD 357	LEYLAND TITAN TD5	PARK ROYAL H26/26R	11/39
258	GCD 358	LEYLAND TITAN TD5	PARK ROYAL H26/26R	11/39
259	GCD 359	LEYLAND TITAN TD5	PARK ROYAL H26/26R	11/39
260	GCD 360	LEYLAND TITAN TD5	PARK ROYAL H26/26R	11/39
261	GCD 361	LEYLAND TITAN TD5	PARK ROYAL H26/26R	11/39
262	GCD 362	LEYLAND TITAN TD5	PARK ROYAL L26/26R	12/39
263	GCD 363	LEYLAND TITAN TD5	PARK ROYAL L26/26R	12/39
264	GCD 364	LEYLAND TITAN TD5	PARK ROYAL L26/26R	12/39
265	GCD 365	LEYLAND TITAN TD5	PARK ROYAL L26/26R	12/39
1472	GCD 372	LEYLAND TIGER TS8	HARRINGTON B32R	11/39
1473	GCD 373	LEYLAND TIGER TS8	HARRINGTON B32R	11/39
1474	GCD 374	LEYLAND TIGER TS8	HARRINGTON B32R	11/39
1475	GCD 375	LEYLAND TIGER TS8	HARRINGTON B32R	11/39
1476	GCD 376	LEYLAND TIGER TS8	HARRINGTON B32R	11/39
1477	GCD 377	LEYLAND TIGER TS8	HARRINGTON B32R	11/39
1478	GCD 378	LEYLAND TIGER TS8	HARRINGTON B32R	11/39
1479	GCD 379	LEYLAND TIGER TS8	HARRINGTON B32R	11/39
1480	GCD 380	LEYLAND TIGER TS8	HARRINGTON B32R	1/40
1481	GCD 381	LEYLAND TIGER TS8	HARRINGTON B32R	1/40
1482	GCD 382	LEYLAND TIGER TS8	HARRINGTON B32R	12/39
1483	GCD 383	LEYLAND TIGER TS8	HARRINGTON B32R	11/39
1484	GCD 384	LEYLAND TIGER TS8	HARRINGTON B32R	2/40
1485	GCD 385	LEYLAND TIGER TS8	HARRINGTON B32R	3/40

All services operate daily except where otherwise stated

Number	Route
1	Worthing Dome - Findon - Storrington
2	Worthing Dome - Findon - Horsham Station
3	East Worthing Ham Hotel - Worthing Station - Goring Church
4	High Salvington - Durrington - Worthing Station - East Worthing Brookdean Road
5	Worthing Pier - Thomas A'Becket - Offington Corner
6	Worthing Pier - South Farm Rd - Thomas A'Becket - Ringmer Road
7	Worthing Pier - Broadwater - Sompting - Lancing - Worthing Dome (Circular in both directions)
7A	Worthing Pier - Broadwater - Sompting - Lancing Manor
8	Worthing Pier - Broadwater - East Worthing Ham Hotel
9	Shoreham - Sussex Pad Hotel - Worthing - Littlehampton - Arundel
9A	Arundel - Littlehampton - Angmering-on-Sea
9B	Arundel - Littlehampton - Angmering on Sea - Angmering Village *(one late evening journey in this direction)*
10	Brighton Pool Valley - Shoreham - Sussex Pad Hotel - Worthing - Arundel Ford Road
11	Worthing Dome - Goring - Ferring-on-Sea South Drive
11A	North Ferring Corner - Ferring-on-Sea South Drive
12	Tongdean - Brighton Pool Valley - Newhaven - Seaford - Eastbourne
12A	Tongdean - Brighton Pool Valley - Peacehaven Annexe
12B	Brighton Station - Saltdean Mount
13	Brighton Pool Valley - Lewes County Hall
13A	Lewes Nevill Crescent - Newhaven
13B	Brighton Pool Valley - North Moulscombe
13C	Newhaven Bridge Street - Denton
13D	Newhaven Bridge St - East Side
	Newhaven Bridge St - Gibbons Road *(Friday, Saturday & Sunday evenings)*
13E	Brighton Pool Valley - East Moulscombe
13F	Brighton Pool Valley - Lower Bevendean Happy Valley
14	Brighton Pool Valley - Hurstpierpoint - Bolney - Haywards Heath Station
15	Eastbourne – Hailsham - Ninfield - Bexhill - Hastings *(Joint service with Maidstone & District)*
16	Brighton Pool Valley - Lewes - Laughton - Golden Cross
17	Brighton Pool Valley - Henfield - Cowfold - Horsham Carfax
18	Brighton Pool Valley - Lewes - Heathfield - Hawkhurst *(Joint service with Maidstone& District)*
20	Brighton Pool Valley - Lewes - Chailey Kings Head
21	Brighton Pool Valley - Southwick Town Hall - Buckingham Park - Shoreham Beach
21A	Southwick Town Hall - Buckingham Park -- Shoreham Station
21B	Brighton Pool Valley - Southwick Town Hall - Southlands Hospital - Shoreham Bridge *(Wednesday & Sunday afternoons)*
22	Brighton Pool Valley - Steyning - Pulborough - Petworth - Duncton Cricketers
23	Brighton Pool Valley - Ditchling - Haywards Heath Station
24	Brighton Pool Valley - Lewes - Ditchling - Hurstpierpoint - Brighton (Circular in both directions)
	Brighton Pool Valley - Lewes - Ditchling - Hurstpierpoint - Henfield *(Early and late journeys only)*
25	Brighton Pool Valley - Lewes - Eastbourne
26	Seaford - Litlington - Alfriston - Berwick Cross Roads
26A	Seaford - High and Over - Alfriston - Berwick Cross Roads - Eastbourne *(Summer only - no morning service)*
27	Brighton Pool Valley - Devil's Dyke Hotel - Poynings - Small Dole - Henfield George
28	Brighton Steine Street - Lewes - Chailey - Chelwood Gate - Forest Row - East Grinstead LIMITED STOP
29	Brighton Pool Valley - Lewes - Plumpton Station - Wivelsfield Green - Haywards Heath Station
30	Brighton Pool Valley - Burgess Hill - Haywards Heath Station - Chelwood Common
31	Brighton Pool Valley - Shoreham - Worthing - Littlehampton - Bognor - Chichester - Emsworth - Havant - Portsmouth Theatre Royal - Southsea South Parade Pier
31A	Emsworth - Havant - Fratton - Southsea South Parade Pier
31B	Havant - Portsmouth Theatre Royal - Southsea South Parade Pier *(Peak times and evenings)*
31C	Farlington - Portsmouth Theatre Royal - Southsea South Parade Pier *(Peak times and evenings)*
31F	Brighton Pool Valley - Shoreham - Lancing - Worthing Dome
31G	Brighton Pool Valley - Shoreham - Lancing - Worthing - Angmering-on-Sea
32	Brighton Pool Valley - Hove Station - Devil's Dyke Hotel *(Summer only)*
34	Hurstpierpoint Chinese Gardens Hotel - Hassocks Station
38	Southsea Clarence Pier - Wickham - Meonstoke (Two journeys extended each way to Hambledon)

39	Southsea South Parade Pier - Stakes - Waterlooville - Hambledon - Worlds End
40	Southsea South Parade Pier - Theatre Royal - Purbrook - Waterlooville - Clanfield - Petersfield
40B	Portsmouth Theatre Royal - Purbrook - Waterlooville - Clanfield Drift Road
41	Southsea South Parade Pier - Fratton - Purbrook - Waterlooville - Horndean
42	Southsea South Parade Pier - Theatre Royal - Purbrook - Waterlooville - Horndean - Petersfield
42B	Portsmouth Theatre Royal - Purbrook - Waterlooville - Horndean - Snell's Corner
43	Southsea South Parade Pier - Theatre Royal - Havant - Westbourne Cricketers OR Churchers Corner
44	Emsworth - Westbourne Square *(No morning service except one early journey on Monday to Saturday)*
45	Southsea South Parade Pier - Theatre Royal - Fareham - Warsash
	Southsea South Parade Pier - Theatre Royal - Castle Street - Fareham
	Southsea South Parade Pier - Fratton - Castle Street - Fareham
46	Hayling Ferry - Eastoke House *(Summer only)*
47	South Parade Pier - Fratton - Havant - Gable Head - Eastoke - Hayling Bus Station - Manor Corner - Havant - Fratton - South Parade Pier
	South Parade Pier - Fratton - Havant - Manor Corner - Hayling Bus Station - Eastoke - Gable Head - Havant - Fratton - South Parade Pier
	Havant - Northney - Gable Head - Eastoke - Hayling Bus Station - Manor Corner - Northney - Havant
	South Parade Pier - Theatre Royal - Havant - Eastoke House *(Summer only)*
48	Horndean - Havant Church - Waterlooville
50	Elmer - Bognor - Smarts Corner - Nyetimber - Pagham Beach
50A	Elmer - Bognor - Rose Green - Nyetimber (extended Summer only to Pagham Beach)
51	Bognor Bus Station - Linden Avenue - Aldwick Road - Bognor Bus Station. (Circular in both directions)
52	Chichester Station - Hunston - Sidlesham - Selsey Seal Road
	Chichester West Street - Donnington - Sidlesham - Selsey Seal Road
53	Chichester West Street - Birdham - East Wittering - West Wittering - Birdham - Chichester West Street (Circular in both directions)
	Chichester West Street - Birdham - Itchenor
54	Chichester West Street - Funtingdon - Churchers Corner - Compton
	Chichester West Street - Hambrook Post Office *(Saturdays)*
55	Aldwick Barrack Lane - Bognor - North Bersted
56	Chichester Railway Station - Old Bosham *(No Sunday morning service)*
57	Chichester West Street - Tangmere - Westergate - Bognor Pier
58	Chichester West Street - Singleton - East Dean
59	Bognor Railway Station - Chichester - Midhurst - Petworth
60	Midhurst - Rogate - Petersfield
61	Petersfield Station - South Harting - Elstead
62	Arundel - Walberton - Middleton on Sea - Bognor Pier *(Summer only)*
63	Horsham Station - Billingshurst - Petworth - Halnaker - Chichester Railway Station
64	Chichester West Street - Barnham - Ford Aerodrome
65	Littlehampton - Arundel - Amberley - Storrington
66	Arundel - Slindon - Chichester - Summersdale
68	Arundel - Littlehampton - Cemetery - Rustington Church - Albert Road - Cemetery - Littlehampton - Arundel
68A	Arundel - Littlehampton - Cemetery - Albert Road - Rustington Church - Cemetery - Littlehampton - Arundel
69	Littlehampton - Arundel - Pulborough - Billingshurst - Horsham Station
70	Storrington - West Chiltington Village - Pulborough Station
71	Storrington - Thakeham Cross Roads
72	Horsham The Common - Carfax - Highlands Estate
72B	Horsham Carfax - The Common *(Saturday afternoons and evenings)*
73	Horsham The Common - Carfax - St. Leonards Hotel
75	Horsham Carfax - Barns Green - Coolham - Shipley OR Billingshurst
78	Slinfold - Horsham - Handcross
79	Slinfold - Horsham - Handcross - Balcombe *(Wednesday, Saturday & Sunday)*
80	Horsham Carfax - West Grinstead - Partridge Green - Steyning White Horse
81	Haywards Heath Station - Bolney - Cowfold - Billingshurst
82	Haywards Heath Station - Cuckfield - Handcross - Crawley
83	Haywards Heath Station - Warninglid - Horsham Carfax
84	Haywards Heath Station - New England Road - Haywards Heath Station (Circular service in both directions)
85	Haywards Heath Station - Sunte Avenue - Lindfield P.O.
86	Haywards Heath Station - Borde Hill - Balcombe - Stoney Lane
86A	Haywards Heath Station - Cuckfield - Balcombe
87	East Grinstead - Kingscote - West Hoathly - Ashdown Forest The Goat *(No Sunday morning service)*
88	Haywards Heath Station - Ardingly - Turners Hill
89	Haywards Heath Station - Chailey - Uckfield
90	Eastbourne Pevensey Road - Hailsham - Hellingly - Horam – Heathfield

91	Eastbourne Pevensey Road - Hailsham - Horam - Heathfield - Uckfield
92	Eastbourne Pevensey Road - Stone Cross - Hailsham - Uckfield - East Grinstead
	Eastbourne Pevensey Road - Hailsham - Upper Dicker
93	Eastbourne Langney Road - Wannock - Jevington
94	Eastbourne Langney Road - Polegate - Dittons Wood Corner
95	Eastbourne Pevensey Road - Stone Cross - Hailsham - Rushlake Green - Heathfield *(extended afternoons and evenings to Waldron)*
96	Eastbourne Pevensey Road - Stone Cross - Pevensey Bay
97	Eastbourne Royal Parade - Beachy Head Hotel
98	Eastbourne Pevensey Road - Pevensey Bay - Pevensey Old Mint House
99	Eastbourne Pevensey Road - Pevensey Bay - Pevensey - Bexhill - Hastings *(Joint service with M&D)*
119	Brighton Pool Valley - Lewes - Uckfield - Maresfield OR Five Ash Down - Crowborough - Tunbridge Wells *(Joint service with Maidstone & District)*
T1	Worthing Splash Point - West Worthing Station - Library
T2	Worthing Splash Point - Grand Avenue - West Worthing Station

SPECIAL HOSPITAL SERVICES

Hove Station - Brighton Pool Valley - Lewes - Golden Cross - Hellingly Hospital
Alfriston Cross - Berwick - Hailsham - Hellingly Hospital
East Grinstead - Uckfield - Golden Cross - Hellingly Hospital
Hurstpierpoint - Ditchling - Lewes - Hellingly Hospital
Seaford - Eastbourne - Hellingly Hospital
Hastings - Bexhill - Hailsham - Hellingly Hospital
(Hellingly services operate every Tuesday, alternate Wednesdays and on the first Sunday of each month except for the Hurstpierpoint service which does not run on Tuesdays)

EXPRESS SERVICES

Eastbourne Royal Parade - Hailsham - Uckfield - East Grinstead - Caterham - London Victoria
Eastbourne Cavendish Place - Seaford - Lewes - East Grinstead - Caterham - London Victoria *(Summer)*
Brighton - Bolney - Handcross - Crawley - Redhill - London Victoria
Brighton - Henfield - Handcross - Crawley - Redhill - London Victoria *(Wednesdays)*
Brighton - Burgess Hill - Cuckfield - Handcross - Crawley - Redhill - London Victoria
Littlehampton - Worthing - Horsham - Crawley - Redhill - London Victoria
Worthing - Horsham - Dorking - Kingston - London Victoria *(All year))* - Kings Cross *(Summer)*
Bognor - Littlehampton - Arundel - Petworth - Dorking - Sutton - London Victoria
Bognor - Chichester - Guildford - Kingston - London Victoria
Hayling Island - Havant - Guildford - Kingston - London Victoria *(Summer)*
Southsea - Portsmouth - Petersfield - Guildford - Kingston - London Victoria - Kings Cross
Gosport - Fareham - Alton - Aldershot - Staines - London Victoria
SOUTH COAST EXPRESS SERVICE Margate - Hastings - Brighton - Portsmouth - Bournemouth
Hove Station - Brighton - Lewes - Ringmer - Heathfield - Robertsbridge Darvell Hall Sanatorium *(Sundays)*
Robertsbridge Station - Robertsbridge Darvell Hall Sanatorium *(Sundays)*

+ Denotes vehicle in process of receiving new body at this date
++ Denotes a coach converted for use as an Ambulance 8/39

1-2	ACD 101-2	LEYLAND CUB KP2	HARRINGTON C14F	1933
3-5	CUF 403-5	LEYLAND CUB KPZ1	HARRINGTON C14F	1936
7-9	DUF 7-9	LEYLAND CUB SKPZ2	PARK ROYAL B26R	1937
10-12	CUF 410-12	LEYLAND CUB SKPZ2	PARK ROYAL B26R	1936
13-15	CUF 313-5	LEYLAND CUB KP3A	PARK ROYAL B20F	1936
16-18	CUF 516-8	LEYLAND CUB KPZ2	PARK ROYAL B20F	1936
19-24	ECD 519-24	LEYLAND CUB KPZ2	PARK ROYAL B20F	1937
25-26	ECD 525-6	LEYLAND CUB KPZ2	PARK ROYAL B20F	1938
30-35	CCD 700-5	LEYLAND CUB KP3A	HARRINGTON C20F	1936
36	CUF 436	LEYLAND CUB KPZ2	HARRINGTON C20F	1936
38	DUF 38	LEYLAND CUB KPZ2	HARRINGTON C20F	1937
40-45	DUF 40-5	LEYLAND CUB KPZ2	HARRINGTON C20F	1937
47-48	DUF 47-8	LEYLAND CUB KPZ2	HARRINGTON C20F	1937
50-54	DUF 50-4	LEYLAND CUB KPZ2	HARRINGTON C20F	1937
55-58	EUF 555-8	LEYLAND CUB KPZ4	HARRINGTON C20F	1938
80-81	FUF 180-1	DENNIS FALCON	HARRINGTON B30C	1939
100-111	BUF 200-11	LEYLAND TITAN TD4	SHORT L26/26R	1935
112-121	BUF 212-21	LEYLAND TITAN TD4c	SHORT H26/24R	1935
122-138	BUF 222-38	LEYLAND TITAN TD4	SHORT H26/24R	1935
139-144	CCD 939-44	LEYLAND TITAN TD4	BEADLE L26/26R	1936
145-150	CCD 945-50	LEYLAND TITAN TD4c	BEADLE H28/24R	1936
151-154	DUF 151-4	LEYLAND TITAN TD5	PARK ROYAL H26/26R	1937
155-180	EUF 155-80	LEYLAND TITAN TD5	PARK ROYAL L26/26R	1938
181-200	EUF 181-200	LEYLAND TITAN TD5	BEADLE L26/26R	1938
201-205	EUF 201-5	LEYLAND TITAN TD5	PARK ROYAL H26/26R	1938
206-211	FCD 506-11	LEYLAND TITAN TD5	PARK ROYAL H26/26R	1939
212-217	FCD 512-7	LEYLAND TITAN TD5	PARK ROYAL L26/26R	1939
218-227	FUF 218-27	LEYLAND TITAN TD5	PARK ROYAL H26/26R	1939
228-239	FUF 228-39	LEYLAND TITAN TD5	BEADLE H26/26R	1939
240-249	GCD 40-9	LEYLAND TITAN TD5	PARK ROYAL H26/26R	1939
250-261	GCD 350-61	LEYLAND TITAN TD5	PARK ROYAL H26/26R	1939
262-265	GCD 362-5	LEYLAND TITAN TD5	PARK ROYAL L26/26R	1939
307-308	AJG 37-8	LEYLAND TITAN TD5	PARK ROYAL L27/26R	1939
322	AJG 22	LEYLAND TITAN TD5	PARK ROYAL L27/26R	1939
324	AJG 24	LEYLAND TITAN TD5	PARK ROYAL L27/26R	1939
326-329	AJG 26-9	LEYLAND TITAN TD5	PARK ROYAL L27/26R	1939
400-401	GCD 974-5	GUY ARAB I 5LW	N. COUNTIES L27/28R	1943
402	GCD 976	GUY ARAB II 5LW	STRACHAN L27/28R	1943
403-404	GCD 689-90	GUY ARAB II 5LW	STRACHAN L27/28R	1943
405-406	GCD 691-2	GUY ARAB II 6LW	STRACHAN H30/26R	1944
407	GUF 37	GUY ARAB II 6LW	STRACHAN H30/26R	1944
408-409	GUF 68-9	GUY ARAB II 6LW	PARK ROYAL H30/26R	1944
410-413	GUF 70-3	GUY ARAB II 5LW	PARK ROYAL H30/26R	1944
414-415	GUF 74-5	GUY ARAB II 5LW	WEYMANN L27/28R	1944
416-423	GUF 116-23	GUY ARAB II 6LW	N. COUNTIES H30/26R	1944
424-426	GUF 124-6	GUY ARAB II 6LW	N. COUNTIES H30/26R	1945
427-441	GUF 127-141	GUY ARAB II 5LW	N. COUNTIES H30/26R	1944
442-443	GUF 142-3	GUY ARAB II 6LW	PARK ROYAL H30/26R	1944
444-445	GUF 144-5	GUY ARAB II 5LW	PARK ROYAL H30/26R	1944
446-447	GUF 146-7	GUY ARAB II 6LW	PARK ROYAL H30/26R	1945
448-451	GUF 188-91	GUY ARAB II 5LW	N. COUNTIES H30/26R	1945
452-462	GUF 152-62	GUY ARAB II 5LW	N. COUNTIES H30/26R	1945
500-504	EUF 500-4	LEYLAND CHEETAH LZ3	PARK ROYAL C24C	1938
505-510	FUF 505-10	LEYLAND CHEETAH LZ4	PARK ROYAL C24C	1939
550-551	AUF 850-1	LEYLAND TIGER TS6T	SHORT B40C	1934
552-553	BUF 552-3	LEYLAND TIGER TS7T	SHORT B40C	1935
801-809	UF 4801-9	LEYLAND TITAN TD1	BRUSH H27/24RO	1929

810	UF 4810	LEYLAND TITAN TD1	BRUSH O27/24RO	1929
811-823	UF 4811-23	LEYLAND TITAN TD1	BRUSH H27/24RO	1929
871/4/6	UF 6471/4/6	LEYLAND TITAN TD1	PARK ROYAL H26/26R (1943)	1930
937-939	UF 8377-9	LEYLAND TITAN TD1	PARK ROYAL H28/24R (1943)	1932
940/2	UF 8380/2	LEYLAND TITAN TD1	EAST LANCS H26/26R (1944)	1932
946	UF 8846	LEYLAND TITAN TD2	WILLOWBROOK L27/24R (1943)	1932
947	UF 8847	LEYLAND TITAN TD2	EAST LANCS H26/26R (1945)+	1932
949	UF 8849	LEYLAND TITAN TD2	WILLOWBROOK L27/24R (1943)	1932
950	UF 8850	LEYLAND TITAN TD2	EAST LANCS H26/26R (1945)+	1933
951	UF 8851	LEYLAND TITAN TD2	WILLOWBROOK L27/24R (1944)	1933
952	UF 8852	LEYLAND TITAN TD2	EAST LANCS H26/26R (1945)	1933
953	UF 8853	LEYLAND TITAN TD2	WILLOWBROOK L27/24R (1944)	1933
954-955	UF 8854-5	LEYLAND TITAN TD2	EAST LANCS H26/26R (1944)	1933
956	UF 8856	LEYLAND TITAN TD2	EAST LANCS H26/26R (1945)+	1933
957	UF 8857	LEYLAND TITAN TD2	WILLOWBROOK L27/24R (1944)	1933
958	UF 8858	LEYLAND TITAN TD2	EAST LANCS H26/26R (1945)+	1933
959	UF 8859	LEYLAND TITAN TD2	EAST LANCS H26/26R (1944)	1933
960-963	AUF 660-3	LEYLAND TITAN TD3c	SHORT H26/24R	1934
964-975	AUF 664-75	LEYLAND TITAN TD3	SHORT H26/24R	1934
1001-1002	UF 5741-2	LEYLAND TIGER TS2	HARRINGTON C32R (1935)	1930
1003-1005	UF 5803-5	LEYLAND TIGER TS2	HARRINGTON C32R (1935)	1930
1008	UF 5808	LEYLAND TIGER TS2	HARRINGTON C32R (1936)	1930
1009	UF 5809	LEYLAND TIGER TS2	HARRINGTON C32R (1935)	1930
1010-1011	UF 5810-1	LEYLAND TIGER TS2	HARRINGTON C32R (1936)	1930
1016-1019	UF 6616-9	LEYLAND TIGER TS2	HARRINGTON C32R (1936)	1930
1021	UF 6621	LEYLAND TIGER TS2	HARRINGTON C32R (1936)	1930
1024	UF 6924	LEYLAND TIGER TS2	HARRINGTON C32R (1936)	1930
1026	UF 6926	LEYLAND TIGER TS2	HARRINGTON C32R (1936)	1930
1029	UF 7329	LEYLAND TIGER TS2	HARRINGTON C32R	1931
1030	UF 7330	LEYLAND TIGER TS2	HOYAL C32R	1931
1038-1039	UF 7338-9	LEYLAND TIGER TS2	HOYAL C32R	1931
1042	UF 7342	LEYLAND TIGER TS2	HARRINGTON C32R	1931
1054-1055	UF 7354-5	LEYLAND TIGER TS2	HARRINGTON C32R	1931
1061	JK 1266	LEYLAND TIGER TS2	PARK ROYAL C32R (1935)	1930
1079	UF 9779	LEYLAND TIGER TS4	HARRINGTON C32R	1933
1086-1088	AUF 786-8	LEYLAND TIGER TS6	HARRINGTON C32R	1934
1090-1091	BCD 890-1	LEYLAND TIGER TS7	HARRINGTON C++R	1935
1093-1096	BCD 893-6	LEYLAND TIGER TS7	HARRINGTON C++R	1935
1097-1100	BCD 897-900	LEYLAND TIGER TS7	HARRINGTON C32R	1935
1101-1102	BUF 401-2	LEYLAND TIGER TS7	PARK ROYAL C++R	1935
1103	BUF 403	LEYLAND TIGER TS7	PARK ROYAL C32R	1935
1104	BUF 404	LEYLAND TIGER TS7	PARK ROYAL C++R	1935
1105	BUF 405	LEYLAND TIGER TS7	PARK ROYAL C32R	1935
1106	BUF 406	LEYLAND TIGER TS7	PARK ROYAL C++R	1935
1107-1112	BUF 407-12	LEYLAND TIGER TS7	HARRINGTON C++R	1935
1113-1115	CCD 713-5	LEYLAND TIGER TS7	HARRINGTON C++R	1935
1118-1119	CCD 718-9	LEYLAND TIGER TS7	HARRINGTON C32R	1935
1120	CCD 720	LEYLAND TIGER TS7	HARRINGTON C++R	1935
1121-1122	CCD 721-2	LEYLAND TIGER TS7	HARRINGTON C32R	1935
1123	CCD 723	LEYLAND TIGER TS7	HARRINGTON C++R	1935
1124	CCD 724	LEYLAND TIGER TS7	HARRINGTON C32R	1935
1125-1126	CCD 725-30	LEYLAND TIGER TS7	HARRINGTON C32R	1936
1128-1129	CCD 728-9	LEYLAND TIGER TS7	HARRINGTON C32R	1936
1131	CCD 731	LEYLAND TIGER TS7	BEADLE C++R	1936
1132-1133	CCD 732-3	LEYLAND TIGER TS7	HARRINGTON C32R	1936
1134-1144	CCD 734-44	LEYLAND TIGER TS7	BEADLE C32R	1936
1145-1146	CCD 745-6	LEYLAND TIGER TS7	HARRINGTON C26R	1936
1147-1149	CCD 747-9	LEYLAND TIGER TS7	HARRINGTON C32R	1936
1151-1159	CUF 151-9	LEYLAND TIGER TS7	BURLINGHAM C32R	1936
1166	DUF 166	LEYLAND TIGER TS7	HARRINGTON C32R	1937
1173	DUF 173	LEYLAND TIGER TS7	HARRINGTON C32R	1937
1177-1178	DUF 177-8	LEYLAND TIGER TS7	HARRINGTON C26R	1937
1179	DUF 179	LEYLAND TIGER TS7	HARRINGTON C32R	1937

1180-1181	DUF 180-1	LEYLAND TIGER TS8	HARRINGTON C32R	1937
1182-1184	EUF 82-84	LEYLAND TIGER TS8	HARRINGTON C32R	1938
1186-1192	EUF 86-92	LEYLAND TIGER TS8	HARRINGTON C32R	1938
1194-1198	EUF 94-98	LEYLAND TIGER TS8	HARRINGTON C32R	1938
1201-1205	EUF 101-5	LEYLAND TIGER TS8	HARRINGTON C32R	1938
1206-1210	EUF 106-10	LEYLAND TIGER TS8	PARK ROYAL C32R	1938
1211-1212	EUF 511-2	LEYLAND TIGER TS8	HARRINGTON C32R	1938
1213-1226	FUF 313-26	LEYLAND TIGER TS8	HARRINGTON C32R	1939
1400-1402	BUF 980-2	LEYLAND TIGER TS7	HARRINGTON DP32R	1935
1403-1404	BUF 983-4	LEYLAND TIGER TS7	HARRINGTON B30R	1935
1405-1406	BUF 985-6	LEYLAND TIGER TS7	HARRINGTON DP32R	1935
1407	BUF 987	LEYLAND TIGER TS7	HARRINGTON B30R	1935
1408	BUF 988	LEYLAND TIGER TS7	HARRINGTON DP32R	1935
1409	BUF 989	LEYLAND TIGER TS7	HARRINGTON B30R	1935
1410	BUF 990	LEYLAND TIGER TS7	HARRINGTON DP32R	1935
1411-1414	BUF 991-4	LEYLAND TIGER TS7	HARRINGTON B30R	1935
1415	BUF 995	LEYLAND TIGER TS7	HARRINGTON DP32R	1935
1416-1418	BUF 996-8	LEYLAND TIGER TS7	HARRINGTON B30R	1935
1419	BUF 999	LEYLAND TIGER TS7	HARRINGTON DP32R	1935
1420-1422	CCD 30-2	LEYLAND TIGER TS7	HARRINGTON B30R	1935
1423	CCD 33	LEYLAND TIGER TS7	HARRINGTON DP32R	1935
1424-1425	DCD 324-5	LEYLAND TIGER TS7	HARRINGTON DP32R	1936
1426-1428	DCD 326-8	LEYLAND TIGER TS7	HARRINGTON B30R	1936
1429	DCD 329	LEYLAND TIGER TS7	HARRINGTON DP32R	1936
1430-1431	FCD 30-1	LEYLAND TIGER TS8	HARRINGTON B30R	1938
1432-1433	FCD 32-3	LEYLAND TIGER TS8	HARRINGTON B32R	1938
1434-1441	FCD 34-41	LEYLAND TIGER TS8	HARRINGTON B30R	1938
1442	FCD 242	LEYLAND TIGER TS8	HARRINGTON B30R	1938
1443	FCD 243	LEYLAND TIGER TS8	METCALFE C32C (1941)	1938
1444-1445	FCD 244-5	LEYLAND TIGER TS8	HARRINGTON B30R	1938
1446	FCD 246	LEYLAND TIGER TS8	HARRINGTON B32R	1938
1447-1448	FCD 247-8	LEYLAND TIGER TS8	HARRINGTON B30R	1938
1449-1452	FCD 249-52	LEYLAND TIGER TS8	HARRINGTON B32R	1938
1453	FCD 253	LEYLAND TIGER TS8	HARRINGTON B30R	1938
1454-1456	FCD 254-6	LEYLAND TIGER TS8	HARRINGTON B32R	1938
1457-1458	FCD 257-8	LEYLAND TIGER TS8	HARRINGTON B30R	1938
1459-1460	FCD 259-60	LEYLAND TIGER TS8	HARRINGTON B32R	1938
1461-1465	FCD 261-5	LEYLAND TIGER TS8	HARRINGTON B30R	1938
1466-1467	FCD 366-7	LEYLAND TIGER TS8	HARRINGTON B30R	1938
1468-1469	FCD 368-9	LEYLAND TIGER TS8	HARRINGTON B30R	1939
1470	FCD 370	LEYLAND TIGER TS8	HARRINGTON B30R	1938
1471	FCD 371	LEYLAND TIGER TS8	HARRINGTON B30R	1939
1472-1479	GCD 372-9	LEYLAND TIGER TS8	HARRINGTON B30R	1939
1480-1481	GCD 380-1	LEYLAND TIGER TS8	HARRINGTON B30R	1940
1482-1483	GCD 382-3	LEYLAND TIGER TS8	HARRINGTON B30R	1939
1484-1485	GCD 384-5	LEYLAND TIGER TS8	HARRINGTON B30R	1940
1802-1804	UF 5850-2	LEYLAND LIONESS LTB1	HARRINGTON C20R	1930
1806	UF 5854	LEYLAND LIONESS LTB1	HARRINGTON C20R	1930
1807-1811	UF 6507-11	LEYLAND LIONESS LTB1	HARRINGTON C20R	1930
1812-1817	UF 8826-31	LEYLAND LIONESS LTB1	HARRINGTON C20R	1933
1818-1823	CUF 318-23	LEYLAND TIGRESS RLTB3	BURLINGHAM C20C	1936

All services operate daily except where otherwise stated

No services operate on Sunday mornings except on the following routes

31A	Hourly service between Emsworth and Portsmouth Theatre Royal (*with some additional early morning journeys*)
31B	Half hourly service between Havant Church and Fratton Bridge.
39	Hourly service between Hambledon and Portsmouth Theatre Royal via Stakes.
40	Hourly service between Clanfield and Portsmouth Theatre Royal.
41	Half hourly service between Horndean and Fratton Bridge.
42B	Hourly service between Snell's Corner and Portsmouth Theatre Royal
43	Hourly service between Westbourne (Cricketers) and Portsmouth Theatre Royal
45	15 minute service between Fareham and Portsmouth Theatre Royal (*apart from 7 early morning journeys, all operate direct through Portchester*)
47	Two hourly service each way round the Hayling loop (*not serving Northney*)

Number	Route
1	Worthing Dome - Findon - Storrington
2	Worthing Dome - Findon - Horsham Station
3	East Worthing Ham Hotel - Worthing Station - Goring Aldsworth Avenue
3A	Worthing Pier - Rowlands Road - West Worthing Station - Library (*Monday to Saturday*)
4	High Salvington - Durrington - Worthing Station - East Worthing Brookdean Road
5	Worthing Pier - Thomas A'Becket - Offington Corner - Findon
5A	Worthing Pier - Littlehampton Road North Star Hotel
6	Worthing Pier - South Farm Road - Ringmer Road - Littlehampton Road North Star Hotel
7	Worthing Pier - Sompting - Lancing Station
7A	Worthing Pier - Sompting - Lancing Manor - Worthing Pier (Circular in both directions)
8	Worthing Pier - Broadwater - East Worthing Ham Hotel
9	Shoreham - Sussex Pad Hotel - Worthing - Angmering Village - Littlehampton
9A	Littlehampton - Angmering-on-Sea
10	Brighton Pool Valley - Shoreham - Sussex Pad Hotel - Worthing - Arundel Ford Road
12	Tongdean Valley Drive - Brighton Pool Valley - Newhaven - Seaford - Eastbourne
12A	Brighton Station - Peacehaven Annexe
12B	Brighton Station - Saltdean Mount
13	Brighton Pool Valley - Lewes County Hall
13A	Lewes Nevill Crescent - Newhaven
13B	Brighton Pool Valley - North Moulscombe
13C	Newhaven Bridge Street - Denton
13D	Newhaven Bridge Street - East Side (*Saturdays*)
13E	Brighton Pool Valley - East Moulscombe
13F	Brighton Pool Valley - Lower Bevendean
14	Brighton Pool Valley - Hurstpierpoint - Bolney - Haywards Heath Station
15	Eastbourne - Hailsham - Ninfield - Bexhill - Hastings (*Joint service with Maidstone & District*)
16	Brighton Pool Valley - Lewes - Laughton - Golden Cross
17	Brighton Pool Valley - Henfield - Cowfold - Horsham Carfax
18	Brighton Pool Valley - Lewes - Heathfield - Hawkhurst (*Joint service with Maidstone & District*)
20	Brighton Pool Valley - Lewes - Chailey Kings Head
21	Brighton Pool Valley - Southwick Town Hall - Shoreham Bridge Hotel - Old Shoreham Erringham Road
1B	Brighton Pool Valley - Southwick Town Hall - Southlands Hospital - Shoreham Bridge (*Wednesday and |Sunday afternoons*)
22	Brighton Pool Valley - Steyning - Pulborough - Petworth
23	Brighton Pool Valley - Ditchling - Haywards Heath Station
24	Brighton Pool Valley - Lewes - Ditchling - Hurstpierpoint - Brighton (Circular in both directions)
	Brighton Pool Valley - Lewes - Ditchling - Hurstpierpoint - Henfield (*Early and late journeys only*)
25	Brighton Pool Valley - Lewes - Berwick - Eastbourne
26	Seaford - Litlington - Alfriston - Berwick Station
27	Brighton Pool Valley - Dyke Road - Poynings - Small Dole - Henfield George
28	Nevill Estate - Lewes High Street - Landport Estate (*Monday to Saturday*)
29	Brighton Pool Valley - Lewes - Plumpton Station - Wivelsfield Green - Haywards Heath Station
30	Brighton Pool Valley - Burgess Hill - Haywards Heath Station - Chelwood Common
31	Brighton Pool Valley - Shoreham - Worthing - Littlehampton - Bognor - Chichester - Emsworth - Havant - Portsmouth Theatre Royal - Southsea South Parade Pier

31A	Emsworth - Havant - Portsmouth Theatre Royal - Southsea South Parade Pier
31B	Havant - Fratton - Southsea South Parade Pier
31C	Farlington - Portsmouth Theatre Royal *(Monday to Saturday early morning)*
31F	Brighton Pool Valley - Shoreham - Lancing - Worthing – Ferring
31G	Brighton Pool Valley - Shoreham - Lancing - Worthing - Angmering-on-Sea
32	Brighton Pool Valley - Burgess Hill - Haywards Heath Station - Fletching - Uckfield
33	Hassocks Station - Ditchling *(extended Monday to Saturday to Westmeston)*
34	Hurstpierpoint Chinese Gardens Hotel - Hassocks Station
35	Petersfield - Clanfield - Hambledon - Fareham *(Monday, Wednesday and Saturday)*
35A	Petersfield - Chalton *(Wednesday and Saturday)*
36	Brighton Pool Valley - Keymer - Burgess Hill - Haywards Heath Station - Horsted Keynes - East Grinstead
37	Portsmouth Theatre Royal - Purbrook - Waterlooville Heroes Inn *(Monday to Saturday)*
37A	Portsmouth Theatre Royal - Purbrook - Stakes - Waterlooville Heroes Inn
38	Portsmouth Theatre Royal - Wickham - Droxford Square - Meonstoke
38A	Portsmouth Theatre Royal - Wickham - Newtown *(Monday to Saturday)*
39	Portsmouth Theatre Royal - Purbrook - Waterlooville - Hambledon
40	Southsea South Parade Pier - Theatre Royal - Purbrook - Waterlooville - Clanfield - Petersfield
40B	Southsea South Parade Pier - Portsmouth Theatre Royal - Purbrook - Waterlooville - Clanfield Drift Road
41	Southsea South Parade Pier - Fratton - Purbrook - Waterlooville - Horndean
42	Southsea South Parade Pier -Theatre Royal - Purbrook - Waterlooville -Horndean - Petersfield
42A	Portsmouth Theatre Royal - Purbrook - Waterlooville - Horndean *(Early morning and evening journeys)*
42B	Southsea South Parade Pier - Portsmouth Theatre Royal - Purbrook - Waterlooville - Horndean - Snell's Corner
43	Southsea South Parade Pier - Fratton - Havant - Westbourne Cricketers OR Racton Corner
44	Emsworth - Westbourne Cricketers
45	Portsmouth Theatre Royal - Fareham - Warsash
	Portsmouth Theatre Royal - Castle Street - Fareham
	Southsea South Parade Pier - Fratton - Castle Street - Fareham
47	Havant Station - Gable Head - Eastoke - Hayling Bus Station - Manor Corner - Havant Station *(certain journeys via Northney)*
	Havant Station - Manor Corner - Hayling Bus Station - Eastoke - Gable Head - Havant Station *(certain journeys via Northney)*
48	Havant Church - Horndean
49	Havant Church - Waterlooville
50	Elmer - Bognor - Smarts Corner - Nyetimber - Pagham Beach
50A	Elmer - Bognor - Rose Green - Nyetimber - Pagham Beach
51	Bognor Bus Station - Linden Avenue - Aldwick Road - Bognor Bus Station (Circular in both directions) *(Monday to Saturday)*
52	Chichester West Street - Hunston or Donnington - Sidlesham - Selsey Seal Road
53	Chichester West Street - Birdham - East Wittering - West Wittering - Birdham - Chichester West Street (Circular in both directions)
53A	Chichester West Street - Birdham - Itchenor
54	Chichester Railway Station - Funtingdon - Racton Corner - Compton
	Chichester Railway Station - Hambrook Post Office *(Saturdays)*
55	Aldwick Barrack Lane - Bognor - North Bersted
56	Chichester Railway Station - Old Bosham
57	Chichester West Street - Halnaker - Westergate - Bognor
58	Chichester West Street - Singleton - East Dean - Goodwood - Chichester West Street (Circular in both directions)
59	Bognor Railway Station - Chichester - Midhurst - Petworth - Billingshurst - Horsham Station
60	Midhurst - Rogate - Petersfield
61	Petersfield Station - South Harting - Elstead - Midhurst
62	Chichester West Street - Chilgrove - South Harting - Petersfield Station *(Wednesday & Saturday)*
63	Petworth - Tangmere - Halnaker - Chichester Railway Station
63A	Petworth - Duncton
63B	Petworth - Sutton *(Tuesdays, Thursdays and Saturdays)*
64	Westergate - Bilsham Corner
65	Bognor - Westergate - Barnham - Walberton - Slindon
65A	Bognor - Westergate - Fontwell - Slindon
66	Arundel - Slindon - Tangmere - Chichester West Street
67	Havant Station - Rowlands Castle - Compton - South Harting - Petersfield Station
68	Littlehampton - Arundel
69	Arundel - Pulborough - Billingshurst - Horsham Station
70	Storrington - West Chiltington Village - Pulborough Station
71	Storrington - Thakeham Cross Roads

72	Horsham The Common - Carfax - Highlands Estate
73	Horsham The Common - Carfax - St. Leonards Hotel
75	Horsham Carfax - Barns Green - Coolham - Buckbarn Cross Roads OR Billingshurst
78	Horsham Carfax - Handcross
79	Horsham Carfax - Handcross - Balcombe *(Wednesday and Saturday)*
80	Horsham Carfax - West Grinstead - Partridge Green - Steyning White Horse
81	Haywards Heath Station - Bolney - Cowfold
82	Haywards Heath Station - Cuckfield - Handcross - Crawley
83	Haywards Heath Station - Warninglid - Horsham Carfax
84	Haywards Heath Station - New England Road - Haywards Heath Station (Circular service in both directions)
85	Haywards Heath Station - Sunte Avenue - Lindfield P.O.
86	Haywards Heath Station - Borde Hill - Balcombe - Stoney Lane
86A	Haywards Heath Station - Cuckfield - Brook Street
87	East Grinstead - Kingscote - West Hoathly - Ashdown Forest, Hindleap Cross Roads
88	Haywards Heath Station - Ardingly - Turners Hill
89	Haywards Heath Station - Chailey - Uckfield
90	Eastbourne Pevensey Road - Hailsham - Hellingly - Horam - Heathfield
91	Eastbourne Pevensey Road - Hailsham - Horam - Heathfield - Uckfield
92	Eastbourne Pevensey Road - Stone Cross - Hailsham - Uckfield - East Grinstead
92A	Eastbourne Pevensey Road - Hailsham - Upper Dicker
93	Eastbourne Pevensey Road - Wannock - Jevington
94	Eastbourne Pevensey Road - Polegate - Dittons Wood Corner - Stone Cross - Eastbourne Pevensey Road (Circular service in both directions)
95	Eastbourne Pevensey Road - Stone Cross - Hailsham - Rushlake Green - Heathfield *(extended Monday to Saturday to Waldron)*
96	Eastbourne Pevensey Road - Stone Cross - Pevensey Bay
99	Eastbourne Pevensey Road - Pevensey Bay - Bexhill - Hastings *(Joint service with Maidstone & District)*
119	Brighton Pool Valley - Uckfield - Five Ash Down - Crowborough - Tunbridge Wells *(Joint service with Maidstone & District)*
119A	Brighton Pool Valley - Uckfield - Maresfield - Crowborough - Tunbridge Wells *(Joint service with Maidstone & District)*
-	Bognor - Chichester - Midhurst - Petworth - Billingshurst - Horsham Station (Limited Stop) *(Monday to Saturday)*

SPECIAL HOSPITAL SERVICES

Hove Station - Brighton Pool Valley - Lewes - Golden Cross - Hellingly Hospital
Burgess Hill - Hurstpierpoint - Ditchling - Lewes - Hellingly Hospital
(The above services operate alternate Tuesdays & Wednesdays and on the first Sunday of each month except the Burgess Hill service does not run on Tuesdays)
Eastbourne - Hailsham - Hellingly Hospital
(The above service operates every Tuesday, alternate Wednesdays and on the first Sunday of each month)

EXPRESS SERVICES

Hove Station - Brighton - Lewes - Ringmer - Heathfield - Robertsbridge Darvell Hall Sanatorium *(Second and Fourth Sundays)*

The following leaflet was issued to members of the public by the government in July 1939.

Civil Defence
Some things you should know if war should come.
Public Information Leaflet No 1
Read this and keep it carefully. You may need it.
Issued from the Lord Privy Seal's Office July 1939.

If war should come:

The object of this leaflet is to tell you now some of the things you ought to know if you are to be ready for the emergency of war.

This does not mean that war is expected now, but it is everyone's duty to be prepared for the possibility of war.

Further leaflets will be sent to you to give you fuller guidance on particular ways in which you can be prepared.

The government is taking all possible measures for the defence of your country, and has made plans for protecting you and helping you to protect yourselves, so far as may be, in the event of war.

You, in your turn, can help to make those plans work, if you understand them and act in accordance with them.

No-one can tell when and how war might begin, but the period of warning might be very short. There would be no time then to begin to think what you ought to do.

READ WHAT FOLLOWS, and think NOW.

1.   Air Raid Warnings:
When air raids are threatened, warning will be given in towns by sirens and hooters, which will be sounded, in some places by short blasts, or in other places by a warbling note, changing every few seconds. In war, sirens and hooters will not be used for any other purpose than this.

The warning may also be given by the Police or Air Raid Wardens blowing short blasts on whistles.

When you hear the warning, take cover at once. Remember that most of the injuries in an air raid are caused not by direct hits by bombs, but by flying fragments of debris or bits of shells. Stay under cover until you hear the sirens or hooters sounding continuously for two minutes on the same note, which is the signal "Raiders Passed".

If poison gas has been used, you will be warned by means of hand rattles. Keep off the streets until the poison gas has been cleared away. Hand bells will be rung when there is no longer any danger. If you hear the rattle when you are out, put on your gas mask at once and get indoors as soon as you can.

Make sure that all members of your household understand the meanings of these signals.

2.   Gas Masks:
If you have already got your gas mask, make sure that you are keeping it safely and in good condition for immediate use. If you are moving permanently, or going away for any length of time, remember to take your gas mask with you.

If you have not yet received your gas mask, the reason may be that it has been decided in your district to keep the masks in store until an emergency is threatened. If, however, you know that your neighbours have got their gas masks, and you have not got yours, report the matter to your Air Raid Warden.

The special anti-gas helmet for babies and the respirator for small children will not be distributed in any district before an emergency arises.

3. Lighting Restrictions:

All windows, sky-lights, glazed doors, or other openings which would show a light, will have to be screened in war time with dark blinds or blankets, or brown paper pasted on the glass, so that no light is visible from outside. You should obtain now any materials you may need for this purpose.

No outside lights will be allowed and all street lighting will be put out. Instructions will be issued about the dimming of lights on vehicles.

4. Fire Precautions:

An air attack may bring large numbers of small incendiary bombs, which might start so many fires that the Fire Brigades could not be expected to deal with them all. Everyone should be prepared to do all he can to tackle a fire started in his own house. Most large fires start as small ones. Clearing the top floor of all inflammable materials, lumber etc., will lessen the danger of fire, and prevent a fire spreading. See that you can reach your attic or roof space readily. Water is the best means of putting out a fire started by an incendiary bomb. Have some buckets handy. But water can only be applied to the bomb itself in the form of a fine spray, for which a hand pump with a length of hose and special nozzle are needed. If you throw a bucket of water on a burning incendiary bomb it will explode and throw burning fragments in all directions. You may be able to smother it with sand or dry earth.

5. Evacuation:

Arrangements have been made by the government for the voluntary evacuation from certain parts of the London area and of some other large towns of schoolchildren, children below school age if accompanied by their mothers or other responsible persons, expectant mothers, and adult blind persons who can be moved.

Parents in the districts concerned who wish to take advantage of the government's evacuation scheme for their children have already received or will receive full instructions what to do, if the need arises.

Those who have already made, or are making arrangements to send their children away to relations or friends must remember that while the government evacuation scheme is in progress, ordinary railway and road services will necessarily be drastically reduced and subject to alterations at short notice.

Try to decide now whether you wish your children to go under the government evacuation scheme and let you local authority know. If you propose to make private arrangements to send your children away do not leave them to the last moment. All who have work to do, whether manual, clerical or professional, should regard it as their duty to remain at their posts, and do their part in carrying on the life of the nation.

6. Identity labels:

In war you should carry about with you your name and address clearly written. This should be on an envelope, card, luggage label, not on some odd piece of paper easily lost. In the case of children a label should be fastened, e.g. sewn, on to their clothes, in such a way that it will not readily become detached.

7. Food:

It is very important that at the outset of an emergency, people should not buy larger quantities of foodstuffs than they normally buy and normally require. The government are making arrangements to ensure that there will be sufficient supplies of food, and that every person will be able to obtain regularly his or her fair share; and they will take steps to prevent any sudden price rises. But if some people try to buy abnormal quantities, before the full scheme of control is working, they will be taking food which should be available for others. If you wish, and are able to lay in a small extra store of non-perishable foodstuffs, there is no reason why you should not do so. They will be an additional insurance. But you should collect them now and not when an emergency arises.

8. Instructions to the public in case of emergency:

Arrangements will be made for information and instructions to be issued to the public in case of emergency, both through the Press, and by means of broadcast announcements. Broadcasts may be made at special times, which will be announced beforehand, or during ordinary news bulletins.

This leaflet was sent to all homes and was produced in co-operation between the War Office and the Ministry of Home Security.

If the INVADER comes
WHAT TO DO – AND HOW TO DO IT

The Germans threaten to invade Great Britain.

If they do so they will be driven out by our Navy, our Army and our Air Force. Yet the ordinary men and women of the civilian population will also have their part to play. Hitler's invasions of Poland, Holland and Belgium were greatly helped by the fact that the civilian population was taken by surprise. They did not know what to do when the moment came. You must not be taken by surprise. This leaflet tells you what general line you should take. More detailed instructions will be given you when the danger comes nearer. Meanwhile, read these instructions carefully and be prepared to carry them out.

I

When Holland and Belgium were invaded, the civilian population fled from their homes. They crowded on the roads, in cars, in carts, on bicycles and on foot, and so helped the enemy by preventing their own armies from advancing against the invaders. You must not allow that to happen here.

Your first rule, therefore, is:

(1) IF THE GERMANS COME, BY PARACHUTE, AEROPLANE OR SHIP, YOU MUST REMAIN WHERE YOU ARE. THE ORER IS "STAY PUT".

If the commander-in-chief decides that the place where you live must be evacuated, he will tell you when and how to leave. Until you receive such orders you must remain where you are. If you run away, you will be exposed to far greater danger because you will be machine gunned from the air as were civilians in Holland and Belgium, and you will block the roads by which our own armies will advance to turn the Germans out.

II

There is another method which the Germans adopt in their invasion. They make use of the civilian population in order to create confusion and panic. They spread false rumours and issue false instructions.

In order to prevent this, you should obey the second rule, which is as follows:

(2) DO NOT BELIEVE RUMOURS AND DO NOT SPREAD THEM. WHEN YOU RECEIVE AN ORDER, MAKE QUITE SURE THAT IT IS A TRUE ORDER AND NOT A FAKED ORDER. MOST OF YOU KNOW YOUR POLICEMEN AND YOU'RE *(sic)* A.R.P. WARDENS BY SIGHT, YOU CAN TRUST THEM. IF YOU KEEP YOUR HEADS, YOU CAN ALSO TELL WHETHER A MILITARY OFFICER IS REALLY BRITISH OR ONLY PRETENDING TO BE SO. IF IN DOUBT ASK THE POLICEMAN OR THE A.R.P. WARDEN. USE YOUR COMMON SENSE.

III

The Army, the Air Force and the Local Defence Volunteers cannot be everywhere at once. The ordinary man and woman must be on the watch. If you see anything suspicious, do not rush round telling your neighbours about it. Go at once to the nearest policeman, police station or military officer and tell them exactly what you saw. Train yourself to notice the exact time and place where you saw anything suspicious, and try to give exact information. Try to check your facts. The sort of report which a military or police officer wants from you is something like this:

"At 5.30 p.m. tonight I saw twenty cyclists come into Little Squashborough from the direction of Great Mudtown. They carried some sort of automatic rifle or gun. I did not see anything like artillery. They were in grey uniforms."

Be calm, quick and exact. The third rule, therefore, is as follows:

KEEP WATCH. IF YOU SEE ANYTHING SUSPICIOUS, NOTE IT CAREFULLY AND GO AT ONCE TO THE NEAREST POLICE OFFICER OR STATION, OR TO THE NEAREST MILITARY OFFICER. DO NOT RUSH ABOUT SPREADING VAGUE RUMOURS. GO QUICKLY TO THE NEAREST AUTHORITY AND GIVE HIM THE FACTS.

IV

Remember that if parachutists come down near your home, they will not be feeling at all brave. They will not know where they are, they will have no food, they will not know where their companions are. They will want you to give them food, means of transport and maps. They will want you to tell them where they have landed, where their comrades are, and where our own soldiers are.

The fourth rule, therefore, is as follows:

> DO NOT GIVE ANY GERMAN ANYTHING. DO NOT TELL HIM ANYTHING. HIDE YOUR FOOD AND YOUR BICYCLES. HIDE YOUR MAPS. SEE THAT THE ENEMY GETS NO PETROL. IF YOU HAVE A CAR OR MOTOR BICYCLE, PUT IT OUT OF ACTION WHEN NOT IN USE. IT IS NOT ENOUGHTO REMOVE THE IGNITION KEY; YOU MUST MAKE IT USELESS TO ANYONE EXCEPT YOURSELF. IF YOU ARE A GARAGE PROPRIETOR, YOU MUST WORK OUT A PLAN TO PROTECT YOUR STOCK OF PETROL AND YOUR CUSTOMERS' CARS. REMEMBER THAT TRANSPORT AND PETROL WILL BE THE INVADER'S MAIN DIFFICULTIES. MAKE SURE THAT NO INVADER WILL BE ABLE TO GET HOLD OF YOUR CARS, PETROL, MAPS OR BICYCLES.

V

You may be asked by Army and Air Force officers to help in many ways. For instance, the time may come when you will receive orders to block roads or streets in order to prevent the enemy from advancing. Never block a road unless you are told which one you must block. Then you can help by felling trees, wiring them together or blocking the roads with cars.

Here, therefore, is the fifth rule:

> BE READY TO HELP THE MILITARY IN ANY WAY. BUT DO NOT BLOCK ROADS UNTIL ORDERED TO DO SO BY THE MILITARY OR LDV AUTHORITIES.

VI

If you are in charge of a factory, store or other workplace, organise its defence at once. If you are a worker, make sure that you understand the system of defence that has been organised and know what part you have to play in it. Remember that parachutists and fifth column men are powerless against any organised resistance. They can only succeed if they can create disorganisation. Make certain that no suspicious strangers enter your premises. You must know in advance who is to take command, who is to be second in command, and how orders are to be transmitted. This chain of command must be built up and you will probably find that ex officers or N.C.O's who have been in emergencies before, are the best people to undertake such command.

The sixth rule is therefore as follows:

> IN FACTORIES AND SHOPS, ALL MANAGERS AND WORKMEN SHOULD ORGANISE SOME SYSTEM NOW BY WHICH A SUDDEN ATTACK CAN BE RESISTED.

VII

The six rules which you have now read give you a general idea of what to do in the event of invasion. More detailed instructions may, when the time comes, be given you by the Military and Police Authorities and by the Local Defence Volunteers; they will NOT be given over the wireless as they might convey information to the enemy. These instructions must be obeyed at once. Remember always that the best defence of Great Britain is the courage of her men and women.

Here is your seventh rule:

> THINK BEFORE YOU ACT. BUT THINK ALWAYS OF YOUR COUNTRY BEFORE YOU THINK OF YOURSELF.

GARAGES, BUS & COACH STATIONS AT 1 SEPTEMBER 1939

EASTBOURNE (E)
Pevensey Road Bus Station
Royal Parade (Buses)
Cavendish Place Coach Station

ALFRISTON	West Street
CHELWOOD GATE	Lewes Road
EAST GRINSTEAD	24 Chequer Road
HEATHFIELD	Tilsmore Road
SEAFORD	Dane Road
UCKFIELD	Mill Road

BRIGHTON (A)
Freshfield Road
Royal Mews, Steine St Coach Station
Edward Street
Manchester Street

BOLNEY	London Road, A23
EAST HOATHLY	London Road, A22
HANDCROSS	London Road, A23
HAYWARDS HEATH	Gordon Road
HENFIELD	Lower Station Road
HURSTPIERPOINT	Mansion House, West Furlong Lane
LEWES	Eastgate
STEYNING	Star Inn

WORTHING (W)
Steyne Mews
Library Place
Bedford Row

BARNS GREEN	Two Mile Ash Road
DIAL POST	A24
HORSHAM	Denne Road South Garage
	Denne Road North Garage
	(let to Fry & Co)
LITTLEHAMPTON	East Street
PULBOROUGH	London Road
STORRINGTON	Amberley Road

BOGNOR REGIS (B)
Fields Garage, Richmond Road
Bus Station, 66-70 High Street

CHICHESTER	Northgate
EAST WITTERING	Longlands Farm
MIDHURST	North Street
PETWORTH	Angel Street
SELSEY	New Inn
	(renamed Neptune Inn c1944)

PORTSMOUTH (P)
Hyde Park Road
Hilsea

CLANFIELD	North Lane
EMSWORTH	Fords Lane
HAMBLEDON	West Street
HAYLING ISLAND	Elm Grove
PETERSFIELD	Station Road
WARSASH	Warsash Road
WICKHAM	Station Road

OFFICES AT 1 SEPTEMBER 1939

ARUNDEL	39 High Street
BOGNOR REGIS	Elmer Bus Stand
BRIGHTON	5 Steine Street
	Royal York Buildings, Pool Valley
	Aquarium Kiosk, Palace Pier
	West Street Kiosk, Kings Road
CHICHESTER	11 West Street
EASTBOURNE	1 Cavendish Place
	Kiosk, Pier Gates
	Claremont Hotel, Cavendish Place
EAST GRINSTEAD	33 High Street
HAILSHAM	45 High Street
HAVANT	3/5 South Street
HAYWARDS HEATH	Railway Station
HORNDEAN	Ship & Bell waiting room
HORSHAM	22 Richmond Terrace, Carfax
HOVE	7 St Aubyn's Gardens
LEWES	174 High Street
LONDON	27 Princes Street, W1
LITTLEHAMPTON	Kiosk, The Parade
MIDHURST	North Street
NEWHAVEN	1 Bridge Street
PETERSFIELD	27 The Square
PETWORTH	The Square
PORTSMOUTH	Southdown Buildings, North End
	69 Commercial Road
SEAFORD	5 Clinton Place
SHOREHAM-BY-SEA	86 High Street
SOUTHSEA	South Parade Pier Kiosk
	241 Albert Road
	No 5 Kiosk near Canoe Lake
	Traffic Regulators Kiosk, South Parade
UCKFIELD	High Street
WASHINGTON	Frankland Arms
WORTHING	23 Marine Parade
	2 New Broadway, Tarring Road
	5 Arcade Buildings
	45 Marine Parade

LICENSED RESTAURANT & BAR   London Road, County Oak, Crawley

CENTRAL WORKS   Victoria Road, Portslade